The Representation of Bodily Pain in Late Nineteenth–Century English Culture

LUCY BENDING

CLARENDON PRESS · OXFORD

OXFORD

UNIVERSITY PRESS

Great Clarendon Street, Oxford OX2 6DP

Oxford University Press is a department of the University of Oxford.
It furthers the University's objective of excellence in research, scholarship,
and education by publishing worldwide in

Oxford New York

Athens Auckland Bangkok Bogotá Buenos Aires Calcutta
Cape Town Chennai Dar es Salaam Delhi Florence Hong Kong Istanbul
Karachi Kuala Lumpur Madrid Melbourne Mexico City Mumbai
Nairobi Paris São Paulo Shanghai Singapore Taipei Tokyo Toronto Warsaw
and associated companies in Berlin Ibadan

Oxford is a registered trade mark of Oxford University Press
in the UK and certain other countries

Published in the United States
by Oxford University Press Inc., New York

British Library Cataloguing in Publication Data

Data available

Library of Congress Cataloging in Publication Data

Data available

ISBN-0-19-818717-3

1 3 5 7 9 10 8 6 4 2

Typeset by Best-set Typesetter Ltd., Hong Kong
Printed in Great Britain
on acid-free paper by
T.J. International Ltd,
Padstow, Cornwall

Acknowledgements

THERE ARE many people who have contributed in diverse ways to this book. I'd like to thank, first of all, Matthew Pateman, for his encyclopedic knowledge of flogging without which the final chapter of this book would not be what it is now. Kate Flint also made her mark—though of a very different kind—as she guided and supported this project, and its author, through a D.Phil with enthusiasm and intelligence, deploying her usual critical acumen and breadth of knowledge. Others contributed when this book was still a dissertation: Molly Baer Kramer, Marcella and Michael Bungay Stanier, Julia Paulman Kielstra, Katie-Louise Thomas, Claire Pettitt, and Karen Luscombe—all of whom discussed the ideas and arguments of this book as they struggled into existence. Jennifer Bending also belongs in this list: her wide-ranging understanding and knowledge of pain in its clinical and philosophical contexts lies at the heart of this project. Roy Porter and Valentine Cunningham responded enthusiastically and helpfully as examiners, and since then Martin Arnold, Fran Brearton, and Matthew Pateman of University College Scarborough provided a convivial and stimulating environment for the closing stages of this project. My thanks also go particularly to Patricia Duncker and Diane Watt of the University of Wales Aberystwyth whose encouragement and advice have proved invaluable as this book went through the press. The Wellcome Institute Library, London, the Bodleian, and the British Library have assisted me in various ways during my research for this book, and the British Library has also kindly granted permissions for the use of illustrations. I am indebted to the British Academy, St Hugh's College, Oxford, and the University of Wales, Aberystwyth, for their financial support in the development of this project, and to everybody at Oxford University Press who have seen this book through the press. Finally, my greatest thanks go to Theo Bloom who has stood by me through all of this, offering unflagging intelligence and good humour, as well as an uncanny knack with footnotes.

Every effort has been made by the author to secure permissions prior to publication. If notified, the publisher will rectify any errors or omissions at the earliest opportunity.

Contents

List of Figures   ix

INTRODUCTION   1

1. CHRISTIAN UNDERSTANDINGS OF
   PHYSICAL SUFFERING   5
   I. Doctrinally Sanctioned Pain   5
   II. The Pains of Earth   27

2. MEDICAL UNDERSTANDINGS OF PAIN   52
   I. The Rise of the Medical Paradigm   52
   II. The Dangers of Diversity   75

3. PAIN AND LANGUAGE   82
   I. The Language of Pain: Virginia Woolf and
      Elaine Scarry   83
   II. Literary and Social Conventions   89
   III. Articulating Pain   104

4. ANTIVIVISECTIONARY RHETORIC
   AND PAIN   116
   I. Vivisection in Practice   117
   II. The Civilized Savage   123
   III. Vivisection on Public Display   135
   IV. Vivisection and Brutalization   152

5. THE QUESTION OF SHARED HUMAN
   SENSIBILITY   177
   I. Evolutionary Hierarchies of Suffering   178
   II. Excluding the Deviant   207
   III. Class and the Infliction of Pain   232

6. THE PLEASURES AND PAINS OF
   FLOGGING 240

Bibliography 275

Index 299

List of Figures

1. Physiological instruments   145
2. Man in Pain   187
3. *a* Du-Bois Reymond's Electrical Algometer; *b* Weber's
   Esthesiometer   219

Introduction

PAIN IS not a brute given with a single, universally accepted meaning. Instead, those who suffer refer their physical discomfort to external systems of value: to suffer is manly, is the result of sin, is a sign of civilization and its attendant sensitivity, is the product of neurology. This book, then, is concerned not with the idea of pain as an ultimate sensation, but with arguments over the meaning and interpretation of pain as they appeared in many different forms of literature, whether novels, medical textbooks, campaigning pamphlets, advertisements, or sermons, primarily in the last two decades of the nineteenth century.

William James, writing in his textbook *Psychology* (1892), began his section on pain with the unequivocal statement: 'The physiology of pain is still an enigma.'[1] The ability to treat pain—with local and general anaesthetics, by means of surgery, or with drugs such as morphine—had, by the end of the century, far outstripped the ability of physiologists to understand why such medical interventions worked, or the nature of the nervous system on which these things acted. Whilst medical understandings remained imperfect, physiologists worked towards connecting the pain of the body with the body itself. In so doing, they undercut the much older Christian belief that pain was in the hands of God: that a beneficent God inflicted pain both for the pragmatic reason that it short-circuited serious bodily dissolution by prompting individuals to start back from the source of pain, and for the metaphysical reason that it kept errant humans on the straight and narrow. This book sites itself in the 1880s and 1890s for a number of reasons, but primary amongst these is the sense that it was a period of confusion when the *meaning* of pain—the reasons attributed to its infliction and endurance—was open to many and varied interpretations, none of which had entirely gained the upper hand.

My overall aim is, therefore, to trace the relationships between different understandings of physical pain by looking at

[1] *Psychology* (Macmillan, 1892), 67.

the language and arguments of those who described it, and to map the changing perceptions of pain against specific medical, theological, anthropological, and technological developments. I shall be arguing for different models of interaction between discourses, as bishops and doctors parted company over the meaning of the pain suffered by those with cholera; criminologists refused, or at least failed, to feed the concurrent and relevant findings of anthropologists into their understandings of the pain of criminals; evolutionary-minded doctors attacked and ridiculed what they perceived to be the falsehoods of their Christian colleagues in the pages of the *Lancet*; and decadents seeking the ultimate sensation turned to that which so many of their contemporaries shunned. These are interactions depending on disagreement, but I also show the coterminous nature of arguments over the meaning or value of pain in different fields of interest. It is, for example, no surprise that Annie Besant despised the idea of a God who demanded the painful sacrifice of his Son, and that she was simultaneously a staunch advocate of euthanasia for those in pain; or that Frances Power Cobbe, equally repelled by a Christian scheme of an eternity of pain for malefactors, was one of the most active and prominent antivivisectionists of the late nineteenth century. Not only did individuals carry their ideas about pain between separate fields, but contemporaneous ideas could leak from one discourse to the other, as the author of *Teleny* (often assumed to be Oscar Wilde) shared his understandings of the neurology of pain with the scientist Francis Galton. In a broader scheme, understandings of pain held by theologians and by physiologists and medical practitioners strongly affected the tenability of their counterparts' positions. In the middle of the century, there is no doubt that Christian theology had a firm, though loosening, grip on the courses open to doctors. Vaccination and anaesthesia both had to fight for survival against the Christian belief that intervention in God's world was blasphemous. The pendulum then swung in the other direction as pain lost its place as a natural part in the universe and became, instead, something to be removed or alleviated at all costs. As I shall argue, medicine took on the role of dominant discourse, and added its strength to the changes that were already under way in the Christian Church: if quotidian pain was no longer either necessary or natural, then other sorts of pain, formerly ordained by God—those of atonement and damnation—also began to lose their analogical rationale. It is no surprise that the Church of England heresy trials in the 1860s, largely brought because of the defendants' refusal to accept eternal damnation, were concurrent with the increasing strength of physiological and neurological knowledge. Whilst these trends, however, were clearly interrelated, it was also the case that there was no general consensus, and that unpopular beliefs were as firmly held as popular ones, as belief refused to bend, in some cases at least, to prevalent scientific formulations.

Pain, and the ways in which it was understood and schematized, far from being abstruse, got to the heart of many important Victorian debates and cultural currents. I have already hinted at the changing status of pain and its importance within the English Church as a determining factor, but perceptions of pain had other far-reaching implications. The newly acquired ability to control pain, at least to some extent, contributed to the professionalization of the medical establishment, and, eventually, the displacement of pain as an integral part of life was seen to play a part in the imperialist anxiety that British soldiers were no longer manly enough for the task they were to undertake. The Victorian craze for classification took up the supposed inability of particular groups to feel pain, and used this to specify sufferers' positions on scales of sensitivity, such that degree of civilization, class, and psychological well-being, were all seen to be predetermined. Such arguments were intrinsically circular, and rested not on observation or empirical evidence, but rather on supposed similarities to groups already assumed to be insensate. This assumed insensitivity was then used to police the boundaries between different groups, as the ability to feel pain was used as a marker of difference between, for example, the law-abiding and the criminal.

My aim throughout has been to bring together understandings of pain (as well as rhetorical strategies for describing pain) drawn from different spheres, and to do this I have brought to the fore practices and collections of ideas that became potent sources of meaning for pain, and which forged complicated links between fields of discourse. The concepts of savagery and civilization, particularly, were both defined by, and defining of, pain, as assumptions about the sensitivity of groups designated 'savage' rested less on empirical evidence than hearsay and received opinion. Groups repeatedly compared to savages, particularly criminals, but also vivisectionists, were then defined by what was assumed to be the leading characteristic of savages: their insensitivity, and this was transferred from the original group to the second group. The penal implications of this for criminals who could not easily feel punishment were marked. Tattooing, which had been the symbol of savagery and criminality, was given a sharp twist as it became a fashionable craze for European aristocracy in the 1880s. The strength of collocated ideas was such that wealthy, upper-class women who would usually fall into the category of the highly sensitive, their luxurious lifestyle subject to another cultural preconception that determined their sensitivity, could have this stripped from them by the Italian criminologist Cesare Lombroso, maintaining that their tattoos necessarily implied their insensitivity.

Pain was not something to be trusted and relied on, a bodily given the same for all who suffered, but instead was part of a complex and unstable system of signification, manipulable by those with power, and powerfully inflected by such diverse categories as class, race, gender, and, in the case of the decadents of the 1890s, desire.

I

Christian Understandings of Physical Suffering

I. DOCTRINALLY SANCTIONED PAIN

Christianity and medicine provided the two dominant, though conflicting, discourses for understanding physical pain in the nineteenth century. As the importance of the former as a widely accepted framing device for understanding physical suffering waned, explanations for pain based on medical understandings came to the fore. In a reciprocal process, the emphasis shifted from one to the other until a gulf—both theological and medical—opened up between understandings of bodily pain in the 1840s and in the 1880s. The last two decades of the century, following on from the upheavals of these forty years, were a time of great uncertainty where physical pain was concerned. Christian justifications, which had largely been accepted for centuries, were widely seen to be inadequate, whilst physiological understanding was not yet advanced enough to give convincing explanations for the neurological functioning of pain.

For Christian theologians two kinds of pain were of importance: the pains of the here and now and the doctrinally sanctioned pains of eternal damnation. Following the widespread overthrow of belief in the physical pains of hell, came a change in the perception of physical pain, both among the clergy and the laity. Harriet Martineau, writing in 1844, was doubtless earnest in her 'supposition—indispensable and . . . almost universal,—that pain is the chastisement of a Father; or, at least, that it is, in some way or other, ordained for, or instrumental to good',[1] though she clearly also recognized that such conventional Christian thinking 'glamorized morbid self-pity and

[1] *Life in the Sick-Room. Essays. By an Invalid* (Edward Moxon, 1844), 7.

sapped the will to be well'.[2] Even without Martineau's ambivalence, her claim, in its inclusiveness, was optimistic even in the 1840s[3] but by the 1880s it was hopelessly outmoded. The Catholic Church, along with Anglo-Catholics and the Evangelical wing of the Church of England, fought against—and indeed needed, if they were to retain their position, to fight against—doctrinal change, specifically where the atonement and eternal damnation were concerned. The Broad Church, on the other hand, took their lead from Unitarians who believed in the universalist doctrine that all would eventually be accepted in heaven after a period in hell to purge away their sins.[4] The casualty of such a position was the unquestioned belief in the plenary inspiration of the Bible, not least when this was used as a vindication of such doctrines as that of a physical hell. Biblical authority was progressively put under pressure.

The Christian Church in Britain had no single doctrinal line on physical pain, and its manifold meanings were pulled sharply this way and that by party and denominational allegiances, remaining unstable even within the boundaries of a single denomination. By the 1870s, what came to be known as the 'problem' of pain, the question of how physical suffering could be reconciled to the idea of a loving God, was widely recognized as a stumbling block to belief in Christianity in its own right. As Charles Voysey, whose claims will play a large part in this discussion, was to argue:

I am literally besieged with letters pressing me for an answer to the questions, Why should there be so much apparently needless suffering in the world? How can we, in the presence of these painful facts, believe in the existence and sovereign control of a good God?

On every hand such and kindred discussions are raised. One hardly ever touches the subject of Religion without the conversation drifting rapidly to this central and vital enquiry.

---

[2] Roy Porter, 'Pain and Suffering', in W. F. Bynum and Roy Porter, *Companion Encyclopedia of the History of Medicine*, 2 vols. (London: Routledge, 1993), ii 1580.

[3] See later discussion of J. A. Froude's broadly autobiographical novel, *The Nemesis of Faith* (1849).

[4] For an excellent statement of the Unitarian position, and indeed many aspects of the Victorian debate over eternal damnation, see Geoffrey Rowell, *Hell and the Victorians: A Study of the Nineteenth-Century Theological Controversies concerning Eternal Punishment and the Future Life* (Oxford: Clarendon Press, 1974), 32–61.

The doubts which cluster around it darken many a soul, alike among the fortunate and the unfortunate. Old men and women shake their heads over it as an insoluble problem, while the young talk flippantly of it as a reason for dismissing the subjects of religion and God altogether from their minds.[5]

For him, and for many others, pain was a problem that hit hard at the foundations of his Christian faith.

The religious meanings of bodily pain largely took shape in relation to other doctrinal argument, as overtly religious, though in secular terms unfeelable, pains—those of the crucifixion or of hell—were held up for examination. Whilst the doctrinally sanctioned pains of Christianity and the pains of earthly existence were clearly related to each other in the minds of theologians and laity alike, there is a great difference between these two sorts of pain—the historical and redemptive pain of Christ and the anticipated retributive pain of hell, and the real pains of the here and now. The pains of eternal damnation could be described in terms of refined and grossly multiplied physical and earthly pains, but their insubstantiality meant that there were few, even of those who wrote invoking eternal damnation, who believed that such suffering could be their own fate. As Anthony Trollope suggested, there was an enormous 'discrepancy between actual beliefs and declarations of faith'. Whilst a clergyman declared aloud ' "a dozen times every year of his life" that he believed in the "fulminating clause of the Athanasian Creed" '—'They that have done good shall go into life everlasting, and they that have done evil into everlasting fire'—very few actually believed it.[6] The pains of eternal damnation simply could not have the same real presence as the pains of the here and now.

The apologies for physical pain which began to be written largely in the late 1870s took at least part of their impetus from the heated debate over the validity of eternal damnation; an argument which, as I shall show, had come to a head in the heresy trials of the 1860s. The idea of *poena sensus* (pain/ punishment of sense) of the Catholic Church, and of the

[5] *The Mystery of Pain, Death and Sin, and Discourses in Refutation of Atheism* (London and Edinburgh: Williams and Norgate, 1878), 29.

[6] See Michael Wheeler, *Death and the Future Life in Victorian Literature and Theology* (Cambridge: Cambridge University Press, 1990), 194.

Evangelical wing of the Church of England of the earlier part of Victoria's reign, widely gave way, under intense pressure of argument, to the idea of *poena damni* (punishment/pain of loss) in the 1880s and 1890s. Those in hell were no longer thought to be suffering physical pains, but rather the spiritual pains of separation from God. As a result, physical pain on earth became harder to justify. The retributive purpose of physical pain was stripped away from eternal damnation, and the theological value attributed to pain—of all kinds—was called into question.

Long-standing justifications of doctrinally supported pain were attacked not only by such secularists as Austin Holyoake,[7] but also by professing Christians, and from the mid-century onwards these assaults came thick and fast from members of the Broad Church.[8] Such attacks did not, of course, concern themselves exclusively with this question of pain, but the proponents of such arguments, whilst calling into question the infallibility of the Bible, brought the question of the *value* of pain to the fore. Largely seeking to replace the idea of the unquestionable Word of God with notions of moral rectitude, such doctrines as vicarious atonement, resting on Christ's 'purchase from God through the price of his bodily pangs', were replaced by the 'salvation from evil through sharing the Saviour's spirit'.[9] The change in emphasis is clear. The doctrine of eternal damnation, that of vicarious atonement, and the cruelty ordained by God in the Old Testament, all became unacceptable to many members of the Broad Church. Acrimonious debate sprang from the increasing disbelief in the idea that a loving God could require an eternity of physical pain for sinners, and attitudes towards physical pain on earth were inextricably entwined with this debate. The fall of the former laid the way for the questioning of the moral rightness of the latter.

---

[7] See Rowell, *Hell and the Victorians*, 2.

[8] For a definition of 'Broad Church' see Alec R. Vidler, *The Church in an Age of Revolution: 1789 to the Present Day* (Harmondsworth: Penguin, 1961), 129: 'the term "Broad Church" is even less specific than High Church or Low Church. Broad Churchmen were not organised as a party, as the Anglo-Catholics and the Evangelicals were. Moreover, for lack of a better word it could be used as a description of any churchman who did not line up with either of those parties.'

[9] Rowland Williams, 'Bunsen's Biblical Researches', in *Essays and Reviews* (John W. Parker, 1860), 87.

The critic W. R. Greg, writing in 1872, made plain the basis of his own disbelief in a physical hell, offering instead a vision of sinners, after death, being forced to recognize themselves and their sins as they really were: 'No other punishment whether retributive or purgatorial will be needed. Naked truth, unfilmed eyes, will do all that the most righteous vengeance could desire.'[10] The sinner, instead of finding himself surrounded by eternal fire, 'shall stand amazed and horror-struck at the low promptings to which he once yielded himself up in such ignominious slavery, and shall shrink in loathing and shame from the reflected image of his own animal brutality'.[11]

Whilst dissenting from the picture portrayed, Greg gathered together the scriptural basis for the supposed existence of hell, and these descriptions provide the basis for the representations of hell that proved so contentious:

throughout the Epistles there is no description of any place or world of punishment; and few references to the existence of such. Paul indeed speaks of the 'day of wrath;' the 'wrath to come;' 'indignation and wrath, tribulation and anguish, upon every soul of man that doeth evil;' and both Paul and the writer of the second epistle of Peter mention incidentally the 'everlasting destruction,' the 'perishing' of sinners;—but this is the sum total of their contributions to the subject, which seems scarcely ever to have been present to their minds. In the Gospels, however, the place of punishment is mentioned in several places, generally as from Christ himself; and it is always described in the same or nearly the same language, as 'Hell fire;' 'flame;' 'the place where the worm dieth not, and the fire is not quenched;' 'a furnace of fire' . . . In the Revelations the same conception is . . . still more materialized: there it is 'the lake that burneth with fire and brimstone,'— the 'lake of fire,' the 'bottomless pit'—&c. In short, wherever Hell is spoken of at all specifically in the Bible, its tortures are described as purely *corporeal*; and Christian writers and preachers in general have faithfully adhered to the representations of their text.[12]

Such delineations of hell as those of Revelations were, for Greg and for many of his contemporaries, risible and 'almost impossible of credence'.[13] Despite this, such biblical description formed a solid foundation for theological teachings on hell and

---

[10] *Enigmas of Life* (Trübner, 1872), 260.   [11] Ibid. 261.
[12] Ibid. 250–1.   [13] Ibid. 250.

was, particularly in the first half of the century, taken very literally.

The Enigmas of Life was written when the doctrine of physical damnation had already lost ground and, as such, it reflected rather than shaped popular opinion. Not only this, but Greg's equivocal religious status made it impossible for his biographer to decide whether to call him a theist or an agnostic,[14] and these two things together make him, perhaps, not the best standard against which to measure Christian responses to Christian doctrine. The main actors in the debate over eternal damnation needed much stronger convictions, not least because several of them were brought to account in the ecclesiastical courts where they were tried for heresy. F. D. Maurice, professor of divinity at King's College, London, and John William Colenso, fellow of St John's College in Cambridge, caused a furore in theological circles, though they escaped the ecclesiastical courts. H. B. Wilson, editor of the highly controversial *Essays and Reviews* (1860), was tried, along with his colleague Rowland Williams, in the ecclesiastical Court of the Arches. Both finally cleared themselves from accusations of heresy, whereas the more outspoken Charles Voysey was found guilty of similar charges and was forced out of the Church of England in 1871. All of these men were brought to task, at least in part, because of their attitudes towards eternal damnation, and as such they show the upsurge of feeling against the doctrine: an upsurge that was willing to forfeit livelihood and reputation for the sake of belief.

Maurice, himself from a Unitarian background, rethought his response to pain supposedly ordained by God, and in so doing distanced himself from the idea of eternal damnation, as well as from those theories of the atonement which involved vicarious suffering. In the last essay in *Theological Essays* (1853), the book that brought about his downfall, he equivocated over eternal damnation, torn between a desire to accept the Bible as literally true, and his revulsion from a doctrine that he found morally repugnant. Whilst denouncing 'frivolous rhetoric',[15] he argued the case that 'Eternity in relation to God has nothing to

---

[14] John Morley, 'W. R. Greg: A Sketch', in *Critical Miscellanies*, 3 vols. (Macmillan, 1886), iii. 252–3.

[15] 'Concluding Essay: Eternal Life and Eternal Death', in *Theological Essays* (2nd edn., Cambridge: Macmillan, 1853), 443.

do with time or duration',[16] so that eternal punishment could not mean 'everlasting' punishment, but rather 'indefinite' punishment. In this way, it became possible for Maurice to claim that eternal pains were, in fact, only temporary.

Such a theory had been propounded before this time in novels. Elizabeth Gaskell, also from a Unitarian background, and the wife of a famous Unitarian minister,[17] envisaged the fate of the murderer John Barton in terms of a temporary spell in hell. Described by Job Legh after his death, Barton's hell is a place of repentance, rather than unending torment. Legh charts the course of Barton's disillusionment, crime, and repentance:

Then he grew bitter and angry, and mad; and in his madness he did a great sin, and wrought a great woe; and repented him with tears as of blood; and will go through his penance humbly and meekly in t'other place, I'll be bound. I never seed such bitter repentance as his that last night.[18]

Gaskell makes clear the foundation for this belief that he will 'go through' his time in hell in the biblical quotation she uses to mark the shared gravestone of John Barton, and his adulterous sister-in-law, Esther: ' "For He will not always chide, neither will He keep his anger for ever." '[19]

Maurice's position was more difficult. As professor of divinity at King's, he had to be seen to uphold the orthodox position of the Church of England. Whilst the equivocations of *Theological Essays* were unacceptable in 1853, they came to mark a great deal of the debate over physical pain during the mid- to late nineteenth century. Arguments such as Maurice's which rely on the redefinition of words, make it clear that the ground was being laid for the widespread dismissal of the Bible as the unadulterated word of God. Maurice's own position, however, as Owen Chadwick argues, was both confused and confusing,[20] for whilst his essay appeared to deny the validity of both eternal

---

[16] Ibid. 450.
[17] See R. K. Webb, 'The Gaskells as Unitarians', in Joanne Shattock (ed.), *Dickens and Other Victorians: Essays in Honour of Philip Collins* (Macmillan, 1988), 144–71.
[18] *Mary Barton: A Tale of Manchester Life*, 2 vols. (Chapman and Hall, 1848), ii. 301.
[19] Ibid. 311, quoting Ps. 103: 9.
[20] See *The Victorian Church*, 2 vols. (Adam and Charles Black, 1966), i. 545 ff.

punishment and atonement, he still taught these doctrines to his students and his book hid the real state of his mind behind unclear phraseology. R. W. Jelf, the principal of King's, was left in the position of having to ascertain Maurice's true stance, being convinced that a man who did not believe in eternal damnation could not be suitable to train clergymen. Bishop Blomfield stepped in, and Maurice was dismissed for his dangerous doctrine on the future punishment of the wicked.

Blomfield had a further part to play, as it was he who was supposed to consecrate Colenso the Bishop of Natal. Colenso, however, had published a letter which praised Maurice as one from whom he had 'derived inestimable blessings'[21] as part of the dedication to his book, *Village Sermons*, published in 1853, the year of Maurice's dismissal from King's. In response to this a petition was collected by those who already opposed Maurice to prevent Colenso's consecration.[22] Colenso was forced to backtrack, claiming that he revered Maurice as a great religious teacher, but that he himself believed in eternal damnation in its conventional sense.[23]

The disturbance aroused by Maurice was the first of several such disturbances, but the publication of *Essays and Reviews* in 1860 caused a religious crisis that surpassed all others of the nineteenth century and which continued to rage for more than four years.[24] This book, which was the idea of H. B. Wilson, tutor at St John's in Oxford, attempted to bring to the Church of England the sort of historical criticism of the Bible that had been common practice in Germany for half a century.[25] Contributors, representing the bravest of the Broad Church, included: Frederick Temple, the headmaster of Rugby, who later became the archbishop of Canterbury; Rowland Williams, the professor of Hebrew at Lampeter; Baden Powell, the Professor of Geometry at Oxford; H. B. Wilson himself; C. W. Goodwin, a layman from Cambridge; Mark Pattison, rector of Lincoln College, who later became an agnostic; and Benjamin Jowett,

---

[21] *Village Sermons* (Cambridge: Macmillan; Norwich: Thomas Priest, 1853), p. vii.
[22] Chadwick, *Victorian Church*, i. 550. But see also Rowell, *Hell and the Victorians*, 118. Rowell argues that Colenso's missionary experience made it impossible for him to believe in eternal damnation for heathens.
[23] Chadwick, *Victorian Church*, i. 550.
[24] See Vidler, *Church in Age of Revolution*, 123.   [25] Ibid. 125.

who was at that time tutor at Balliol, where he later became master. The book was attacked on all fronts, as Vidler details.[26] The first major opponent was Frederic Harrison, the British proponent of positivism, who wrote anonymously in the *Westminster Review* that he found himself unable to see how the authors reconciled their modern and critical views with their position inside the Church of England.[27] Samuel Wilberforce joined the attack, arguing against what he saw as the authors' scepticism, verging on atheism,[28] and in so doing made it clear that those inside the Church were as opposed to the book as those outside. A meeting of bishops, urged on by Wilberforce, were so scandalized that they felt compelled to prosecute. Williams, whose review of 'Bunsen's Biblical Researches' had provoked the most outrage in its open claims for a critical reading of the Bible, stood trial alongside Wilson, the editor. Both were initially found guilty in the Court of Arches of denying the inspiration of Scripture, with Wilson facing further charges of denying the doctrine of eternal damnation, but both were later exonerated on appeal to the Judicial Committee of the Privy Council in February 1864. In response to this judgement, a statement of refutation addressed to the Archbishop of Canterbury was organized and offered by a collection of 11,000 clergymen and 137,000 laymen, led by Pusey. The signatories declared their

firm belief that the Church of England and Ireland, in common with the whole Catholic Church, maintains without reserve or qualification, the Inspiration and Divine Authority of the whole Canonical Scriptures, as not only containing but being the Word of God; and further teaches, in the Words of our Blessed Lord, that the 'punishment' of the 'cursed' equally with the 'life' of the 'righteous' is everlasting.[29]

Belief in the plenary inspiration of the Bible went hand in hand with belief in hell and everlasting punishment. The mounting

---

[26] Ibid. 125 ff.

[27] 'Neo-Christianity', *Westminster and Foreign Quarterly Review*, NS 36 (1860), 295: 'In object, in spirit, and in method, in details no less than in general design— this book is incompatible with the religious belief of the mass of the Christian public, and the broad principles on which the Protestantism of Englishmen rests. The most elaborate reasoning to prove that they are in harmony can never be anything but futile, and ends in becoming insincere.'

[28] See 'Essays and Reviews', *Quarterly Review*, 109 (1861), 248–305.

[29] See Vidler, *Church in Age of Revolution*, 128.

opposition to such linkage, and the revolt against eternal
damnation as a moral idea, hit hard at the basis of Evangelical
and High Church Christianity. Wilson, in similar vein to
Gaskell, claimed, concerning hell, that

The Roman Church has imagined a *limbus infantium*; we must rather
entertain a hope that there shall be found, after the great adjudication,
receptacles suitable for those who shall be infants, not as to years of
terrestrial life, but as to spiritual development—nurseries as it were
and seed-grounds, where the undeveloped may grow up under new
conditions . . . and the perverted be restored.[30]

It was largely this statement, and its refusal to accept an eternity of punishment, that landed Wilson in the ecclesiastical
courts.[31] The Church of England, which had largely cast aside
the idea of a physical hell by 1880, was clearly not ready to do
so in the 1860s when Wilson was writing.

Charles Voysey, himself brought up as a strict Evangelical,
took courage from the vindication of Williams and Wilson, as,
indeed, did many members of the Broad Church. Ignoring the
fact that their fairly mild statements had led to prosecution,
however successfully defended, Voysey began publishing
sermons under the title *The 'Sling and the Stone.'* with the freethinker Thomas Scott in 1864. These ranged widely, but were
largely concerned with proving that the Bible should not be
taken literally, and, indeed, that the Church had much to answer
for in treating the Bible as the indisputable word of God:

Both the Bible and the Church have been presented to us under false
pretences.

The Bible has been presented to us as one homogeneous book
written by one author, no less than God Himself, and therefore to be
accepted as infallible and true in every one of its statements. To this
fundamentally false pretence has been added a threat of grievous,
perhaps endless, punishment against every one who deliberately rejects
the authority of any part of it.[32]

---

[30] *Essays and Reviews* (John W. Parker, 1860), 206.
[31] See M. A. Crowther, *Church Embattled: Religious Controversy in Mid-
Victorian England* (Newton Abbot: David and Charles, 1970), 120.
[32] 'Address to the Reader', in *The 'Sling and the Stone.' Aimed not against Men,
but Opinions. Free Speaking in the Church of England*, 10 vols. (London: Trübner;
Ramsgate: Thomas Scott, 1867), vol. ii, p. 3. This address is bound at the beginning of the British Library copy.

From this position Voysey questioned the morality of the Old Testament, and denied that such stories as that of Jehu murdering the priests of Baal could have significance for contemporary Christians. Instead of being edified, readers were being lead astray by tales of divinely sanctioned cruelty.[33] He further suggested that the 'core of truth' that ' "sin bears bitter consequences," and that "from those consequences we shall be ultimately saved" ' had been surrounded by 'many erroneous notions'.[34] Salvation, as a word, had been misrepresented, and as such had led to cruelty. Amongst such erroneous notions was the 'most false of all the false meanings of salvation, viz., that salvation is being somehow rescued and delivered from that endless life in torment—that salvation is being saved from everlasting hell'.[35] Voysey's insistence on biblical criticism[36] gave him a platform to reject such doctrines as that of eternal damnation on the grounds that it was immoral. In the series of sermons *The 'Sling and the Stone.'* he did just this, claiming that no sin, however terrible, could deserve endless punishment, and that if this were the case, then God would be a sadist rather than a benevolent Father. Wilson had not gone nearly so far: he had expressed hope that no one would be consigned to hell for ever, but he certainly did not deny hell's existence. Voysey not only did this, but also claimed that a God who demanded such eternal suffering could not be one worthy of worship. We shall see this attitude replicated in his approach to the necessity of physical pain in Section II of this chapter.

Voysey did not stop here. As Geoffrey Rowell argues of the debate over eternal punishment following Wilson's trial, 'in the minds of many, there was an inverse correlation between the intensity of the pains of hell and the status of the Saviour':[37] to deny hell was, in effect, to suggest that Christ could not save. This was exactly the position that Voysey found himself in by 1868, when he explicitly rejected the idea that Christ's crucifixion brought about man's salvation. Voysey's printed works caused such offence that he was tried in the Chancery Court of York in December 1869. The court case was lengthy, and in it

---

[33] See *'Sling and Stone.'*: vol. I, pt. xi, *Jehu and Hezekiah*, p. 12.
[34] Ibid.: vol. II, pt. ii, *Salvation*, p. 5.   [35] Ibid. 6.
[36] See Ibid.: vol. III, pt. iv, *Bribes and Threats*, p. 79.
[37] *Hell and the Victorians*, 123.

Voysey depended on the precedent of Wilson's victory, claiming that he was only making more explicit claims that Wilson, and his fellow-writers in *Essays and Reviews*, had already made. The precedent was ineffectual, and in 1871 he was found guilty and deprived of his living.

If Voysey stood as an example of the boldest[38] or, perhaps, the most belligerent of the Broad Church, J. C. Ryle stands as a prime example of an influential Evangelical clergyman who stood firm against the attacks of Voysey and the other 'heretics', and whose long life enabled his influence to be felt over a period of upwards of fifty years. Considered to be the leader of the Evangelical wing of the Church after the furore aroused by *Essays and Reviews*, he set himself against both the High and the Broad Church, until eventually becoming bishop of Liverpool in 1880. Ryle never faltered in his faith, always believing in the plenary inspiration of the Bible, and the central importance of the atonement to the Christian religion. As such, by the end of his life, marked in theological terms by the publication of Charles Gore's *Lux Mundi* (1889) the year before his death, he was out of line with the main thrust of Church of England thought. Gore's book—the 1880s' acceptable equivalent of the controversial *Essays and Reviews*—marked this change. Dean Church, the leader of English Liberal Catholicism, reviewed the book, and in so doing recognized the radical change that the Church had undergone as the turn of the century approached: 'Things are, no doubt, changed; & the Bishops are changed, & most of them, except perhaps Liverpool, accept as truisms what their ignorant predecessors in 1840–45 held up to execration as scoundrelly dishonesty & treason.'[39] As Boyd Hilton argues, by 1870 'it was commonplace for Anglicans to assert that a theological transformation had recently taken place, whereby a worldly Christian compassion, inspired by the life of Jesus, had alleviated such stark evangelical doctrines as those of eternal and vicarious punishment'.[40]

Ryle is an appropriate figure to suggest what Evangelical attitudes were—indeed he wrote between two and three hundred

---

[38] See Crowther, *Church Embattled*, 127–8.

[39] G. L. Prestige, *The Life of Charles Gore: A Great Englishman* (London and Toronto: William Heinemann, 1935), 85.

[40] *The Age of Atonement: The Influence of Evangelicalism on Social and Economic Thought, 1785–1865* (Oxford: Clarendon Press, 1988), 5.

tracts which sold twelve million copies in his lifetime[41]—and I
shall be using his attitudes towards the pains of hell, those of
the atonement, as well as the pains of earth, to suggest the inter-
connectedness of these three in his arguments, and the ways in
which the lessening hold of the two former affected the treatment of the latter. It has already become clear that theological
pain became problematic for members of the Broad Church,
and I want here to suggest the ways in which it was valued by
Evangelicals.

Ryle came from a tradition which believed in the efficacy of
pain as an active process: by dying on the cross Christ was able
to reconcile wayward man to God. As Ryle claimed in one of
his many tracts, 'Depend upon it, the cross of Christ,—the death
of Christ on the cross to make atonement for sinners,—is the
centre truth in the whole Bible':[42] without this, there could be
no redemption, no escape from the pains of hell. Ryle, basing
his faith on the biblical depictions outlined by Greg earlier in
this chapter, believed in a hell of physical torments which would
last for ever, deserved by sinners who refused to accept Christ
during their lifetime, and a warning to those tempted to stray.
He is unequivocal on this point:

Let us settle it, for another thing, in our minds, that the *future misery*
of those who are finally lost is eternal. This is an awful truth, I am
aware, and flesh and blood naturally shrink from the contemplation
of it. But I am one of those who believe it to be plainly revealed in
Scripture, and I dare not keep it back in the pulpit.[43]

Here Ryle displays a different attitude towards suffering: the
pain of crucifixion and atonement could be seen as redemptive,
whilst the pains of hell were clearly retributive. Ryle makes this
point when he asks the question: 'What was the use of God's
Son becoming incarnate, agonizing in Gethsemane, and dying
on the cross to make atonement, if men can be finally saved
without believing on Him?'[44] *Use* is the issue here. Ryle

---

[41] Marcus L. Loane, *John Charles Ryle, 1816–1900: A Short Biography* (James Clarke, 1953), 22.
[42] *The Cross. A Tract for the Times* (5th edn., Ipswich: Hunt; London: Wertheim and Macintosh; Nisbet, 1852), 12–13.
[43] *Eternity! Being Thoughts on 2 Cor. iv. 18. Spoken in Peterborough Cathedral, on Dec. 23rd, 1877. With a Postscript containing some remarks on Canon Farrar's 'Eternal Hope.'* (William Hunt, 1877), 8.
[44] Ibid. 11.

embraces the Evangelical reading of the Bible—that the pain of crucifixion was required and useful—whilst simultaneously recognizing that 'flesh and blood naturally shrink from the contemplation of it'. In a process often repeated, and outlined in the discussions of religious rationalizations of physical pain in Section II of this chapter, Ryle is content to classify such inflictions of pain—here wreaked on the Son of God—as a mystery, something beyond the power of man's imagination to fathom: 'I always expect to find many mysteries in revealed religion, and I am not stumbled by them. I see other difficulties in the world which I cannot solve, and I am content to wait for their solution.'[45] Pain requires no vindication on earth, because it is the essence of divinity to be mysterious.

Up until this point, the discussion of Ryle's thought has been confined to pain that has no specific earthly referent, but he also deliberately read the pains of the here and now in accordance with his theological perspective. The outbreak of cholera in the 1860s was, for Ryle, 'The Hand of the Lord!' working on earth: a divine policy for bringing man's actions into line with God's will. Cholera, of course, had, and still has, other aspects to it than simply pain—death being not the least of these—but it is, all the same, a painful disease. As Ryle writes:

Cholera is a most *severe and trying visitation to men's bodies*. . . . It is often attended by such fearful pains, that the mind can attend to nothing in the hour of death. Few diseases do their fatal work with such terrific torment to the body as Asiatic cholera.[46]

It seems probable from such description that Ryle had first-hand knowledge of the effects of cholera, and the thrust of his tract is to enable his readers to place such pain in a religious framework, thereby understanding it as part of the deliberate purpose of God. He did not, as we shall see G. A. Rowell argue later in this chapter, suggest that such pains did not exist, being

[45] *Eternity!* 24.
[46] *'The Hand of the Lord!' Being Thoughts on Cholera. 2 Sam. xxiv.* 14 (London and Ipswich: William Hunt, [1866]), 4. For the severity of the cholera epidemics of the 19th cent., see Anthony S. Wohl, *Endangered Lives: Public Health in Victorian Britain* (London, Melbourne, Toronto: J. M. Dent, 1983), 118–19. For a strikingly different reading of the 1832 cholera outbreak in Manchester, see Mary Poovey's discussion of James Phillips Kay in *Making a Social Body: British Cultural Formation, 1830–1864* (Chicago and London: Chicago University Press, 1995), 56 ff.

smoothed away by the loving hand of God as death approached. Ryle is adamant that dying of cholera makes deathbed repentance impossible as it is simply too painful to concentrate on anything outside the body's immediate sufferings: the time for repentance is whilst one is still in health. Similarly, and more important in terms of his own theology, he insists that 'cholera, like every other pestilence, is a *direct visitation from God*'.[47] Pain and death must simply be accepted as one of the simple tenets of faith. Ryle continues:

I shall not spend much time in proving this. I believe it to be a Scriptural principle, and one that cannot be overthrown. In fact, I am persuaded there is no real standing ground between this view and downright infidelity.[48]

It is here that the nature of Ryle's Evangelicalism comes to the fore. Just as God laid the heavy affliction of plague on King David's kingdom, such that 70,000 men died in three days,[49] so too did Ryle read cholera as part of God's ongoing concern and engagement with mankind:

Believing these things, I see the hand of God in all the great events which happen in the world. The rise and fall of nations, the discoveries of art and science, the outbreak of wars, famines, and pestilences,— all these things are planned, arranged, timed, and managed by an all wise God. The great Architect above us will one day show that all happened by His appointment, and all worked together for man's good and His glory.[50]

In true Evangelical fashion, Ryle cites a list of confirming Old Testament texts which speak of God sending pestilence to his people[51] and uses these to provide a rationale for nineteenth-century outbreaks of pestilence. Not only does Ryle hold firmly to Jeremiah's explanation for such illnesses—'They have rejected the word of the Lord'[52]—but also refuses to countenance any other:

Some men will tell us confidently that cholera arises entirely from second causes. Bad drainage, bad water, want of cleanliness, want of sufficient food,—all these are enough in the eyes of these men to

---

[47] *Cholera*, 5.   [48] Ibid.   [49] 2 Sam. 24: 15.   [50] *Cholera*, 6.
[51] Lev. 26: 25, Num. 14: 12, Ps. 78: 50, Jer. 24: 10, Ezek. 14: 19, Amos 4: 10.
[52] Jer. 8: 9.

explain the present visitation. But unfortunately for these people there
was no drainage at all in former days! The streets of our great cities
were dirty and unpaved! The water supply was miserably defective!
The sanitary condition of the people was in every respect disgracefully
bad. Yet in these days there was no cholera.

No! it will not do. Second causes, no doubt, may help on cholera
when cholera begins. But second causes will not account for its
beginning.[53]

The primary cause of cholera is not, for Ryle, bad sanitation,
but the national sins of 'drunkenness, Sabbath-breaking, and
infidelity'.[54] The pain and death of cholera are read as chastise-
ments with which God draws errant man back to the narrow
path of Godliness and Evangelicalism, so that 'painful as the visitation may be at the time, it is for the good . . . let us not doubt
that the health of the body politic needs it . . . There is mercy
even in this outbreak of cholera.'[55] Christianity's peculiar power
where physical pain is concerned lies, Ryle suggests, in the fact
that the Hand of the Lord that inflicts such chastising pain is
also 'The hand that was nailed to the cross of Calvary'.[56] As
such it 'is too loving to lay on us more than we can bear'.[57]

Ryle's arguments are important not simply because, as the
acknowledged voice of Evangelicalism, he demonstrates the way
in which readings of pain were firmly tied to a belief in the literal
truth of the Bible, but, in terms of my own argument, because
of the unresolved signs of equivocation seen in his tracts.[58] Pain,
for Ryle, is a mystery that will only be solved after the Second
Coming, but whilst pain is a visitation intended to chastise and
emend, it is also the duty of the Christian to run errands for the
sick and to give money; to eat wisely and to avoid polluted
water; to

Wage war against all bad smells and heaps of dirt, as you would against
a poisonous serpent. Complain at once to the parish authorities if nui-
sances near you are not removed. Be very careful about your own
eating and drinking, and the eating and drinking of all the members

---

[53] *Cholera*, 7.   [54] Ibid. 16.   [55] Ibid. 9.   [56] Ibid. 8.
[57] Ibid. 8.
[58] See G. H. Lewes, 'On the Dread and Dislike of Science', in *Versatile Victorian:
Selected Writings of George Henry Lewes*, ed. Rosemary Ashton (Bristol: Bristol
Classical Press, 1992), 317–26, for a scathing denunciation of such 'logical incon-
sistency' (325).

of your family. Forbid green apples, unripe plums, and cheap stale fish to come within your doors.[59]

Ryle clearly does not see these injunctions to avoid impending doom as equivocations, claiming instead that 'God Himself gave [regulations] for preserving cleanliness and health among His chosen people'[60] in Deuteronomy, and he establishes such evasion as sound good sense. But such an attitude surely questions, implicitly at least, the ability of God to inflict at will. The secondary causes which Ryle acknowledges have a curiously shifting status in the face of a deliberate visitation of cholera. If it is the duty of Christians to alleviate the disease in others, and to avoid it for themselves, then it is hard to see how this fits in with God's plan of chastisement. Pain was envisaged in terms of purpose, but it was a purpose that could be thwarted. This, indeed, is the problem that confronted many of the medical innovations of the nineteenth century, whether doctors were trying to introduce vaccinations or to use chloroform in child-birth, both of which ran into the religious objection that illness and pain were part of a biblical injunction and that it was impious to relieve them. James Young Simpson, largely responsible for popularizing anaesthetic childbirth in the late 1840s, laughed at religious injunctions that parturitional suffering was the curse of Eve[61] and as such should not be tampered with. His arguments against such biblical injunctions ridicule those who hold such views and demolish what he sees as spurious arguments for the plenary inspiration of the Bible.[62]

Such disregard of the Bible and the elevation of humankind's facility to judge the rights and wrongs of bodily suffering is vital to my argument. For Evangelicals, as indeed for Catholics, the righteous trinity of atonement, eternal damnation, and physical

---

[59] *Cholera*, 13. See Wohl, *Endangered Lives*, 120: 'Cholera was contracted by swallowing water or food which had been infected by the cholera vibrio, a minute bacillus. The vibrio could last up to five days in meat, milk, or cheese, less in green vegetables, and up to sixteen days in apples, and it could dwell up to a fortnight in water. It was most often spread by water contaminated by the excreta of cholera victims, or by flies which hatched in or fed upon the diseased excrement.'

[60] *Cholera*, 13.   [61] Gen. 3: 16.

[62] See esp. James Young Simpson, *Answer to the Religious Objections advanced against the Employment of Anæsthetic Agents in Midwifery and Surgery* (Edinburgh: Sutherland and Knox; London: Samuel Highly, 1847).

chastisement was unbreakable, having an outlet for Evangelicals in the saying 'spare the rod and spoil the child' and, predominantly for Catholic clergy, in beating themselves to mortify
the flesh. Such positions were not as simply confined to denom-
inations as this might suggest, as the Anglo-Catholic Anthony
Froude found out to his cost when beaten by his father,[63] and
as Gladstone flogged himself after night visits amongst prostitutes.[64] But pain of these kinds relied on there being divine
purpose behind it. Christian attitudes towards physical suffering suggested that pain was both profoundly useful—the atonement brought God and humanity back into alignment, as the
fear of hell kept it on the straight and narrow[65]—and retributive—beating recalcitrant children could serve as a prefigure-
ment of what they would suffer if their final destination turned
out to be hell. The Catholic priest the Revd J. Furniss[66] displays
this attitude in an extreme form in his horrifying book *The Sight
of Hell* (1861), published for the instruction of 'children and
young persons' and 'recommended to be used along with the
Catechism in Sunday-schools as part of a course of religious
instruction'.[67] In this book, which sold in its millions,[68] Furniss
describes in abhorrent detail the fate of those destined to spend
eternity in hell:

The sinner lies chained down on a bed of red-hot blazing fire! When
a man, sick of fever, is lying on even a soft bed, it is pleasant sometimes to turn round. If the sick man lies on the same side for a long
time, the skin comes off, and the flesh gets raw. How will it be when
the body has been lying on the same side on the scorching, boiling fire
for a hundred millions of years? Now look at that body lying on a bed
of fire, [*sic*] All the body is salted with fire. The fire burns through

---

[63] Herbert Paul, *The Life of Froude* (Sir Isaac Pitman, 1905), 12.
[64] See Roy Jenkins, *Gladstone* (London and Basingstoke: Macmillan, 1995),
103–7.
[65] E. B. Pusey, writing to A. C. Tait, 25 Dec. 1863, claimed: 'I am sure that
nothing will keep men from the present pleasures of sin, but the love of God or the
fear of Hell; and that the fear of Hell drives people back to . . . God.' Quoted in
Crowther, *Church Embattled*, 132.
[66] Revd J. Furniss CSSR (Congregation of the Most Holy Redeemer) was a
Redemptorist: one of a community of priests and lay brothers, whose 'special
concern is the preaching of the Word of God, especially by means of missions,
retreats, and novenas'. See the *New Catholic Encyclopedia*, 15 vols. (New York:
McGraw-Hill, 1967), xii. 161–4: 'Redemptorists'.
[67] Greg, *Enigmas*, 251 n.   [68] See Wheeler, *Death and the Future Life*, 180.

every bone and every muscle. Every nerve is trembling and quivering with the sharp fire. The fire rages inside the skull, it shoots out through the eyes, it drops out through the ears, it roars in the throat as it roars up a chimney.[69]

This is precisely what such writers as Voysey were reacting against. Such description is not just repulsive to the late twentieth-century reader, but was equally held up for execration at the time of its publication. T.R., writing in *Hell and its Torments* (1870), expressly aimed to drag the reader away from belief in such sadistic fantasies as those portrayed in *The Sight of Hell*.[70] Despite the strength of T.R.'s opposition, Furniss was not moving outside his ambit as a Catholic priest in his representations of a physical and eternal hell, as is made clear in Kenelm Digby Best's translation of H. Hurter's Jesuit *Compendium of Dogmatic Theology*. In this, Catholic doctrine concerning hell is elucidated: '*Transgressions of the divine law not pardoned in this life are punished by God in the next*'; '*The fire with which the impious are punished is true and real, not metaphorical*'; '*The pains of the damned are eternal*.'[71] Such doctrine has moved on from simply the biblical descriptions cited by Greg, and, as Hurter makes clear, the doctrine has been reinforced by the interpretations of the Church Fathers, and rests on the word of such men, on 'the voice of tradition and the testimony of the martyrs',[72] and on such formulations as the Athanasian Creed, which contained its infamous damnatory clause, 'They that have done good shall go into life everlasting, and they that have done evil into everlasting fire.'[73] T.R. objected strongly to such doctrine, particularly as portrayed for the young by Furniss, and fought against it by making it public. As T.R. wrote:

[69] T. R., *Hell and its Torments, as described by Eye-witnesses and Others. With remarks by T.R., Author of 'Substitution.'* (London: Geo. John Stevenson; Manchester: John Heywood; Glasgow: W. Love; Edinburgh: H. Robinson, 1870), 19.

[70] T. R. was far from alone in his objections to this particular book. See also Annie Besant, *On Eternal Torture* (Thomas Scott, [1874]), 7–8 and Greg, *Enigmas*, 251–2 n.

[71] *The Catholic Doctrine About Hell. From the Compendium of Dogmatic Theology*, trans. Kenelm Digby Best (London: Burns and Oates; New York: Catholic Publication Society, 1887), 3, 6 and 11.

[72] Ibid. 12–13.

[73] For parallel Evangelical justifications of the doctrine of hell, including the witness of the language of the Bible, the Prayer Book, the Catechism, and the Burial Service, see Ryle, *Eternity!*, 8–9.

We imagine few who have read this description carefully and thought-fully will find their faith in this horrible dogma much increased thereby; on the contrary, we think, if the thoughtful reader will only try to *realise* the true nature of the horrible torments here depicted, and whether such *endless* misery can be productive of any permanent good whatever to any of God's creatures, living or dead, his better feelings and his sense of justice will revolt at the dogma and at the very idea of a human soul being kept in such perpetual misery without any hope of release.[74]

T.R.'s sharp denunciation of such physical depictions of hell by no means stood alone, but constituted a part of the moral objections to Christianity that began to be voiced in the second half of the century. As Howard Murphy argues, the idea that the decline of belief in orthodox Christianity stemmed *mainly* from the rise of evolutionary thought after the publication of Darwin's *Origin of Species* in 1859 is largely unfounded.[75] He cites the cases of J. A. Froude, Francis Newman, and Mary Ann Evans[76] to suggest that, despite their upbringing in the Established Church, these three lost their formerly strong faith, largely because of

a growing repugnance toward the ethical implications of what they had been taught to accept as essential Christian dogma . . . None of them appears to have read Lyell, and each made his [sic] decisive break with orthodoxy from ten to twenty years before the appearance of *The Origin of Species*.[77]

Froude's Anglo-Catholicism and Evans's Evangelicalism, though widely divergent in other ways, revolved around the same central set of tenets, including the particularly repellent, to them and to many others, assertion of vicarious atonement, and eternal damnation.[78]

---

[74] *Hell and its Torments*, 36.

[75] 'The Ethical Revolt against Christian Orthodoxy in Early Victorian England', *American Historical Review*, 60 (1955), 800–17. See also Robin Gilmour, *The Victorian Period: The Intellectual and Cultural Context of English Literature, 1830–1890* (London and New York: Longman, 1993), 87 ff.

[76] Such discussion of well-known figures turning against their former faith is widely replicated. See Chadwick, *Victorian Church*, on Dickens (i. 528) and Thackeray (i. 529); Gilmour, *Victorian Period*, on Frances Power Cobbe (74), Beatrice Webb (92), and Darwin (89).

[77] Murphy, 'Ethical Revolt', 801.

[78] For Eliot's positive response to Froude's book, see George Eliot, 'J. A. Froude's *The Nemesis of Faith*', *Coventry Herald and Observer*, 16 Mar. 1849, 2; repr. in George Eliot, *Selected Essays, Poems and Other Writings* (Penguin, 1990), 265–7.

James Anthony Froude, in *The Nemesis of Faith*, gives to his mouthpiece, Markham Sutherland, an impassioned rejection of the doctrine of hell:[79]

I mean that the largest portion of mankind, these very people who live about us, feel with us, act with us, are our daily companions—the people we meet at dinner or see in the streets, that are linked in with us with innumerable ties of common interests, common sympathies, common occupations—these very people are to be tortured for ever and ever in unspeakable agonies. My God! and for what? They are thrown out into life, into an atmosphere impregnated with temptation, with characters unformed, with imperfect natures out of which to form them, under necessity of a thousand false steps, and yet with every one scored down for vengeance; and laying up for themselves a retribution so infinitely dreadful that our whole soul shrinks horror-struck before the very imagination of it; and this under the decree of an all-just, all-bountiful God—the God of love and mercy.[80]

Here God is portrayed as being less rather than more compassionate than his creation, who acknowledge the causes of wrongdoing and recognize that such people deserve 'not anger and punishment, but tears and pity and forgiveness'.[81] The fictional Sutherland—Froude staunchly denied that the book was autobiographical in the preface to the second edition—revolts, as Murphy suggests, ethically against the Church of which he was a member. Pain inflicted eternally on the poor, or, indeed, on anyone cannot, in Sutherland's eyes, be right. Susan Budd, in *Varieties of Unbelief*, opens up the issue, broadening Murphy's argument from three exceptional—if broadly representative—thinkers, to examine the patterns of thought of working-class Victorian secularists, for whom, she claims, 'the revolution in scientific and theological thinking seems largely irrelevant. The loss of faith was not an intellectual but a moral matter'[82] based, once again, on the revolt against eternal damnation, vicarious atonement, and damnation for unbelievers.

This issue of ethical revolt against the pain inflicted and required by God is critical. It was shared by those content to

---

[79] For the biographical background to the writing of this novel, see Chadwick, *Victorian Church*, i. 535–7.

[80] *The Nemesis of Faith* (2nd edn., John Chapman, 1849), 15.

[81] Ibid.

[82] *Varieties of Unbelief: Atheists and Agnostics in English Society, 1850–1960* (Heinemann, 1977), 123.

rebel against it from inside the Church of England (Thackeray, whom I shall discuss further, stands as an example of these), as well as those who felt themselves forced to leave (Annie Besant's *My Path to Atheism* includes angry essays on the atonement and eternal damnation), as well, indeed, as those, such as Charles Voysey, ejected forcibly from the ministry for their 'heretical' opinions. Nothing is simple, and a whole series of factors— the ethical revolt against atonement and eternal damnation; the concomitant decline in belief in the plenary inspiration of the Bible; the rise of science and the influence of geological and bio- logical findings which shattered assumptions about Genesis and miracles—worked together to unpick the hold that Christianity had formerly held over the minds of the English, until, as Susan Budd argues,

By 1880, infallibilist interpretations of Scripture had largely been aban- doned, and the main drift of theological debate was over whether there was a future life at all. The post-Darwinian attack on the special status of man in creation and the erosion of the Cartesian dualism of body and soul led to increasing doubt about all doctrines of personal immor- tality. By the early twentieth century, samplings of popular opinion showed that religion had been ethicized. Most people had abandoned a scriptural hell for a vague belief in an unspecific afterlife, regulated not by religious beliefs but by behaviour.[83]

Opinions that were dangerous and heretical in the 1840s had become mainstream by the 1880s, largely through the agency of the series of trials, both professional and legal, of Maurice, Wilson, Williams, and Voysey.

Thackeray's letter of 23–31 December 1830 to his mother is important in bringing together the idea of a vague theologi- cal pain, sited in the afterlife, with the pains of the here and now:

There is to be sure the horrible Hell Fire, w^h declares Pain to be eternal and obliges God thus perpetually to sanction Evil: just fancy it—we who know how intolerable a minute's pain of body or a single stroke of sorrow is, we who, the worst of us, have *some* good in us fancy a scream of agony through eternal ages, and an ever present sorrow to be our ultimate boon from God or the ultimate condition of any single brother man! Judas Iscariot came into the world with diseases from

---

[83] Budd, 117.

his mother, and phrenological bumps—who shall visit the sins of his carcass upon his immortal soul?[84]

Thackeray here reverses Ryle's position in his tract on cholera. Ryle argued that pain in this life was necessary and appropriate as it was God's means of chastising and warning errant man. He approached the worldly from the vantage point of Christian theology, using Christ's pain as a validation of human pain. Thackeray argues from the other end: 'a minute's pain of body' is held up as something intolerable, and as such is taken as the measure for eternal suffering. Judas Iscariot, providing Thackeray with the ultimate sinner, is bound to the things of earth, and his sin is read as the fruit of his inheritance, not something for which his body is bound to pay in suffering through all eternity. Thackeray, in the vanguard of theological thought, offered quotidian pain as a test of the acceptability of theological pain, rather than, as it was for Ryle, the reflection of heavenly suffering. Robin Gilmour suggests a similar equation, when he argues that for Frances Power Cobbe (of whom much more in Chapter 4) her rejection of the atonement and eternal damnation were inextricably linked with her embracing the antivivisectionary cause and its antipathy towards the deliberately inflicted suffering of animals;[85] the same is true of Annie Besant who simultaneously rejected eternal punishment, and advocated euthanasia for those who suffered terribly.[86]

II. THE PAINS OF EARTH

The pains of earth came to the fore as the century progressed, partly as a result of chloroform's undercutting the status of pain as a *natural* phenomenon, partly in response to the new Darwinian paradigm, and partly to fill the gap left by the decline of

---

[84] *The Letters and Private Papers of William Makepeace Thackeray*, ed. Gordon N. Ray, 4 vols. (Oxford: Oxford University Press, 1945), i. 402–3: 'To Mrs. Carmichael-Smyth 23–31 December 1839'.

[85] Gilmour, *Victorian Period*, 74–5. For Cobbe's own description of her relationship to 'the dogmas of Original Sin, the Atonement, a Devil and eternal Hell', see Frances Power Cobbe, *Life of Frances Power Cobbe, as Told by Herself. With Additions by the Author*, posthumous edn. (Swan Sonnenschein, 1904), 102.

[86] [Annie Besant], *Euthanasia* (Thomas Scott, [1875]).

religion as a viable justification for physical suffering. The universally acknowledged unpleasantness of physical pain became a measure of the pains of eternal damnation, rather than, as it was for Furniss, a foreshadowing of such pains. Christian understandings of physical pain in the late nineteenth century were forced to confront the ethical revolt against theologically based pains, and once these latter lost their rationale—as the pains of hell became the spiritual horrors of being shut out from God and from hope for all eternity, and atonement lost ground to the vision of a Christ of compassion—the sustaining religious arguments that had supported quotidian pain came under question. Pain, which had been seen as an expression of God's justice, became by the end of the century the expression of God's injustice. The idea of an eternal damnation with real flames, physical torment, and devils, which had been such an easy target for secularists in the 1840s and 1850s, largely collapsed under the strain of a public who refused to accept the Bible literally, and who were horrified at its moral implications. In this theological upheaval, the moral basis of physical pain itself was also largely undermined. If there was no longer universal acceptance of the justice of the infliction of pain after death, then the immediate assumption of justifiable physical pain during life was equally brought into question.

Theological writers in the last third of the century inherited doubt over the status of physical pain from their immediate predecessors, and were forced into rationalizing and justifying the physical pains of the world in which they lived. Sermons and religious books are two of the very few places in late Victorian writings where authors acknowledged and faced up to bodily pain in a direct way. Rationalizing pain was of the utmost importance for the Church in a society where many of its members were suffering physically at any given time, and where belief in pain with innate value and significance was being seriously undermined, not just by the attrition of once firmly held theological positions, but also by the concurrent encroachment of medical knowledge into a field which had previously been considered almost exclusively theological. It is significant that sermons on pain as a *problem* that needed to be resolved started to be published in the mid-1860s when the debate over eternal punishment was coming to a head, the trials of Wilson and

Williams were just over, and Voysey was preparing the ground for his own heresy trial in his series of outspoken sermons, *The 'Sling and the Stone.'*.

In *God's Thoughts not Our Thoughts* (1867), Voysey sited his own position with regard to physical pain within the broader spectrum of nineteenth-century theological thought. The problem of pain, as Voysey saw it, was that humans, if given the ordering of the universe, would not have allowed physical suffering a place. If God ordains pain, then the question must be asked, 'Are God's thoughts about human pain and sorrow lower than our thoughts, or are they higher?'[87] In asking this question, Voysey's thought, as with his sermon on Jehu, had been deeply influenced by the ongoing ethical revolt against mainstream Christianity. Still within the Church of England at this time, Voysey refused to accept orthodox explanations of pain, turning instead to rationalizations based on thoughtful exploration of the ethics of human suffering. Asking the question of whose thoughts are higher, God's or humankind's, Voysey makes plain his objection to unthinking acceptance:

And for answer to this question, it will not do to follow the example of those who think it wrong to reason, and say, 'Who art thou that repliest against God?' . . . It will not do thus to evade one of the most profound and formidable of all the problems of this age. Better at once to own the truth, and say, 'We are hopelessly puzzled by this painful life, and it robs us of all trust in God.' Better to say this, shocking as it is, than to pretend to acquiesce in God's plan, and to call it good only because we will not look at it. I think God is now mercifully appealing to our reasons, stimulating our enquiries by His own Holy Spirit, in order that we may arrive at higher truth, in order that we may gain a nobler trust, than we had before, when we lay still in darkness and sleep. He wants us, I believe, to make sure the foundation of our faith and hope; to build it on the rock of reason, instead of building, as we have hitherto done, on the treacherous sand of human authority and tradition.[88]

For Voysey, 'God is *now* . . . appealing to our reasons', 'now' being the 1860s when biblical criticism and ethical revolt were undercutting orthodox belief. Pain, in the light of such a belief,

---

[87] *'Sling and Stone.'*: vol. III, pt. viii, *God's Thoughts not Our Thoughts*, pp. 165–6.   [88] Ibid., 166.

became not simply, as it was for Ryle, the mysterious Hand of the Lord at work on earth, but instead a problem that needed to be thought about and resolved.

This change of approach towards pain is seminal in understanding late nineteenth-century ways of making sense of pain. As pain became a problem rather than a mystery, and as such open to interpretation in the theological sphere, it also lost its sure footing in the minds of the public. Harriet Martineau's comfortable assertion that pain is 'in some way or other, ordained for, or instrumental to good' became less and less tenable. From the late 1860s onwards, pain was left open to interpretation in ways that had been impossible when Christian theology had a firm grip on the meaning of physical suffering, and a wholesale reinterpretation of pain became necessary to fill the gap. If, as James Hinton, the surgeon and devotional author, claimed, pain is to be seen in the positive light that makes it acceptable, it always requires 'an entire inversion of our attitude'.[89] It is this 'entire inversion' that is to be seen at work in both religious and non-religious explanations of pain.

No general consensus existed among Christian writers as to the meaning of pain: Evangelicals believing in eternal damnation accepted pain that was retributive and admonitory, whilst their faith in the atonement suggested the redemptive power of their suffering; Unitarians, and other Christian groups that tended towards universalism, saw pain as reformatory and purgative. Acceptance of pain was tied in with infallibilist readings of the Bible. None of these attitudes had any simple relation to physical pain, for they had nothing other than an imaginary presence, their object being a putative future hell, or a non-verifiable historical crucifixion. Theological beliefs, however, clearly did affect people's responses to physical pain. As I have argued, Voysey saw the problem of pain very much as an issue of the day, related directly to more abstruse doctrinal argument. In justifying physical pain as part of God's plan, he also managed to justify its infliction on earth:

We resent soon enough the interference of weak, indulgent, or inexperienced relatives, who say 'Oh don't let the poor child cry—give it

---

[89] [James Hinton], *The Mystery of Pain: A Book for the Sorrowful* (Smith, Elder, 1866), 13.

what it wants—don't whip it,' etc.; and we know then and there how much more we love our children than any one else can, and how much more true love it requires to brace our courage to give them pain and sorrow, than to give them joy. And we know, too, that children always love those best . . . who inflict pain upon them for their good.[90]

Voysey's belief in the rightness of a heavenly Father inflicting pain spills over into his sense of the rightness of the same action by an earthly father, but it is equally the case that God's infliction of pain is justified by the effectiveness of human punishment. Without this justifying rationale, as Voysey wrote seven years after his heresy trial, pain was pointless: 'Without God, and without a perfect issue to all our pains, we are the sport of forces in nature, which are abysmally cruel. No words of indignation and fierce passion could express one's sense of the outrage daily and hourly inflicted on sensitive beings.'[91]

Voysey was far from alone in the 1870s in suggesting that 'the problem of pain' and the seeming indifference behind its infliction, was one of the major stumbling blocks to a faith that upheld the beneficence of an omnipotent God. Much as biblical criticism had questioned, and largely overthrown, the belief in a physical hell, the scriptural texts that supported physical pain were not enough in themselves to justify such suffering.[92] As the theological usefulness of the pain of atonement and hell became unmoored, physical pain—instead of being immediately referred back to 'the Hand of the Lord' as it was with Ryle— floated freely, accruing many different meanings as it went; meanings which sought to make it acceptable. The widespread collapse of unquestioning belief in the Bible meant that the clergy and members of the laity who sought to find an acceptable meaning for pain were forced into eclecticism, as they reached into other spheres—stoicism, biological necessity, Darwinism—for a resanctified pain. The consequence of this was that Christian justifications of physical pain written from

[90] *God's Thoughts*, 171–2.   [91] Id., *Mystery*, 40.
[92] 'He that soweth iniquity shall reap calamity' (Prov. 22: 8); 'Whatsoever a man soweth, that shall he also reap' (Gal. 6: 7); 'we glory in tribulations also: knowing that tribulation worketh patience; And patience, experience; and experience, hope' (Rom. 5: 3–4) etc. See Mircea Eliade (ed.), 'Suffering', in *The Encyclopedia of Religion*, 16 vols. (New York: Macmillan; London: Collier Macmillan, 1987), for a survey of biblical texts used to sustain an argument for useful suffering.

the mid-1860s onwards until the end of the century were much less bound up with denominational allegiances than the parallel arguments over eternal damnation of the 1840s. The old guard, such as Ryle, stuck to outmoded ways of accepting physical suffering, whilst those—the vast majority—who moved on from old-style Evangelicalism, found themselves framing their arguments in much the same terms as equally concerned members of the Broad Church. In the hunt for acceptable meanings, physical pain lost its denominational specificity, and lines of division were drawn up much more sharply between those who refused to accept a Christian paradigm, and those who struggled to maintain it.

Voysey, in his 1878 volume *The Mystery of Pain, Death and Sin*, offered as a hideous possibility a model of a fierce and merciless nature, but worse—for the theologian—was possible. Many Christian apologists acknowledged, and subsequently attempted to refute, the idea that the God who inflicted pain was a sadist, a position also taken by opponents of the doctrine of hell. Daniel Chatterton, the author of a number of atheistic, anti-monarchist pamphlets, writing in 1875, put the case strongly against a sadistic God:

We ask you how can you go down on your bended knees and say 'Oh God thy will be done' in return for God having cast some loved being—say your wife or your child, the flesh of your own loins into a seething lake of hell burning blazes where that flesh shall hiss, quiver, and wither in the boiling lake of flame and torture with the devil to stir them up, as every hellish passion agitates his heart, Mr. Devil and Mr. God Almighty vying with each other to inflict the greatest or most horrid torture, each brute gloating over the agony they are causing?[93]

It is easy to see that once the Christian framework that had sustained the assumed rectitude of hell had fallen apart, physical pain, suffered before death, became questionable in the same terms. The question Christian apologists sought to answer in the negative was: 'Has the Author of all things created us merely to gloat over our sufferings?'[94] The positions I outline here are

---

[93] *Hell, Devils, and Damnation, or The Deeds of a Blood-Stained God and his Pioneer of Priggery, Jesus Christ, if True* (D. Chatterton, [1875]), 5.

[94] J. Edgar Foster, *Pain: Its Mystery and Meaning. And Other Sermons* (James Nisbet, [1891]), 8.

attempts at answering this question to the glory of God. I have chosen people, predominantly ordained ministers, but some lay writers, to articulate and represent particular popular stances: their arguments are reproduced widely across the range of late Victorian religious writing. These writers cross the denominational spectrum, from Voysey's ex-Broad Church theism to J. R. Illingworth's Anglo-Catholicism, but what joins them is that they all defined themselves, in the broadest terms, as Christians.

There is wide acceptance in such writing of the belief that writer and reader share a common understanding of the nature of physical pain, an understanding that the celebrated Wesleyan minister James Dixon[95] makes clear: 'Although we cannot define pain, nor give it colour, form, and substance, yet we are sensible of its existence'[96]—sensible mentally of its existence in others, but physically sensible through our nervous sensibility of its hold on our own bodies. But this, for Christian apologists of pain, was not enough. The brute existence of physical pain needed no further explanation—all had experience of bruising or cutting themselves, even, perhaps only through inference, of breaking a bone or having gallstones—but what did need explanation was the sort of glorified pain, pain with religious significance, advocated by the writers described in this section. Voysey's arguments in *The Mystery of Pain* become significant at this point. In an attempt to explain that God's ways are indeed higher than man's ways, he argues:

We are trained to look at all sorrowful events from *our* side—our narrow, human, earthly side of the question. We feel a present pain and we can only call it by its right name and be impatiently restless till it is removed. But if we would be more than animals, more than mere children, if we would be *men*, we ought to school ourselves ... to look on pain in all its forms as serving a purpose in the plans of an Almighty and All-wise Father quite as indispensable and sacred as that of His choicest gifts.[97]

[95] Dixon was an itinerant preacher for over fifty years, and in this time became the elected representative of the English Conference, the representative of the Conference in the USA, as well as the President of the Canadian conference. See *Dictionary of National Biography*.

[96] *The Pain of the Present and the Happiness of the Future Life. A Sermon, Preached in Cheetham Hill Chapel, on Sunday Morning, April 10th, 1859* (Alexander Heylin, [1859]), 3.

[97] *Mystery*, 7.

Voysey's argument is paradigmatic of much writing that seeks to make sense of pain. It is, perhaps, ironic that one forced out of the Church of England as a heretic, should find himself defending the position of such a staunch Evangelical as Ryle, though Voysey is insistent that the sufferer needs to be *schooled* in the ways of God: blind adherence to dogma is not enough.[98] Pain may be the Hand of the Lord at work, as Ryle believed, but, for Voysey, this had to be thoughtfully, rather than unconditionally, accepted. But the crossover in argument, whatever the doctrinal position, does suggest the flexibility of argumentation where bodily pain was concerned, and the way in which the desire to justify overrode all other considerations.

Voysey's argument is particularly significant in terms of my overall argument because of his desire to relate pain to hierarchical structures: *men*—and it is hard to know exactly how far such a claim is intended to exclude *women*—are more able to pierce the mysteries of God, and therefore more duty-bound to do so, than children, and again than animals: to languish in pain is a sign of the unredeemed brute in the adult man. It is a sign of 'present pain' rather than a pain that is related to eternity in a Christian framework. Voysey, who attached an explanatory appendix to his book detailing scales of sensitivity, ranging from the insensateness of the worm to the painful vulnerability of the human,[99] clearly perceived heightened physical sensitivity and Christian manliness to be linked. In aspiring to be Voysey's ideal man, the sufferer had to leave the relative and projected insentience of the animal and the child behind and embrace not just the means of dealing with suffering, but the suffering itself.

James Hinton, the most single-minded of the religious writers represented here, though himself a surgeon who underwent numerous spiritual crises rather than a member of the clergy,[100] took this argument further. He chose to ground his claim that pain may—and indeed should—be subsumed in religious fervour in the physical and experiential: 'Though we speak of pleasure and pain as fixed and definite things, yet they are truly by no means fixed. It is matter of familiar experience that

---

[98] See *Dogma* versus *Morality. A Reply to Church Congress* (Trübner, 1866).
[99] See Ch. 5 Sect. I for further discussion of this appendix.
[100] See Phyllis Grosskurth, *Havelock Ellis: A Biography* (New York: New York University Press, 1985), 42.

various circumstances may modify our sensibility in respect to things which are, in our ordinary state, painful.'[101] Soldiers in battle failing to notice their wounds, the insignificance of accidents when concentrating deeply, the extreme example of martyrs going 'through their flaming death in ecstasy' and 'eastern sects' who hold glowing metal to their lips without pain,[102] all proved that pain may be subsumed by factors that have a greater power over the mind. For Hinton this power was belief in God.

This, of course, sounds better than it feels in practice. Christian apologists did not uniformly simply expect sufferers to overcome their pain through the power of God, but rather rationalized the presence of pain in the world in different ways. Two broad rationalizations may be educed from the range of religious writing: that pain is a mystery—Ryle's single-mindedly held position—or that pain is a problem. Most Christian apologists, whilst recognizing the difference between the two and, indeed, the implications of such difference, rarely stuck to a single line. Ryle, believing that physical suffering needed no other explanation than biblical sanction to explain its presence, was rare amongst those who wrote about pain. Writers such as J. Edgar Foster (pain is a 'dense and awful mystery')[103] or the missionary C. W. Butler ('There is a mystery of pain which extends beyond the bounds of human life')[104] relied in these statements on the impenetrability of God: a belief in his innate goodness which did not necessarily extend to the earthly comprehensibility of the goodness of his plan. Such attempts to delineate the mystery of pain shore themselves up with biblical quotation. Instead of the 'present pain' of which Voysey speaks, these pains are referred to the future. As Butler writes, citing St Paul (Rom. 8: 22): 'the whole Creation "groans in pain;" but it is waiting as if in earnest and expectancy for a brighter period'.[105] Butler sites the referent of pain that gives it meaning in the redemptive future, and similar quotations from Revelations (16: 4: 'Neither shall there be any more pain') were used

---

[101] *Mystery of Pain*, 33.   [102] Ibid. 34.   [103] *Pain*, 8.
[104] *The Light of Hope in the Mystery of Pain. A Sermon by the Rev. C. W. Butler. Preached in the Congregational Church, Eastwood, on Sunday Evening, June 23rd, 1878, on behalf of the London Missionary Society* (Langley Mill: Augustus Tucker, 1878), 59.   [105] Ibid. 62.

by the clergy to place the meaning of pain outside the realms of the experiential. To justify such claims, it was only necessary, as Ryle had done, to call on the suffering and subsequent exaltation of Christ: 'do not forget that His humility and trust were fully justified, for God raised Him again the third day from the dead'.[106] What this meant was that the inexplicable did not need to be explained.

Arguments over pain were, however, rarely clear cut. Whilst Charles Voysey determinedly sought reasons for pain, he was equally willing to accept that God is good, but mysterious. For him, 'what makes some brave makes others craven. It is contrary, however, to all analogy that we should be able satisfactorily to account for every anomaly and exception to the general order of the Divine Providence.'[107] To destroy the problem of pain, for Voysey and for many others, it seemed at times only necessary to redefine it as a mystery.

But it is clear from Voysey's own writing and, indeed, the writings of many others, that such pushing of anomalies to the other side of a metaphorical veil was not enough to resolve the problem of pain. By categorizing pain as a 'problem' rather than a mystery, such writers referred to the ways in which pain was lived with from day to day, as it was felt on the pulse of the individual sufferer. J. Edgar Foster may have called his book *Pain: Its Mystery and Meaning*, but it is with the *problem* of pain that he was largely concerned, asking what possible function 'present pain' could serve. 'Suffering', he wrote, aligning himself with post-infallibilist readings of the Bible,

is the most stupendous fact in human experience; it is the most difficult problem in our religion. Alas! it is not necessary to prove its existence. We see it everywhere, and it presses us on every side; and our own experience will interpret to us the symbols of pain and agony which we find in every house.[108]

It is this belief in the *painfulness* of pain, rather than its spiritual referent, that began more and more to work itself out in

---

[106] A. Maitland Wood, 'Are the Pain and Sorrow in the World Inconsistent with a Belief in God's Power and Goodness?', in Walsham How, Espin and A. Maitland Wood (eds.), *Hard Questions. A Course of Mid-day Addresses at St. Peter's, During the Mission at Chester, 1877* (Chester: Phillipson & Golder; London: Griffith & Farran, [1877]), 18.
[107] *Mystery*, 25.   [108] *Pain*, 1.

the writings of theologians in the latter part of the century. From the mid-1860s onwards, most apologists for pain found it necessary to look to other modes of justification than the Bible as the justifying Word of God, and formulations for resolving the problem of pain, 'the most stupendous fact in human experience', varied widely. Most, however, took the form of suggesting that pain was in some way beneficent: that it was prophylactic, or that it built up the character, this latter including the idea that pain was punitive and forced wayward man to see the error of his ways. Unitarian views on the invidiousness of eternal damnation, which had preceded and to some extent prompted the ethical revolt against an orthodox hell, survived in these attitudes towards a reformatory physical pain, and it is in such interchanges that the relatedness of the two arguments may clearly be seen.

G. A. Rowell, meteorologist, expert on drainage, and assistant in Oxford's Ashmolean Museum, took the first of these two lines—that pain is useful—in *An Essay on the Beneficent Distribution of the Sense of Pain* (1857). His argument, though it clearly self-defines as Christian, is much more nearly related to biological works of the same period, such as, for example, G. H. Lewes's reading of the insensibility of sea anemones in his 1858 book *Sea-side Studies*. Rowell resolutely claimed that pain is never excessive, that it always serves a useful purpose:

the sense of pain is not an infliction, but one of the most useful and important senses we possess . . . it is given to animals only in as great a degree as is necessary, and . . . no creature has a higher sense of pain than is required for the preservation of the class to which it belongs.[109]

These, largely biological, ideas that pain 'is the will of the Creator, and is evidence of merciful and benevolent design',[110] were subsequently used by Christian writers, ransacking the field of biology looking for solutions to the problem of pain, and as such the book serves as a resumé, and anticipation, of many such arguments. Rowell's main claim, that 'every part of the body is susceptible of pain, wherever that sense is necessary to indicate disease or injury',[111] is used to suggest that the pain

---

[109] *An Essay on the Beneficent Distribution of the Sense of Pain* (Oxford: G. A. Rowell, 1857), 2.
[110] Ibid.   [111] Ibid. 4.

of burning means that hot objects that would destroy body
tissue are dropped; that a sprained ankle that needs rest for its
recovery is too painful to walk on; that 'improper food' is
guarded against by stomach pain; and, slightly differently, that
pain prompts man to adapt to his climate by making him take
shelter from excessive cold or heat. The possible examples are
endless, and, indeed, undeniable: pain clearly does serve this
protective function:

> there would be no end to our dangers, if not possessed of this useful
> monitor, which is *a guard against injury*, and *a check to excesses*. There
> may be pain and suffering, the use of which it may be difficult to see;
> but I would rather attribute this to a want of knowledge, than believe
> that the rule which holds good in so many cases does not hold good
> in all.[112]

Rowell, here, relies on the same argument as those who describe
pain in terms of mystery, but instead of seeing the veil that sep-
arates the sufferer from the reason for his suffering in terms of
religion, it is envisaged in terms of physiological knowledge.
Given time, all these things will become clear. He insists, further,
that not only will the reason behind medically mysterious pains
become apparent, but also that many instances of physical
damage which would be painful under normal circumstances
prove not to be so. In so doing they give 'evidence of Divine
mercy': 'pain ceases when it becomes useless, and drowsiness,
insensibility, and a painless death, are the natural consequences'.[113] The prime example of such painlessness in the
Victorian period was that of David Livingstone when he was
attacked by a lion in 1843.[114] This scene almost invariably forms
a significant part of the tales of the explorer's adventures
recounted in the Victorian period and on into the twentieth
century.[115] Livingstone records the experience in his diary:

---

[112] *An Essay on the Beneficent Distribution* 6.   [113] Ibid. 7.
[114] See Anne Hugon, *The Exploration of Africa: From Cairo to the Cape*, trans.
Alexandra Campbell (Thames and Hudson, 1993), 87.
[115] See also, e.g. William H. G. Kingston, *Travels of Dr. Livingstone* (Routledge,
[1886]), 3; [J.] Macaulay, *Livingstone Anecdotes: A Sketch of the Career and Illustrations of the Character of David Livingstone, Missionary, Traveller, Philanthropist*
(Religious Tract Society, [1886]), 34–7; M. Douglas, *In Lionland: The Story of
Livingstone and Stanley* (London, Edinburgh, New York: Thomas Nelson, 1900),
10–11; R. B. Dawson, *Livingstone: The Hero of Africa* (Seeley, Service, 1918), 52–5.

I saw the lion just in the act of springing upon me . . . he caught my shoulder as he sprang, and we both came to the ground below together. Growling horribly close to my ear, he shook me as a terrier dog does a rat. The shock produced a stupor similar to that which seems to be felt by a mouse after the first shake of the cat. It caused a sort of dreaminess, in which there was no sense of pain nor feeling of terror, though quite conscious of all that was happening. It was like what patients partially under the influence of chloroform describe, who see all the operation, but feel not the knife. This singular condition was not the result of any mental process. The shake annihilated fear, and allowed no sense of horror in looking at the beast. This peculiar state is probably induced in all animals killed by the carnivora, and, if so, is a merciful provision by our benevolent Creator for lessening the pain of death.[116]

J. R. Illingworth, religious philosopher and one of the contributors to *Lux Mundi*,[117] writing in 1889, assumed the widespread knowledge and acceptance of Livingstone's explanation of his experience. He condensed this story into a few words in which he affirmed his belief in the Christian referent of pain: 'then there are the phenomena of fascination, which may well resemble the experience of Livingstone in the lion's mouth.'[118] He needs to say nothing more than this as he tacitly assumes that the story is a matter of general knowledge.

Rowell uses phenomena such as fascination to suggest the variability of pain, that it is not always a constant but is subject to the purposes of God. Pain will warn of the early stages of disease so that appropriate action may be taken, but is withdrawn in the latter stages when it would serve no useful purpose.[119] Similarly, Rowell argues that, 'as in the case of the

---

[116] *Livingstone's Travels and Researches in South Africa; including a Sketch of Sixteen Years' Residence in the Interior of Africa, and a Journey from the Cape of Good Hope to Loanda on the West Coast, thence across the Continent, down the River Zambesi, to the Eastern Coast. From the Personal Narrative of David Livingstone, LL.D., D.C.l. To which is added A Historical Sketch of Discoveries in Africa* (Philadelphia: J. W. Bradley, 1859), 15.

[117] For an appraisal of the significance of this volume, see Geoffrey Wainwright, *Keeping the Faith: Essays to Mark the Centenary of* Lux Mundi (SPCK, 1989).

[118] 'The Problem of Pain: Its Bearing on Faith in God', in Charles Gore (ed.), Lux Mundi: *A Series of Studies in the Religion of the Incarnation* (John Murray, 1889), 115.

[119] This argument was ridiculed by evolutionary-minded doctors of the 1880s, as we shall see in the next chapter. The notebooks that the American surgeon S. Weir Mitchell kept during the Civil War, between three and ten years after Rowell was

blind rat, we see a sense withheld where useless, it may be presumed that the sense of pain would be withheld where unnecessary, as it would not only be useless, but an infliction'.[120] But this is where writers such as Rowell whose arguments rested entirely on the beneficence of God put their heads straight into the lion's mouth, for if pain without a purpose can be pointed to and yet remain unexplained, then the answer to the question 'Has the Author of all things created us merely to gloat over our sufferings?' can only be yes. Hinton, writing about pain surplus to prophylactic requirement recognized just such a possibility, claiming that pain 'is liable to exceed, in an immense degree, the amount which is needful to secure its beneficial influence',[121] and himself, as shall be argued, chose very different grounds to resolve the problem of pain.

Rowell was, in effect, saying that pain was inconsequential and negligible. Other religious writers, on the other hand, chose to ground their arguments on the premiss that character was forged in the smithy of seemingly useless pain. Foster makes this point graphically in his image of sculpture which combines the process of the infliction of pain with the production of a beautiful object:

To the eye of a sculptor in every block of stone there is a statue; but to make it visible to every eye it must be cut out of the block with mallet and chisel. But the stone does not see the end in view, it only feels the rough treatment which it querulously resents. It wishes to be left alone. It is quite satisfied with itself as it is. It cares nothing for statuary. 'Oh dear! don't!' says the stone to the chisel; 'these heavy blows are very terrible to bear; besides, I am at a loss to imagine where the necessity is for my being subjected to such coarse and severe treatment. Oh dear! pray, do desist!' 'You are intended to be as beautiful

---

writing, and which he recorded in *Injuries of Nerves and their Consequences* (Philadelphia: J. B. Lippincott, 1872) also suggest very pointedly Rowell's romanticization of physical suffering: 'Perhaps few persons who are not physicians can realize the influence which long-continued and unendurable pain may have upon both body and mind. The older [note]books are full of cases in which, after lancet wounds, the most terrible pain and local spasms resulted. When these had lasted for days or weeks, the whole surface became hyperæsthetic, and the senses grew to be only avenues for fresh and increasing tortures, until every vibration, every change in light ... brought on new agony. Under such torments the temper changes, the most amiable grow irritable, the soldier becomes a coward, and the strongest man is scarcely less nervous than the most hysterical girl', 196.

[120] *Essay*, 9.   [121] *Mystery of Pain*, 26.

as the Apollo Belvidere,' [*sic*] answers the chisel, with another sharp stroke. 'Oh dear! worse and worse!' cried the stone, shuddering under the blow which strikes off a rough projection. 'But if such be my destination, why not put me into my place at once, without this suffering?' 'You are not fit for it,' replies the chisel, still going on with its work. 'Don't you see that every statue has undergone this process?' 'How long must I suffer?' asks the stone sorrowfully. 'Only till all that is unsuitable and improper shall be removed,' rejoins the chisel; 'and when made meet for the high situation you are to occupy, you will be placed amongst the others, and be as beautiful as they are.'[122]

It is worth quoting this passage at some length for the image of the strangely polite, anthropomorphized block of stone is particularly effective at conveying the idea of the necessary part pain plays in a process of reformation. Without the deliberately inflicted pains of the sculptor which form the object of beauty, the rock, or the stony heart, of those who begrudge their suffering, remains in its rough state. The image involves the omniscience of the creator and the recalcitrance of the created, as well as invoking an image for pain—the strike of an external implement to convey internal suffering—commonly used to describe unpleasant physical sensation.

Similar to this is a sentiment expressed in *Lucile*, a poem by Owen Meredith, the pseudonym of Bulwer Lytton's son. Here Lucile claims:

There is purpose in pain,
Otherwise it were devilish. I trust in my soul
That the great master hand which sweeps over the whole
Of this deep harp of life, if at moments it stretch
To shrill tension some one wailing nerve, means to fetch
Its response the truest, most stringent, and smart,
Its pathos the purest, from out the wrung heart,
Whose faculties, flaccid it may be, if less
Sharply strung, sharply smitten, had fail'd to express
Just the one note the great final harmony needs.[123]

What becomes clear from both of these images—of sculpture and of music—is that pain is aestheticized in such a way that what becomes important is not the pain in itself, but the result

---

[122] *Pain*, 11–12.
[123] *Lucile* (Chapman & Hall, 1860), II. v. viii. 290–1.

of that pain: here, the effect that it has on character.[124] As pain is perceived as a problem, rather than as an unquestionable given, images are used to help make sense of the suffering. Both images include the physicality of pain—the action of the chisel and the plucking of the string—but subsume such physicality in a greater end. Foster, picking up the image of making music, claims that not only does pain tune the various chords of the heart allowing it to add to the divine harmony, but it also enlarges and ennobles the heart: 'by pain man is thus raised from sheer animalism to Divine manhood, [and] his capacity for suffering is not diminished, but immeasurably increased.'[125] This leads us back to Voysey's position, for again the ability to suffer, conjoined with the ability to withstand such suffering, is linked to manhood, and set against 'sheer animalism' which is figured as being lower down in a scale of value.

Where the process of character-formation by pain was concerned, the ends were seen to justify the means, not just because of the resultant statuary or music, but for a number of subsidiary reasons. To a large extent, theologians were concerned with the *amount* of suffering involved, and what became important was the ratio of pain to the useful results of such suffering. The amount of pain was seen to be small in relation to the amount of pleasure encountered in the course of life, whilst pain, being suffered only on an individual, rather than a cumulative basis, did not mount to enormous proportions, and indeed, was absurdly short in relation to eternity. The argument of Australie's poem 'The Balance of Pain', the title poem of a collection published in 1877, is intimately connected with such weighings up of pain. Theodore, the poem's hero, denounces the unfairness of the intensity of his own physical suffering, placing it in the context of the unavoidable pains of life:

> Pain and still pain! pain at each turn of being!
> Pain at life's opening and the last dark hour!
> Pain in the flesh and in the soul's vague depths—

---

[124] See G. J. Barker-Benfield, *The Culture of Sensibility: Sex and Society in Eighteenth-Century Britain* (1992; Chicago and London: University of Chicago Press, 1996), 20–3. Barker-Benfield links the language of music—vibrations, thrills, strings—with the language of sensibility, and suggests the interplay between the two.   [125] *Pain*, 15.

Pain as the law of growth—the due of change—
Pain as the needful attribute of life.
Where shall it end? With body and with form?
Not so, e'en joy itself must come to man
Temper'd with pain; beauty, the more intense,
The keener, thrills us with the pleasure-pang.
Music and love, ay, holiness itself,
Hold pain for ever in their essence bound.
From first to last no hope and no escape!
Yet could I bear it, were the throes assign'd
In equal measure to each human soul.
But 'tis not thus; on one the woes are heap'd,
While others pass with strange immunity
From all save that engrain'd in very living.
It is a grand injustice of the Lord
In whom, alike, all move and have their being.[126]

Agatha, Theodore's interlocutor in the course of the poem, teaches him that pain is always balanced by other God-given gifts, that despite seeming disparity in amounts of pain suffered, every pain is balanced by an equivalent pleasure, as an 'intenser depth of joy' comes with 'pain itself, that sanctifying cross'.[127] Theodore initially sees his own suffering as an impediment to Christian belief:

But mine own self, so rack'd in flesh and mind,
Seemeth a contradiction. Could you prove
Your words to me, thenceforth would I adore
The God I ne'er can worship, love, the while
I feel He hath unjustly marr'd my being.[128]

Agatha succeeds in her task of persuasion in large part by making Theodore realize that he is so intimately concerned with his own pain, that he fails to see it in others. He knows 'the ache | Its pressure brings on some most tender nerve'[129] in his own case, but obdurately fails to recognize pain in anyone else. He

---

[126] Australie [pseudonym of Emilie Matilda Australie Heron], *The Balance of Pain: And Other Poems* (George Bell, 1877), 1. This book is Australie's only published work.
[127] Ibid. 3.   [128] Ibid. 4.   [129] Ibid. 7.

> Sees but the outward mien, and deems that he
> Who walks more bravely, or whose burden seems
> Of easier form, or richer fashion, is
> Therefore more favour'd by the Lord, who gives
> To each as He thinks best.[130]

Recognizing the 'thread of love [that] run[s] through the woof of pain'[131] is, Agatha argues, the only way to find one's own pain acceptable. In a process that was repeated over and again over the course of the nineteenth century, pain is referred outwards from itself, and its meaning is established in relation to something not itself. As Theodore is brought to claim:

> Because at last
> The bitterness is past. I read in faith
> God's dealings with his children. He is just,
> And gives to all some cross. 'Tis *in themselves*
> There lies the power of turning to a joy,
> Or bearing, as a fretting load, the pain
> To each appointed as his human test.[132]

It is this process of 'turning to a joy' that is important; of redefining pain in terms of spiritual advantage.

To make such claims more palatable, justifications of pain that flattered the individual sufferer were made, and it was argued that the sensitivity that allowed one to feel pain also allowed one to perceive the purpose behind, or beyond, that suffering. The flexibility of religious arguments becomes apparent when the counter-claim—that pain could also teach the stupid ('the value of pain is this, that it compels attention, whether we will or no, to the disturbance it accompanies')[133]—is urged with equal force. In this sense of compelling the attention, pain was also widely seen to be penal, as it was in the case of eternal damnation. However much academic clergymen, such as Illingworth, argued 'that suffering . . . introduced into the world by sin . . . is not a Christian dogma, though it is often thought to be so',[134] many of his fellow clergymen persisted in preaching to this effect: 'that there should be suffering and death among

---

[130] *Australie*, 7.   [131] Ibid. 22.   [132] Ibid. 22–3.
[133] F. A. Dixey, *The Necessity of Pain* (Oxford House Papers, no. 19; Rivingtons, 1888), 6.
[134] 'Problem of Pain', 117.

men we can easily understand—for men have sinned, and pain and death are the wages of sin'.[135] Josiah Oldfield, writing shortly after the end of Victoria's reign, makes the case for the penal function of pain—pain as the wages of sin—most straightforwardly, using what he saw to be the pointless inflictions of pain by vivisection, hunting, and butchering meat as the framework for the infliction of pain by God:

Until man has learnt those lessons of self-sacrifice and mercy, which God is ever teaching, there will be no end to the dominion of Brother Pain.

If I inflict pain selfishly and wantonly upon the lower creation to which I am as God, then will my prayers for ease from pain remain unheard, and the great Lord whose servant I am must needs hand me over to the prison house of Brother Pain to learn my lessons.[136]

Oldfield's position is extreme, but in its extremity it effectively positions arguments for the punitive function of pain that will be discussed more fully in the final chapter. Illingworth himself claims that 'a vast amount of the suffering in the world is obviously punishment',[137] not just for 'obvious vices punished with remorse, and disease, and shame'[138] (which presumably Illingworth thinks of as sexual), but also 'ignorance, impatience, carelessness, even mistakes of judgment'.[139] Again it is clear that positions taken up in the debate over eternal damnation were reinvested with meaning in arguments over the value of physical pain. The punitive here begins to shade into the 'corrective and purgatorial'[140] as pains and penalties inflicted on the innocent 'tend to correct and purify the character'.[141] Illingworth sums up this argument by calling on the idea behind Foster's block of stone carved by the artist's hand, that 'when we say that men learn wisdom by experience, we mostly mean by experience [of] something painful'.[142]

Theologians worried by the harshness of such punitive infliction of pain sought ways of making it more palatable, a favourite justification being that of God's analogical relationship to parents who chastise their child for its own sake. As we

---

[135] Butler, *Light of Hope*, 59.

[136] *Myrrh and Amaranth. Two Lectures. I. Brother Pain and His Crown. II. Sister Drudgery and her Roses* (Sampson Low, Marston, 1905), 30.

[137] 'Problem of Pain', 117.   [138] Ibid.   [139] Ibid.   [140] Ibid.

[141] Ibid.   [142] Ibid. 117–18.

have already seen, Voysey argues for the parental need to punish children physically, claiming that 'It is where love is highest and purest that we are fortified to crucify ourselves by punishing our children'.[143] In a deft move, the physical pain of the punished child is transferred to the sympathetic pain of the parent, under-cutting the reality of such physical suffering. The pain of mankind is not so important as the pain suffered by God at man's waywardness, and, as the next move, the sympathetic pain of the parent becomes the real pain of the crucified Christ, again stripping the reality from human physical suffering and referring it to the greater and redemptive suffering of God. Using the model of parental discipline to serve for God's just chastisement is effective, too, as it calls on the mystery of God: those things which the child cannot understand will become clear to the adult. Pain may seem pointless, but as the child grows into adulthood and understanding, it will see pain's purpose and value its efficacy.

Foster nearly founders on the rock of pain in children them-selves, rather than adults figured as children, as he wrestles with the idea of the power of pain to teach the young:

Walk through the lengthy wards of a children's hospital. Look at the tiny sufferers, lying helpless on their little beds, debarred by their dis-eased and stunted bodies from all childish sports. There is no disci-pline there. Poor children! they are too young to be its fitting subjects. Is not pain in their case a dense and awful mystery? Does it not look like some flaw in God's machinery?[144]

What becomes clear from his subsequent explanation of physi-cal pain is the way in which such apologists were willing to reach outwards into other disciplines for explanations of physi-cal suffering: making pain acceptable was more important than rigid adherence to a single line of argument. Pain may be a mystery, but it is also referable to a strangely confuted Dar-winism and doctrine of original sin: 'We are told that God made man free, the arbiter of his destiny; but that when put to the proof he failed, yielded to temptation, and chose evil for his good. Here you have the origin of pain.'[145] This is Butler's argu-ment, that 'men have sinned, and pain and death are the wages of sin', but, as with Butler who found this hard to reconcile with

---

[143] *Mystery*, 38.   [144] Foster, *Pain*, 7–8.   [145] Ibid. 9.

the suffering of innocent children, Foster finds a way out of the rigorous confines of such an argument by looking to contemporary science:

By the law of heredity, each successive generation receives the mental disorders and the physical infirmities of the one immediately preceding it. To humane minds . . . the doctrine of original sin . . . seemed arbitrary and incomprehensible, until the Darwinian theory of development showed that sin can be transmitted from parent to child. The mind recoiled from the belief that, because one man sinned, all men should be sinners. Now, however, in the light of science, the doctrine is seen to be just, the conclusion inevitable. Man being the creature of sin, disease, and pain, his posterity, from the hour of birth, must have inherent in their nature the elements of multiform suffering.[146]

As the generations pass, the weight of accumulated pain and suffering grows larger and larger, much as diseases such as syphilis pass from one generation to the next, until, Foster claims, 'every pore of the body, every thought, imagination, feeling, and possession may be an inlet to suffering'.[147] Pain, in this way, was taken out of the hands of God: it is the result of the abuse of free will. But it should be remembered that it was Foster who offered the vision of God as sculptor, banging away at unredeemed man, intent on making him the Apollo Belvedere, and from this the malleability of the arguments about pain may be inferred. Without belief in an almighty and loving God, Foster sees only despair, and it is clear from the flexibility of his arguments the lengths to which he will go to sustain this position. Foster is far from alone in this, and I use him to suggest that pain was used as a counter in argument to sustain particular positions.

Pain was envisaged positively in a wide variety of different ways in Christian discourse. Not only was it seen as the necessary result of sin, and as the remedy for that sin, but was also recognized as a spur to action. The sight of painful suffering in others was assumed to prompt onlookers to charitable action,

---

[146] Ibid. 9–10.

[147] Ibid. 10. For the way diseases were understood to be passed on to the next generation in the wake of Benedictin Augustin Morel's *Treatise on the Degeneration of the Human Species* (1857) see Kelly Hurley, *The Gothic Body: Sexuality, Materialism, and Degeneration at the* Fin de Siècle (Cambridge: Cambridge University Press, 1996), 177 n.

whilst suffering in oneself became a measure of the degree to which one was found wanting. As Hinton argued, 'The reason we are made, or seem as if we were made, for pain, is that we are made for love . . . Our feeling it as pain, proves something wanting in ourselves.'[148] An individual's suffering becomes a sign of his need for reformation as well as the process that allows for such reformation.

And this leads to Agatha's final position in 'The Balance of Pain', where pain is finally 'hail'd | As a new gift, enabling us to feel | More fully with some fellow'[149] as 'each new pang | Bring[s] us one step still nearer to the Christ'.[150] This is where explanations of pain become unique to Christian discourse. J. R. Illingworth comments on Christianity's eclecticism in gathering together current justifications for suffering halfway through his own article on pain:

Now, though all these considerations naturally lead on into theology for their further treatment, yet it should be noticed that they are in no sense exclusively theological. The penal, the corrective, the preventive, and the stimulating uses of pain are all recognised in the average man's philosophy of life.[151]

Where Christianity makes its mark on pain is not in its claim that pain plays an essential part in the formation of character—for this is equally a tenet of stoicism—but in its claims for Christ's redemption through suffering. Not only, as J. Thain Davidson claims, is it the case that 'Jesus knows the dart of every pain'[152] for he has suffered himself and can sympathize through personal experience, but these very sufferings are the means through which redemption is effected. Davidson continues:

You know they used to wound the balsam-tree in order to obtain from it the healing essence, and in like manner we are reminded by the prophet, that Christ, this tender plant, from which the balm exudes, was 'wounded for our transgressions' and that 'by His stripes we are healed.'[153]

---

[148] *Mystery of Pain*, 38.   [149] Australie, *Balance of Pain*, 23.
[150] Ibid. 24.   [151] 'Problem of Pain', 118–19.
[152] 'Jesus Christ, the Healer of the Body. A Sermon', revised by the author in *Catholic Sermons No. V., June 1873. Preached in Islington Presbyterian Church, London, On Sunday Evening, April 20, 1873* (Edward Curtice and F. Pitman, 1873), 54.   [153] Ibid. 60.

The process of the infliction of pain becomes, through its association with Christ's scourging and crucifixion, a part of the healing process itself. In suffering for others, theologians argue, Christ sets up a model which suggests that the feeling of pain provides an impetus to action as it allows the sufferer to understand and to compassionate the sufferings of others. By feeling pain 'we become partakers of God's holiness—of His exquisite compassion and sensibility'.[154]

Sensibility to pain is of the utmost importance as participation in it involves participation in Christ's sufferings and consequent compassion. There is, however, also a move away from physical suffering itself in justifications of pain: a suggestion that in a Christian framework it is both important in the ways I have just suggested and, also, profoundly unimportant. As Maitland Wood argues, there is no pain from which good cannot spring. Taking as his most extreme case the seemingly unjustifiable pain of a baby who cannot have deserved pain on its own account, Maitland Wood argues that for the baby who dies in pain there is eternal life, and its suffering is as nothing. If the baby lives the pain will be forgotten, and if the baby becomes an empained cripple, then it will bring the family together in love, and its pain will thus serve a purpose.[155] Whilst this is absurdly optimistic, it follows the pattern of the most purely theological arguments for pain. James Hinton offers a strange mixture of the biological and the pointedly theological in *The Mystery of Pain*, for he recognizes the prevalence of pain in the world instead of trying to explain it away, as Voysey, amongst most others, does by finding moral justifications for physical suffering. Hinton argues that 'There is no adequate explanation . . . to be found in pain in the beneficial effects which it produces in respect to our physical existence.'[156] Pain may prompt man to act, but far more pain is suffered than could ever be required for this purpose. Likewise pain may be said to follow wrongdoing and serve as a punishment for sin, but, Hinton argues, 'Nights spent in dissipation bring ruined health; nights spent in fond watchings by beds of pain bring a like and equal ruin.'[157] Hinton accepts none of the justifications suggested by contemporary

---

[154] Foster, *Pain*, 12.   [155] 'Pain and Sorrow', 16.
[156] *Mystery of Pain*, 27.   [157] Ibid. 27–8.

theologians, complaining that in justifying pain in physical terms, they are missing its essential point:

All these we have enumerated are secondary purposes served by pain. They do not conduct us to its source, nor reveal to us its meaning . . . For pain often paralyses instead of stimulating and reduces to impotence energies of the utmost value.

We must, therefore, accept pain as a fact existing by a deep necessity, having its root in the essential order of the world.[158]

Hinton is the only writer discussed here who deeply believes that philosophical explanations of pain are completely valueless. Instead, he suggests that man should aim to subsume pain in sacrifice, that 'Our feeling it as pain, proves something wanting in ourselves.'[159] He is not suggesting that pain is not felt physically, but that the Christian should be able to interpret pain in such a way that 'It lies hidden and unfelt in the form of devoted sacrifice; but it is there, and it would make itself felt as pain if the love which finds joy in bearing it were absent.'[160]

This is a paradigm for pain control, the many shapes of which will be traced over the course of these chapters. Pain without a supportive structure to give it meaning seems at best futile and at worst malign. Early nineteenth-century Christian theology, taking the Bible as the direct Word of God, provided just such a sustaining structure that made sense of their pain for those who suffered. A single meaning—albeit mysterious—could be ascribed to physical pain: it was the Hand of the Lord at work, and as such was unquestionable. With the slow collapse of such faith, reflected in the downfall of the doctrine of a physical hell, pain began to be seen as a problem, and, defined in this way, was open to numerous solutions, drawn from many different discourses. One such discourse was that of medicine and in the next chapter, which deals with medical understandings of pain, predominantly in the 1880s and 1890s, I shall be looking at the process that ran alongside the loosening grip of Christianity on physical suffering, and which played some part—by offering a contrary rationale—in that loosening process. But if Christianity as the framing discourse for physical pain was on the decline, then medicine, by the 1880s, had not yet reached a position of

---

[158] Ibid. 30.   [159] Ibid. 38.   [160] Ibid. 35–6.

absolute supremacy. I shall be arguing that very little was actually known about the processes and physiology of pain. A gap was left between the medicalization of pain and the decline of a widely held Christian rationale for suffering, and in this gap the meaning of pain was open to all comers.

2

Medical Understandings of Pain

I. THE RISE OF THE MEDICAL PARADIGM

Medical explanations for pain, based on the body and its neurological organization, both created and went some way towards filling the gap in conceptualizing physical suffering left by the failure in Christian rationales of benevolently inflicted pain. Advances in medical knowledge breached Christian certitude as they undermined the naturalness of pain and put in its place a bodily function that could be removed, or at least alleviated, by chemical or surgical interference. Christianity was forced by its nature to accept pain not as a function of the body in distress, but rather as a counter in God's interaction with humankind. The rising medical profession of the nineteenth century—rising not only in its increasing professionalization but also in the depth and range of its knowledge—sought ways of addressing the problem of pain in a very different arena. Instead of defining pain as a mystery, medical practitioners began to look for its method of functioning and to acknowledge that, in many cases, painfulness far outstripped any putative beneficent value. From asking, in Christian terms, what value pain could have to a particular suffering individual, the medical profession began to ask the questions, what is pain? what is its specific link, neurological or otherwise, to the body? To understand its functioning and to cure, rather than to justify and suffer, was the aim of the medical profession.

Roselyne Rey's *The History of Pain* (1993) charts medical understandings of pain from Graeco-Roman times until the 1950s. Her title for the chapter on the nineteenth century is revealing, for she calls it the age of 'The Great Discoveries'. It was indeed a time of rapidly increasing physiological knowledge as well as one of great therapeutic advances, though, perhaps strangely, the latter ran ahead of the former as the ability to alleviate pain far outstripped medical understandings of its functioning. It is not my aim to chart the course of medical science in detail—Rey does this effectively—but rather to suggest that despite ongoing therapeutic advance, pain was little understood and as a result of this was the object of sharply conflicting medical explanations.

Increasingly, as the century advanced, pain was seen to be tied to the body.[1] The emergence of physiology as an experimental science, prompted by the work of Charles Bell and François Magendie in the 1820s on sensory and motor nerves, led to the scientific study of sensation in general and pain in particular. Johannes Müller, writing in 1840, further rendered pain the object of scientific enquiry in his 'Doctrine of Specific Nerve Energies', where the brain was seen as the recipient of information from the nerves, carried in a form of energy specific to each sensation.[2] Over the course of the nineteenth century physiological knowledge was increasingly linked to neurology, so that pain began to be seen unequivocally as a function of the body rather than of the mind. Despite his lack of direct anatomical experience, Alexander Bain, the founder of the psychological journal *Mind*, and author of the enormously influential volumes *The Senses and the Intellect* (1855) and *The Emotions and the Will* (1859), clinched the corporeality of pain, insisting on the physiological basis of mental phenomena. As Gardner Murphy writes: 'In Bain we have for the first time physiological explanations sufficiently elaborate to be taken quite seriously. The psychologist began to think of experimental physiology as fundamental to his science.'[3] Bain represents a turning point in the ability to understand pain, as he provided

[1] The attempts by physiologists to connect pain to neurology were, of course, not conceived of in a vacuum, and over the course of the 19th century physiological organization became increasingly important as a way of understanding or, at least, rationalizing a wide range of phenomena. Franz Gall invented phrenology which tied behaviour to cranial bumps, whilst Lombroso and other criminal anthropologists (see Ch. 5) extended this to a complex system of bodily measurements as a way of explaining criminal propensity. See also Stanley Joel Reiser, *Medicine and the Reign of Technology* (Cambridge: Cambridge University Press, 1978). Reiser outlines the technology—laryngoscopes, opthalmoscopes, specula, amongst others—which made it possible for doctors to see the mechanical causes of bodily complaints.

[2] See John J. Bonica, 'History of Pain Concepts and Pain Therapy', *Seminars in Anesthesia*, 4 (1985), 196.

[3] *An Historical Introduction to Modern Psychology* (London: Kegan Paul, Trench, Trübner; New York: Harcourt, Brace, 1929), 110.

the basic framework for understanding it in terms of the body on which the later arguments over the precise nature of pain to be discussed in this chapter were built. As Lorraine Daston argues, however, 'Although he laced his explanations liberally with physiology, Bain nonetheless couched his explanations in psychological terms: pain and pleasure were ultimately feelings, not neural tremors.'[4] Pain and pleasure were together seen by Bain 'almost to comprehend the entire sum of conscious states',[5] and as polar opposites were perceived as the motivations to particular courses of action, whether reflex or volitional. 'Pain is what we avoid, repel, flee from; pleasure is what we cling to, and labour to increase.'[6] In these terms pain includes itchiness or the response to bad smells—unpleasant things to be avoided—and Bain refused to engage with a fully neurological explanation for physical suffering, depending rather on a vision of pain as the marker of a body's adaptedness to its environment. As Grant Allen wrote in *Physiological Æsthetics* (1877)— which, the author claimed, compiled and interpreted the thinking of Bain, Henry Maudsley, and Herbert Spencer—'every organism, in proportion to the completeness of its adaptation, energetically resists any act which interferes with its efficiency as a working machine: and such interferences are known subjectively as Pains'.[7]

Such explanations as Allen's are not directly connected to the sense of pain as the fruit of nervous activity, but Bain's research did, nevertheless, provide the impetus to physiological understandings of physical suffering, and the following generations of physiologists turned away from observation as the primary method of neurological research and turned towards direct anatomical knowledge and vivisection as a source of knowledge. The marked disproportion between levels of understanding of the physiological nature of pain and the ability to treat it— whether surgically or pharmacologically—remained, and classifying pain as a neurological phenomenon did not imply an

---

[4] 'The Theory of Will versus the Science of Mind', in William R. Woodward and Mitchell G. Ash (eds.), *The Problematic Science: Psychology in Nineteenth-Century Thought* (New York: Praeger, 1982), 97–8.
[5] *The Senses and the Intellect* (John W. Parker, 1855), 87.
[6] Ibid. 89.
[7] *Physiological Æsthetics* (Henry S. King, 1877), 17.

understanding of the nature of this classification. John Bonica usefully traces the course of the diverse inventions and technological advances that together allowed for the effective treatment of pain:

Among the most important [advances] were the isolation of morphine from crude opium by Serturner in 1806, which was followed by the development of techniques of getting pure crystalline drugs from previously crude and uncertain mixtures and allowed other opium alkaloids to be isolated, including codeine in 1832. In 1828 Wohler reported the synthesis of urea and Leroux reported the isolation of saline which years later led to the introduction of salicylic acid, sodium salicylate, and acetanalid. In 1899 Dreser produced acetyl salicyctic acid that became marketed by the Bayer Company as aspirin. A milestone in the prevention and treatment of pain was the public demonstration of the anesthetic properties of ether by Morton in 1846 which led to the development of general anesthesia. At about this time, Rynd developed the hollow needle and somewhat later, Wood and Pravaz developed the syringe which permitted the injection of analgesics. This development, together with the isolation and pharmacologic studies of cocaine, eventually led to the demonstration of its local anesthetic efficacy by Karl Koller in 1884, and the subsequent widespread use of regional analgesia and anesthesia, not only for surgery but also for diagnosis and therapy of nonsurgical pain . . . The advent of anesthesia and aseptic surgery and the evolution of the specificity theory led to still another method of relieving chronic intractable pain—neurosurgical operations on sensory pathways in peripheral nerves and the spinal cord.[8]

Such a catalogue of pharmacological and clinical advances being made largely at a time before the possibility of understanding their modi operandi is valuable, for it suggests both the inventiveness of physicians and chemists, and their relative inability to understand the functioning of such palliatives. During the nineteenth century great advances had been made in the alleviation of pain, but the mechanics of physical suffering were largely not understood—a position reflected in the doctor's answer to Margaret Hale's question about the imminent death of her mother in Elizabeth Gaskell's *North and South*:

---

[8] 'Pain Concepts', 196. For the surgical treatment of chronic pain, see also A. D. Hodgkiss, 'Chronic Pain in Nineteenth-Century British Medical Writings', *History of Psychiatry*, 2 (1991), 27–40.

'Will there be much suffering?'

He shook his head. 'That we cannot tell. It depends on constitution; on a thousand things. But the late discoveries of medical science have given us large power of alleviation.'[9]

North and South, published between 1854–5, eight years after the introduction of chloroform, suggests both this inability to understand the nature of pain itself, to know how the body will respond, and the optimism of newly acquired medicinal weapons to be aimed at pain. The introduction of anaesthetic surgery was of critical importance not simply because of its pain-relieving properties. It changed the perception of pain, not just on the operating table where it was primarily used, but also in general terms, and brought about a reversal in what seemed to be the natural order of things. Before the introduction of chloroform and similar anaesthetics, pain could be seen as a part of life, a natural state, whereas after its uptake—though this was not entirely unproblematic[10]—chemical intervention into the state of pain became the 'natural' one.

An article in the *Lancet* of 1887 shows both great certainty and great ambivalence in trying to define, or even to describe, pain. The article approaches a definition of pain whilst at the same time claiming that such definition is impossible, and employs a curious, yet fruitful, mixture of the modern nomenclature of science and older modes of expression of religion and philosophy. It ends, however, by confusing the why and the how of bodily pain, assuming that these are identical: that a medical description of nervous pathways also gives a philosophical answer to the problem of the existence of pain.

The *Lancet*'s unsigned editorial begins with a series of what it posits as 'unanswered, perhaps unanswerable, questions'—'"what is pain?" "what is pleasure?" "what is life?" "what is death?"'[11]—and suggests that despite the attempts of thinkers to solve such mysteries, even in the light of modern scientific

---

[9] *North and South* (1854–5), ed. Angus Easson (London, New York, Toronto: Oxford University Press, 1973), 126.

[10] See Martin S. Pernick, *A Calculus of Suffering: Pain, Professionalism, and Anesthesia in Nineteenth-Century America* (New York: Columbia University Press, 1985). Pernick effectively charts the course of the uneven uptake of anaesthesia, specifically in the USA.

[11] 'What is Pain?', *Lancet*, 13 Aug. 1887, 333.

advances, such questions remain insoluble. The writer's ambivalence is deep for he refuses to accept that despite a perceived
inability to define pain, there is a quality which we understand—
through experience—to be pain and with which we can identify
and sympathize: 'We think we know what it is to live and feel
pleasure or pain, but when we attempt to express our thoughts
by words we discover that the feat is impracticable. The answer
to the question, "What is pain?" must therefore be, "No one
knows." '[12] Such an assumption goes to the heart of this argument, for it suggests that it is possible for particular powerful
groups to define pain in such ways as to invalidate the claims
of others to feel and to suffer. Here, the inability of the medical
profession to find a definition for pain is seen to invalidate
private experience. It was certainly the case—as indeed it still
is—that no one knew *exactly* what pain was in scientific terms—
that is, how it works rather than how it feels—but such a claim
is, nevertheless, an aggressive denial of experiential understanding. Mary Poovey, in her chapter on the medical treatment
of Victorian women in *Uneven Developments*, makes clear the
implications of just such overriding of voice, particularly of
women's voices, in the mid-century debate over the introduction of anaesthesia into childbirth. Her claim is that the representation of the female body and its suffering was almost
exclusively in the hands of male medical practitioners able to
manipulate their treatment, even to the extent of refusing to
administer painkilling drugs in childbirth, in accordance with
their own convictions and desires rather than in accordance
with women's suffering.[13] Such practice has important reso-
nances and, to a large extent, I shall be tracing just such ethical
implications of reading pain in the light of particular frameworks of expectation throughout this book.

[12] Ibid.
[13] See *Uneven Developments: The Ideological Work of Gender in Mid-Victorian
England* (Virago, 1989), 43 ff. For a striking example of the power relationship
between doctor and female patient, see H. Arthur Allbutt, *The Wife's Handbook:
How a Woman should Order Herself during Pregnancy, in the Lying-in Room, and
after Delivery. With Hints on the Management of the Baby, and on other Matters
of Importance, necessary to be known by Married Women* (R. Forder, 1887), 22:
'When labor is tedious and painful, many medical men let their patients inhale
a little chloroform during the pains. This gives wonderful relief. If the doctor
proposes it, the woman must not demur.'

The author of the *Lancet* piece overrides personal, lay experience in a similar fashion, but from suggesting that 'no one knows' what pain is, he goes to some lengths to synthesize state-of-the-art medical thinking on the nature of pain:

> This is how far we have proceeded in the quest for a definitive answer. Pain is a sensation[14] which more or less rapidly and acutely assails the faculty of endurance. In its commonest forms it is suffering produced by nerve excitation, the elements of the nervous apparatus being either directly or by a transmitted irritation mechanically disturbed . . . It is not of course always the fact that these mechanical injuries to nervous tissue take place at the point to which pain is referred, because, being a sensation, pain is *felt* at some seat of sensation that is in connexion with the sensory apparatus affected, although it may be remote from the point where the impression is produced. In short, pain may be a message of suffering sent from some injured part through a chain of nerve-elements as a message of word-symbols is transmitted by a telegraphic wire.[15]

There is in this a curious mixture of the language of science and the language of popular understanding and religion. For whilst the author is insistent on the medical terminology of sensation, referral and excitation; on the ability to classify and ascertain pain's 'commonest forms'; and on unquestionable assertion ('it is not *of course* always the fact . . .') there is a concurrent veering of his terminology towards much less scientific representations. On one hand he claims to want a 'definitive answer', and on the other recognizes in his use of language that this is impossible, not least because 'pain is a sensation which *more or less*' does many different things. There is no one single entity that can be called pain. This recognition undercuts the certainty of his language, but it is also clear that the author is falling back on an older and much less scientific mode of expression. The search for a meaning for pain is a 'quest' and the 'faculty of endurance'—a conjunction of the language of science and that of stoical acceptance—is assailed, envisaging pain not as the

---

[14] See Lightner Witmer, 'Pain', in Thomas L. Stedman (ed.), *Twentieth Century Practice: An International Encyclopedia of Modern Medical Science by Leading Authorities of Europe and America*, 20 vols. (Sampson Low, Marston, 1897), xi. 905–45, where he defines a sensation as 'a simple unanalyzable mental content', 940.

[15] 'What is Pain?', 333–4.

product of firing nerves as he purports to be suggesting, but as a malign external agent that attempts to break down the barriers of the body. The writer has overthrown Aristotelian notions of pain as an emotional process, 'a passion of the soul', and sought to ground pain in neurology. There is, nonetheless, in this passage a disturbing conjunction of suffering and pain that undercuts just this distinction. If pain is hurt or strong discomfort in some part of the body and suffering is the ability to bear it, the author of this *Lancet* article elides the two. For the author, 'suffering [is] produced by nerve excitation', suggesting not just the painful results of nerve transmission, but the effect of this pain on the mind and life of the sufferer as a direct consequence of such excitation.

Towards the end of the article such confusion becomes more acute as the writer becomes both more didactic and less scientific. The image of the telegraph wire courts popular understanding as it looks back to an invention generally available in the middle of the 1840s.[16] Whilst suggesting the electrical nature of neurological transmission, the image of telegraphic communication simplifies the complexity of the nervous system, envisaging a direct and constant connection between the message received and that transmitted. It relies on an assumption of beneficent pain teaching the child to drop a hot coal, rather than on chronic pain which has long since lost its monitory function. Sir Alfred Power's poem on 'The Nervous System', from his series *Sanitary Rhymes*, uses just this image of the telegraph wire to explain painful neurological firings:

> These fibres so thickly pack under the skin,
> That you can't put between them the point of a pin,
> Which appears from it's [*sic*] sending a sharp thrill of pain,
> As by telegraph wire, to the seat of the brain.[17]

[16] The *Lancet* author was by no means unique in using this image. See also Bain, *Senses*, 30; Henry Hayman, 'Why We Suffer, An Attempt to Show the Economy of Pain', in '*Why We Suffer*', *And Other Essays* (W. H. Allen, 1890), 37, and Karl Pearson, *The Grammar of Science* (Walter Scott, 1892), 53. In this, Pearson uses the related image of the telephone exchange. See also J. Munro, 'The Nerves of the World', *Leisure Hour* (1895), 18–22, 96–102, 183–7.

[17] 'The Nervous System', in *Sanitary Rhymes. The Present Series Consists of Personal Precautions against Cholera, and all kinds of Fever; and contains:- No. I.—The Skin. No. II.—The Blood. No. III.—The Nervous System* (T. Richards, 1871), 6.

The telegraph system is brought into play by the introduction of harmful and alien matter in the shape of a pin. The analogy is the preferred one of those who argue that pain is the necessary gift of a loving God whose aim is to save mankind from physical dissolution at the cost of a small amount of pain. Power simplifies to convey his message, concerning the avoidance of cholera (it is noticeable how markedly different his explanation of the pain of cholera is from that of J. C. Ryle in the previous chapter), in the form least resistant to understanding. The simplification, where the writer of the *Lancet* article is concerned, is more confusing, for it suggests a purpose for pain, a benevolent transmission of a message. It is from this point onwards that the editorial writer begins to make assertions about the purpose of pain rather than its mechanics. If, as he earlier suggested, 'The true test of success' in finding an answer to the question of what pain is, is 'the possibility of shaping a satisfactory definition of the thing sought for',[18] then the last section of the article suggests the failure of the enterprise:

The purpose of pain is doubtless protective. The sensation is the warning sign of injury, and cries for relief, not simply for the avoidance of suffering, but for the remedy of a state or condition which threatens the integrity of the tissue or organ in distress. It is in this light that pain should be regarded. It may be heroic to bear necessary pain, but to turn a deaf ear to the warning cry of pain is to commit an act of folly.[19]

Such commentary in no respect provides a definition: it is rather an assertion of the telegraphic view of the beneficence of pain—'the purpose of pain is doubtless protective'—which fails to pay due, or even any, attention to pain that cannot be forced into such an overtly simplified category. What is particularly telling about such comment is the attempt to place the reading of pain in a specific moral context: 'It is in this light that pain *should* be regarded.' That is, it is imperative to read pain in a particular way. But there is a deep-seated confusion at work here, as the writer tries to draw a distinction between 'necessary pain' that should be borne heroically, and a category he calls the 'warning cry of pain'. But if this is the case, then there are problems with the nomenclature, for surely warning pain is neces-

---

[18] 'What is Pain?', 333.   [19] Ibid. 334.

sary pain, and the type of pain that needs to be borne heroically is not working on the telegraphic system, but rather is chronic pain that has long since passed the admonitory stage, if, indeed, it ever fulfilled that function.

The didacticism of a commentary that tries to override such confusion betrays the lack of knowledge as to the nature of pain pertaining at the end of the nineteenth century, when the debate over the nature of pain—its psychological or neurological status—was being fought out by exponents of the three prevailing modes of thinking. Using Lightner Witmer's article 'Pain'—an entry in *Twentieth Century Practice*, a late nineteenth-century encyclopedia of medicine—I shall be teasing out the strands of these various schools of thought. First, the traditional Aristotelian idea of pain as an emotion, like joy, was taken over by psychology, and pain was seen as ' "a state of mind without any physical basis in the body" ',[20] an understanding of pain that relied on the acceptance of 'mental and neural parallelism'; that 'every mental state or process has a correlated neural process'.[21] Such a view relies not at all on the notion of pain pathways, where nerves conduct an impulse from the site of injury to the brain where it is interpreted as pain. Witmer angrily refutes the validity of such thinking, citing the case of a 19-year-old girl diagnosed according to such psychological principles as having ' "subconscious pain" ' which took the form of pains in her arms. The physician concerned, failing to find any cause, described this pain as ' "hysterical, subjective, mental, delusional, and not to be ascribed, therefore, as due to any physical external cause" '.[22] It is in this refusal to find the basis of pain in neurological pathways that this understanding of pain differs sharply from the two other medical theories prevalent at the end of the century. Both of these ground their understanding of the nature of pain in neurology, but differ in their understanding of the nature of pain pathways. As such,

---

[20] Witmer, 'Pain', 905. See such medical works as Daniel Hack Tuke, *Illustrations of the Influence of the Mind Upon the Body in Health and Disease, Designed to Elucidate the Action of the Imagination*, 2nd edn., 2 vols. (J. and A. Churchill, 1884). See esp. ch. 9, sect. I, 'Influence of Mental States upon Disorders of Sensation' in which the author cites numerous cases where the patient's pain is perceived to be of purely mental origin, and being caused by 'Imagination' can also be cured by the 'imagination', ii. 180–4.
[21] Witmer, 'Pain', 907.   [22] Ibid. 938.

they may be called the specificity theory and the intensity theory.[23]

The specificity theory—the one which Witmer himself held—suggested that impulses resulting from a painful stimulus travelled along nerves specific to pain, nerves distinct from those which transmitted, say, touch or heat. Whilst this could not be physiologically proven, specificists attempted to find such pain tracts and indeed a nervous end organ for pain. Those, however, who adhered to the intensity view, denied the presence of specific pain tracts, but rather suggested that any sensation could cause either one of the two extremes, pleasure or pain, the intensity of the stimulus being the deciding factor. A model was proposed whereby at a particular level a sensation could cause first pleasure, but then—passing through a series of stages—would be at first indifferent, then disagreeable, and finally would cross a threshold and become painful. Witmer ridicules this theory by pushing it to extremes: the intensity 'theory presupposes that a bitter taste of adequate intensity must give a pleasure equal in degree to that of the satisfaction of the sexual instinct, while the odor of violets if sufficiently intense must arouse a pain as decided as the agony of angina pectoris'.[24] Put in this way it does indeed sound absurd, but the intensity theory was popular both in medical circles and in popular understandings of the way that pain worked. To make this point, Francis Galton's pronouncements on the nature of sensation and pain can be set against those of the author of *Teleny*, who, probably wrongly, is widely assumed to be Oscar Wilde.[25] Galton writes:

Sensation mounts through a series of grades of 'just perceptible differences.' It starts from the zero of consciousness, and it becomes more intense as the stimulus increases (though at a slower rate) up to the point when the stimulus is so strong as to begin to damage the nerve apparatus. It then yields place to pain, which is another form of sensation, and which continues until the nerve apparatus is destroyed.[26]

---

[23] This is not my own terminology, but is widely used and recognized. See Keith Budd, *Pain* (Update, 1984), 4.

[24] Witmer, 'Pain', 912.

[25] See Serge O. Cogcave's entry, '*Teleny* (Wilde [?] and Others)', in G. A. Cevasco (ed.), *The 1890s: An Encyclopedia of British Literature, Art, and Culture* (New York and London: Garland, 1993).

[26] *Inquiries into Human Faculty and its Development* (Macmillan, 1883), 27–8.

Teleny's hero thrills to the sound of the piano and his sensations follow the course described by Galton: 'That thrilling longing I had felt grew more and more intense, the craving so insatiable that it was changed to pain.'[27] Sexual desire aroused by the music and by the pianist who becomes his lover are apparent here at the beginning of the novel, but when the two finally meet sexually the same pattern is followed, and 'the pleasure he felt was so sharp that it verged upon pain'.[28]

Medical understandings of pain in the last decades of the nineteenth century were, at best, shaky, there being little decisive neurological evidence to substantiate any particular approach. This said, however, an enormous amount of medical optimism existed. Frederick Treves, writing in *The Elephant Man, and Other Reminiscences*, suggested the enormous change between pre- and post-anaesthetic surgery:

Treatment was very rough. The surgeon was rough. He had inherited that attitude from the days when operations were carried through without anæsthetics, and when he had need to be rough, strong and quick, as well as very indifferent to pain. Pain was with him a thing that had to be. It was a regrettable feature of disease. It had to be submitted to. At the present day pain is a thing that has not to be. It has to be relieved and not to be merely endured.[29]

The reality of the change between pre- and post-anaesthetic surgery is not to be disparaged, and is painfully marked in a letter from the Edinburgh chemist George Wilson, written in 1855 to James Young Simpson, which looks back to an operation on Wilson's left foot in 1843. Wilson laments the necessity for an operation three years before the introduction of ether, and details the 'cruel cutting through inflamed and morbidly sensitive parts'.[30] The operation 'could not be despatched by a

---

[27] *Teleny or, The Reverse of the Medal. A Physiological Romance of To-day*, 2 vols. (Cosmopoli, 1893), i. 15.

[28] Ibid. ii. 47. See also Rhoda Broughton, *Belinda* (1883; Richard Bentley, 1887), 100: 'For a moment she closes her eyes, as one faint with a bliss whose keenness makes it cross the borderland and become pain, and so is gathered into his strenuous embrace.' It is no big step from here to the conflation of pleasure and pain found in the pornographic and flagellatory writings of the 1880s and 1890s discussed in Ch. 6.

[29] *The Elephant Man and Other Reminiscences* (London, New York, Toronto, Melbourne: Cassell, 1923), 54.

[30] Cited in Victor Robinson, *Victory over Pain: A History of Anesthesia* (Sigma Books, 1947), 211.

few swift strokes of the knife',[31] and was performed whilst Wilson was entirely conscious, his only palliative being a cup of tea taken beforehand. The letter was written to thank and praise Simpson as the primary instigator of anaesthetic surgery in Scotland, and is important in rendering very real the sufferings of those who went under the surgeon's knife before 1846. Whilst there is no doubt that, as Wilson wrote, 'From all this anguish I should of course have been saved had I been rendered insensible by ether or chloroform . . . before submitting to the operation',[32] it is equally the case that some of the claims made for the eradication of pain towards the end of the century were absurdly optimistic. Treves's comment that 'pain is a thing that has not to be' is bold in the broadness of its application, and one which he would have found impossible to substantiate. Such claims are, however, a clear sign of the mastery of anaesthesia in ways of thinking about pain, and of the emergent confidence in the ability of medicine to treat a problem of the body. Medicine may not have had all of the answers to the problem of pain, but it was certainly in the ascendant—as Christianity found itself in the descendant—as the primary mode of explanation for physical suffering.

As I argued in the previous chapter, rationalizations of pain that fought shy of the eclecticism of the Broad Church and relied on an exclusively Christian framework became increasingly outmoded as moral objections were raised to a God who deliberately inflicted pain, or for whom all pain was attributed to beneficence. But even if such rationalizations could have been sustained against moralists, such ways of attributing meaning and purpose to pain could not for long ward off the encroachments of science. In a process epitomized in a vehement exchange of letters that appeared in the correspondence pages of the *Lancet* for August and September 1887, Christian justifications for pain were brought into contact with evolutionary and medical thought. In this altercation, H. Cameron Gillies, using the pages of the medical journal to air a series of articles called 'The Life-saving Value of Pain and Disease', left himself open to the ridicule of his fellow doctors. Following in the footsteps of such Christian apologists as G. A. Rowell, who, as we

---

[31] Robinson, 211.   [32] Ibid.

have seen, based his arguments solely on the beneficence of God, Gillies offers the utility of pain as its God-given purpose, couching his argument in specifically religious terms, as he approvingly cites Sir James Paget's definition of pain as ' "the prayer of a nerve for food" '.[33] He recites the arguments that had become standard in the defence of pain: that it is of use as a warning, for example, to drop the red hot poker before the skin is burned, or to stop drinking port once the first twinges of gout suggest worse things to come. He makes the somewhat surprising claim that 'I do not concern myself with definitions of pain. It is not the Whence nor the How of pain that is of practical interest, but the Wherefore—its meaning, intention, and purpose',[34] suggesting that its much-vaunted utility is a question of being able to read and interpret the sensation of pain in the light of Christian revelation. Alongside this, he made the further claim, hotly disputed in a series of letters over the next two months, that *Pain never comes where it can serve no good purpose.*[35] It is this claim, in particular, that incited a number of medical practitioners into writing refutations, picking up particularly on cases of painful breast cancer, and other intractable diseases, for which pain appears too late to be of any diagnostic value, but rather makes dying an agonizing experience. As W. J. Collins writes:

Pain, [Gillies] says, in such cases would 'serve no good purpose; there is no pain.' Is this the grim comfort he would bring to a suffering woman tortured slowly to death by a sloughing scirrhus of the breast, or to a man, made almost unhuman and killed by inches by the slow yet sure ravages of a rodent ulcer?[36]

Collins points to a failure in medical procedure here: doctors believing in such rationalizations of pain and its meaning *must* fail to recognize suffering in the patients who come to them. Whilst Collins is angry at this ability to wish away pain in the desire to read it in terms of the beneficence of God, his argument runs deeper. Such blindness to the suffering of patients involves a necessary blindness to current scientific and evolutionary thought: 'It is too late in the day to attempt to prop up

[33] 'The Life-saving Value of Pain and Disease', *Lancet*, 13 Aug. 1887, 305.
[34] Ibid.   [35] Ibid. 306.
[36] 'Pain and its Interpretation', *Lancet*, 20 Aug. 1887, 391.

a theory of the invariable and direct beneficence of pain, shut-
ting the eyes to facts to save a teleological theory which experience and reason have alike discredited.'[37] For him, and for
many others, pain was the by-product of evolution; the necessary corollary of the sensitivity required for progress. As he
argued, 'It has thus come about that the advantage in the race
which the sharp reprimand of pain on danger's approach
bestowed has, with the intensified susceptibilities which we
prize, also afforded us increased possibilities and opportunities
of suffering.'[38]

This was not a new argument, and the intricate relationship
between pain and civilization is one which I shall be exploring
in some detail in the final chapters of this book, but it becomes
clear that religious justifications for suffering had become
largely outmoded by this time, amongst medical practitioners at
least. The vast majority of the letters printed in the *Lancet* in
response to Gillies's article concur with Collins that 'pain is . . .
bound up with the progress of the race'. Collins clarified this
claim in a later letter when he takes up the issue of pain in childbirth; an issue which, as I have already suggested, was fought
over and won by the medical profession, with James Young
Simpson in the vanguard, forty years earlier. Collins refused to
accept religious rationales of parturitional pains as evidence of
the Fall, and denigrated what he labelled the ' "blessing in disguise theory" ',[39] which claims that not only is the pain of childbirth ordained by God, but that it also binds mother to child,
and more impressively 'vice-hardened men, although . . . lost to
all other feeling' to their mothers.[40] William Morris tried out a
similar argument when the older Hammond in *News From
Nowhere* (1891) claims: 'Surely it is a matter of course that the
natural and necessary pains which the mother must go through
form a bond of union between man and woman, an extra stimulus to love and affection between them, and that this is universally recognised.'[41] What Collins asserted in the place of such
thinking is the evolutionary idea that suffering arises in child-

---

[37] 'Pain', 20 Aug., 391.   [38] Ibid.
[39] 'Pain and its Interpretation', *Lancet*, 10 Sept. 1887, 543.
[40] See Hayman, 'Why We Suffer', 9.
[41] *News from Nowhere or, An Epoch of Rest, Being Some Chapters from a
Utopian Romance* (Reeves & Turner, 1891), 67.

birth because of the gradual transition that man, or more specifically, woman, has undergone from quadruped to biped:

Man has not gained the upright posture and his cerebral development without paying heavily for these distinctions. These two factors are responsible for most, if not all, of the obstetric difficulties which woman experiences over and above the normal pains of parturition (if such there be).[42]

There is no purpose to physical suffering: 'Pain is a universal human legacy. It is the penalty we pay for our high state of development.'[43] Most important in this series of letters is the insistence on the part of doctors that evolutionary thought be taken seriously and accepted not as the province of cranks but rather as that of all right-thinking and serious-minded physicians. Evolutionary theory had won the battle, and Christian rhetoric was forced to shape its own arguments in the light of its claims. As Harry Campbell concluded his letter of 10 September 1887, which had already claimed a shared belief that 'there is no doubt that the capacity for pain has largely evolved by natural selection',[44] the medical profession should take note that 'it behoves us, if we write upon the philosophy of [pain], to be most careful that we approach the subject from a strictly scientific point of view',[45] a view that aimed to alleviate and to understand pain without ascribing to it a purpose.[46]

By the 1880s pain, which had been part of a fixed conceptual framework that chose to read physical suffering in terms of the

---

[42] 'Pain', *Lancet*, 10 Sept. 543. See also Simpson, *Answer to Religious Objections*, 9–10.

[43] E. R. Williams, 'Pain and its Interpretation', *Lancet*, 17 Sept. 1887, 593–4. I shall be arguing that pain was not, however, accepted as a 'universal human legacy' in all forms of discourse, particularly in my discussion of the desensitization of savages and criminals in Ch. 5, Sect. II. In question in these last two cases is, of course, the 'high state of development' of which Williams speaks.

[44] 'Pain and its Interpretation', *Lancet*, 10 Sept. 1887, 543.

[45] Ibid.

[46] G. C. Lippincott, contributing to the series of letters 'Pain and its Interpretation', *Lancet*, 17 Sept. 1887, 594, laughs at the notion that pain is something that requires to be defined in terms of purpose: 'So pain is a consequence, a sign of failure of function of nerve or other tissue; and, as a failure, as a defective performance, it has no more *purpose* than hæmorrhage or any other failure or deficiency has. "Purpose" is surely confined to normality, and when the natural conditions under which an organ or a tissue does its work are changed to the extent of causing, for example, hæmorrhage, or pain, or what not, is it not beside the question to talk of "purpose" in it all?'

beneficence of God, or at least as a part of God's plan, had largely buckled leaving a void in the common cultural understanding of what it meant to suffer. As one referent for pain lost its value as a framing discourse, something had to be found to fill its place. Pain simply as pain—a meaningless bodily suffering—was not to be endured, and sufferers had to find new ways of contextualizing their suffering. If pain was not to be seen as a sign of their own depravity, then perhaps it was a sign of sensitivity and of medical need. Roselyne Rey recognizes the necessity of attributing meaning to pain, and argues that in the eighteenth century pain, though assuaged in every way possible, was seen as an overwhelming sign of vitality. After the introduction of anaesthetics into surgery this was seen to change, and pain became of the utmost importance, needing to be alleviated at all costs, even at the cost of life. As Rey writes:

a study published in Great Britain put the number of deaths attributed to anaesthesia in England and Wales between 1846 and 1946 at more than 25,000, with approximately a quarter of these occurring around 1880. It is thus obvious that pain had to be totally unacceptable if an individual would choose to put his life at risk in order to be free of it.[47]

Whilst Pernick argues that most of the deaths were attributable not to anaesthetics, but to the contemporaneous industrialization—accidents on railways and in factories often proved fatal—this does not alter the apprehended danger of chloroform.[48] The perceived cost of changing the dominant explanation for pain was clearly not trivial.

The tendency to glorify the painless becomes apparent in many different ways over the course of the century, but perhaps most noticeably in dental advertisements, epitomized by Messrs Gabriel in their claims for the wonders of 'Anæsthesia by Narcotic Spray'. 'The means whereby operations may be performed without pain must be regarded as among the most important discoveries of the age'; 'To relieve the bodily anguish

---

[47] *The History of Pain* (1993), trans. Louise Elliot Wallace and J. A. and S. W. Cadden (Cambridge, Mass and London: Harvard University Press, 1995), 174.

[48] Pernick, *Calculus of Suffering*, 218. For a 19th-cent. evaluation of the dangers of anaesthetics, see Edward T. Tibbits, *Medical Fashions in the Nineteenth Century: Including a Sketch of Bacterio-Mania and the Battle of the Bacilli* (H. K. Lewis, 1884), 20–2.

of humanity is the noblest undertaking that can engage the attention'; physical courage is 'but an animal quality'; 'Zeno-crates denied that pain was an evil; but few of our readers will agree with the stoic.'[49] Such statements convey a clear under-standing of the way in which pain had fallen through a network of thought that made it sustainable. By 1867 when this dental advertisement appeared—and when Voysey was writing his heretical '*Sling and Stone*.' sermons which overtly questioned the Christian value of physical suffering—the stoical endurance of pain was no longer widely considered to be an admirable attribute, and pain itself was becoming something to be avoided at all costs.

By 1898 a backlash was under way, a backlash underpinned by the eugenicist stress on the healthy body[50] but one that by its very existence suggested the distance travelled since 1846 in the perception of pain. G. W. Steevens, war correspondent on the *Daily Mail*, writing an article, 'The New Humanitarianism', in *Blackwood's Edinburgh Magazine*, professed his horror at the inability of modern man to look pain in the face. His series of books detailing the course of British wars, and praising the manliness, coolness, and marksmanship of the British soldier, suggest that his ideal man matches Rider Haggard's fictional Sir Henry Curtis in *King Solomon's Mines*,[51] or the real figure of Colonel Frank Rhodes, correspondent of *The Times*, who

[49] Messrs Gabriel, *Painless System of Dentistry* (J. & A. Reeves, 1867), 1, 3, 10.

[50] For a fictional representation of the eugenic ideal, see Ménie Muriel Dowie, *Gallia* (Methuen, 1895). Gallia, the novel's New Woman heroine, suppresses her attraction towards Dark Essex who suffers from a heart complaint, and instead marries the robust, though staid, Mark Gurdon: ' "I have wanted the father of my child to be a fine, strong, manly man, full of health and strength" ', 321. Aes-theticism, too, though differently, allowed a sensitive self to disregard the suffering of others: Oscar Wilde's Lord Henry claims that ' "There is something terribly morbid in the modern sympathy with pain" ' and that ' "the nineteenth century has gone bankrupt through an over-expenditure of sympathy" ' (*The Picture of Dorian Gray* (London, New York, Melbourne: Ward Lock, [1891]), 59 and 60); George Moore goes a step further in his *Confessions of a Young Man* (Swan Sonnenschein, Lowrey, 1888), 190–1: 'What care I that some millions of wretched Israelites died under Pharaoh's lash or Egypt's sun? It was well that they died that I might have the pyramids to look on, or to fill a musing hour with wonderment. Is there one amongst us who would exchange them for the lives of the ignominious slaves that died?'

[51] See H. Rider Haggard, *King Solomon's Mines* (London, Paris, New York & Melbourne: Cassell, 1885), esp. ch. 14, 'The Last Stand of the Greys', for Sir Henry in battle, pp. 216–39.

bore a bullet wound in his shoulder 'with his usual humorous fortitude'.[52] Instead of admiring the ethics of the Gabriel brothers, he deplored them, summing up what for him seemed to be the spirit of the age:

It may be the essence of civilisation, or an accident of it; but all our Victorian sentiments, all our movements, all our humanitarianist talk, trend in one direction—towards the conviction that death and pain are the worst of evils, their elimination the most desirable of goods.[53]

Steevens does not attempt to suggest reasons for this turnabout in the relationship to pain, but he does make it plain that such a 'gospel of painlessness'—a notable change from the gospel of painfulness prevalent at the beginning of the century—was 'throttling patriotism' and the 'virility of individual character'.[54] It showed itself in the unwillingness of mothers to have their children vaccinated in case they were hurt by the process; in anti-vivisectionists who refused to pay the price of an animal's pain for a human cure;[55] and, perhaps most important, in the weakness and lack of virility of men unwilling to kill to sustain the Empire.[56] For Steevens, the forces of civilization had had an enervating effect on the formerly manly Briton. He claims: 'We make bicycle records, but we are not prepared to converse coolly while having our legs cut off, as was the way of our great-grandfathers.'[57] This may seem like foolishness or bravado, but the desire for an anaesthetic to remove all traces of pain from life was, for Steevens, debilitating, enfeebling, and dishonest. George Wilson, in his letter to Simpson, somewhat surprisingly, broadly agrees, and abuses himself for his own response to pain, deliberately feminizing his pronounced sensitivity, so that he stands, even in his own eyes, in counterdistinction to Steevens's manly ideal:

---

[52] G. W. Steevens, *With Kitchener to Khartum* (William Blackwood, 1898), 288.

[53] Id., 'The New Humanitarianism', *Blackwood's Edinburgh Magazine*, 163 (1898), 98.   [54] Ibid.

[55] It is interesting that Steevens, in 'Two Hospitals' (from a *Daily Mail* article of 28 June 1888), takes up a stance almost directly contrary to that of 'The New Humanitarianism' when he shies away from describing an operation: 'Faithful accounts of operations do not suit all palates, so we will glide over these lightly.' Repr. in *The Works of George Warrington Steevens*, ed. G. S. Street, 7 vols. (Edinburgh and London: William Blackwood, 1900–2), i. 302.

[56] See Athena Vrettos, *Somatic Fictions: Imagining Illness in Victorian Culture* (Stanford, Stanford University Press, 1995), 124 ff.

[57] 'New Humanitarianism', 104.

I belong ... to that large class, including most women, to whom cutting, bruising, burning, or any similar physical injury, even to a small extent, is a source of suffering never willingly endured, and always anticipated with more or less of apprehension. Pain in itself has nothing tonic or bracing in its effects upon such. In its relation to the body, it is a sheer and unmitigated evil, and every fresh attack of suffering only furnishes a fresh proof of the sensitiveness possessed to pain, and increases the apprehension with which its attacks are awaited.[58]

Wilson's particular misfortune was that he had attained this nadir of virility four years before the widespread use of anaesthetic surgery. But in ways that the advocates of anaesthetics largely failed to acknowledge, even with chloroform to assuage the suffering of surgery, pain remained a fact of life: cutting, bruising, and burning remained as a part of quotidian existence. As Ann Dally suggests, 'Until the late nineteenth century, in every household at any one time, there was likely to be at least one person in severe pain.'[59] This is a view corroborated by George Stoker, Bram's brother, in his pamphlet *Clergyman's Sore Throat* (1884)—a type of pain common enough to become the subject of chit-chat in *Little Dorrit*[60]—in which Stoker's prefatory comment is, 'I believe it is a fact that more human suffering arises from the smaller rather than from the greater bodily ills, and that, taken in the aggregate, the former far outweigh the latter.'[61]

Mrs Humphry Ward, as presented by John Sutherland in his 1990 biography,[62] suffered from a painful mixture of the smaller and the greater ills and in this way provides a remarkable

---

[58] Robinson, *Victory over Pain*, 212.

[59] *Women under the Knife: A History of Surgery* (London, Sydney, Auckland, Johannesburg: Hutchinson Radius, 1991), 3.

[60] Charles Dickens, *Little Dorrit* (1857), ed. Harvey Peter Sucksmith (Oxford: Clarendon Press, 1979), 550: 'He [the Bishop] conversed with the great Physician on that relaxation of the throat with which young curates were too frequently afflicted, and on the means of lessening the great prevalence of that disorder in the church. Physician, as a general rule, was of opinion that the best way to avoid it was to know how to read, before you made a profession of reading.'

[61] *Clergyman's Sore Throat and Post-nasal Catarrh. Causes, Symptoms, and Treatment for Speakers and Singers* (J. & A. Churchill, 1884), 5.

[62] *Mrs Humphry Ward: Eminent Victorian, Pre-eminent Edwardian* (1990; Oxford and New York: Oxford University Press, 1991). See esp. ch. 17, 'Health: 1890–1900', 203–14.

showcase of some of the long-term, bodily afflictions available to the Victorian sufferer, as well as some of the means of coping with such chronic suffering. In the course of her life she suffered from headaches, rheumatism, writers' cramp, neuralgia, piles, an ulcerated stomach, excruciating gallstones, 'delayed complications from childbirth', eczema, styes, and boils, most of which plagued the writer throughout her life, for long stretches at a time. She fought back against these complaints in diverse fashions, in ways largely typical of the ameliorative strategies of Victorian sufferers, though some of her attempts to assuage pain were clearly connected to her status and wealth. Drug-based remedies for her various pains included sal volatile, linseed oil and laudanum,[63] arsenic tonic, strychnine compounds, and what came to be known in 1899 as aspirin. She tried to cure toothache by plunging her head in a bowl of cold water,[64] and attempted to alleviate the pain of writers' cramp with 'Swedish

---

[63] See also Virginia Berridge and Griffith Edwards, *Opium and the People: Opiate Use in Nineteenth-Century England* (London: Allen Lane; New York: St Martin's Press, 1981), and the chapter 'Tradition' in Alethea Hayter, *Opium and the Romantic Imagination* (Faber, 1968). Berridge and Edwards's book is particularly good at establishing the broad base on which opium and its derivatives were administered as pain relief, the lack of restriction on its use, its free availability to all classes, and its popularity as a self-administered drug suitable for all complaints. They write: 'Medical reliance on the drug to combat cholera or dysentery was paralleled by its popular currency as a remedy for diarrhoea. It was as popular for earache as for toothache . . . For stomach cramp, "flatulencies, or wind", headaches, and nervous diseases in general, it was at least a palliative' (32), and add that it was also used for non-specific 'pains in [the] limbs', menstrual pain, gout, and rheumatism. See also Thomas Hardy, *The Trumpet-Major. A Tale*, 3 vols. (Smith, Elder, 1880). Robert Loveday, escaping from the press-gang, receives a serious blow to the head and self-medicates with opium: 'the pain in my head was so great that I couldn't get to sleep; so I picked some of the poppy-heads in the border, which I once heard was a good thing for sending folks to sleep when they are in pain. So I munched up all I could find, and dropped off quite nicely', iii. 68.

[64] See W. C. Honeyman, 'Toothache: A Detective's Story', in *Toothache and Other Interesting and Amusing Stories. By Eminent Authors* (Edinburgh: William P. Nimmo, [1867]), 5–6: 'I had spent the afternoon at home in a state of maniacal frenzy, which increased as evening wore on. I had held my jaw with my hands, and cried, 'Oh-ah-ee-em-m-m-m!' with touching shrillness, and had kicked and stamped on the floor till the people below sent up to inquire, with a horrible facetiousness, 'If I had comed into a fortin', and was dancin' for joy?' I had tried three infallible toothache tinctures, and had thrown each of them aside, heaping anathemas on their lying inventors; I had looked out while the street lamps were being lit, and wondered how the lamplighter could go about his business so unconcernedly when *I* had toothache; and finally had plunged my head into cold water, and after drying it hurriedly, tumbled into bed to try and sleep. I didn't sleep.'

rubbers' or masseurs, as well as 'electric vibration treatment' which went appallingly wrong.[65] She tried preventative medicine, stayed out of cold winds, and propped up her painful arm in more comfortable positions. She was waited on assiduously by her family and secretary, but was also forced into bizarre popular remedies such as eating raw beef sandwiches and following an all-milk diet,[66] the latter of which almost certainly contributed to her pain by reinforcing her gallstones. It should be clear from this catalogue that a mixture of popular remedies and (largely unsuccessful) medical treatments was available, but that at the same time Mary Ward spent a great deal of her life in considerable amounts of pain. One of her strategies for dealing with such pain outside a medical framework was the giving of a name to her suffering in an attempt to make it bearable. Her recurrent fits of pain from gallstones, repeatedly misdiagnosed as 'internal catarrh', 'floating kidneys', 'loose liver',

---

[65] See Donald Baynes, *Auxiliary Methods of Cure. The Weir Mitchell System. Massage. Ling's Swedish Movements. The Hot Water Cure. Electricity* (Simpkin, Marshall, 1888). Baynes suggests many of the procedures tried by Mrs Humphry Ward. Whilst massage was always of therapeutic use, it became popular after S. Weir Mitchell made it a part of his 'Rest Cure', describing its operation and merits in *Fat and Blood: and How to Make Them* (Philadelphia: J. B. Lippincott, 1877). An abundance of books about massage techniques sprang up in the 1880s and 1890s. See Wilkie Collins, *The Legacy of Cain*, 3 vols. (Chatto & Windus, 1889) where the practice is moved into fiction: 'Mrs T[enbruggen]'s marriage had turned out badly, and . . . she had been reduced to earn her own bread. Her manner of doing this was something quite new to me. She went about, from one place to another, curing people of all sorts of painful maladies, by a way she had of rubbing them with her hands. In Belgium she was called a 'Masseuse.' When I asked what this meant in English, I was told, 'Medical Rubber,' and that the fame of Mrs. T.'s wonderful cures had reached some of the medical newspapers published in London' (i. 267). Massage as a technique is presented by Collins in an equivocal light, being both the 'torturing [of] the poor old gentleman's muscles' (ii. 256) and the relief of tortured muscles (iii. 136). See also ii. 253 and iii. 50–1, 53. Cyril Bennett, in his novel *The Massage Case*, 2 vols. (T. Fisher Unwin, 1887), i. 238 is much less equivocal about the adverse effects of badly administered massage and of electrical treatments: 'To put it plainly, [massage] simply consisted of violent pinching from head to foot, and was a torture worthy only of the Spanish Inquisition.' See also Dowie, *Gallia*, 189–90: 'Papa has his masseur every day; . . . Alfred has his electric shock person and galvaniser—he can't raise a slipper before eleven, when this person comes, and afterwards he's awfully larky until it wears off', 189–90.

[66] A very similar sounding diet as a cure for painful ulcers was followed by Richard Jefferies. See Walter Besant, *The Eulogy of Richard Jefferies* (Chatto and Windus, 1888), 346: ' "He put me on milk diet, malt bread, malt extract, malted food, meat shredded and pounded in a mortar, raw beef, and so on. In forty-eight hours the pain was better." '

or 'rheumatic gout', became known within the family as 'side' or, more interestingly, 'the old enemy'[67] as a name is given to the condition in an attempt to familiarize and to understand it. Mary Ward set her physical suffering into a scheme which envisaged pain attacking and her body defending, and in so doing she gave pain meaning, in this case demonizing her suffering to render fighting back part of the battle between Good and Evil. Nietzsche took a similar course with the pain he suffered, writing, in *The Gay Science*, in 1887, 'I have given a name to my pain and call it "dog."' It is just as faithful, just as obtrusive and shameless, just as entertaining, just as clever as any other dog—and I can scold it and vent my bad mood on it, as others do with their dogs, servants, and wives.'[68]

Steevens's claim that pain should be dealt with and not avoided is reflected in the strategies of these two writers, who acknowledge and name their suffering as a way of coming to terms with it. Steevens, however, pushed this further, claiming that it is necessary not to see pain just as a part of life, but also to recognize in it a force for good, not in any religious sense, but rather as the force that was to put the backbone back into late Victorian man: 'We became and are an Imperial race by dealing necessary pain to other men, just as we become powerful men by dealing necessary pain to other animals.'[69] This is an argument George Meredith expounds in *The Egoist*, when Dr Middleton suggests that a flogging is the only answer for the book-shy Crossjay: 'No, sir, no; the birch! the birch! . . . We English beat the world because we take a licking well.'[70] George Gissing's Harvey Rolfe, with far less conviction, intellectually recognizes the necessity of dealing pain out to others and of taking it oneself, but, in the psychological and social whirlpool of late Victorian London, is both horrified and attracted by the idea of his son's sensitivity born of the conditions Steevens so adamantly deplores:

---

[67] See also Charles Dickens, *Bleak House* (1852–3), ed. Osbert Sitwell (London, New York, Toronto: Oxford University Press, 1948), 788: suffering from the gout, Sir Leicester Dedlock finds that 'his old enemy is very hard with him'.

[68] *The Gay Science, with a prelude in rhymes and an appendix of songs* (2nd edn. 1887), trans. Walter Kaufmann (New York: Vintage Books, 1974), 249–50.

[69] 'New Humanitarianism', 104.

[70] *The Egoist: A Comedy in Narrative*, 3 vols. (C. Kegan Paul, 1879), i. 147–8.

'It's natural for a boy to be a good deal of a savage, but our civilisation is doing its best to change that. Why, not long ago the lad asked me whether fishing wasn't cruel. He evidently felt that it was, and so do I; but I couldn't say so. I laughed it off, and told him that a fish diet was excellent for the brains!'[71]

Young Hugh Rolfe, child of the degenerate *fin de siècle*, would clearly not be capable of 'convers[ing] coolly while having [his] legs cut off'. In the final chapter of the book, Rolfe looks to imperialism as a way out of such weakness, and reading *Barrack-Room Ballads* (1892), he recognizes in Kipling the ' "strong man made articulate" ',[72] voicing the unexpressed thoughts of ' "Millions of men, natural men, revolting against the softness and sweetness of civilisation" '.[73] As Steevens suggested, civilization was regarded as having corrupted modern men, such that they became feeble and feminized. The price, however, as Rolfe sees it, of regaining vigour and virility is a return to ' "brute savagery" ', and 'The tongue of Whitechapel blaring lust of life" '.[74] This is one of the central problems dealt with in this book, as the ability to withstand pain is joined to vulgarity and brutalization, both of life and of language. It is a problem that I shall discuss in terms of H. G. Wells's *Island of Doctor Moreau* and Stevenson's *Ebb-Tide*, both of which were written in the mid-1890s. It is in this conjunction that we see another emergent meaning for pain, different both from the sanctified and reformatory pain of Christianity and the evolutionary and physiological pain of medical discourse.

II. THE DANGERS OF DIVERSITY

Whatever the discourse involved, whether medical or theological, the diversity of explanations offered for pain was enormous. I want to change direction slightly to recognize the implications of such diversity in explanations by discussing some twentieth-century theorists of pain. Of particular interest is Ivan Illich, and his claim that the shift of emphasis from enduring pain to curing it adversely affected the ways in which people suffered. This

---

[71] *The Whirlpool* (Lawrence and Bullen, 1897), 342.   [72] Ibid. 449.
[73] Ibid.   [74] Ibid.

opens the way for my later discussions of the abuse of those in
pain by those who define physical suffering.

Illich claims that in the late twentieth century people have
largely abnegated responsibility for their own pain and have
handed it over to the medical profession. Partly, he argues, this
is through no fault of their own. The means of dealing with and
transmuting pain—those which 'traditionally enabled people to
recognize painful sensations as a challenge and to shape their
own experience accordingly'[75]—open to their forebears, in the
form of patience, forbearance, courage, resignation, meekness,
and other virtues expected of them by society, have been
stripped away leaving them without the necessary transformative powers that would make pain bearable without medication.
Illich writes:

> cultures always have provided an example on which behaviour in pain
> could be modelled: the Buddha, the saint, the warrior, or the victim.
> The duty to suffer in their guise distracts attention from otherwise all-
> absorbing sensation and challenges the sufferer to bear torture with
> dignity.[76]

Illich goes on to argue that modern medicine 'has rendered
either incomprehensible or shocking the idea that skill in the art
of suffering might be the most effective and universally acceptable way of dealing with pain'[77] and aims instead at palliative
medicine, the primary aim of which is to remove the patient's
pain by means of anaesthetics or analgesics. In this way, pain
loses its position as an integral part of human existence, and
becomes an unwanted and unnecessary evil. Such a claim is
vital to this project since I am charting the strategies, or lack of
strategies, for dealing with pain in the tail-end of the gap left
between the introduction of anaesthetics in surgery, specifically
chloroform, in 1846, and the commercial production of aspirin
as a household drug in 1899. Illich claims that by the end of the
nineteenth century the rot had already begun to set in, 'pain had
become a regulator of body functions, subject to the laws of
nature; it needed no more metaphysical explanation'[78]—a claim
mirrored by the determinedly evolutionary series of letters,

---

[75] *Medical Nemesis: The Expropriation of Health* (Harmondsworth: Penguin,
1977), 141.
[76] Ibid. 152.   [77] Ibid.   [78] Ibid. 157.

already discussed, that appeared in the *Lancet*. Whilst Illich's claim represents some part of the truth—pain's status did indeed change radically after the introduction of anaesthesia—it is to some extent misleading in suggesting the complete absence of conceptual frameworks for physical suffering after the shift in importance of the Christian paradigm. Former ages had provided religious models for suffering which had largely, though not entirely, dissolved by the end of the nineteenth century, but writers—whether professional or private, medical or lay—alarmed by the presence of a pain emptied of Christian meaning, continued to try to find ways of making sense of physical suffering. Of particular interest, here, is what pain could mean if it were something that could be taken away chemically; if it were not, as hitherto perceived, a constant and ineradicable part of the human condition. Instead of mapping the ability to withstand pain onto Christian virtue, or, indeed, entirely onto neurological wiring, in the following chapters I shall be discussing the ways in which pain came to be seen as an index to other qualities, such as degree of civilization, artistic ability, or class.

There is, however, a different set of ethical problems inherent in opening pain up to such diverse readings. In a critical reading of Richard Sternbach's article 'Strategies and Tactics in the Treatment of Patients with Pain', the implications for such opening up of physical pain to diverse interpretations in the period when Christianity waned and medicine waxed as frameworks of definition become apparent. Whilst broadly aligning myself with Sternbach's argument, I have important reservations concerning its implications. Sternbach claims that pain is not a single entity that can be defined in a single way, but rather is defined in different ways by the different groups of people who lay claim to it. It will be differently defined and will acquire a different terminology for the psychiatrist who may treat pain as an emotion, the neurologist who sees it as the fruits of certain neurological pathways and structures—these two have been seen to come into conflict in Witmer's assessment of late nineteenth-century understandings of pain—or the biologist who highlights its prophylactic function. The groupings Sternbach chooses are clearly indicative of the nature of his study. He is writing about the treatment of pain, rather than the

personal endurance of it, and it is clear that many other
categories could be added to those who demand the right to des-
ignate the terminology of pain: sufferers themselves or their
families; theologians contemplating the divine origin of pain;
anthropologists investigating the capacity for suffering of specific ethnological groups; and so on, in groupings that will
become more apparent in the course of this book. Sternbach's
point is that the ways of thinking about pain institutionalized
by a particular profession, or group of people, can be restrictive, in such a way that the 'choice of what pain *is* will depend,
mostly, upon your profession'.[79] Whilst there is supportive data
for each professional definition it cannot be claimed that any of
them is wrong, which leads Sternbach to his claim that 'the
word "pain" is an abstraction that we use to refer to many different phenomena'.[80] As Sternbach points out, the term covers
a number of different phenomena, from the subjective and
non-verifiable experience of burning or stinging, through the
stimulus of tissue damage of various kinds, which could be
described as 'hurting', to the type of behaviour elicited by such
stimulation, whether it be on the level of neurochemistry, avoidance behaviour, or verbalization. From here Sternbach argues,
rightly, I think, that 'None of these events has any inherent
relationship to any other. It is we who have arbitrarily imposed
on all of them the common concept, "pain".'[81] Where his argument becomes problematic is in his subsequent argument that
therefore

There need not be any arguments about which is the 'right' approach,
because all these parallel approaches are 'right'. That is, each describes
some different things in different ways, and each approach is internally
consistent and follows the rules of its own game of investigation.[82]

This seems fair at first, but there are major difficulties inherent
in such an approach, and they are problems to some extent
teased out by Elaine Scarry in *The Body in Pain*. As she writes:

It is not simply accurate but tautological to observe that given any two
phenomena, the one that is more visible will receive more attention.

---

[79] 'Strategies and Tactics in the Treatment of Patients with Pain', in Benjamin L.
Crue (ed.) *Pain and Suffering: Selected Aspects* (Springfield, Ill.: Charles C. Thomas,
1970), 176.
[80] Ibid. 177.   [81] Ibid. 180.   [82] Ibid.

But the sentient fact of physical pain is not simply somewhat less easy to express than some second event, not simply somewhat less visible than some second event, but so nearly impossible to express, so flatly invisible, that the problem goes beyond the possibility that almost any other phenomenon occupying the same environment will distract attention from it. Indeed, even where it is virtually the only content in a given environment, it will be possible to describe that environment as though the pain were not there.[83]

Such remarks are intended to set the scene for Scarry's discussion of torture, and the ways in which I disagree with her terminology and, indeed, her arguments, will become clear in my subsequent discussion of the introduction to Scarry's book. It is, however, helpful to use the concept of the quietness or invisibility of pain, as opposed to the noisiness or visibility of almost any other stimulus, to understand the ways in which pain may be manipulated and defined by those who are not directly suffering. This is where the problem with Sternbach arises, for it is far too easy to neglect the possibility of abuse in saying that any definition of pain is acceptable as long as it is 'internally consistent and follows the rules of its own game'. Choosing to define pain in particular ways—either for oneself, or for groups deemed somehow other—has consequences. In the remainder of this chapter, I shall be using George du Maurier's immensely popular novel *Trilby* (1894) to suggest the manipulability of those in pain. Du Maurier's Svengali may be seen to fill the position of manipulative medical practice, as the relief of the heroine's pain is not his primary end: this rather is to obtain power over her.

In the novel, Trilby, the eponymous heroine, suffers a maddening, neuralgic pain in her eyes, a pain which only Svengali can remove through his mesmeric power. We see the beginnings of his manipulation of Trilby through her pain when he accepts her statement, in a way surprisingly like that of Jesus for such an anti-Semitic novel, that he has ' "taken all [her] pain away" ' and adds of his own accord that ' "I have got it myself; it is in my elbows. But I love it, because it comes from you." '[84] The relief of her pain is not, however, his primary

[83] *The Body in Pain: The Making and Unmaking of the World* (New York and Oxford: Oxford University Press, 1985), 12.
[84] *Trilby*, 3 vols. (Osgood, McIlvaine, 1894), i. 108.

goal—it is a means to an end, a way of making her come to him whenever she is in pain. She fights against this, but turns to Svengali as to her fate, when spurned by the artist whom she loves. In this way he gains ascendancy over her through her pain. That this process is about his power, rather than her suffering, and his desire to sing through the instrument that is her fine body, the ' "flexible flageolet of flesh and blood" '[85] that he makes her, is all too apparent. The price of taking away her pain is that she ' "*shall see nothing, hear nothing, think of nothing but Svengali, Svengali, Svengali!*" '[86] The workings of this novel may be seen as a paradigm for the ways in which pain can be manipulated and defined by those with power, both inside and outside of fictional writings. An authorial comment in du Maurier's novel declares, 'Such was Svengali—only to be endured for the sake of his music—always ready to vex, frighten, bully, or torment anybody or anything smaller and weaker than himself—from a woman or a child to a mouse or a fly.'[87] Readers are given both the nature of Svengali's power— his size advantage—and the rationale behind his abuse of it, as his musical prowess is seen to a large extent to exonerate him. *Trilby* was not written in a cultural vacuum, and it is only a short step from here to the subject matter of my fourth chapter which deals with the rhetoric of the antivivisection movement in the 1880s and 1890s. Just as Trilby's pain was redefined in terms of Svengali's power, so too was the pain of animals pushed aside in favour of physiological knowledge: as Wilkie Collins's vivisectionist claims, 'Knowledge sanctifies cruelty.'[88] The pioneering antivivisection campaigner and novelist Mona Caird, writing in 1893—the year before *Trilby*—is alarming in this context. She claims, 'there is unquestionably growing up a singular spirit of toleration for the practice of painful experiments on hospital patients' and adds as a note to this, 'The recent scandalous disclosures of such experiments on a grand scale at the Chelsea Hospital for women, have been made since the above

---

[85] *Trilby*, iii. 174.
[86] Ibid. i. 113.   [87] Ibid. i. 171.
[88] *Heart and Science: A Story of the Present Time*, 3 vols. (Chatto & Windus, 1883), ii. 157.

sentence was written.'[89] The pain of the female patients here is clearly considered much less significant than the possibility of scientific advance resulting from such experimentation. In Sternbach's terms, the logic of those involved is 'internally consistent and follows the rules of its own game', and the physiologists concerned are willing to consider the suffering of their patients to be of less importance than their own scientific aggrandizement, or increase in knowledge.

To be without power is dangerous where pain is concerned, since the openness of physical suffering to interpretation leaves it liable to abuse from those who choose to define it in particular ways. Not only is pain open to changing cultural conditions, but it is also liable to be represented or misrepresented by powerful groups aiming to manipulate those with less power.

From this point onwards, I shall be opening outwards from the two primary discourses of Christianity and medicine to the broader question of pain's expressibility. To answer the question of what other options were available to the sufferer, it is necessary to consider the modes of communication open to other groups trying to define pain. The next chapter, on the relationship between language and pain, and the supposed inexpressibility of physical suffering, will act as a bridge between the closing hypothesis of this chapter—that those in pain are liable to abuse by those in power—and my discussion of this in action in my chapter on the rhetoric of vivisection.

---

[89] *A Sentimental View of Vivisection* (Bijou Library, no. 3; William Reeves, [1893]), 22 n. See also Mark Thornhill, *Experiments on Hospital Patients* (Hatchards, 1889); [Edward Berdoe], *Dying Scientifically: A Key to St. Bernard's. By Æsculapius Scalpel* (Swan Sonnenschein, Lowrey, 1888). Blanche Channing's *The Madness of Michael Stark: A Story not drawn from Imagination* (James Clarke, 1900) tells the tale of a man who murders a doctor who has painfully experimented on, and killed, both his wife and child.

3
Pain and Language

It has become a commonplace that pain defies language and, as such, that it is unique as a sensation that cannot be described or shared: sufferers suffer alone, unable to translate their physical pains into words. In this chapter I shall be looking at the arguments of those who promote this line of reasoning, most notably Virginia Woolf and Elaine Scarry, and shall be refuting their claims both theoretically and by arguing from the rhetorical strategies of Victorian writers. The flaw in such arguments is that their proponents refuse to accept that pain can enter into language and be accommodated by its structures—whether descriptive or metaphorical—in the face of a paucity of directly expressive words for painful sensations. In response, I shall be schematizing the conventional attitudes towards physical pain, outside the realms of medicine and Christianity, that were open to the Victorian sufferer and writer. Pain, as a subject, simultaneously resisted representation and provided a widely used counter that carried immediately recognizable cultural designations. It both could and could not be written about, since social conventions and physical and linguistic incapacity silenced individuals, whilst novelistic conventions gave physical suffering free rein, but in so doing to a large extent took the physicality out of that suffering and turned it into an empty convention.

Two Victorian theories of the shared nature of pain suggest the clash between popularly held, yet contradictory, beliefs about physical suffering. On the one hand pain was seen as 'our lot', something that 'braces us and does us good',[1] something that draws humankind together in a band of communal suffering. On the other was Alice James's vision of her friend who 'stood at the foot of the sofa, but . . . had no gift to divine that

---

[1] [Elizabeth von Arnim], *Elizabeth and her German Garden* (Macmillan, 1898), 101.

pain was as the essence of the Universe to my consciousness'.[2]
I shall be steering a path between these two seemingly contradictory beliefs about pain: that pain is a universal condition and
as such a shared understanding of it is inevitable; and that pain
is such an intensely private experience that it is incommunicable even to one's closest friends.

The aim of this chapter, therefore, is to consider the fraught
relationship of pain to language, and I shall start by evaluating
Woolf's theory of pain expression. Moving on from Woolf, I
shall suggest the limitations of Elaine Scarry's more recent formulations, then turn away from these to a detailed examination
of the ways in which late Victorians expressed their physical suffering in words. This chapter will be a chapter of refutations
and of suggestions, as I point towards possibilities and practices
of writing about physical pain denied by the formulations of
modern theorists, and suggest that problems caused by the
scarcity of direct language for pain do not automatically mean
that there is no viable mode of expression. It is clearly not possible to cover every conceivable method of expressing pain: I do,
however, show a range of representational tactics, and in this
way refute the claim that there is no language for pain.

I. THE LANGUAGE OF PAIN:
VIRGINIA WOOLF AND ELAINE SCARRY

Virginia Woolf's much-cited essay 'On Being Ill' (1926) is used
as verification of the ineffability of pain by diverse writers who
take the rationalization of suffering as their subject, from Elaine
Scarry and *The Body in Pain* which insists on the complete
disintegration of language in the face of pain, through Ronald
Melzack and Patrick Wall in their ground-breaking medical book
The Challenge of Pain (1982), to Norman Autton's very differently slanted book *Pain: An Exploration* (1986), a manual of
how to listen to those who suffer physically. These, and indeed
many other writers,[3] cite just one phrase from Woolf's essay:

[2] *The Diary of Alice James* (1964), ed. Leon Edel (Harmondsworth: Penguin, 1982), 77.
[3] See David B. Morris, *The Culture of Pain* (1991; Berkeley and Los Angeles: University of California Press, 1993), 72; Kat Duff, *The Alchemy of Illness* (1993;

English, which can express the thoughts of Hamlet and the tragedy of Lear, has no words for the shiver and the headache . . . The merest schoolgirl, when she falls in love, has Shakespeare, Donne, Keats to speak her mind for her; but let a sufferer try to describe a pain in his head to a doctor and language at once runs dry.[4]

This has largely been taken as gospel in recent years, and in the face of such wholesale acceptance it is important to reorient this comment, putting it back into its context in the essay from which it comes. I shall be using the terminology of 'On Being Ill' as a way of approaching the problems of and limitations to writing about physical pain, suggesting that Woolf's sophistication was far greater than many of those who followed her, lifting just this one decontextualized phrase from her essay.

Woolf's major contention is that it is surprising, considering the prevalence of illness and pain, that these have not become the subjects of literature, superseding love, battle, and jealousy as 'the prime themes of literature': 'Novels, one would have thought, would have been devoted to influenza; epic poems to typhoid; odes to pneumonia, lyrics to toothache.'[5] There *are*, as I argue throughout, 'lyrics to toothache',[6] though assuredly not so numerous as those to love, and spread across a wide range of literary forms. This said, the disproportion between the lyrics of love and those of pain is marked, and Woolf's insight into the barriers to the writing of such lyrics is helpful as a means of discussing the difficulties inherent in writing about pain.

Woolf recognizes two distinct barriers to writing about pain: the first involving taste, decorum, and fear; the second the inability of language adequately to express pain. For Woolf, literature is heavily invested in the life of the mind, so much so that the struggles of the body are overlooked, and 'of all this daily drama', of illness and cold and pain, 'there is no record'.[7]

Virago, 1994), p. xiii; Gert H. Brieger, review of *The History of Pain* by Roselyne Rey, *Nature Medicine*, 1 (1995), 1207.

[4] 'On Being Ill', in *The Essays of Virginia Woolf*, ed. Andrew McNeillie, 4 vols. (Hogarth, 1994), iv. 318.

[5] Ibid. 317.

[6] See Robert Burns, 'Address to the Tooth-Ache', in *Poems and Songs*, ed. James Kinsley (Oxford: Oxford University Press, 1969), 624. The poem begins: 'My curse on your envenom'd stang, | That shoots my tortur'd gums alang, | An' thro' my lugs gies mony a bang, | Wi' gnawin vengeance; | Tearing my nerves wi' bitter twang, | Like racking engines.'   [7] 'On Being Ill', 318.

Not only this, but courage is needed to look pain in the face. The reason for silence in the face of physical suffering is not hard to discover:

To look these things squarely in the face would need the courage of a lion tamer; a robust philosophy; a reason rooted in the bowels of the earth. Short of these, this monster, the body, this miracle, its pain, will soon make us taper into mysticism, or rise, with rapid beats of the wings, into the raptures of transcendentalism.[8]

There are two major points here. The first, the lack of courage in facing pain, is something to which I shall return, whilst the second problem, that of the 'poverty' of language, is perhaps more intractable. Woolf, however, does suggest a way out, as the describer of pain, faced with the absence of appropriate language, is compelled to move outwards from the direct description of pain itself into a metaphorical and explanatory realm in which pain is fitted into another and distinct framework of reference. There may be few directly descriptive words both specific and reproducible, but, as Woolf writes, pain rises 'with rapid beats of the wings' or 'taper[s] into mysticism'. This process shows the description of pain moving into a sphere where a metaphorical language can be found, dependent not on painful experience, but rather on ways of making sense of that experience. Again Woolf writes that in language 'there is nothing ready made' for the sufferer: 'He is forced to coin words himself, and, taking his pain in one hand, and a lump of pure sound in the other (as perhaps the inhabitants of Babel did in the beginning), so to crush them together that a brand new word in the end drops out.'[9] We will see this idea taken up by Scarry, and it is one (as I shall discuss later) with which I am not altogether happy, but we do see Woolf tying this in with the outward movement of pain description. But when Woolf moves on she shows the greater degree of sophistication in her own writing than that of those who cite her, for she writes:

Yet it is not only a new language that we need, primitive, subtle, sensual, obscene, but a new hierarchy of the passions; love must be deposed in favour of a temperature of 104; jealousy give place to the pangs of sciatica; sleeplessness play the part of the villain, and the hero

[8] Ibid. [9] Ibid. 318–19.

become a white liquid with a sweet taste—that mighty Prince with the moths' eyes and the feathered feet, one of whose names is Chloral.[10]

Woolf looks for a way of attributing importance to physical suffering at the expense of other sensations and emotions, pushing these latter further down a hierarchical structure. In so doing she recognizes a way of making sense of pain by referring it to other experiences.

Elaine Scarry, the most influential of modern theorists of pain, refuses to accept this referential quality of pain—the need in describing it to fit it in to other frameworks of reference—and it is this refusal that lies at the centre of my disagreement with her argument in the introduction to *The Body in Pain*. She writes:

If one were to move through all the emotional, perceptual, and somatic states that take an object—hatred for, seeing of, being hungry for—the list would become a very long one and, though it would alternate between states we are thankful for and those we dislike, it would be throughout its entirety a consistent affirmation of the human being's capacity to move out beyond the boundaries of his or her own body into the external, shareable world. This list and its implicit affirmation would, however, be suddenly interrupted when, moving through the human interior, one at last reached physical pain, for physical pain—unlike any other state of consciousness—has no referential content. It is not *of* or *for* anything. It is precisely because it takes no object that it, more than any other phenomenon, resists objectification in language.[11]

In this she is wrong. People have consistently chosen to read pain in referential terms as a way of making sense of its inherent lack of meaning. Pain is always what I shall call in this chapter referential. By this I do not mean that it refers directly to a specific thing, but rather that although pain has no innate meaning, it is given meaning—has meaning imposed on it—when the sufferer, or someone acting either benevolently or malevolently on behalf of the sufferer, draws suffering into association with something else. In Scarry's terms, we feel dislike *for*, we are angry *about*, but we are in pain *because*: because we have sinned, because we are not manly enough, because we are civilized. Scarry chooses to argue from the extremes of torture

---

[10] 'On Being Ill', 319.   [11] *Body in Pain*, 5.

and war, and it is almost certainly true in these cases that language disintegrates, that nothing can be said from such extremity of pain. I do not choose this ground. Rather I aim to show that physical pain in all its forms, from a stubbed toe through flogging to cancer, is hard to convey, that there is a necessity for overcoming squeamishness, decorum, and the recalcitrance of language in writing about pain, but that it is a subject that offers itself as a problem for the expressibility of language, and as such is an important field of literary study. Scarry, however, writes:

> To witness the moment when pain causes a reversion to the pre-language of cries and groans is to witness the destruction of language; but conversely, to be present when a person moves up out of that pre-language and projects the facts of sentience into speech is almost to have been permitted to be present at the birth of language itself.[12]

But isn't this sophistry? Why is it the birth of language when what is happening is that the person in pain is finding the resources to express that pain? Language has been learnt before the infliction of pain, and is being used as a means of expression in the midst of that pain. We are in a strange realm again, where Scarry can write: 'physical pain has no voice, but when it at last finds a voice, it begins to tell a story'.[13] Either it has a voice or it hasn't. How can it find a voice that does not exist? I point to this as an indication of the ways in which the argument from extremes makes little sense, and the ways in which, as a consequence of her rhetorical stance, Scarry loses some of the force of her argument. In pushing things to the position where she claims that there is no language available to the sufferer—'physical pain does not simply resist language but actively destroys it, bringing about an immediate reversion to a state anterior to language, to the sounds and cries a human being makes before language is learned'[14]—she denies the variability of pain, and confounds two strands of argument. There is no sense of degree in Scarry's introduction to *The Body in Pain*, nor any means of judging the severity of pain necessary to validate her claims. Does toothache, for example, bring about this 'immediate reversion', or does it take childbirth or torture to do this? While there is recognition of the difference between the resistance to and the destruction of language by pain, these

---

[12] Ibid. 6.   [13] Ibid. 3.   [14] Ibid. 4.

two seem to play little part in Scarry's thinking. The approbation with which Scarry cites Woolf's famous claim for the lack in the English language of 'words for the shiver or the headache' suggests this confusion. Either language is at fault and does not provide enough words for what would otherwise be expressible since pain is inimical to language, or the experience of pain breaks down the ability to find the right words: the two things are not the same. Scarry proffers the first as a possibility, but gives the second explanation as a certainty.

Scarry claims that in hearing about another's pain we are as distant from it as from far-flung galaxies in which 'violent events of unknown nature occur from time to time', and that as such it has no reality for those not in pain themselves. In this way she suggests a corollary between the inability to experience the events of outer space, and the inability to recognize the pain of an individual sitting in the chair next to one. She goes on to suggest that such metaphorical thinking is at fault in deflecting attention from such individual suffering, writing:

Physical pain happens, of course, not several miles below our feet or many miles above our heads but within the bodies of persons who inhabit the world through which we each day make our way, and who may at any moment be separated from us by only a space of several inches. The very temptation to invoke analogies to remote cosmologies (and there is a long tradition of such analogies) is itself a sign of pain's triumph, for it achieves its aversiveness in part by bringing about, even within the radius of several feet, this absolute split between one's sense of one's own reality and the reality of other persons.[15]

Again, I would contend that Scarry is wrong in this instance. There is confusion in her thinking here, and it is necessary to recognize this in understanding the nature of her claims. The analogy that she draws is intended to suggest something comparably distant and hard to understand as physical pain—the events taking place in very distant Seyfert galaxies, or 'some deep subterranean fact, belonging to an invisible geography that . . . has no reality because it has not yet manifested itself on the visible surface of the earth'.[16] Such things are hard to understand because so far removed from human experience and indeed so physically distant that there can be no direct experi-

---

[15] *Body in Pain*, 4.   [16] Ibid. 3.

ential relationship to them, but not because they are painful and therefore hard to describe. Furthermore, they bear no relation to the nature of pain itself, nor are they intended to express it metaphorically. The images of distance are a red herring, for whilst it is true that one cannot necessarily know that a nearby person is suffering physical pain, this is of a different nature from the physical space between oneself and a distant galaxy: whilst proximity is not necessarily noisier than distance, the reasons for its seeming silence are radically different. There is a shift in the second sentence of the quotation to a belief that these analogies are expressive in the second sense that I have suggested; that they are similar in quality to the nature of human suffering. Scarry refuses to accept that pain is a shared cultural phenomenon and that, as such, it can be incorporated into structures of language and expression, and it is on these grounds that I shall be most fiercely contesting her arguments. In the face of Scarry's unnecessary mystifications about pain, I shall show over the course of the chapter the uneasy, though definitely present, tensions between expressibility and inexpressibility where physical pain is concerned.

II. LITERARY AND SOCIAL CONVENTIONS

The experience of pain was, of course, not uncommon to the Victorians, as I made clear in my discussion of Mrs Humphry Ward's physical sufferings in the previous chapter. It is, then, no surprise that such pain was reflected in a multitude of ways in the stories that they wrote and read, and that Victorian fiction was awash with physical suffering. In the first section of this chapter I outlined the theoretical antagonism towards the idea of physical suffering shared through language; here I shall be suggesting not only that such sharing could be effected, but that it was effected as a matter of course, for a variety of literary ends, in the works of Victorian novelists. In ways that Virginia Woolf failed to see, 'lyrics to toothache', or at least expressions of such pain, filled the pages of the nineteenth-century novel.

In the most blatant sense, it was widely understood that pain was the subject of a common assumption, and that physical suffering lay at the root of human existence. The readership of a novel was clearly expected to share such assumptions, not least because that very readership was expected to share, to some extent at least, the experience of pain itself, as well as the conventional ways of responding to it. A great many novels voiced just this belief: ' "To live is to suffer" ',[17] 'Poor human nature, so richly endowed with nerves of anguish, so splendidly organised for pain and sorrow, is but slenderly equipped for joy';[18] 'Evelyn . . . watched beside her till the poor buffetted soul had escaped from its earthly tenement in the house of pain'.[19] All of these, typical of the approach of Victorian novelists, suggest not just that pain is the lot of the individual sufferer, but also that its endurance is required of all humans. Pain in these examples avoids the difficulties of representation, for the authors simply assume that their readership understands and shares such suffering.

The understanding that physical suffering was shared is reflected, too, in the ways in which authors used the widespread nature of pain as the ground of metaphors. Dickens, particularly, used physical pain not so much as an instrument of plot—though Oliver Twist's pain and debility after being shot means that he is taken into the Maylie household—but as a marker of shared cultural understanding. In *A Tale of Two Cities*, Jarvis Lorry finds that 'the coach (in a confused way, like the presence of pain under an opiate) was always with him',[20] whilst a wherry in *The Old Curiosity Shop* 'looked like some lumbering fish in pain',[21] and Quilp's smile is what 'in any other man would have been a ghastly grin of pain'.[22] All of these similes depend on the reader's understanding of both the visual appearance of physical suffering and its bodily sensations, and mark the author's belief that such understandings are shared and may be used as a cultural given.

---

[17] Ella Hepworth Dixon, *The Story of a Modern Woman* (William Heinemann, 1894), 264.

[18] George du Maurier, *Peter Ibbetson, with an Introduction by His Cousin Lady ***** ('Madge Plunket'). Edited and Illustrated by George du Maurier*, 2 vols. (James R. Osgood, McIlvaine, 1892), i. 84.

[19] Frederic Vynon, *In a House of Pain* (London and Sydney: Remington, 1894), 191.

[20] *A Tale of Two Cities* (1859), ed. John Shuckburgh (London, New York, Toronto: Oxford University Press, 1949), 12.

[21] *The Old Curiosity Shop* (1841), ed. Earl of Wicklow (London, New York, Toronto: Oxford University Press, 1951), 41.   [22] Ibid. 45.

Miriam Bailin's *The Sickroom in Victorian Fiction* (1994), endorses the idea of physical pain as the ground of a metaphor. Her claim is that the suffering so prevalent in novels of the early and mid-Victorian period is the sign of psychological trauma transposed into bodily breakdown. 'Emotional crises articulate themselves with great lucidity and promptitude on the bodies of those who experience them',[23] and the sickroom acts as a 'kind of forcing ground of the self—a conventional rite of passage issuing in personal, moral, or social recuperation'.[24] The sickroom provides a kind of pastoral space, the safe, consolatory atmosphere of which allows for the re-establishment of the sufferer in social terms, and in ways that novelistic convention would not allow outside the physically narrow, but psychologically broad atmosphere of the sickroom. Bailin goes on to cite numerous actual individuals, from George Eliot to Florence Nightingale, who read their sickroom experiences and those of their friends and relations as positive experiences which allowed for their own mental growth and happiness. Bailin carefully refutes the claim that her own reading denies the validity of physical suffering, suggesting that 'the representation of the sickroom as haven provided remedial therapy for pain itself—a strategy for presenting and containing the awful and ever-present fear of physical vulnerability'.[25] Whether this is accurate or not, it is certainly the case, as I shall argue, that much of the pain in Victorian fiction became so much an indicator of other qualities—class, moral rectitude, or whatever—that its physical reality was often lost. It is important, in understanding Victorian representations of pain, to take seriously the claim that metaphors of pain as lover, as music, as doting pet, are attempts both to express the reality of painful bodily experience and to provide means of understanding and enduring such physical suffering. Bailin's book is interesting in its treatment of illness in the early and mid-Victorian period, but I shall be reversing her insights and looking not at pain as a sign of the 'troubled self, ... [with] desires which are not legitimated in the society at large',[26] that is, pain as a metaphor, but rather at the metaphors of pain.

---

[23] *The Sickroom in Victorian Fiction: The Art of Being Ill* (Cambridge: Cambridge University Press, 1994), 10.
[24] Ibid. 5.   [25] Ibid. 13.   [26] Ibid. 21.

Throughout the novel form, and across the Victorian period, a widely accepted set of literary conventions that relied, in a multitude of ways, on physical pain existed. Much as Lawrence Rothfield argues that Mme de Merteuil's smallpox scars disclose her true nature,[27] or the possession of a piano called on a set of conventions and assumptions that suggested the wealth and social status of the owner,[28] so too did the presence of pain in a novel reflect on those who suffered and those who inflicted suffering. Ways of inflicting and of enduring pain provided an immediately understandable index to character. Lady Audley, belying her seeming sensitivity, did 'cruel things with [her] slender white fingers, and laugh[ed] at the pain she inflicted'[29]— a laugh that betrays her inner life—whilst Mrs Humphry Ward's Marcella, nursing the painful foot of a patient, shows her true sensitivity in her gentleness.[30] Physical suffering, rather than a response to the physical suffering of another, too, had its novelistic point. Frederick Fairlie's claim that 'movement of any kind is exquisitely painful'[31] points directly to his cultivated valetudinarianism, and precedes, though in a diametrically opposed fashion, Rhoda Broughton's *fin de siècle* aesthete who can see 'nothing so beautiful as the passionate pulsations of pain!'[32] This process of reading physical pain is epitomized by Lucy Snowe's exegesis of Miss Marchmont's physical suffering: 'I . . . had learned from the manner in which she bore this attack, [a paroxysm of pain] that she was a firm, patient woman'.[33] Pain in this way was easy to read and denoted very specific attributes, both for characters within a novel and for readers of the novel.

Not only could the endurance of pain be read directly against individual character, but its presence could also be directly connected to class. A whole series of books of the 1880s and

---

[27] *Vital Signs: Medical Realism in Nineteenth-Century Fiction* (Princeton: Princeton University Press, 1992), 3.

[28] See Mary Burgan, 'Heroines at the Piano: Women and Music in Nineteenth-Century Fiction', *Victorian Studies*, 30 (1986), 51–76.

[29] Mary Elizabeth Braddon, *Lady Audley's Secret*, 3 vols. (Tinsley, 1862), i. 209.

[30] *Marcella*, 3 vols. (Smith, Elder, 1894), iii. 45–6.

[31] Wilkie Collins, *The Woman in White*, 3 vols. (new edn., Sampson Low, 1860), i. 61.

[32] *Second Thoughts* (1880; new edn., Richard Bentley, 1893), 5.

[33] Charlotte Brontë, *Villette* (1853), ed. Herbert Rosengarten and Margaret Smith (Oxford: Clarendon Press, 1984), 49.

1890s—Gissing's early novels, *The Unclassed* (1884) and *The Nether World* (1889), for example, Arthur Morrison's *Child of the Jago* (1896), Somerset Maugham's *Liza of Lambeth* (1897), and William Pett Ridge's *Mord Em'ly* (1898)—used the recurrent pains of hangovers and of wife-beating to delineate the brutality of working-class life. The aristocratic counterpart to such class-revealing pain was gout: Sir Leicester Dedlock's had 'come down, through the illustrious line, like the plate, or the pictures, or the place in Lincolnshire'.[34] Not only, then, is the way in which characters suffer indicative of their personality, but the type of pain that falls to their lot is also revealing. Mord Em'ly, the product of a fictional imagination and conventional restrictions, could never be a victim to gout which required not only a hereditary disposition to it, but also the intake of rich food and plentiful alcohol. George Eliot makes this point sharply in *Romola* with Bartolommo Scala's gout: 'Meantime he had got richer and richer, and more and more gouty, after the manner of successful mortality; and the Knight of the Golden Spur had often to sit with helpless cushioned heel.'[35]

The conventions that accrued to pain existed not just in terms of the delineation of character, but had ramifications in the process of plotting and of legitimizing the telling of the story. Rider Haggard rationalized the time Allan Quatermain takes off from big-game hunting and adventuring to write the story of *King Solomon's Mines* by making him suffer physically. 'Not a literary man, though very devoted to the Old Testament',[36] he is given time to write by 'the pain and trouble in [his] left leg'[37] which prevented any other activity, and in this way the presence of pain provides a fairly convincing excuse for the telling of the story. Not only, however, did pain provide the impetus to write, but it also provided a way of turning the plot. John Loveday's burns, in Hardy's *The Trumpet-Major*, received in protecting Anne from a stream of boiling water, win—temporarily at least—her affections and, in so doing, twist the plot,[38] whilst

---

[34] Dickens, *Bleak House*, 218. See Jan B. Gordon, ' "The Key to Dedlock's Gait:" Gout as Resistance', in David Bevan (ed.), *Literature and Sickness* (Amsterdam and Atlanta, Ga.: Rodopi, 1993), 25–52. For a somewhat uninspiring discussion of gout as a rich man's disease see also Rey, *History of Pain*, 233–5.

[35] *Romola* (1863), ed. Andrew Brown (Oxford: Clarendon Press, 1993), 75.

[36] *King Solomon's Mines*, 7.

[37] Ibid. 8.   [38] *Trumpet-Major*, iii. 171–2.

Collins's Herr Grosse, in a way typical of many of his novels, is unable to prevent disaster in *Poor Miss Finch* (1872) because 'he had been attacked by "a visitation of gouts"'.[39] Pain, too, provided an excuse, as well as a means, of deceit. Rudolf Rassendyll, in Anthony Hope's *Prisoner of Zenda*, recognizing the potential of pain as a means of disappearance, swathes his face in clothing as a form of disguise—'feigning a toothache, [he] muffled [his] face closely'[40]—and in this way escapes discovery without arousing distrust. Headaches, too, formed an excuse of this kind, and entered the conventions of the Victorian novel, both as shorthand for acute sensibility and as an acceptable excuse for non-appearance at crucial moments of the plot. The headache, too, could be used as shorthand for other, perhaps unacceptable, forms of distress. Lucy Snowe's 'headache', caused by Paul Emanuel's departure, is 'read' and understood by Madame Beck, as it is by the reader, though designated a physical rather than emotional disturbance.[41] Victor Radnor, in Meredith's *One of Our Conquerors*, uses just this ploy when his supposed wife is found, in reality, to be his mistress: 'He told Nesta not to disturb her mother, and murmured of a headache.'[42] She is, in fact, upstairs bewailing the fact that her secret has finally been uncovered. Not only did headaches provide a suitable cover for emotional disturbance, but they also provided the polite face of less publicly acceptable distress.

Thus pain largely lost its physical reality when it appeared in novels and became purely a literary device in ways that Valerie Ann Bystrom acknowledges and delineates in her article 'The Abyss of Sympathy: The Conventions of Pathos in Eighteenth and Nineteenth Century British Novels'. In looking at the conventions of pathetic scenes—of deathbeds, of underfed children, of 'gentility in temporary straits'[43]—Bystrom finds that 'suffering in pathetic scenes tends to prettiness and not much pain',[44]

---

[39] *Poor Miss Finch: A Novel*, 3 vols. (Richard Bentley, 1872), iii. 255.
[40] *The Prisoner of Zenda: Being the History of Three Months in the Life of an English Gentleman* (Bristol: J. W. Arrowsmith; London: Simpkin, Marshall, Hamilton, Kent, [1894]), 96.
[41] Charlotte Brontë, *Villette*, 649.
[42] *One of Our Conquerors*, 3 vols. (Chapman and Hall, 1891), iii. 188.
[43] 'The Abyss of Sympathy: The Conventions of Pathos in Eighteenth and Nineteenth Century British Novels', *Criticism: A Quarterly for Literature and the Arts*, 23 (1981), 213.   [44] Ibid.

a claim surely born out by Dickens's depiction of the death of Little Nell: 'She was dead. No sleep so beautiful and calm, so free from trace of pain, so fair to look upon.'[45] Such painless death clearly reflected the theological and medical attitudes of those such as Gillies who, as I suggested in the previous chapter, believed in a God-given anaesthetic for the good at the moment of death. Pain at death, in novels, became an index to moral character as much as pain in life. Nell slips away without suffering, whereas Jocelyn Quilp in his bizarre novel *Baron Verdegris* (1894) recognized in his readership the desire for fair play: 'In view of the evils attendant upon the scheme for which Nalyticus was responsible, it may be some satisfaction to my contemporaries to know that this Philosopher died a lingering and extremely painful death.'[46] This point is made forcibly in *Mord Em'ly*, in which the eponymous heroine, making up stories to amuse her friends, draws heavily on the techniques and conventions of sensation fiction:

'Who married the countess,' asked Mrs. Wingham confidentially, 'in that tale you were telling the girls last night, Mord Em'ly?'

'The countess? Oh, she married the painter chap.'

'Thought so,' said Mrs Wingham. 'Her 'usband died, then?'

'Drowned,' said Mord Em'ly. 'Drowned by a collision with an iceberg in the Mediterranean Sea.'

'Phew!' Mrs. Wingham gave a whistle of surprise. 'That was rough on him. He was a good bit older, though, than her, wasn't he?'

'Twice her age.'

'And the will that that old beggar of an uncle perduced? How did they get over that? She wouldn't 'ave a penny to call her own, poor soul!'

'Turned out he'd forged it,' explained the young *raconteuse*. 'There was a water-mark on the paper, with a date *after* the date of the will.'

'Well, I never did!' declared Mrs. Wingham amazedly. 'Did they lock him up for it?'

'How could they when he went and swallowered a mugful of poison d'rectly minute he was found out? He died,' added Mord Em'ly, with a relish, 'enduring 'orrible agonies.'

'Serve him jolly well right, too,' declared Mrs. Wingham. 'He deserved all he got. Now, you girls, off you go to school . . .'[47]

[45] *Curiosity Shop*, 538–9.
[46] *Baron Verdegris. A Romance of the Reversed Direction* (Henry, 1894), 18.
[47] W. Pett Ridge, *Mord Em'ly* (C. Arthur Pearson, 1898), 89–90.

Mord Em'ly, conversant in the conventions of sensation fiction—the older husband, the forged will, the suicide *in extremis*—exploits painful death in the story that she tells, and in the wicked uncle's ''orrible agonies' gives her listeners exactly what they want to hear. Mrs Wingham's responses—'Thought so', 'Serve him jolly well right, too'—suggest the complicity between storyteller and listener, and the ways in which particular literary conventions were expected, and to a large extent required, by a novel's readership.

The 'relish' that Mord Em'ly displayed in the painful denouement of her story is reflected widely in Victorian fiction as pain became not a grossly unpleasant physical sensation too painful to write about, but rather a way of manipulating reactions to character or a source of enjoyment to the reader. Mord Em'ly delights in the come-uppance of the villain, whilst Trollope goes one step further in his story 'A Ride Across Palestine', using the presence of pain as a source of titillation for the reader. A married man, calling himself Jones, meets a woman disguised as a man, calling herself John Smith, and both travel together on horseback across Palestine. The story flirts with gender confusion as Jones advises Smith to arm himself with a ridiculously phallic pistol to '[hang] over [his] loins',[48] and then in a scene of protracted sexual tension recognizes that ' "that confounded Turkish saddle has already galled your skin" ', and the only relief for such saddle sores, Jones claims, is brandy ' "externally applied" '.[49] Pain and sex are inextricably mingled as Jones complains: ' "You should have let me rub in that brandy . . . You can't conceive how efficaciously I would have done it." '[50]

While one set of conventions depended on understanding pain as a shared experience, diverse contrary conventions of silence also accrued to the description of physical pain. The difficulties of writing specifically about physical suffering come into focus when drawn alongside the difficulties in describing any other emotional experience. Queen Victoria, for example, suggests just such a difficulty when Albert accepts her proposal of marriage in 1839: 'Oh! to *feel* I was, and am, loved by *such* an Angel as Albert was *too great delight to describe!* he is *perfection*; per-

---

[48] 'A Ride Across Palestine', in *Tales of All Countries*, 2nd ser. (Chapman and Hall, 1863), 243.
[49] Ibid. 246.   [50] Ibid. 248.

fection in every way—in beauty—in everything!'[51] This is the language of convention: the breathiness of the queen leads her to choose *not* to look for a mode of expression, but rather to suggest that a lack of language is more expressive than words. The root of the inability to find language lies here in convention rather than in any incapacity of language or physical incapacity. Victoria clearly could have spelt out the admirable qualities she saw in Albert; indeed, she goes some way towards this before expressively drawing back.

Rider Haggard, writing in *She* and drawing on a Burkean model of inexpressibility,[52] employs a similar tactic as he plays with the conventional impossibility of describing pain in order to draw on a Gothic blankness more horrible than any direct description. Holly, the narrator, describes the 'cave of torture' in a footnote:

The only objects in the cave itself were slabs of rock arranged to facilitate the operations of the torturers. Many of these slabs, which were of a porous stone, were stained quite dark with the blood of ancient victims that had soaked into them . . . But the most dreadful thing about the cave was that over each slab was a sculptured illustration of the appropriate torture being applied. These sculptures were so awful that I will not harrow the reader by attempting a description of them.[53]

The apologetic form of the last sentence will become familiar in the next chapter in the context of the antivivisection movement of the 1880s, where the details of what protesters saw as the systematic torture of animals were synchronously evoked and turned away from. Haggard is here exploiting the convention of assumed readerly sensibility to provide a blank screen onto which such readers can project their own hideous imaginings and fears, possibly worse than those he could evoke through

[51] Journal entry for 14–15 Oct. 1839. Cited in Cecil Woodham-Smith, *Queen Victoria: Her Life and Times, 1819–1861* (Hamish Hamilton, 1972), 184.

[52] See Edmund Burke, *Philosophical Enquiry into Our Ideas of the Sublime and the Beautiful* (1757), ed. Adam Phillips (Oxford: Oxford University Press, 1992), 54: 'To make any thing very terrible, obscurity seems in general to be necessary. When we know the full extent of any danger, when we can accustom our eyes to it, a great deal of the apprehension vanishes. Every one will be sensible of this, who considers how greatly night adds to our dread, in all cases of danger, and how much the notions of ghosts and goblins, of which none can form clear ideas, affect minds, which give credit to the popular tales concerning such sorts of beings.'

[53] *She: A History of Adventure* (Longmans, Green, 1887), 175.

direct description. Andrew Lang, explicitly recognizing such conventions of Gothic silence, brings irony to his depiction of the techniques of the supernatural novel:

> You may describe a ghost with all the most hideous features that fancy can suggest—saucer eyes, red staring hair, a forked tail, and what you please—but the reader only laughs. It is wiser to make as if you were going to describe the spectre, and then break off, exclaiming, 'But no! No pen can describe, no memory, thank Heaven, can recall, the horror of that hour!' So writers, as a rule, prefer to leave their terror (usually styled 'The Thing') entirely in the dark, and to the frightened fancy of the student.[54]

The question I ask in this chapter is whether the description of pain and the silence that surrounds it is of a different order from that of the description of the horrors of 'ghosts and goblins'— things that don't exist—that Burke evokes, and that Lang here draws on. Lang's words, 'No pen can describe, no memory . . . can recall', take on a peculiar reality rather than a purely conventional status as they pertain to the description of pain by one who actually suffers physically. The description of pain must necessarily be different from the description of 'ghosts and goblins' as its physical reality was impressed hour by hour on the bodies of sufferers, rendering its description not just a game, a stimulating frisson of horror, but an important means of conveying the painful reality of adverse physical sensation.

Just as describing Albert's virtues would have been possible for Queen Victoria, so, too, *could* Holly have described the horrors of the torture cave: both invoke silence and impossibility for their own particular descriptive ends. The example from *She*, however, also calls on the sympathetic responses of its readership, who would supposedly find the description of the infliction of pain too harrowing to read. It is clear from this that the possibility of writing about pain is more complicated than it at first appears. It is not simply a question of the incapacity of language—that 'language at once runs dry'[55] in the face of physical suffering—but is also caught up in the sensibilities of those who read. As Virginia Woolf recognized: 'to look these things

---

[54] 'The Supernatural in Fiction', in *Adventures among Books* (Longmans, Green, 1905), 273.
[55] Woolf, 'On Being Ill', 318.

squarely in the face we need the courage of a lion tamer.' Holly
is not describing pain itself and facing the inadequacies of language directly, but is fighting shy of describing the act of torture
which would evoke a pained response in the reader. As Alexander Bain wrote in *The Senses and the Intellect*: 'The place of
attachment of the nails is the seat of a violent form of acute
pain, which has a fatal facility of seizing on the imagination,
and exciting revulsion even in idea.'[56] Such 'revulsion even in
idea' is a potent force in preventing the direct expression of
painful experience, completely different from the inadequacies
of language, and it relies on the sympathetic response of the
readership who cannot bear to face such suffering. It is,
however, also a sign that pain is not suffered alone, that it can
be shared and is a sensation to which people at large respond
sympathetically.

Alongside the Burkean convention of Gothic silence lay
another culturally constructed barrier to writing about pain that
faced the Victorian sufferer, for it was also broadly considered
to be far more Christian and brave to resist the urge to complain about physical suffering than it was to voice it. In an
alarmingly anodyne poem by B. F., 'A Tale of a Hospital Ward.
A True Story', published in 1898, the narrator tells the story of
a boy, Jim, 'So badly burnt he suffered agony'.[57] Jim, 'incapable
of self-control . . . cried out like a little child'[58] every time his
dressings were changed, and despite his youth is presented as
pitifully weak in his inability to withhold his screams. Matters
change when another patient teaches him the words ' "I can do
all things thro' the strength | of Christ Who strengthens me" '[59]
and Jim subsequently finds the inner strength to suffer in silence:
'So morning after morning lay the boy | Silently strong to bear
the bitter pain,'[60] whilst his 'lips were moving as in silent
prayer'.[61] To shout at pain is to question the providence and
beneficence of God, whereas to be silent under its infliction is
to accept the rightness of the pattern of creation.

This insistence on suffering in silence is by no means a unique,

---

[56] *Senses*, 181.
[57] 'A Tale of a Hospital Ward. A True Story' (no publication details, [1898]), l.
14.
[58] Ibid., ll. 18–19.   [59] Ibid., ll. 40–1.   [60] Ibid., ll. 77–8.
[61] Ibid., l. 65.

or even a rare, position and reverberates as a trope denoting just such Christian fortitude throughout Victorian fiction. Mrs Henry Wood's Rupert Trevlyn experiences a horrible moment of pain shortly before his premature death when his Aunt Edith, intending to soothe his fevered brow, lets a drop of eau de Cologne fall into his eye: 'It smarted very much, but Rupert smiled bravely. "Just a few minutes' pain, Aunt Edith, and it will all be gone." '[62] Rupert, dying, has recognized that all things 'pass away' and so too will his pain: his ability to suffer, without complaining, is a mark of his willingness to trust in God.

Elizabeth Gaskell, describing Mrs Hale's imminent death in *North and South*, sets such stoicism in the face of suffering not in the context of an unwitting infliction of pain, as is the case with Rupert Trevlyn, but in terms of her own organically generated pain:

But with the increase of serious and just ground of complaint, a new kind of patience had sprung up in her mother's mind. She was gentle and quiet in intense bodily suffering, almost in proportion as she had been restless and depressed when there had been no real cause for grief.[63]

In the deep-seated illness which does indeed kill her, the formerly self-indulgent Mrs Hale finds the strength to stay silent.

Victorian sufferers who valued the tenets of orthodox Christianity were caught in a double bind. If they were truly dying their pain would be taken away by godly anaesthetic—as Gillies argued, 'pain never comes where it can serve no good purpose'—whereas if they felt pain then they were not dying and it was their duty to suffer in silence, showing their allegiance in this way to the suffering Christ. As Gissing's Miss Bystrom puts it, 'The more the body suffers, the greater should be the delight of the soul.'[64] William Hale White, in *The Autobiography of Mark Rutherford* (1881), picks up on the ambivalence of not speaking about pain when suffering and the misleading consequences this may have. He then reverts, however, to the belief that silent suffering is better and more noble. Rutherford,

---

[62] *Trevlyn Hold; Or, Squire Trevlyn's Heir*, 3 vols. (Tinsley, 1864), iii. 296.
[63] *North and South*, 104.
[64] *The Unclassed* (1884; new edn., Lawrence and Bullen, 1895), 35.

having spent the evening with his friend Mardon and Mary, Mardon's daughter, 'Mentally . . . accused her of slightness, and inability to talk upon the subjects which interested Mardon and [himself]',[65] until he realized that she had been suffering from severe neuralgia all evening and 'had said nothing about it . . . [but] had behaved with cheerfulness and freedom'.[66] Rutherford's response to his discovery encapsulates many of the attitudes towards the vocal expression of pain:

and I thought, too, that if I had a fit of neuralgia, everybody near me would know it, and be almost as much annoyed by me as I myself should be by the pain. It is curious, also, that when thus proclaiming my troubles I often considered my eloquence meritorious, or, at least, a kind of talent for which I ought to praise God, contemning rather my silent friends as something nearer than myself to the expressionless animals. To parade my toothache, describing it with unusual adjectives, making it felt by all the company in which I might happen to be, was to me an assertion of my superior nature. But, looking at Mary, and thinking about her as I walked home, I perceived that her ability to be quiet, to subdue herself, to resist the temptation for a whole evening of drawing attention to herself by telling us what she was enduring, was heroism, and that my contrary tendency was pitiful vanity.[67]

Silence is heroic; complaints irreligious, arrogant, and self-aggrandizing. But whilst the expectation of heroic silence held for both men and women, there was a gender divide in the shapes such heroism took. Mary Mardon and Mrs Hale are heroic in their gentle, cheerful, and subdued passivity, whilst Rupert Trevlyn explicitly behaves 'bravely' in facing up to his physical suffering. The prime example of such male heroism in the face of pain comes from the '*ne plus ultra* of the muscular School of fiction',[68] G. A. Lawrence's *Guy Livingstone* (1857). In a book that seems determined to emphasize the seemingly indestructible nature of its hero, the acknowledgement of Livingstone's horrendously painful death stands out. In the closing chapters of the book, as Livingstone lies slowly dying after a

---

[65] *The Autobiography of Mark Rutherford, Dissenting Minister. Edited by his Friend, Reuben Shapcott* (Trübner, 1881), 67.
[66] Ibid.   [67] Ibid. 67–8.
[68] John Sutherland, *The Longman Companion to Victorian Fiction* (Harlow: Longman, 1988), 268.

hunting accident, Lawrence suggests the hero's undiminished courage, and the onlookers' horror at such suffering:

When Powell's [the doctor's] self-command gave way so completely, after he saw the nature of Guy's case, it was not because he knew it must end fatally, but because his skill told him what fearful agonies must precede the release . . . The colossal strength and vital energy of Livingstone's frame and constitution yielded but slowly to a blow which would have crushed a weaker man instantly . . . I cannot go through the details; I will only say that, sometimes, none of us could endure to look upon sufferings which never drew a complaint or a moan from him.[69]

Hammond, the narrator, 'could [not] endure to look upon [Guy's] sufferings', whilst Guy himself is so heroic in adversity that no verbal complaint escapes him. Both the onlooker and the sufferer collude in repressing the verbalization of suffering—whilst in so doing, of course, also flagging its presence—much as in a parallel way Christianity and an ideal of manliness, although for different reasons, worked together to the same end. This coming together of separate—though, no doubt, related—forces is common in assumptions made about pain. Christian desire not to question the ordinances of God and a manly fortitude coincide with each other, demanding the same silent response from sufferers. Women suffered with quiet gentleness as men bit the bullet and suffered with silent bravery, but the end result is the same, and an ideal of non-verbalized suffering was held up to those who suffered physically.

   That social conventions acted to repress the direct expression of physical suffering was not the only problem in writing about pain. The words of the novelist and essayist Richard Jefferies, who suffered terrible pain from a combination of intestinal ulcers, fistula, and starvation—'I can hardly write of it'—undergo a gruesome twist as his physical suffering becomes such that he physically cannot write. Queen Victoria's coy incapacity at 'too great a delight to describe' becomes a physical incapacity as the writer literally cannot hold the pen: '"My great difficulty is the physical difficulty of writing. Since the spine gave way, there is no position in which I can lie or sit so as to use a pen without distress. Even a short letter like this is

---

[69] *Guy Livingstone; or, 'Thorough'* (1857; Leipzig: Bernhard Tauchnitz, 1860), 299.

painful." '[70] It is for this reason, that the process of writing is directly interfered with, amongst others, that there are few first-hand accounts of physical pain: Fanny Burney's 1810 sickening account of her mastectomy;[71] W. E. Henley's series of poems concerning his experience of amputation in Edinburgh in the 1870s, *In Hospital*[72]—both composed looking back at painful experience after some years had elapsed—and the diaries of Alice James, Gideon Mantell,[73] and Emily Shore,[74] all of whom recounted their painful illnesses in some detail in their journals. Such accounts are not just striking in themselves, but because they are by their very existence unusual.

There is, too, another problem in the direct depiction of pain, and it is one that Harriet Martineau picks up in the introduction to her book *Life in the Sick-Room*. As Martineau claims of her own physical suffering:

Where are these pains now?—Not only gone, but annihilated. They are destroyed so utterly, that even memory can lay no hold upon them. The fact of their occurrence is all that even memory can preserve. The sensations themselves cannot be retained, nor recalled, nor revived; they are absolutely evanescent, the most essentially and completely destructible of all things. Sensations are unimaginable to those who are most familiar with them. Their concomitants may be remembered, and so vividly conceived of, as to excite emotions at a future time: but the sensations themselves cannot be conceived of when absent. This pain, which I feel now as I write, I have felt innumerable times before; yet, accustomed as I am to entertain and manage it, the sensation itself is new every time; and a few hours hence I shall be as unable to represent it to myself as to the healthiest person in the house. Thus are the pains of the year annihilated. What remains?

All the good remains.[75]

---

[70] Letter to Charles Longman, May 1885. Cited in Walter Besant, *Eulogy*, 331.

[71] *Journals and Letters of Fanny Burney (Madame D'Arblay)*, ed. Joyce Hemlow with George G. Falle, Althea Douglas, and Jill A. Bourdais de Charbonnière, 12 vols. (Oxford: Clarendon Press, 1975) vi. 596–615: 30 Sept. 1811, 'To Esther (Burney) Burney'. See also Julia L. Epstein, 'Writing the Unspeakable: Fanny Burney's Mastectomy and the Fictive Body', *Representations*, 16 (1986), 131–66.

[72] *In Hospital*, in *Poems, 1898* (Oxford and New York: Woodstock, 1993). For details see John Connell, *W. E. Henley* (Constable, 1949) and Mary MacCarthy, *Handicaps: Six Studies* (Longmans, Green, 1936).

[73] *The Journal of Gideon Mantell, Surgeon and Geologist. Covering the Years 1818–1852*, ed. E. Cecil Curwen (London, New York, Toronto: Oxford University Press, 1940).

[74] *Journal of Emily Shore* (new edn., Kegan Paul, Trench, Trübner, 1898).

Martineau places the inability to recall the sensation of pain amongst the providences of God, but such claims leave those who would write about pain once again in a double bind. Either they are in suffering so intense, as with Jefferies, that the holding of the pen is an impossibility, or pain is an alien experience even to sufferers themselves, becoming 'unimaginable to those who are most familiar with them'.

III. ARTICULATING PAIN

Scientific work done on the expressibility of pain by Ronald Melzack and W. S. Torgerson,[76] pioneers in the verbal description of pain, serves as a way of approaching the various ways in which pain may be shared through language, rather than just through an amorphous idea of shared cultural understanding or acknowledged novelistic or Gothic conventions. These two doctors compiled the McGill pain questionnaire as a way of overcoming the difficulty of finding words to express painful experience. Whilst they conclude that much pain expression falls into the 'as if . . .' structure we will see Elaine Scarry discuss, they also suggest that there are words which directly correlate with particular pain sensations. To create a diagnostic tool, they took words from patients' descriptions of the pain they felt, and words used in scientific literature, and, asking people to evaluate the relative intensities of these words, evolved chains of descriptors qualitatively similar but varying in intensity, such as hot, burning, scalding, searing. This provided a means of measurement and assessment essential to scientific enterprise. More important for this study were the implications of their other conclusion, that particular causes of pain correlate with a particular constellation of descriptive words. That is, for example, in a high proportion of cases toothache is described as being throbbing, boring, sharp, sickening, annoying, constant, and rhythmic; whilst the pain of cancer is shoot-

---

[75] *Life in the Sick-Room*, 4.
[76] I am predominantly using the overview of their 1971 work as a source, as it appears in Ronald Melzack and Patrick Wall, *The Challenge of Pain* (1982; rev. edn., Penguin, 1988). See ch. 3, 'The Varieties of Pain'.

ing, sharp, gnawing, burning, heavy, exhausting, unbearable, and constant.

This conception of pain as a communicable experience—something that may be shared—is of vital importance in undercutting Scarry's theoretical mystifications about the essential insularity of the experience of pain. As the McGill pain questionnaire suggests, there *are* ways to encode pain directly in language, or at least to register different degrees of painful experience, and to mark these differences linguistically. Language presents other possibilities than those of direct expression. These rely to a large extent on the cultural understanding that the pain of another may be understood through one's own pain, and that the visual and oral signs of pain may be read and understood.

Bain's comment—'The place of attachment of the nails is the seat of a violent form of acute pain, which has a fatal facility of seizing on the imagination, and exciting revulsion even in idea'—is vital in understanding the nature of the sympathetic transference between sufferer and non-sufferer. Such transference relies on the fact that non-sufferers have at some time or other suffered themselves, and can, if not explicitly, recall the experience of hurt in such a way that it calls up a visceral response. Walter Besant in his biography of Richard Jefferies calls on exactly this technique to convey the reality of Jefferies's sufferings to his readership, demanding that they refer his pain to their own suffering: 'You know how painful an ulcer is anywhere—say on your lip—now for over two years this ulceration had been burning its way in the intestines.'[77]

Such an understanding of the shared nature of pain also allowed writers to convey physical suffering in a multitude of ways. Bernard Shaw, with considerable brevity, simply states the fact of pain over the dead body of Henrietta Trefusis in his novel *An Unsocial Socialist* (1884). In answer to the question, ' "Did she suffer?" ' comes the answer, ' "For some hours, yes" '.[78] Nothing more needs to be said.

But more can be said. Writers depended not just on the naming of acknowledgedly painful diseases—Mr Shelton in Mrs

---

[77] Besant, *Eulogy*, 346.
[78] *An Unsocial Socialist* (Swan Sonnenschein, Lowrey, 1887), 123.

Humphry Ward's *Marcella* suffered 'a peculiar and agonising form of neuralgia'[79]—but drew on the external appearance of pain and the description of the cries caused by physical suffering. Laura Fountain, in Ward's *Helbeck of Bannisdale* (1898), betrays the intensity of her suffering in the cry she cannot suppress. 'Pitched against the railing of the dogcart... her wrist was painfully twisted' and she finds that the 'first cry of pain' she uttered was 'beyond her control'.[80] In acknowledging the cry, and evoking the convention of silence in the face of physical suffering that it breaks, Ward suggests very quickly the intensity of the pain felt by Laura. Ward's other tactic in this scene is to suggest the cause of her pain—being pitched against the railing of the dogcart—to evoke the pain suffered, and again in so doing she suggests the suffering it induces. Father Furniss, described in Chapter 1, evoked the pains of hell by claiming that ' "It is easy to understand the . . . pains of hell, because there are pains like them on earth" '.[81] The fate of an 18-year-old girl condemned to eternal damnation is gruesomely detailed in ways that suggest the ability of the reader to understand a pain that is written about rather than personally experienced:

'On her head she wears a bonnet of fire; it is pressed down close all over her head; it burns her head; it burns into the skin; it scorches the bone of the skull, and makes it smoke. The red-hot fiery heat goes into the brain, and melts it. . . . You do not, perhaps, like a headache. Think what a headache that girl must have.'[82]

The description of an eternal pain is, perhaps, futile because it is entirely unverifiable, but other kinds of inflictions clearly have the same effect, as the beatings in *Tom Brown's School Days* or *Lady Gay Spanker's Tales of Fun and Flagellation* suggest. The consequences, too, of physical suffering also attest to its painfulness, whether this be the inability to sit down after a beating, Martia Josselin's insomnia—'she could not always sleep for her pain',[83]—or John Hewett's 'bad attack of rheumatism . . . [which] made [him] incapable of earning anything at all'.[84] The

---

[79] *Marcella*, iii. 348.
[80] *Helbeck of Bannisdale* (Smith, Elder, 1898), 419.
[81] T. R., *Hell and its Torments*, 21.   [82] Ibid. 22.
[83] George du Maurier, *The Martian: A Novel* (1897; Harper, 1898), 466.
[84] George Gissing, *The Nether World: A Novel*, 3 vols. (Smith, Elder, 1889), iii. 258.

consequences of pain validate the reality of the suffering and suggest it to those who read. Gissing's description of the vitriol attack on Clara Hewett brings together many of these ways of conveying the physical sense of pain: 'something [was] dashed violently in her face,—something fluid and fiery,—something that ate into her flesh, that frenzied her with pain, that drove her shrieking she knew not whither.'[85] The aggression of the action—the vitriol is 'dashed violently'—and its incomprehensibility—'something' is thrown, Clara does not know what—give edge to Clara's pain. The violence with which the vitriol is thrown clearly has little to do with the pain inflicted, but in describing the incident in these terms Gissing calls on the established associations of violence and pain, feeding these into the reader's understanding of Clara's suffering. Similarly, Gissing describes her actions and appearance: she is 'frenzied', she shrieks, and she runs aimlessly hither and thither. But Gissing takes his description of pain a step further as he gives it a metaphorical life—the vitriol 'ate into her flesh'—and sets it into a hierarchical structure—the pain became her master as it 'drove her . . . she knew not whither'.

Richard Jefferies, writing of his personal experience, admits both his own inadequacy and the inadequacy of language in describing pain in a letter to C. P. Scott, Jefferies's friend and the editor of the *Manchester Guardian*. In so doing, however, he effectively transmits an idea of his suffering in a number of ways:

If I wrote a volume I could not describe it to you, this terrible scorching pain, night and day. There is nothing in medical books like it, except the pain that follows corrosive sublimate which burns the tissues. It was at times so maddening that I dreaded to go a few miles alone by rail lest I should throw myself out of the window of the carriage.[86]

Words alone cannot come close to a literal description of such pain, and the only language available to the writer is that of analogy. The pain is like that of burning as it seems to scorch his tissues. Throughout Jefferies's descriptions of his pain, his comparisons are of this type: 'Sometimes it seemed like a rat always gnaw, gnaw, night and day';[87] 'I can compare it to

---

[85] Ibid. ii. 215. [86] Cited in Walter Besant, *Eulogy*, 345.
[87] Ibid. 344.

nothing but the flame of a small spirit lamp continually burning within me';[88] he spends 'cursed months ground by pain';[89] and then, somewhat differently, he writes: 'suddenly I went down as if I had been shot';[90] and the experience was 'awful, like lightning through the brain'.[91] Largely these are images of burning, but the overwhelming impression is of relentless pain, the constant gnawing of the rats, the months of grinding, but punctuated by sharp interjections of acute pain, the flash of lightning, or the crack of the gunshot.

It is valuable to return at this point to Melzack and Torgerson and their description of the pain of cancer as shooting, sharp, gnawing, burning, heavy, exhausting, unbearable, and constant. Such description, compared to Jefferies's own descriptions of his physical discomfort, leaves little doubt as to a possible mapping of physical sensation onto particular constellations of language: that despite an inability to find exact words for pain, there is a possibility of suggesting the nature of pain through a series of words.[92] Jefferies picks up on nearly all of these descriptors, though in largely metaphorical terms: the rat gnaws and the spirit lamp burns constantly, whilst the lightning and the gun shoot, and the whole is so unbearable that Jefferies is unable to trust himself with the open windows of a railway carriage. I have no intention of retrospective diagnosis, but I would suggest that Melzack and Torgerson's work recognizes a possible way of describing pain sensation and of cutting through the insularity of pain.

Jefferies suggests just this insularity in the dual sense of the words 'There is nothing in medical books like it.' Here he reveals not only his own inability to know if anyone else can suffer in the same way as him, but also a sense that pain is not the primary concern of the medical profession, particularly true in Jefferies's own case where he was consistently diagnosed as hysterical, and in consequence was told 'All you have to do is

---

[88] Walter Besant 344.

[89] Samuel J. Looker and Crichton Porteous, *Richard Jefferies: Man of the Fields. A Biography and Letters* (John Baker, 1964), 208.

[90] Walter Besant, *Eulogy*, 339.

[91] Looker and Porteous, *Richard Jefferies*, 193.

[92] See Jonathan Miller, *The Body in Question* (London and Basingstoke: Papermac, 1978), 38. Here Miller describes the difficulties of using metaphorical language to convey pain.

not to think of it'[93] and to drink a glass of water when in pain. In invoking his insularity, Jefferies calls up the spectre of Gothic blankness, and in this way—as well as in his metaphoric representations—calls up an idea of the intensity and physical reality of the pain he suffers.

Writing about pain does, and in many ways must, align itself to such metaphoric modes of expression or ways of referring pain's meaning to structures outside itself. I want here to return to Elaine Scarry and her arguments in the introduction to *The Body in Pain*, where she claims that 'the very temptation to invoke analogies to remote cosmologies (and there is a long tradition of such analogies) is itself a sign of pain's triumph'. This book, to a large extent, sites itself in Scarry's parenthesis—'(and there is a long tradition of such analogies)'—but refuses to accept the negative connotation of such attribution. The proliferation of metaphor is not a 'sign of pain's triumph' but instead is a mode of coming to terms with the nature of pain, a way of explaining and of understanding, both in personal terms, and for others. Whilst Scarry's is a profoundly interesting book, it is limited in its understanding of the ways in which the metaphors of pain can work and refuses to accept the shared basis of pain. Her tendency to argue from extremes pushes her towards gross simplification, the value of which is very dubious. She goes on to write:

Because the existing vocabulary for pain contains only a small handful of adjectives, one passes through direct descriptions very quickly and . . . almost immediately encounters an 'as if' structure: it feels as if . . . ; it is as though . . . On the other side of the ellipse there reappear again and again (regardless of whether the immediate context of the vocalisation is medical or literary or legal) two and only two metaphors, and they are metaphors whose inner workings are very problematic. The first specifies an external agent of the pain, a weapon that is pictured as producing the pain; and the second specifies bodily damage that is pictured as accompanying the pain. Thus a person may say, 'It feels as though a hammer is coming down on my spine' even where there is no hammer; or 'It feels as if my arm is broken at each joint and the jagged ends are sticking through the skin' even where the bones of the arms are intact and the surface of the skin is unbroken.[94]

---

[93] Looker and Porteous, *Richard Jefferies*, 196.
[94] *Body in Pain*, 15.

That this claim for two metaphors of pain has solid grounding in actual descriptive practice is born out by the descriptions of pain by chronic pain patients, gathered over the course of six months between June and December 1993 by J. C. Bending of the National Hospital for Nervous Diseases. The patient's pain is variously described in metaphorical terms. It feels as if the patient is being beaten up with a lot of sticks; like an internal injury, as though something is out of place; like a tight band of pressure; like violent toothache; like a knife stabbing the patient's back; like a blowtorch running up and down the patient's leg; like walking on a bucket of hot coals; as if in a vice; as though the bones have fallen apart and need to be gathered together; like a large football getting bigger; like being continuously buggered; like dull toothache and headache all in one; as though the patient's head has been cut in two and not put back together correctly; as though the patient's back is in a clamp with someone tightening it.[95] Scarry's metaphors are clearly at work here, as the external agent—the knife, the blowtorch, or the vice—acts on the sufferer's body, and this body itself feels as though it is falling apart.

Whilst Scarry's formulation of 'two and only two' metaphors of pain clearly covers some instances of pain, it is not, as I shall argue, all-inclusive as she so vehemently claims. My aim now is to show the ways in which writers opened up the metaphors of pain, and in so doing, found ways of rendering their suffering, and its meaning, in language.

Annie Besant, though writing outside a Christian framework, reflects J. Edgar Foster's sculptural analogies of Chapter 1. She writes theosophically of passing through materiality into spirituality in terms of sculpture: 'the Soul takes the pain in hand as a sculptor might take a chisel, and with this instrument of pain he strikes at his own personality'.[96] One might say, here, that the chisel is a weapon, but it is clear that it is not being used aggressively or destructively, but rather as the creator of a thing of beauty, and, as such, clearly calls on the theosophical idea of

---

[95] 'Pain Descriptions', MS notes, in possession of author, 1993.

[96] *The Meaning and the Use of Pain* (Adyar Pamphlets, 168; Adyar: Theosophical Publishing House, 1932), 18–19. This lecture was first delivered at Blavatsky Lodge in 1894.

shedding outer layers to arrive at a spiritual core that Besant expounds throughout this lecture. Besant is providing a way of understanding pain that allows readers to make sense of it, to come to terms with their own suffering, and to move beyond purely physical pain into a different and more spiritual understanding of the agony of the body. This said, Scarry's argument could conceivably, though I think wrongly, claim Besant's image as one that fits into the first of her 'two and only two metaphors', but images that clearly cannot be fitted into such a scheme are provided by Coventry Patmore in his poem 'Pain' (published in the same volume as 'The Angel in the House' in 1886). Patmore's opening stanza finds numerous analogies to his titular subject in an attempt to understand:

> O, Pain, Love's mystery,
> Close next of kin
> To joy and heart's delight,
> Low Pleasure's opposite,
> Choice food of sanctity
> And medicine of sin,
> Angel, whom even they that will pursue
> Pleasure with hell's whole gust
> Find that they must
> Perversely woo,
> My lips, thy live coal touching, speak thee true.[97]

The tactics this poem uses to convey the reality of physical pain suggest the many and varied ways in which pain was read in the late nineteenth century, and demonstrably annihilate Scarry's conception of the metaphors available to the expression of bodily pain.[98] The poem begins with an invocation and reification of pain as an entity in itself, rather than just as the product of bodily lesion, the result of physical damage. It is then placed in alignment with a number of things: it is 'kin to joy' in a way that recalls many of the Victorian attempts to find the provenance of pain, whom its parents are, where its dwelling

---

[97] 'Pain', ll. 1–11, in *Poems*, 2 vols. (2nd collective edn., George Bell, 1886), ii. 100–2.

[98] It is ironic that Scarry herself (*Body in Pain*, 11) cites the example of Nietzsche calling his pain his dog, an example which clearly falls outside her own schematization of the metaphors of pain.

place.[99] It is placed in opposition to pleasure in a manner which was explored in physiological writing at the close of the nine-teenth century, being defined not as bad in itself but as part of a continuum of sentience, one end of which could not exist without the other; and it becomes food and medicine, the thing that sustains life and allows growth and well-being. Perhaps most interesting in this opening stanza—particularly in the light of the angriness of Scarry's book, and her demand that the truth be told about pain, and that reticence and unpleasantness must not stand in the way of the denunciation of torture—is the allu-sion to Isaiah 6 and the touching of the mouth with a hot coal. It is worth quoting the verses in question, for they throw light on the matter when read in conjunction with Patmore's poem:

Then flew one of the seraphims unto me, having a live coal in his hand, which he had taken with the tongs from off the altar:
     And he laid it upon my mouth, and said, Lo, this hath touched thy lips; and thine iniquity is taken away, and thy sin purged.
     Also I heard the voice of the Lord, saying, Whom shall I send, and who will go for us? Then said I, Here am I; send me.[100]

Pain is apostrophized in Patmore's poem as Angel, and repre-sents the seraphim of Isaiah, carrying the live coal which both purifies and pushes the narrator into his prophetic role. The pain of that encounter stimulates the response to pain that Scarry craves, the move from suffering into speech, but the narrator is not moved to the denunciation of pain, but rather to its exul-tation. The next few lines of Patmore's poem fit more conven-tionally into Scarry's scheme, suggesting what she calls the language of agency, as pain is described in terms of an infliction by means of external implements:

Thou sear'st my flesh, O Pain,
But brand'st for arduous peace my languid brain,
And bright'nest my dull view . . .[101]

Melzack and Torgerson would clearly have had no difficulty reg-istering this kind of language on the McGill questionnaire scale, but Patmore does not leave it at this. Pain is acknowledged as

---

[99] See James Henry's 1854 poem, 'Pain', in D. J. Enright (ed.), *The Faber Book of Fevers and Frets* (Faber, 1989), 65.
[100] Isa. 6: 6–8.   [101] 'Pain', ll 12–14.

'searing' and 'branding', but at the same time it is given a function: it 'bright[ens] my dull view'. This is not seen as a pay-off, but rather a positive thing, and we see in this phrase the vestiges of some of the terminology that was to give shape to the understanding of pain in the late Victorian period. Pain claims the language of acuity, it is sharp and piercing, whilst that which it acts on is seen as blunt and dull. The interaction between the two is such that pain awakens the sufferer from his torpor into an active life of perception. In the language of Isaiah it makes possible the statement and demand 'Here am I; send me.'

Lines from near the close of Patmore's poem suggest one more possible way in which pain may be seen that falls outside the parameters set by Scarry:

> What mockery of a man am I express'd
> That I should wait for thee
> To woo!
> Nor even dare to love, till thou lov'st me.
> How shameful, too,
> Is this:
> That, when thou lov'st, I am at first afraid
> Of thy fierce kiss,
> Like a young maid;
> And only trust thy charms
> And get my courage in thy throbbing arms.[102]

Pain emerges as lover, a far remove from the Angel in the House, the femme fatale who needs only the slightest of pushes to emerge as Swinburne's Delores, *Notre Dame des Sept Doulours*. Pain is read in terms of sex and sexual relations, as modesty is reinvented as the attribute of the man in relation to pain's 'fierce kiss',—the touch of the live coal on the lips of the loved one. We see in these lines the deconstruction effected by pain that Scarry fears, the falling apart of the structures the mind builds in the face of pain, and the undoing of the manhood of the narrator, but we see also a response to this, an attempt to understand what is going on, through the language of metaphor. The poem's narrator expresses his perceived weakness in the face of pain through stereotypical gender role reversal, as he becomes the coy 'young maid' who must wait for the advances of her

---

[102] Ibid., ll. 44–54.

brutal lover. He hints at the physicality of the relationship as he claims to get his 'courage in [pain's] throbbing arms'—such throbbing expressing not just the nature of the pain involved, as earlier it was 'searing', but also the sexual passion involved, and the power of the embrace.

This chapter has been concerned with the private language available to those who suffer—the ways of making sense in personal terms of pain—whether of fictional or of human sufferers. Claiming, as Scarry does, that there is no language for pain, has adverse implications for those in pain, as a discussion of Richard Rorty's claims about pain, language, and silence makes clear. Rorty bases his 'liberal ironist' vision, delineated in *Contingency, Irony, and Solidarity*, on the assumption that 'the imaginative ability to see strange people as fellow sufferers'[103] is what matters, and is, rather than any metaphysical quality, that which will manage to establish solidarity among the human race. This is questionable in itself,[104] but where the argument of *Contingency, Irony and Solidarity* becomes particularly feeble is in Rorty's assumptions about the nature of the pain of which he writes. His claim that 'pain is nonlinguistic'[105] is clearly, and acknowledgedly, derived from Scarry's work, and he relies heavily on the belief that the act of suffering in one's body makes the physical act of speech impossible, as well as on its corollary—equally disabling—that there is no language available for sufferers to describe their pain. But Rorty, whilst he uses these ideas, shifts the conceptual framework by redefining what he means by pain, claiming that 'the best way to cause people long-lasting pain is to humiliate them'.[106] Clearly he and Scarry are writing about two fundamentally different things tied together by the same terminology. Rorty's elision of these two different kinds of pain makes nonsense of his claims that

victims of cruelty, people who are suffering, do not have much in the way of a language. That is why there is no such things [*sic*] as the 'voice of the oppressed' or the 'language of the victims.' The language

---

[103] *Contingency, Irony, and Solidarity* (1989; Cambridge: Cambridge University Press, 1994), p. xvi.

[104] See Bradford T. Stull, *Religious Dialectics of Pain and Imagination* (Albany, NY: State University of New York Press, 1994), 18–19.

[105] Rorty, *Contingency*, 94.   [106] Ibid. 89.

the victims once used is not working anymore, and they are suffering too much to put new words together. So the job of putting their situation into language is going to have to be done for them by somebody else. The liberal novelist, poet, or journalist is good at that.[107]

This seems to me to be a fundamental error, and while Rorty aims at empowering the empained, he is, in fact, denying them the ability to speak for themselves and shifting the responsibility to other groups. Whilst it may be the case that those humiliated by having 'the things that seemed most important to them' made to 'look futile, obsolete, and powerless'[108] are silenced by political structures, it is certainly not the case that their 'pain' is 'destroy[ing] language itself'.[109] His unthinking elision of physical and mental suffering falsifies his logic, and makes his position untenable. This matters little when he confuses the pain of Jo, the crossing sweeper in *Bleak House*, with the senseless torture of an 8-year-old boy in Nabokov's *Bend Sinister*, for both are fictional and suffer no consequences. As Scarry herself suggests, however, trying to find structures to accommodate physical pain in language is a 'project laden with practical and ethical consequences'.[110] Rorty's confusion of terms feeds back into Scarry's own assumptions that pain is essentially incommunicable and lays bare the dangers of her position. In assuming there is no language for pain, on whatever grounds, and passing authority over to some other group, however benign (as, doubtless, are the liberal novelists, poets, and journalists of Rorty's vision), those who suffer lose control over their own suffering.

[107] Ibid. 94.   [108] Ibid. 89.   [109] Ibid.   [110] *Body in Pain*, 6.

4

Antivivisectionary Rhetoric and Pain

This chapter brings together the theoretical concerns of the previous chapter and close readings of the literature of vivisection of the 1880s and 1890s, to establish the ways in which the pain of others, whether animal or human, was thought too painful to recognize, and the pain of animals too lowly to value. The debate over vivisection raised difficult questions of literary representation as the tension between what could be said—and what could not—rested not so much on the possibilities of language itself, as on the dictates of decorum and sensibility. I shall be tracing how far antivivisectionists could go in delineating physical suffering without alienating their readership.

Anna Sewell's talking horses in *Black Beauty* (1877), brought to the fore sensate creatures who lacked the power to communicate their sufferings forcibly enough for their pain to be taken seriously by those who inflicted it: tails are docked and heads held too high by the bearing-rein in the name of fashion, and horses are worked into the ground as an expendable commodity. But whilst Ginger clearly has a hard life, full of cruelty, her suffering is not such that it cannot be written about in a novel.[1] Not so the fate meted out to the worn-out horses of the French Army, which became the staple objects of investigation in the vivisectionary laboratories of Paris.[2] A vivisected Black Beauty,

---

[1] *Black Beauty: His Grooms and Companions. The Autobiography of a Horse. Translated from the Original Equine by Anna Sewell* (Jarrold, [1877]). See esp. chs. 8, 'Ginger's Story Continued' and 40, 'Poor Ginger'.

[2] Paul Elliott, 'Vivisection and the Emergence of Experimental Physiology in Nineteenth-Century France', in Nicolaas A. Rupke (ed.), *Vivisection in Historical Perspective* (1987; London and New York: Routledge, 1990), 52: 'professors of veterinary medicine had free access to almost limitless supplies of animals and horses in particular. It should be remembered that in the nineteenth century the horse was still an essential weapon of war and so governments were always willing to allow scientists to carry out research that was intended to improve their effectiveness. Consequently, old and diseased horses were routinely sent from the army stables to the veterinary schools for use in experiments or anatomical demonstrations.'

directly depicted, is unimaginable in Sewell's story:[3] sharp bits that tear at the horses' mouths, whilst upsetting, do not lie outside the possibilities of representation. In this chapter, I shall be evaluating the possibilities and potentialities of fiction and non-fiction used as polemical weapons in the antivivisectionary cause.

I. VIVISECTION IN PRACTICE

Vivisection was not a new method of scientific investigation in the 1880s. As Andreas-Holger Maehle and Ulrich Tröhler suggest, the cutting up of live animals has been performed and recorded, to a greater or lesser extent, since 450 BC, when Alcmaeon of Croton cut through the optic nerve of a living animal and demonstrated its consequent blindness, until the nineteenth-century upsurge in the practice.[4] In France and Germany, by the 1850s, vivisection was firmly established as a valued scientific procedure, and chairs in experimental physiology had been established in many universities. Vivisection provided a way of moving on from anatomy with its emphasis on looking, a way of legitimizing and professionalizing the medical profession by giving it a much firmer scientific and experimental basis. In contemporary England things were different. As Gerald Geison argues, by the early 1870s there was a general recognition amongst English physiologists that they had played little or no part in the recent advances in physiological knowledge. Physiology in England was left to amateurs rather than professionals, and there were, indeed, neither laboratories nor university positions in which experimental physiologists could carry out vivisectional investigations.[5] Whilst Geison offers the broad-based acceptance of natural theology and strong antivivisection sentiment as reasons for the lack of English

---

[3] Though see Coral Lansbury, 'Gynaecology, Pornography, and the Antivivisection Movement', *Victorian Studies*, 28 (1985), 413–37.

[4] 'Animal Experimentation from Antiquity to the End of the Eighteenth Century: Attitudes and Arguments', in Rupke (ed.), *Vivisection in Historical Perspective*, 14–47.

[5] 'Social and Institutional Factors in the Stagnancy of English Physiology, 1840–1870', *Bulletin of the History of Medicine*, 46 (1972), 30–58.

experimental physiology, he largely fails to substantiate these claims. James Turner, however, charts the course of an increasingly sentimental and empathic attitude towards animals, giving substance to Geison's claims. He traces the movement from an eighteenth-century emphasis on the pitying subject who weeps at the sight of suffering to a late nineteenth-century recognition of the pitiful object as worthy of recognition in its own right.[6]

A 'benevolent tide of sympathy'[7] washed through prison reform, harsh public schools, and the slave trade, recognizing the suffering of those involved, and, by the time of the Industrial Revolution, and partly because of it, compassion was put on the agenda. A general 'revulsion from suffering'[8] ensued, which included groups other than humans. The first statutory protection for animals came in England in 1820, with societies for the protection of animals growing up shortly thereafter.[9] Sentiment of this kind was certainly strong, and, as Geison argues, was almost certainly the reason why experimental physiologists in England were the exception rather than the rule before the 1870s. In the early 1870s, however, when Michael Foster—one of the contributors to John Burdon-Sanderson's important *Handbook for the Physiological Laboratory* which I shall discuss later in this chapter—was establishing his own laboratory in Cambridge,[10] things began to change. By the time the 1876 Cruelty to Animals Act was introduced to regulate and restrict animal experimentation, enough support could be found amongst the research and medical communities, who recognized in vivisection a means of professionalizing science in general terms, to force amendments to the bill, rendering it, as Judith Hampson claims, so ' "innocuous" . . . that it might serve the purpose of soothing the agitated public while imposing no real

---

[6] See also Harriet Ritvo, *The Animal Estate: The English and Other Creatures in the Victorian Age* (1987; Penguin, 1990), esp. ch. 3, 'A Measure of Compassion', pp. 125–66.

[7] James Turner, *Reckoning with the Beast: Animals, Pain, and Humanity in the Victorian Mind* (Baltimore and London: Johns Hopkins University Press, 1980), 4.

[8] Ibid. 34.

[9] For the rise of animal protection societies in England see ibid. 39.

[10] For the paucity of professional English vivisectionists at work in the early 19th century see Diana Manuel, 'Marshall Hall (1790–1857): Vivisection and the Development of Experimental Physiology', in Rupke (ed.), *Vivisection in Historical Perspective*, 78–104.

restrictions on fundamental or medical research'.[11] Such an evaluation makes clear both the public concern over the practice of animal experimentation, and the flexing muscles of the youthful science of professional English physiology as these emerged at the end of the last century. Would-be physiologists were forced to fight their corner, and out of this purportedly restrictive legislation sprang a consolidated defence of experimental physiology. The testimony offered by physiologists before the Royal Commission of 1875 was printed in scientific and medical journals, and, as Nicolaas Rupke argues, 'in the early 1880s, the scientists launched an organised publicity campaign in defence of animal experimentation'.[12] The International Medical Conference (IMC), held in London in 1881, justified vivisection as a technique, claiming that its benefits far outweighed the suffering involved, and that the infliction of pain was properly compensated by a consequent medical elimination of pain. At the end of the conference a general resolution was unanimously passed:

That this Congress records its conviction that experiments on living animals have proved of the utmost service to medicine in the past, and are indispensable to its future progress; that, accordingly, while strongly deprecating the infliction of unnecessary pain, it is of opinion, alike in the interests of man and of animals, that it is not desirable to restrict competent persons in the performance of such experiments.[13]

The IMC's resolution makes it plain that doctors were prepared to reassess the value of pain, particularly the pain of a non-verbal group, and, indeed, that they were so confident of their position that they were willing to make public their rationale. In March 1882 the Association for the Advancement of Medicine by Research was set up, the avowed aim of which was to bring justifications for vivisection into the public arena and to counter the swelling tide of antivivisection rhetoric. Animal

---

[11] 'Legislation: A Practical Solution to the Vivisection Dilemma?', in Rupke (ed.), *Vivisection in Historical Perspective*, 315. For details of the debate over legislation, see E. Westacott, *A Century of Vivisection and Anti-vivisection: A Study of their Effect upon Science, Medicine, and Human Life during the Past Hundred Years* (Ashingdon: C. W. Daniel, 1949).

[12] 'Pro-vivisection in England in the Early 1880s: Arguments and Motives', in id. (ed.), *Vivisection in Historical Perspective*, 190.

[13] Cited ibid. 191–2.

experimentation became the subject of vast amounts of propaganda as both sides in this acrimonious debate put forward their case in numerous books, pamphlets, and articles. Whilst many antivivisectionists were concerned with what they saw to be needless and cruel pain inflicted on animals, by no means all of the arguments of this debate centred on physical suffering. Cartesian Christianity denied animals a soul and the capacity to suffer,[14] and in this way Christian rhetoric removed pain from the equation: animal screams were directly analogous to the noises made by badly oiled machinery, and as such were inconsequential.[15] If no pain was felt, then there was no reason not to carry out the experiment. Equally unconnected to the suffering of animals was the prevalent Kantian claim that vivisection was wrong not because of the infliction of pain, but rather because such infliction brutalized those who practised it.[16] Those who could bring themselves to cut up a living dog would almost inevitably move on to murdering humans, or, indeed, experimenting on them whilst they were alive. Vivisectionists themselves were also largely unconcerned with animal pain,[17] and saw it as a means to an end: the widespread use of curare as a drug that removed an animal's ability to struggle rather than its ability to feel strongly suggests this. 'Unnecessary pain' may be deplored, but pain that contributes to medical knowledge is necessary, and as such not just acceptable but vital; vital not just in its possible translation into a cure, but also in the part it plays in the professionalization of the medical profession. As these diverse motives were bandied about, particular stereotypes of the proponents of each side of the argument emerged: antivivisectionists were characterized as sentimental women,

[14] René Descartes, *Discourse on Method* (1637), pt. V, trans. John Veitch (La Salle, Ill.: Open Court, 1989), 44–63.

[15] See L. C. Rosenfield, 'Descartes' Denial of Soul in Animals', in *From Beast-Machine to Man-Machine* (New York: Oxford University Press, 1940), 3–26. Rosenfield gathers together Descartes's published and unpublished thoughts on animal automatism and sets them in their historical context.

[16] See Immanuel Kant, *Lectures on Ethics*, trans. Louis Infield (Methuen, 1930), 240. Kant's lectures of *c.*1780 are reconstructed from lecture notes taken by his students.

[17] Though see Manuel, 'Marshall Hall', 78–104. Manuel describes the way Marshall Hall, very much out on a limb as a professional English physiologist in the 1830s, sought to restrict and codify the practice of vivisection.

whilst vivisectionists were callous and brutal men. I shall be examining this dichotomy in the course of this chapter.

The debate over vivisection in England was very much a live issue from the 1870s until the turn of the century, and onwards. Not only did it emerge in the medical press, particularly after the 1881 IMC,[18] but it also became the subject of debate in widely different kinds of journals. The *Nineteenth Century* published articles from advocates and adversaries alike, whilst the feminist journal *Shafts* denounced the practice, and *Punch*, in a series of items in 1874, sneered at vivisectionists and their pretensions to advanced knowledge, laughing at the way in which physiologists proved that alcohol made dogs drunk.[19] Vivisection took on a metaphorical life as A. V. Dicey, reviewing *Daniel Deronda* in 1876, wrote of 'something absolutely painful in the kind of vivisection to which [Deronda's] physical and moral qualities are subjected',[20] and as Oscar Wilde used the same metaphor for psychological insight in his description of Lord Henry in *The Picture of Dorian Gray*.[21] Not only did novelists use vivisection in this metaphorical fashion, but, as I shall establish in the course of this chapter, the evil vivisectionist also became the stock villain in a number of late Victorian novels.[22]

The controversy over vivisection was not, however, just fought out on paper, though the verbal depiction of pain will be the major concern of my argument. Animal experimentation evoked strong feelings, and had repercussions in the field of action. Much as vivisection played a key part in giving medicine the power and prestige of scientific investigation, the antivivisection cause became one of the keynotes of the feminist movement.[23] Antivivisection was a cause supported by Queen

[18] See Rupke, 'Pro-vivisection', 189–91.

[19] See esp. 'Vivisection and Cheek', *Punch*, 17 Jan. 1874, 28; and 'Vivisection and Science', *Punch*, 19 Dec. 1874, 257.

[20] Review of *Daniel Deronda* by George Eliot, *Nation*, 19 Oct. 1876, 245.

[21] *Dorian Gray*, 83–4. See also Hardy, *Trumpet-Major*, i. 147; and H. G. Wells, *The Wonderful Visit* (London: J. M. Dent; New York: Macmillan, 1895), 143–5.

[22] See Coral Lansbury, *The Old Brown Dog: Women, Workers, and Vivisection in Edwardian England* (Madison: University of Wisconsin Press, 1985). See esp. ch. 8, 'The Truths of Fiction'.

[23] See the chapter on Frances Power Cobbe in Barbara Caine, *Victorian Feminists* (Oxford: Oxford University Press, 1992), 103–49.

Victoria, Lord Shaftesbury, R. H. Hutton, the Bishop of Manchester, Thomas Carlyle, John Bright, John Ruskin, Lewis Carroll, Alfred, Lord Tennyson,[24] and Robert Browning, among many others in the military, the Church, and the House of Commons.[25] For Ruskin—representative in the strength of his feeling—the appointment of John Burdon-Sanderson as the Waynflete Professor of Physiology in Oxford in 1882, and the subsequent monetary grant supporting his laboratory in 1885, led directly to Ruskin's resignation as Slade Professor of Art.[26] These few examples suggest the widely diverse intellectual and political allegiances of those who opposed vivisection, as well as the strength of conviction held by opponents and the force of dispersion antivivisectionary thinking had behind it.

This chapter will look specifically at the conflicting forces at work in the description of bodily pain in the 1880s and 1890s, using literature of all kinds—sermons, medical textbooks, campaigning pamphlets, novels—focusing on vivisection. Taking as a starting point one of the arguments of the previous chapter, I shall argue that overt description of the infliction of pain, written in an attempt to make known, and thereby suppress, the practice of vivisection, could be counter-productive. That is, such description expressly excluded those readers whose sensibility was honed to such a degree that they responded sympathetically to those in pain, and, through a process of transference, found such description too painful to read. Father Furniss, the advocate of eternal damnation, recognized at the beginning of *The Sight of Hell*, the problems of detailed description of the infliction of pain: 'The false delicacy of modern times in keeping back the searing images of Hell, while in the case of children, it has often marred a whole education, is a formidable danger to the sanctity as well as to the faith of

---

[24] For Tennyson on vivisection, see *The Princess*, iii. 288–303. Whilst Tennyson profoundly disliked the practice of vivisection, this is also, and importantly, a view projected onto a *female* community. *Tennyson: A Selected Edition*, ed. Christopher Ricks (Harlow: Longman, 1989).

[25] See the signatories to the 'memorial' that Frances Power Cobbe drew up and presented to the RSPCA in an attempt to force the society into exerting their influence to restrict the practice of vivisection through legislation. Cited in Richard D. French, *Antivivisection and Medical Science in Victorian Society* (Princeton and London: Princeton University Press, 1975), 65.

[26] See Richard D. Ryder, *Victims of Science: The Use of Animals in Research* (Davis-Poynter, 1975), 203–4.

men.'[27] Furniss, driven by Redemptorist conviction, provided hideous descriptions of an imaginary hell, based on a handful of biblical texts and the authority of the Church Fathers, for the good of those who read them, whilst antivivisectionists, recognizing the necessity of upsetting their readership, described real scenes and procedures of the infliction of pain, often described in their own terms as 'hellish'. Furniss writes of 'false delicacy', calling on the convention of a sensibility born of civilization too refined to cope with day-to-day living. Wilkie Collins, however, pushed at the boundaries of the notion of such 'false delicacy' and the limits to what it was acceptable to write about the practice of vivisection, as I shall suggest in the course of this chapter, in a discussion of his 1883 novel *Heart and Science*.

Of particular concern is the dual concept of feeling as it relates to pain rather than to any other emotional subject, and the overlap between words denoting feeling in both the moral and the physical sphere; the place where the emotional delicacy of sensibility merges with the physical acuteness of sensitivity. Collins's *Heart and Science*, Stevenson's *Strange Case of Dr. Jekyll and Mr. Hyde* (1886), Edward Berdoe's *St. Bernard's* (1887), and H. G. Wells's *The Island of Doctor Moreau* (1896) will be read alongside various antivivisectionary tracts written in the 1880s and 1890s by such prominent writers and campaigners as Frances Power Cobbe, Ouida, Mark Thornhill, and Mona Caird, to suggest ways in which these authors entered the propaganda battle over vivisection, using and subverting the language of physiology, and reclaiming words associated with physiological research as weapons against it. By reading different forms of writing—fiction as well as polemical works—against each other, I shall show the different possibilities and achievements of different forms of writing, and establish the interplay between the two.

II. THE CIVILIZED SAVAGE

The concepts of sensitivity and sensibility, the ability to feel both physically and emotionally, are of great importance in

---

[27] Cited in Wheeler, *Death*, 180.

understanding the ways in which pain was perceived and written about in the late nineteenth century. The ability to feel pain became for civilized Christians one of the keynotes of civilization, the attribute that separated them from the so-called savage. The relationship between savagery and civilization is a complex one. On the one hand, savages are presented as near brutes. Lower down the evolutionary scale than civilized westerners, they are less sensitive to refinements of feeling, both emotionally and physically, and necessarily so, for it is their sensitivity that has allowed evolution to take place at a more advanced rate in civilized people. This increased sensitivity, however, has two negative aspects: the first of these is a hyperaesthesia that allows the civilized to suffer pain in contexts that are pain-free for the savage; and the second is a consequence of this, that supersensitive civilized people will eschew all painful encounters and will choose to live an 'unnatural' and luxurious life, thus allowing, and, indeed, precipitating, the enervation of their faculties.

John Conquest in his childcare manual, *Letters to a Mother* (1848), suggests the imperviousness of the savage to pain, in contrast to the oversensitivity of the modern wealthy European, and in so doing suggests the future path of much of the discussion over sensitivity of the second half of the century:

It is ... obvious that the difficulty and danger which so often attend childbearing in civilized society are attributable, principally, to unnatural customs and habits of living, in which women, in this and other countries, indulge from their infancy, and which operate by preventing the constitution from acquiring its proper firmness and vigour and by producing a weak, feeble, and irritable state of body.[28]

---

[28] *Letters to a Mother, on the Management of Herself and Children in Health and Disease; embracing the Subjects of Pregnancy, Childbirth, Nursing, Food, Exercise, Bathing, Clothing, Etc., Etc. With Remarks on Chloroform* (1848; 5th edn., rev. Longman, 1858), 41. See also [von Arnim], *German Garden*, 66–7: 'they [the German working women] have to produce offspring, quite regardless of times and seasons and the general fitness of things; they have to do this as expeditiously as possible, so that they may not unduly interrupt the work in hand; nobody helps them, notices them, or cares about them, least of all the husband. It is quite a usual thing to see them working in the fields in the morning, and working again in the afternoon, having in the interval produced a baby. The baby is left to an old woman whose duty it is to look after babies collectively. When I expressed my horror at the poor creatures working immediately afterwards as though nothing had happened, the Man of Wrath [Elizabeth's husband] informed me that they did not suffer

The enervation and feebleness of body and spirit G. W. Steevens described as a *fin de siècle* malaise has its precursor here. The obverse of such supersensitivity of the 'civilized' nations is the lack of pain of the 'savage', which takes form in a slightly earlier passage from Conquest:

The same simplicity, expedition, and freedom from danger, attend this natural process [childbirth] amongst the natives in most parts of Asia, Africa, the West Indies, and America, where the mode of living among the natives is more simple and abstemious, and their occupations and general habits more laborious, than in more civilised countries.[29]

The underlying assertion is that savages do not feel pain, whereas the citizens of civilized nations do—a belief that had many invidious imperialist applications.[30] Weir Mitchell, the American Civil War surgeon and writer, makes explicit the link between the inability to feel pain and a 'savage' state in his straightforward claim that 'in our process of being civilized we have won, I suspect, intensified capacity to suffer'.[31]

Savagery, in this way, provided a potent image of the unfeeling for late Victorians.[32] Lack of feeling came to be strongly associated with a backward step, with degeneration and devolution. The infliction of pain *brutalized*, made those who practised it more like the brutes and savages from whom the civilized had dissociated themselves evolutionarily over the course of time. Civilized Christians became brutish when their level of sensibility was somehow lowered: hence the dangers of vivisection. Not only did the animals experimented on suffer pain, but the vivisectionist was degraded by watching, and creating, that suffering. The result of this process was the creation of such

because they had never worn corsets, nor had their mothers and grandmothers. We were riding together at the time, and had just passed a batch of workers, and my husband was speaking to the overseer when a woman arrived alone, and taking up a spade began to dig. She grinned cheerfully at us as she made a curtsey, and the overseer remarked that she had just been back to the house and had a baby.'

[29] *Letters*, 40.

[30] See H. J. Bigelow, 'Vivisection', in *Surgical Anæsthesia: Addresses and Other Papers* (Boston: Little, Brown, 1900), 374: 'There can be little doubt that an intelligent dog has at least the same thoughts, emotions, and suffering under vivisection as a Bushman or a Digger Indian would experience.'

[31] *Characteristics* (6th edn., Macmillan, 1899), 13. Also quoted in id., 'Civilization and Pain', *Annals of Hygiene*, 7 (1892), 26.

[32] See my discussion of tattooing in Ch. 5, Sect. II.

monsters of callousness as *Heart and Science*'s Doctor Benjulia, a man prepared to expedite the death of a young girl for the furtherance of his scientific studies.

The conjunction of savagery, criminality, and brutality was a powerful one in the last two decades of the nineteenth century, and the three things were almost inextricably tied up together, and used collectively as the antithesis to civilization. The mention of savages was, therefore, not peripheral as brutality necessarily called on savagery for the late Victorians. The concept of the 'civilized savage'—the French or English experimental physiologist—appears in much antivivisection literature, as the insensitivity of those considered savages by the western world was turned inside out into an emotional, rather than a purely physical, insensibility, as it came to refer to such men as Collins's Dr Benjulia.

There was, however, another side to the question of savagery and the inability to feel pain, and that is the inability of savages to feel *sympathetically* any pain they might inflict: an argument antivivisectionary writers were quick to seize upon. It was a link Havelock Ellis forged in 1889, in the related field of criminal anthropology, when he claimed that the physical and concomitant psychical analgesia of criminals went hand in hand, allowing criminals to inflict pain at their pleasure.[33] Perhaps the clearest exposition of the links between civilization and savagery in terms of a sympathetic response to pain appears in Mona Caird's article 'The Evolution of Compassion' (1896). Here Caird, a prolific antivivisection pamphleteer and novelist, claimed that over the course of time humans are progressing from the positive enjoyment of cruelty and the infliction of pain to a point where they sympathize with the sufferings of their fellows and refuse to partake in such cruelty. Caird by no means considered this process to be at an end, and had no doubt that 'The savagery of our ancestors still rages in our blood',[34] finding its explicit expression—among other places—in the 'cool-nerved Professor with his dissecting-knife'.[35]

Not only does this article trace the trajectory of compassion, but it also offers a defence against the attacks on antivivisec-

[33] See ibid.
[34] 'The Evolution of Compassion', *Westminster Review*, 145 (1896), 636.
[35] Ibid. 637.

tionists by such men as Max Nordau. Nordau's book *Degen-eration*, in which, amongst many other debased *fin de siècle* activities, he derides those who oppose vivisection, was first translated into English in 1895.[36] His attack on the 'morbid sen-timentalism . . . concerning the sufferings of the frog, utilized in physiological experiments'[37] denounces what, for Nordau, was a kind of megalomania. The nature of his attack, and its struc-tural similarities to, though its profound difference in emphasis from, antivivisectional writing, makes clear the interrelatedness of the opposing rhetorics of the two parties in the debate. Nordau sneered at what he saw as crazes—vegetarianism, anti-vivisection, 'barefoot perambulations on wet grass'[38]—and argued that anyone silly, or sick, enough to take up one of these causes would be inextricably caught up in all of the others: 'As a rule, all these derangements appear simultaneously, and in nine out of ten cases it is safe to take the proudly strutting wearer of Jaeger's garments for a Chauvinist, the Kneipp vision-ary for a groats-dieted maniac, and the defender of the frog, thirsting for the professor's blood, for an anti-Semitist.'[39] Femi-nist journals such as *Shafts* would, no doubt, refuse some of the categories Nordau introduced, but they did bring together, in a remarkably similar fashion, collections of what might be called 'isms'—vegetarianism, antivivisection, rational dress for women, universal suffrage—and used these together to instigate a feeling of solidarity amongst women who shared these con-victions. What for Nordau were a group of symptoms denoting derangement became in *Shafts* the nexus of important social and political concerns.

Women, as Mary Ann Elston argues, were persistently asso-ciated with sentimentality, with feelings rather than with reason, in the debate over vivisection, and much as savagery and civi-lization were seen as polar opposites, so too were the attitudes of women and men polarized. As Elston schematizes: 'Sentiment versus science: women versus men.'[40] Edward Berdoe, satirizing

---

[36] For the popularity, as well as the adverse medical reception of Nordau's *Degen-eration*, see Hurley, *Gothic Body*, 76 n.
[37] *Degeneration* (William Heinemann, 1895), 209.
[38] Ibid.   [39] Ibid.
[40] 'Women and Anti-vivisection in Victorian England, 1870–1900', in Rupke (ed.), *Vivisection in Historical Perspective*, 259.

the attitudes of vivisectionists, and using the terminology of being inside or outside a wall of sensibility that will come to the fore in this chapter, describes a situation from his novel *St. Bernard's* in just these terms: 'Outside "some sentimentalists, weak-brained lords and hysterical women," as they were termed by the men of science, were making a noise over these very things.'[41] Unreason, sentiment, and hysteria were deemed by those in favour of vivisection the province of women, and of men little better than women, whilst women sought to affirm such sensibility as a positive value. This was not, however, always an easy claim to sustain, and Frances Power Cobbe was forced to caution 'women supporters against excessive displays of emotion, calling instead for vigorous denunciations of injustice, based on women's moral superiority, not their womanly "privileges"'.[42] Such claims provide the rationale for mirroring the techniques and rhetorical strategies of pro-vivisectionists by antivivisectionary writers.

The explicit linking of savagery and civilization and the debate over vivisection was widespread. Emily Brontë, writing *Wuthering Heights* in 1847, at the same time as vivisection was coming very much to the fore in French medical schools, makes the links between cruelty, vivisection, and savagery very clear in her portrayal of Heathcliff. John Sutherland, writing in his essay 'Is Heathcliff a Murderer?', catalogues Heathcliff's many physical cruelties,[43] but Brontë's Isabella, driven by Heathcliff's cruelty to escape from him after her marriage, goes one step further, and puts his cruelty into the context of vivisection. She describes his predilection for ' "Pulling out the nerves with red hot pincers" ',[44] and, in saying this, recognizes a quality that Heathcliff finds in himself: ' "It's odd what a savage feeling I

---

[41] *St. Bernards: The Romance of a Medical Student.* By Æsculapius Scalpel (Swan Sonnenschein, Lowrey, 1887), 115.

[42] Elston, 'Women and Anti-vivisection', 264.

[43] 'Is Heathcliff a Murderer?', in *Is Heathcliff a Murderer? Great Puzzles in Nineteenth-Century Literature* (Oxford and New York: Oxford University Press, 1996), 53–8. See also J. B. Bullen, 'Figuring the Body in the Victorian Novel', in id. (ed.), *Writing and Victorianism* (London and New York: Longman, 1997), 250–65. Bullen describes the 'dismembered and dislocated . . . bruised, broken, lacerated, torn, cut and beaten' (258) bodies in *Wuthering Heights*, but fails to connect these to Heathcliff's vivisectional tendencies.

[44] *Wuthering Heights* (1847), ed. Hilda Marsden and Ian Jack (Oxford: Clarendon Press, 1976), 211.

have to anything that seems afraid of me! Had I been born where laws are less strict, and tastes less dainty, I should treat myself to a slow vivisection of those two, [the young Catherine and Linton] as an evening's amusement." "[45] Savagery, daintiness or 'delicacy', vivisection and the ability to enjoy vivisection, as well as the slowness of the procedure, all fed into the debates at the heart of this chapter.

Caird's claim is that savagery and civilization can, and do, coexist, and that 'at the back of all the apparent civilisation of modern life lies always this chaos of greedy instincts',[46] whether aggressive, sensual, or parental, which may rise up and over-whelm the more rational and spiritual nature hitherto in command. Heathcliff, happy with violent, primitive urges, is held back from human vivisection by the structures of civiliza-tion—taste and law—rather than by any innate goodness. For Caird, the way forward involves the fight against such retro-gressive urges:

The taming and ruling, and, in some cases, the destruction of these primitive forces is the task that lies before the human race; and all who make that task more difficult are in truth its bitterest enemies. Among the most dangerous of these 'ravening creatures of the prime' is the hideous instinct of cruelty which we have been trying to trace to its origin, and to recognise in some of its disguises.[47]

So it is that cruelty, and the inability to feel vicarious pain—in ways that Brontë clearly recognized thirty years before the fight over vivisection was taken up in earnest—are the corner-stone of savagery. Caird substantiates her claim by arguing that as 'we penetrate further into the past, we find the sense of humour depending always more obviously and solely upon the enjoyment of the pain, misfortune, mortification or embarrass-ment of others',[48] and this is, for her, the defining trait of the savage, whilst the 'soft under-murmur of pity'[49] is to be seen as the hallmark of true civilization. For Caird, cruelty of this sort can hide itself under the mask of civilization, and it is this idea of the coexistence of the savage and the civilized in a single

---

[45] Ibid. 328.   [46] 'Evolution', 637.   [47] Ibid. 638.
[48] Ibid. 636. Mitchell employs very similar arguments in his article 'Heroism in Every-day Life', *Century Illustrated Monthly Magazine*, 43 (1902), 217–20.
[49] Caird, 'Evolution', 636.

person, with the savage hiding under a veneer of civilization, that takes shape in the notion of the 'civilized savage'. It is no coincidence that Jekyll's alter ego in Stevenson's book is called Hyde: the savage and the cruel hiding behind the largely civilized façade offered by Dr Jekyll himself.

The portrayal of the vivisectionist Benjulia in *Heart and Science* shows how this opposition between civilization and savagery, sensibility and insensibility, could be manipulated by a novelist. Collins makes it very clear that Benjulia, far from being personally insensitive, suffers from physical torments—his gout becomes 'Ten thousand red-hot devils . . . boring ten thousand holes through [his] foot'[50]—but the vivisectionist clearly does not feel any sympathy with the animals on which he experiments, nor with the broader field of human suffering in general. He clearly does not feel bound by sympathy to society,[51] claiming that 'Now that he was out of pain for awhile, the doctor's innate insensibility to what other people might think of him, or might say to him, resumed its customary torpor in its own strangely unconscious way.'[52]

His insensibility, or 'unconsciousness', another term with applications in anaesthesia, is such that he does not feel bound by social mores—as Heathcliff is only very tentatively bound—and neither does he vicariously feel the pain that he inflicts on the animals he vivisects. Collins, caught up in conventions of decency, refuses to discuss this openly, but it is clear that Benjulia feels no revulsion when he is literally caught with the blood of experimental animals on his hands.[53] The contrary response of those surgeons who operated before anaesthetics were brought into use offers a fitting comparison. The use of anaesthesia not only rendered surgery painless for the patient, but one of its major advances was seen to be the alleviation of the surgeon's suffering, partly because he no longer had to contend with the struggles of the patient, but also—and more

---

[50] *Heart*, i. 265. Suffering from gout is a common problem in Collins's novels, probably because it was based on one of the author's own afflictions. See Catherine Peters, *The King of Inventors: A Life of Wilkie Collins* (Secker and Warburg, 1991), 257.
[51] See Caird, 'Evolution', 638 in which Caird makes explicit the link between social cohesion and sensibility, and cruelty and social disintegration.
[52] Collins, *Heart*, i. 267.   [53] Ibid. ii. 142.

important—because he no longer had to experience the sufferings of the patient vicariously. Weir Mitchell loathed operating before the introduction of anaesthetics, claiming: 'surgery was horrible to me. I fainted so often at operations that I began to despair'.[54] His case was by no means unique.

Pre-anaesthetic surgeons needed to disregard the pain they inflicted if they were to do their job, and there was a great deal written by surgeons after 1846—the year when anaesthetics were introduced—on the vicarious pain they felt before this date as they cut into sentient flesh. Protheroe Smith's comment is, perhaps, more smug than most, but conveys this dislike of inflicting pain:

And the practice [of administering chloroform] is not a great blessing to the patient merely; it is a great boon, also, to the practitioner. For, whilst it relieves the former from the dread and endurance of agony and pain, it both relieves the latter from the disagreeable necessity of witnessing such agony and pain in a fellow-creature, and imparts to him the proud power of being able to cancel and remove pangs and torture that would otherwise be inevitable.[55]

Smith is, no doubt, pleased with himself at his ameliorative powers, but there is at the bottom of this a huge amount of relief at the termination of the need to feel pain at the patient's pain. Smith's self-satisfaction, set against its antithesis, is shown to advantage by Ouida's assessment of the vivisectionist inflicting pain:

The comedy of high and pure intentions; the scenic effect of the healer doing violence to his own nature in causing pain that he may cure it; the theatrical *mise-en-scène* of the arch-benevolence forcing itself to hurt, that it may thus acquire power to soothe and save; these are what with the greatest care and caution are put before the world in general, by the priesthood of physiology. Nothing can be farther from fact. Throughout Europe and America, and in many parts of Asia and Africa, the pursuit of physiology is a profession like any other, a career, a means to an end; that end, like other men's, being money, celebrity, and success.[56]

---

[54] Quoted in Anna Robeson Burr, *Weir Mitchell: His Life and Letters* (New York: Duffield, 1929), 45.

[55] *Scriptural Authority for the Mitigation of the Pains of Labour, by Chloroform, and Other Anæsthetic Agents* (S. Highly, 1848), 40.

[56] Ouida [Marie Louise de la Ramée], *The New Priesthood* (E. W. Allen, 1893), 28.

Benjulia's ability not to feel the pain he inflicts vicariously is what makes him a 'scientific savage'—one who does not feel pain—though Collins does, perhaps generously, credit his character with a desire for knowledge, rather than just the pecuniary interest Ouida avers. It is apparent from antivivisection pamphlets in general that this usage is not restricted to Collins's novel, and the opposition between the humane doctor who seeks human good through his caring bedside technique—the way in which the major breakthrough in brain disease in *Heart and Science* is actually made—and the self-serving solipsism of the savage vivisectionist, is pronounced. Ouida marks out the separation between doctor and vivisectionist with considerable firmness, though suggesting confusion in public perceptions of the two categories:

The public ideal of the doctor or surgeon is of one who approaches human suffering in tenderness and mercy, being only anxious to alleviate it; the reality of the scientific experimentalist, whether surgeon or doctor, is one who regards all suffering with curiosity, inquisitiveness, and absolute indifference except as to the character of its various phenomena.[57]

The splitting up of vital beings into their component phenomena which can then be *looked at* and examined will be discussed later in a fuller discussion of *The New Priesthood*. The ability of vivisectionists to look at living creatures in this disjunctive fashion is that which ensures that inevitably practitioners 'must become entirely brutalised and hardened to such sufferings',[58] for as they look at individual phenomena they fail to see the suffering of the whole. While the brutalized vivisectionist feels nothing, the brutes he experiments upon are in unnoticed agony.

Sensibility and insensibility[59] are pitted against each other, with the supposed evolutionary high point of the vivisectionist swapping places with the lowly animal, the object of his inves-

---

[57] *Ouida, Priesthood,*.   [58] Ibid. 16.

[59] Whilst I have distinguished between emotional and sensory perception using the words sensibility and sensitivity respectively, it is clear that late Victorian writers, and, indeed, their 18th-century precursors, linked the two terms. It is impossible to keep them completely separate in this discussion, not least because sensibility was reliant on the delicate and refined body. See my discussion of neurological sensibility in ch. 5.

tigation. An evaluation of Collins's use of the interplay in the pairing sensibility/insensibility may be used to indicate moral aspects of his book. At the beginning of *Heart and Science*, before Carmina has got to know her aunt, her response to Ovid's question as to her happiness is a conventional one: ' "Haven't you seen my pretty rooms—my piano—my pictures—my china—my flowers? I should be the most insensible creature living if I didn't feel gratitude to your mother." '[60] Carmina is talking of emotional feeling here, but the irony of her comment is that by the time Mrs Gallilee has behaved so atrociously that Carmina can no longer feel anything that even approaches gratitude, she has fallen into a fit that has indeed rendered her devoid of all feeling:

A ghastly stare, through half-closed eyes, showed death in life, blankly returning her look. The shock had struck Carmina with a stony calm. She had not started, she had not swooned. Rigid, immovable, there she sat; voiceless and tearless; insensible even to touch[61]

This catatonic state, reworking the idea of insensibility, sheds light on Benjulia's brutalized state. The terms of description suggest the primacy of sensation over emotion—she is 'insensible *even* to touch', but touch is the last thing, and the most primitive, to which she is expected to respond. Benjulia's responses, however, are entirely in the realm of the physical, and the only pain to which he responds is his own. A great deal of stress is put on Benjulia's ability to look, but what he sees is not carried over into emotional response.[62]

In the light of the horrified reviews of Arthur Machen's *The Three Impostors* (1895) and Wells's *The Island of Doctor Moreau* (1896), both of which revelled in the gruesome,[63] it is

---

[60] *Heart*, i. 246.   [61] Ibid. iii. 49.

[62] The number of references to Benjulia's eyes and his mode of observation is large. One example will serve. Carmina falls under Benjulia's care, and his response, after realizing that she may provide a useful case study in the search for a cure for brain disorders, is ' "Don't be afraid; I'll look after her" ' (ibid. 66). The phrase is, of course, a conventional one, but it becomes clear that his intention is only to watch her degenerative course whilst she is treated by an incompetent doctor, and to gather information from her regression.

[63] See my later discussion of *The Island of Doctor Moreau* and the reprinted reviews of Machen's book that appear in the back of the 1995 Everyman edn. Arthur Machen, *The Three Impostors* (1895; London: J. M. Dent; Vermont: Charles E.

no surprise that Wilkie Collins, writing a decade earlier in *Heart and Science*—a book which overtly professed to expose the brutalizing effects of vivisection—would not go into detail, or even provide the vaguest outline, of vivisectionary practice. Collins acknowledges in the preface 'To Readers in General' the help of Frances Power Cobbe, one of the leading exponents in the fight against vivisection. Her style, as will be shown in the discussion of one of her remarkably open antivivisection pamphlets, is by no means so evasive as that of the novelist. Collins's preface, however, is firm on this matter:

> From first to last, you are purposely left in ignorance of the hideous secrets of Vivisection. The outside of the laboratory is a necessary object in my landscape—but I never once open the door and invite you to look in. I trace, in one of my characters, the result of the habitual practice of cruelty (no matter under what pretence) in fatally deteriorating the nature of man—and I leave the picture to speak for itself.[64]

This is paradigmatic of the approach of many Victorian writers to the portrayal of pain, and whilst the metaphors change, the position remains the same. Readers are led up to the point of pain, and then there is a turning away and a failure to look at the pain itself and to describe it: a stopping at the door of the laboratory, though a faint wailing of animals can be heard from within. Descriptions of the approach to pain and some of the externals of illness are given, and then there is a sudden transference and the sensitivity of the sufferer is subsumed in the sensibility of the watcher. As Turner terms it, the pitying subject becomes paramount, whilst the pitiful object takes second place to the emotion it engenders.

In the previous chapter I established the ways in which the depiction of pain evoked a particular set of conventional responses. Sarah Grand's *The Beth Book* (1898) pushes these conventions so that what might be a Gothic tale of horror takes on realistic import, and then draws back from a full statement of the infliction of pain. Beth, the unhappily married heroine— soon to be still more unhappy—hears moans of pain emanating

---

Tuttle, 1995). See also id., *Precious Balms* (Spurr and Swift, 1924) which amusingly gathers together adverse reviews of Machen's own books, many of which express horror at his subject matter.

[64] *Heart*, vol. i, p. xi.

from her husband's surgery and goes downstairs to find that her husband, a doctor, has been cutting up a live dog on the kitchen table. Her immediate response to this discovery is typical:

Beth, checked again in her search, was considering what to do next, when the horrid cry was once more repeated. It seemed to come from under the calico sheet. Beth lighted the gas, put down her candle, and going to the table, took the sheet off deliberately, and saw a sight too sickening for description. The little black-and-tan terrier, the bonny wee thing which had been so blithe and greeted her so confidently only the evening before, lay there, fastened into a sort of frame in a position which alone must have been agonising. But that was not all.

Beth had heard of these horrors before, but little suspected that they were carried on under that very roof[65]

Words fail the author in the face of pain, and Beth is faced with a 'sight too sickening for description'. The vivisected dog is mentionable as a 'little black-and-tan terrier', but in its vivisected state it becomes 'a sight too sickening for description'. The mutilated dog is there, but only in the silences of the text. It becomes a 'horror'—something that raises sensation in the watcher rather than a suffering being in its own right—as the silence between paragraphs offers the blank space for imaginative horrors evoked by Holly's description of the torture chamber in *She*. The next part of this chapter will deal with the ways in which authors, starting with Wilkie Collins, and then moving on to the works of antivivisectionary polemicists, found, or failed to find, ways of overcoming this problem.

III. VIVISECTION ON PUBLIC DISPLAY

Collins's novel *Heart and Science* is interesting partly because it stands between fact and fiction, continuing his 'propagandist phase' begun in 1870 with *Man and Wife*[66] (a novel which deals primarily with British marriage laws, but also with another civilized savage, this time the sportsman Geoffrey Delamayn). Collins made clear in *Heart and Science* his didactic aim. His

---

[65] *The Beth Book: Being a Study from the Life of Elizabeth Caldwell Maclure. A Woman of Genius* (Heinemann, 1897), 437.

[66] John Sutherland, 'Collins, [William] Wilkie', in *Longman Companion to Victorian Fiction*, 142.

ambition was to make use of every advantage the novel form offered him to put forward antivivisectionary arguments: Benjulia's altercation with his brother (enlightened by Morphew's proposed antivivisectionary book) exposes the working of the vivisectionist's mind, whilst the unnamed dying foreigner's own book leads Ovid to the discovery of a cure for brain disease, the malaise for which Benjulia has failed to find a cure in vivisection. From just these two examples, the importance antivivisectionists placed on laying bare the counter-arguments to animal experimentation in the form of documents is apparent. Ouida puts forward this argument in her antivivisectionary book *The New Priesthood*, vital in this respect, as it urges the reading public to read and learn, rather than be delicate and avoid:

By their own words let . . . [vivisectionists] be judged: the records of their acts are published, and may be measured by all who can read, although doubtless much still remains hidden which takes place in the many secret places of their labours, and which they would be afraid to reveal to the public conscience, sluggard though that be.[67]

James Turner questions the efficacy of such a technique, claiming that

antivivisectionists had only the faintest notion of what scientists were actually about. Animal lovers who tried to expose the horrors of vivisection by citing chapter and verse from scientific journals (a favourite ploy) usually only exposed their own incomprehension . . . they invoked medical evidence obsolete for decades: 'a ridiculous fagot of antediluvian oracles' as William James put it.[68] They were forever finding themselves the butt of ridicule for their ignorance of the most basic physiological facts, such as the insensibility of the brain.[69]

There were, no doubt, weaknesses in the knowledge of antivivisectionary writers, as the famous altercation over the use of anaesthesia between Victor Horsley, one of the most hated animal experimenters, and Frances Power Cobbe suggests,[70] and it is also the case that much of the information gathered by anti-

---

[67] *Priesthood*, 19.
[68] [William James], 'Vivisection', *Nation*, 20 (1875), 128.
[69] Turner, *Reckoning with the Beast*, 106.
[70] See E. E. A. W.—One who attended the Church Congress Debate, 'A Sketch of the Church Congress Debate on Vivisection, October 6th, 1892', *Shafts*, 3 (1892), 12; and J. B. Lyons, *The Citizen Surgeon: A Biography of Sir Victor Horsley F.R.S., F.R.C.S., 1857–1916* (Peter Dawnay, 1966), 130 ff.

vivisectionists related to French vivisectional practice of the 1850s rather than pertaining directly to English practice in the 1870s and 1880s. Nevertheless, as I made clear in my discussion of Nordau's *Degeneration*, it was too easy for male experimental physiologists to write off female intervention as irrational and a symptom of derangement. As Craig Buettinger argues, by the early twentieth century women were being diagnosed as 'zoophil-psychotic' as a means of disarming their protest, and in this way the legitimate concerns of the antivivisection lobby were rendered worthless in a pseudo-scientific manner.[71] In the same way that Havelock Ellis claimed that criminals were able to commit brutal crimes because they had had a 'psychical analgesia' matching their (supposed) physical analgesia,[72] what could be termed the 'psychical hyperaesthesia' of antivivisectionists was pathologized and labelled irrational and therefore ignorable.

Antivivisectionary writers, aiming to throw open the doors of the laboratory that Collins kept so firmly closed, took up the language of observation of physiologists, and used the power of sight, and the ability to *show* something through language, to uncover what they perceived to be the iniquities of physiologists' laboratories.

Attack, using 'their own words' and their own actions, was the technique favoured by antivivisectionary writers to bring the condemnation of their readers down on the heads of physiologists. Collins, shivering on the shore rather than taking the plunge into unadulterated antivivisectionary rhetoric, claims for his book 'temperate advocacy to a good cause'.[73] He will not depict the horrors of the laboratory, but in *Heart and Science* we do see Benjulia portrayed in exactly the fashion that Ouida suggests. Collins uses various strategies to depict the physiologist through his own words, and the reader is guided through the logic of antivivisectionary thought through the workings of Benjulia's mind:

The Law which forbids you to dissect a living man, allows you to dissect a living dog. Why?

---

[71] 'Antivivisection and the Charge of Zoophil-Psychosis in the Early Twentieth Century', *Historian*, 55 (Winter 1992), 277–88.
[72] See Ch. 5, Sect. II. [73] *Heart*, vol. i, p. xii.

There was positively no answer to this.

Suppose he said, Because a dog is an animal? Could he, as a physiologist, deny that man is an animal too?

Suppose he said, Because a dog is the inferior creature in intellect? The obvious answer to this would be, But the lower order of savage, or the lower order of lunatic, compared with the dog, is the inferior creature in intellect; and, in these cases, the dog has, on its own showing, the better right to protection of the two.[74]

These are Benjulia's own words, but both the reader of the novel and Benjulia find 'the very questions with which his brother had puzzled him—followed by the conclusion at which he himself had arrived' in Morphew's letter proposing the subject matter of his book. Collins is fond of these layers of books within books—it is, after all, the technique of *The Moonstone* and *The Woman in White*—and it is in this way, to a large extent, that the didactic purpose of the book is worked out. This interrogative form of self-analysis allows the presentation of a logical argument, and the questions asked are, indeed, the questions found in almost any antivivisectionary tract written at the time.[75] This is given an added irony in that both the vivisectionist and the antivivisectionist are forced, by logic, to arrive at the same conclusion, although the vivisectionist is happy to ignore the conclusions that he reaches.

In Morphew's letter to Benjulia's brother, Lemuel, the reader is told that his antivivisectionary work will 'address itself to the general reader', and, to a certain extent, there is an affinity of stated aim in this respect between author and character. Collins clearly uses the synopsis of Morphew's book to give his novel a backbone of science ('I should also like to ask what proof there is that the effect of a poison on an animal may be trusted to inform us, with certainty, the effect of the same poison on man')[76] without having to be any more explicit than this. Morphew's proposed plan of procedure raises important issues:

'Briefly stated, you now have the method by which I propose to drag the scientific English Savage from his shelter behind the medical inter-

---

[74] *Heart*, vol. ii. 150.

[75] See e.g. Mona Caird, *Beyond the Pale. An Appeal on Behalf of the Victims of Vivisection* (Bijou Library, no. 8; William Reeves, [1897]), 37 ff for the exposition of very similar arguments.

[76] *Heart*, ii. 153.

ests of humanity, and to show him in his true character,—as plainly as the scientific Foreign Savage shows himself of his own accord; *He doesn't shrink behind false pretences. He doesn't add cant to cruelty. He boldly proclaims the truth:—I do it, because I like it!'*[77]

The openness of a character's or, indeed, a real physiologist's life is at stake here, as well as the related question of the openness of a text to the reader. *Heart and Science's* Mrs Gallilee, led astray by the observance of science, exemplifies the process of being dragged from shelter. Bursting in on her niece in a state of distress, her 'look and manner showed serious agitation, desperately suppressed. In certain places, the paint and powder on her face had cracked, and revealed the furrows and wrinkles beneath.'[78] What is suggested here is the true inner life of the character, and the falling away of the mask: in other terms, a looking beyond the outside walls of the laboratory to the horrors within. The face underneath will break through, for such people have been brutalized. The performative aspect of the scientist is picked up in the earlier quotation from Ouida, where she stresses the theatrical nature of the physiologist's art—'the scenic effect of the healer', 'the theatrical *mise-en-scène*', 'these are . . . put before the world'—in her choice of terms of description. The 'Foreign Savage *shows* himself' and is open to interpretation in a way that the English vivisectionist, such as Benjulia, who disingenuously claims that his studies are in chemistry, is not.[79] In terms of antivivisectionary rhetoric, to 'drag the scientific English Savage from his shelter' it was only

---

[77] Ibid. ii. 154–5.   [78] Ibid. iii. 44.

[79] The 'Foreign Savage' of whom Morphew is speaking is probably based on the Austrian histologist Emanuel Klein, lecturer in physiology at St Bartholomew's Hospital. Klein horrified the Commissioners at the First Royal Commission into vivisection in 1875 by his callous answers to their questions, and almost certainly affected the legislative outcome of the Commission. See Ryder, *Victims*, 198:

Question: When you say that you use (anaesthetics) for conveniences' sake, do you mean that you have no regard at all for the suffering of the animals?
Klein: No regard at all.
Question: You are prepared to establish that as a principle which you approve?
Klein: I think that with regard to an experimenter, a man who conducts special research and performs an experiment, he has no time, so to speak, for thinking what will the animal feel or suffer. His only purpose is to perform the experiment, to learn as much as possible and to do it as quickly as possible.
Question: Then for your purpose you disregard entirely the question of the suffering of the animal in performing a painful experiment?
Klein: I do.

necessary to bringing his words to the attention of the reading public.

This was, however, much more difficult than it at first appears. In the previous chapter I discussed the barriers to free expression of painful human experience, and the case of pain inflicted on animals was scarcely different. A similar metaphor to that of the impenetrability of the physiologist's laboratory is found in Lord Shaftesbury's view of social responsibility and interaction. Jo Manton describes the situation thus:

So sacred was the home and family life to Victorians, that Lord Shaftesbury, archpriest of humanitarians, considered cruelty or neglect there 'of so private, internal and domestic a character, as to be beyond the reach of legislation'.[80]

Shaftesbury's comment on the sanctity of the home is both telling and representative, for it shows that he recognized boundaries that should not be crossed, and that the crossing of them, however necessary in terms of the alleviation of pain, was to be regarded as a breach of decorum. That such boundaries *were* surmountable was the contention of antivivisectionists who found such concepts of decorum inimical to the openness needed to display physiologists in their own words. Such writers, therefore, had to establish a new concept of decorum, writing in a style decorous only in that it was fitting to its subject, but indecorous in that it accepted language and subject matter that could not be accommodated by the social proprieties of the novel form. If Collins's novel was 'temperate advocacy', many antivivisectionary tracts could only be seen as 'heated advocacy'. There is little doubt that such writers felt qualms at the strength of the language they felt forced to use, whilst simultaneously recognizing that this was unavoidable if they were to avoid the greater evil of silence. Thus it is that the usually verbally restrained clergyman Mark Thornhill comes to write the following defence of heated language in the cause of antivivisection:

But, when leaving the theories of vivisection, we contemplate the practices in which those theories have resulted; when, in the laboratories of the physiologists, we behold the torn flesh, the quivering muscles;

---

[80] *Mary Carpenter and the Children of the Streets* (Heinemann, 1976), 249.

when we see the hapless victims of experiment boiled alive, flayed alive, roasted alive, their brains seared with heated wires; when, in short, we see them subjected to every refinement of torment that modern science can devise, that modern appliances can effect; when we behold all this, then I think we may be permitted to abandon the quiet tone appropriate to philosophical discussion, and to denounce these horrors in language whose warmth shall be commensurate with our feelings.[81]

Thornhill carefully establishes the supremacy of his 'feelings' as set against the callousness of vivisectionists, and uses his own ability to sympathize to validate the immediacy of his own writing. This is very different from Collins's approach, where the nearest one gets to a physical representation of the animals' plight is the sounds of their death as they are killed by Benjulia just before he himself commits suicide.[82]

Following accepted antivivisectionary rhetoric, Thornhill's pamphlet *The Morality of Vivisection*, from which the above quotation comes, is parasitic upon another pamphlet—written by George Gore and published by the Association for the Advancement of Medicine by Research[83]—and shows the fallacies of vivisectionary thought by working through Gore's own argument. Gore contends that physiologists recognize the taboo nature of the work that they do, but suggests that the infliction of pain is necessary in order that knowledge is acquired:

Dr. Gore thus argues: The acquisition of all possible knowledge being a duty, so also must the performance of physiological experiments be a duty, inasmuch as it is only by the performance of these experiments that physiological knowledge can be acquired. To object to the performance of these experiments because they occasion pain, is to object to the fulfilment of a duty because it happens to be unpleasant; which is, assuredly, no valid ground for objection. It is, in fact, placing ourselves in opposition to the Creator, who has so constituted things that no knowledge can be acquired without labour, pain, or sacrifice of some kind.[84]

The unpleasantness of such claims becomes apparent when one realizes that a transference has been effected: the pain involved in the search for knowledge is no longer that of the searcher,

[81] *The Morality of Vivisection* (Hatchards, 1885), 19.
[82] *Heart*, iii. 287.
[83] *The Utility and Morality of Vivisection* (J. W. Kolckmann, 1884).
[84] Thornhill, *Morality*, 6.

but rather that of the animal subject to vivisection. As the Bishop of Manchester, who was directly involved in the anti-vivisection cause, put it: ' "the Law of Sacrifice is truly the law of life, but it is the sacrifice of *yourself* and not of another!" '[85] Such painful self-sacrifice was left, as Lisa Cartwright argues, to such as Elihu Thomson, an electrician who carried out tests on the safety of Rontgen rays in 1896 using his own body and at the cost of terrible sores on his fingers.[86]

That pain, or work, as Gore argues, are concomitants of the acquisition of knowledge, or, indeed, of any purposeful striving is, to a certain extent, a commonplace.[87] Negotiating the language of pain becomes problematic, as becomes apparent in Thornhill's seemingly offhand remark that any reader who may 'be at the pains to investigate the subject'[88] will discover the nature of the physiologist's art. The pains here are pains of effort or attention, but there is clearly also a less superficial meaning: readers of sensibility will find the act of reading such literature a painful experience since they will suffer the pain vicariously. This is an issue to which I shall return.

Mona Caird recognized the price of what seemed to her the needless infliction of pain as 'an unspeakably awful inheritance of suffering for the race that is guilty of these deeds of selfishness and violence'.[89] Deliberately inflicted pain gathers this inheritance, not in vague spiritual terms, but in the effects it has on those who practise it:

it is not difficult to see how the curse will descend and *has* descended; for the conscience must of necessity be blunted and hardened by our participation in these practices, either in body or in spirit—either with the instruments of torture in one's hands, or the decree of torture on one's lips,—even in the case where one has consented to remain igno-

---

[85] E. E. A. W., 'Sketch', 12.

[86] *Screening the Body: Tracing Medicine's Visual Culture* (Minneapolis and London: University of Minnesota Press, 1995) 126–7. See also Elston, 'Women and Anti-vivisection', 276: Anna Kingsford, a leading antivivisectionist, offered her own body for vivisection rather than have animals cut up.

[87] Such gain of knowledge at the expense of another's pain is exemplified in the following quotation: ' "Certainly, I killed forty or fifty people before I acquired my present dexterity with the knife; everyone buys experience." He, fortunate person, had bought it at the expense of other people instead of at his own.' Ouida, *Priesthood*, 67.

[88] *The Clergy and Vivisection* (Hatchards, [1883]), 15.

[89] *Sentimental View*, 23.

rant of the evil, in order to avoid the pain of knowing it, and for the sake of escaping the discomfort of possessing a conscience that urges us to action which we have no intention whatever of taking.[90]

The 'pain of knowing' represents another turnaround of the commonplace that the acquisition of knowledge and pain go hand in hand. It is just this that writers of antivivisection pamphlets had to contend with, and this that caused the breach of decorum in their writing. Thornhill's comment—'I will not sicken my readers with the details'[91]—lies at the heart of the matter.

It is this obstacle to the propagation of their message that antivivisectionists, such as Frances Power Cobbe, were seeking to break through by holding up the brute fact of pain in its most naked form to the reading public. Outrage at such cruelty, and fear at its expected consequences, allowed and, indeed, necessitated their mode of address. As a result, antivivisectionary texts were structured to show—much more clearly by demonstration than insinuation—the type of pain, and the ways that it was inflicted, on the animals that found themselves in the physiologist's laboratory.

The opening paragraphs of Cobbe's *Light in Dark Places*, following the technique at which Turner scoffs, present in some detail her rationale and plan of attack:

The following pages are intended to convey, in the briefest and simplest form, ocular illustration of the meaning of the much disputed word *Vivisection*. Some of the tools and some of the furniture of the physiological laboratory, various modes of fastening the victims, and a selection of instances of divers experiments, have been arranged with the view of affording the reader by a few moments' inspection a truer idea of the work of the 'torture-chambers of science' than can be obtained by the perusal of a vast quantity of letter-press description.

Every one of the illustrations is a reproduction, in most cases of reduced size, by photo-zincography, of the engravings and wood-cuts in the standard works of the most eminent physiologists. In every case the reference to the original work is given, and the perfect accuracy of the reproduction guaranteed. Nothing has been added and nothing has been taken away, except somewhat of the strength and vividness of the larger originals, which have been lost in the reproduction. Thus every illustration in this pamphlet may be taken with certainty to be a

[90] Ibid.   [91] *Clergy*, 23.

Vivisector's own picture of his own work, such as he himself has chosen to publish it.[92]

In these paragraphs the reader is presented with a clear demonstration of the way that Cobbe, and writers like her, went to work, turning observation, which was the stock in trade of the physiologist, against him. The emphasis on looking is clear: the reader is given 'ocular illustration'; photographs of pictures taken directly from physiological handbooks; and the wherewithal to 'inspect' the vivisectionist's laboratory.[93] The whole pamphlet is built on this principle—sources are cited, with publisher, page number, and date; pages of vivisectionary instruments and equipment are drawn and stand with prefatory description only, for it is assumed that they will speak for themselves:

I now proceed to show what are the simplest tools of vivisectors.

The following are taken (much reduced) from Bernard's last great work, the *Physiologie Opératoire*, Paris, Bailliere et Cie, 1879. They consist of various forms of scissors, pincers with claws, crooked pincers, scalpels, crooks with single and double claws, crochets with thread and weights attached, saws and knives. [see fig. 1][94]

This is the rhetoric of display, and its openness is a deliberate attack on the hidden nature of much physiological work. The title, *Light in Dark Places*, is carefully chosen and appropriate, for this is exactly the nature of the antivivisectionary enterprise: to bring to light abuses that go on, but which are not seen because carried on behind closed doors, at the same time putting this in a moral context of good and evil, light and dark.

---

[92] *Light in Dark Places* (Victoria Street Society for the Protection of Animals from Vivisection, [1883]), 3.

[93] Such practice was not restricted simply to the printing of such pictures in pamphlets. Westacott (*Century*, 132) suggests that such pictures were projected onto huge screens at antivivisection meetings. See also William Schupbach, 'A Select Iconography of Animal Experiment', in Rupke (ed.), *Vivisection in Historical Perspective*, 351–4. Schupbach describes the public use of Michael Joseph Holzapfl's painting *Der Vivisector*. The picture, painted in 1883, 'went on tour to Dresden, Hamburg, Düsseldorf and Vienna, provoking public discussion of the vivisection question at each venue. In the first half of 1885 it was exhibited in London . . . , where, however, its fame had run before it, for the anti-vivisection pressure group the Victoria Street Society had already sold many mounted photographs of the picture at 2s. 6d. each, adorned with explanatory verses', 351.

[94] *Light*, 7.

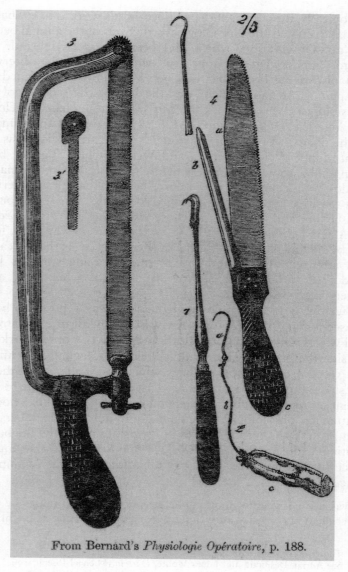

From Bernard's *Physiologie Opératoire*, p. 188.

FIG. I. Physiological Instruments

Source: Frances Power Cobbe, *Light in Dark Places* (Victoria Street Society for the Protection of Animals from Vivisection, [1883]), 7.

Ironically, the nature of the vivisectionist's work is to lay bare; to make obvious the physiological structures of the animal being cut up. Observation, which had been the stock in trade of doctors, underwent a change as it began to mean the observation of a living body that was being cut into: as I argued in Chapter 2, Alexander Bain was the last of the old school of physiologists who did not carry out vivisection. Henry Bigelow, the American surgeon who died in 1871, stands as an example of the doctor who taught his students ' "the art of diagnosis by sight alone" '.[95] Like Darwin and Weir Mitchell, Bigelow had been unable to witness surgery before the introduction of anaesthetics,[96] and, similarly, could never bear 'the needless fingering of a sensitive region'[97] as a means of diagnosis. His repulsion at vivisection, and its effects on those who practise it, is recorded by Albert Leffingwell: 'Watch the students at a vivisection. It is the blood and suffering, not the science, that rivets their breathless attention. If hospital service makes young students less tender of suffering, vivisection deadens their humanity and begets indifference to it.'[98]

Bigelow, working inside the profession, was exposed to both vivisection and the literature of vivisection in all its explicitness and was repulsed and horrified. Frances Power Cobbe, working outside the physiological establishment, was equally horrified, but recognized that those things which she, and many others, considered to be the infamies of vivisection did not come to the attention of the public for the simple reason that those books written by physiologists circulated only amongst members of that profession. Berdoe's claim in *Dying Scientifically*, the book written as the key to *St. Bernard's*,[99] that fiction is the strongest force of dissemination of unpalatable knowledge is of importance here:

It was not possible to draw public attention to these abuses by any other method than that of writing a story, as interesting as might be,

---

[95] Turner, *Reckoning with the Beast*, 81.
[96] See Adrian Desmond and James Moore, *Darwin* (Michael Joseph, 1991), 25.
[97] Turner, *Reckoning with the Beast*, 81.
[98] *The Vivisection Question* (New Haven: Tuttle, Morehouse & Taylor, 1901), 48–9.
[99] *Dying Scientifically* cites journal titles and page numbers of corroborative evidence for the claims made in *St. Bernard's*.

embracing all the facts. A treatise on hospital management would have fallen still-born from the press. The abuses complained of in St. Bernard's have been ventilated over and over again in the medical and lay papers, and nothing has been done to rectify them.[100]

Ouida demanded more of her readership in her summing up of *The New Priesthood* than just an engagement with antivivisectionary novels. Her aim was to make the reader face up to the facts of vivisection directly:

In conclusion, I would only implore any reader who may doubt the truth of my statements, or the logic of my deductions, to procure and study the published text of scientific transactions, in any and in all languages they may prefer: they will find confirmation of all which I have stated, and of all which I consider of so dire a menace to the nations; and they will also find details so hideous, of torture so horrible, that I have refrained from quoting the descriptions of them in these pages.[101]

Such writing demanded active involvement on the part of the reader: a direct confrontation of things thought too painful for public knowledge. Whilst a Sarah Grandian refusal to describe the horrors of vivisection may seem to be a bowing to convention, the realities of vivisection were, indeed, truly shocking, even to those within medical practice.[102] Ouida inherits the trope of sensibility—'details so hideous . . . that I have refrained from quoting . . . them'—but is left with the problem of trying to transcend it, to write the unwritable, and partly she does this by using, as she claims, the vivisector's own words.

Such physiological detail as that which Ouida baulked at, was, as I have suggested, openly portrayed by vivisectionists whose aim was to disseminate physiological knowledge. There is an openness in the following quotation, but it is an openness that operates within the closed world of 'scientific transactions'.

---

[100] Ibid. 5.   [101] *Priesthood*, 76.

[102] See George Hoggan's letter to the *Morning Post*, 2 Feb. 1875, cited in Ryder, *Victims*, 173. Hoggan had worked under Claude Bernard, but found the practice of vivisection both cruel and repulsive: 'We sacrificed daily from one to three dogs, besides rabbits and other animals, and after four years' experience I am of the opinion that not one of those experiments on animals was justified or necessary. The idea of the good of humanity was simply out of the question, and would be laughed at, the great aim being to keep up with, or get ahead of, one's contemporaries in science, even at the price of an incalculable amount of torture needlessly and iniquitously inflicted on the poor animals.'

As such its text was hidden from the public, and in bringing it forward, Cobbe renders it appalling by the comparison with the homely cookery book:

In the editor's Preface (Dr. Burdon-Sanderson) to the English *Handbook of the Physiological Laboratory*,[103] he says: 'This book is intended for beginners in physiological work. It is a book of methods ... designed for workers ...' The whole large volume is in the form of a receipt-book for cookery. 'Proceed as above' ... 'Divide the lingual nerve' ... 'For this purpose, (Asphyxia) a cannula must be fixed air-tight in the trachea,' ...—and so on through 558 pages.[104]

Cobbe's comparison with the recipe book is a clever one. Claude Bernard's own terminology is deliberately picked up—biological science 'is a superb and dazzlingly lighted hall which may be reached only by passing through ... [the] long and ghastly kitchen'[105] that is the vivisectionist's laboratory, and in this way the vivisectionist is again attacked with his own words. She also suggests both that the quotidian life of the vivisectionist is utterly different from that of the person of sensibility who abhors the infliction of pain, and that the way in which vivisectionists look and see is of a different nature. A comment by Mary M'Kinnel, published in *Shafts*—a journal serving as a forum for a great deal of antivivisectionary debate—is enlightening in this context, for she suggests that despite their keen powers of observation, the senses of physiologists have been trained, and tainted, by the nature of their work:

Man's moral and spiritual attributes are those which chiefly distinguish and raise him above the lower animal creation, those which ought also to give to the former their special claim upon his humanity, but if this part of his being is stunted in growth,[106] or becomes perverted, while still intellectually superior, he becomes less than human, a demon in short, and society is demoralised. Could we have any school in which the former can more surely graduate, than that of vivisection, where

---

[103] J. Burdon-Sanderson (ed.), *Handbook for the Physiological Laboratory*, 2 vols. (J. & A. Churchill, 1873).

[104] *Light*, 4.

[105] Claude Bernard, *An Introduction to the Study of Experimental Medicine*, trans. Henry Copley Greene (New York: Macmillan, 1927), 15. (*Introduction à l'étude de la médicine experimentale* (Paris: J. B. Baillière, 1865), 28: 'un salon superbe tout resplendissant de lumière, dans lequel on ne peut parvenir qu'en passant par une longue et affreuse cuisine'.)

[106] This metaphor is taken very literally in *Jekyll and Hyde* (see Ch. 5, Sect. II).

the student is taught to be deaf to the cry of torture, and blind to the dumb beseeching look of helpless creatures stretched there under the knife of the vivisector.[107]

It is for this reason, in the eyes of antivivisectionary writers— that they are 'blind to the dumb beseeching looks' of the animals on which they experiment—that experimental physiologists can write vivisection manuals in the form of recipe books without feeling vicarious pain. In Bain's words, the damaged bed of a fingernail, so long as it is not one's own, no longer has the power to excite revulsion, nor even to stir sympathy.

Cobbe is insistent on the necessity of recognizing the implications of various speeds of procedure. Her book is intended to convey information in 'the briefest and simplest form'—'a few moments' inspection' will render up the truth—and this accessible information is set against the 'perusal of a vast quantity of letter-press description', surely a leisurely or scholarly pursuit, and one which does not promote swift action. There is an immediate reason for such brevity on Cobbe's part as a review of *The New Priesthood* makes clear. M.S.S., the author of the review, suggests that all men and women should discover the truth behind vivisection, and discover it quickly: 'This we must do speedily, remembering that while we lose time, while we pause and consider, the agony of these our fellow creatures goes on without ceasing.'[108]

This is a practical and humanitarian reason for the emphasis on speed, but Cobbe is also using the emphasis on the decisive nature of quick action to undercut the procedures of physiologists. A comment of hers, again from *Light in Dark Places*, highlights the differences between the humane doctor and the devilish vivisectionist:

It is well also to bear in mind as differentiating the operations of Vivisection from those of ordinary surgery, that whereas the latter is always conducted with the utmost celerity, and the pride of the humane and skilful surgeon is to complete his task in a few minutes or seconds, the vivisector is expressly cautioned not to hurry himself, but to perform all his operations slowly, noting each incident which may arise, and each exhibition of suffering by the animal under the knife.[109]

---

[107] Mary M'Kinnel, 'Vivisection', *Shafts*, 2 (1894), 340–1.
[108] Review of *The New Priesthood* by Ouida, *Shafts*, 2 (1893), 173.
[109] *Light*, 4.

The terms here are loaded: 'ordinary' surgery is that done by medical practitioners, not vivisectionists, and the opposition between the 'task' of the surgeon and the primarily visual nature of the vivisectionist's diffuse business is marked. John Elliotson, who became Professor of Medicine at the University of London, described François Magendie—the founder, according to Claude Bernard, of experimental physiology—very much in these terms. Appalled at the savagery he witnessed in Magendie's laboratory at the Collège de France, Elliotson claimed that 'Dr Magendie, . . . cut living animals here and there with no definite object, but just to see what would happen.'[110] As with Benjulia, the fictional representative of such men as Magendie, the vivisectionist was trained to look, but he was expressly trained not to see pain, or the signs of pain.

There is a curious simplicity of conception in the belief of anti-vivisectionary writers that the reader who faced the pain of reading the works of physiologists would immediately see the infamy of the procedure, and act on this knowledge. Ouida did, however, expressly mention sympathetic pain amongst the reasons why the general public did not become acquainted with vivisectionary practice: 'It is this reluctance to suffer pain from hearing of it, which, yet more than either indifference or collusion, has enabled the practice to attain the continually increasing proportions that it has done in this century.'[111] There is clearly a problem here, however, and it is one raised in the review of *Heart and Science* in the *Academy*:

and here he [Collins] is not less successful than in *Man and Wife* in the difficult task of mixing art and argument. That he is wholly successful cannot be said, for *Heart and Science* will be found more entertaining than convincing, save by those who do not need to be convinced.[112]

That is, Wilkie Collins is preaching to the converted. There is, however, more at stake here. Antivivisectionists *are* more likely to read a novel written from an antivivisectionary perspective than those unconcerned with, or ignorant of, the practice, but those with the sensibility to feel the pain of laboratory animals

---

[110] Cited in Ryder, *Victims*, 170.   [111] *Priesthood*, 53.
[112] James Ashcroft Noble, review of *Heart and Science* by Wilkie Collins, *Academy*, 28 Apr. 1883, 290.

vicariously are also those who will find it too painful to read of their suffering. An article, published in *Shafts*, and written by Arthur Ebbels, raises just these questions of sensibility, taking a line directly opposed to most of those published in this journal. Ebbels contends that advocates of an antivivisectionary ethic are 'affected by a delicate sensibility' and should instead be 'listen[ing] to the calm but impartial voice of reason'.[113] This would persuade them that medical progress can only come through vivisection, and that therefore experimental physiology should be regarded in a positive light. Whilst admitting its necessity, however, they should also refrain from acquainting their 'susceptible minds' with such things:

it is perhaps fortunate for sensitive individuals that they are not compelled to steep their minds in the minute particulars of the cancer ward and the operation theatre. Perhaps, also, it would be as well if they abstained from harrowing their feelings into a condition of unreasonable strain by searching out the facts regarding vivisection.

It requires a strong and able mind to stand face to face with Nature in some of her more dreadful aspects, for which aspects, indeed, we are in no wise responsible, but which, nevertheless, some of us must face. Surely, it seems to me, these are scarcely the subjects with which tender and unprepared women should seek to interfere. I grant their repulsive character. But that does not absolve those of us who are strong enough from the necessity of grappling with the most repulsive and filthy details *for the good of mankind*. The moral evil falls upon those who, without compulsion and without preparation, seek out these matters. And the greatest moral evil they are made to suffer, by thus incontinently plunging into a terrible question, is the effectual blunting of their sense of truth, in consequence of the distortion of their moral perspective.[114]

Ebbels wrote to the pattern recognized by Mary Ann Elston as a directing principle in the debate over vivisection: 'Sentiment versus science; women versus men.' For Ebbels facts are not for the sensitive, and 'tender . . . women' are excluded by their natures from the painful responsibilities of scientific investigation.

Mary M'Kinnel, writing a refutation of this article in the same issue of *Shafts*, was quick to point out the fallacy of his claim,

[113] 'On Vivisection', *Shafts*, 3 (1895), 10.   [114] Ibid.

arguing that medicine and vivisection are by no means similar categories, though Ebbels deals with them as though they are interchangeable: the former deals with the world as it is and its agonies, whilst the latter creates those pains for its own (fruitless) observation. *Shafts* was an ill-chosen place for Ebbels to publish his paternalist attitudes: as M'Kinnel pointed out, women's sensibilities were not so tender that they could not face pain in hospitals and, indeed, work for its alleviation.

Ebbels used the language of the antivivisection debate, though turning it and changing its valence. 'Searching out the facts' and 'seek[ing] out . . . matters' are conceptualized as negative things. Wilkie Collins's claim that he will not 'open the door [of the laboratory] and invite you to look in' is an obvious physical corollary to Ebbels's own paternalistic restriction on the intellectual freedom of women. I have argued that Collins's closed door was, to some extent at least, a matter of decorum, but there was clearly more to it than this. Decorum may be seen as just a social convention, a pandering, however serious the intention might have been, to custom, but the laboratory wall—that which stopped the general public from finding out about the practices of vivisectionists—might more importantly be seen as a wall of sensibility, and the response to pain had a great deal to do with the constitution of such a wall. Those inside inflicted pain, but failed to feel it vicariously, whilst those outside were kept outside by their sympathetic apprehension of it. The requirement to face up to pain broadcast by antivivisectionists thus cut two ways: vivisectionists faced pain by becoming insensible and brutish, whereas antivivisectionists had to overcome the promptings of sensibility, and deal with the consequences. Ebbels wrote of 'moral evil', by which he meant a distortion of the 'truth' brought about by a misunderstanding of the ways of science, whereas Cobbe and others saw this 'moral evil' as the bluntening of sympathetic response.

IV. VIVISECTION AND BRUTALIZATION

It is this bluntening of perception, and the way that it was thought to be brought about, to which I now turn. Ouida realized the fictional possibilities of the problem she addressed, and that the nature of those whom she described lent itself easily to the portrayal of fictional villains. Not content to rely on the effectiveness of such fictional works as her own 1894 story *Toxin*, Ouida calls on the reader's imagination to bring forth such a beast as she describes, and then insists on his reality in the reader's world:

Think of a practical physiologist, rising every day and going to the same hideous employment with the morning light, keeping the tortured and mutilated creatures beside him week after week, month after month, refusing them even the comfort of a drop of water, if thirst will increase the 'interest' of his experiment; think of him, eating and drinking, jesting and love-making, filling his belly and indulging his desires, then returning to his laboratory to devise and execute fresh tortures, his hands steeped in blood, his eyes greedily watching the throes he stimulates; think of what his daily and yearly existence is, and then judge if he be fit to consort with men of gentle temper and decent habitudes, or if he and such as he, be fit to be trusted with the care of sick and suffering humanity. Let the general public try and realise what the hourly life of such a physiologist is, and it will no more trust its children to him, than to the mercies of the whirlpool or the flames of the fire.

Let the world realise that this man, as I have drawn him here, is no fictitious character, no creature of phantasy, no figure of imagination, but is a fact; that he, and such as he, exist in scores and hundreds and thousands; that they are working from year's end to year's end in all the cities and towns of the earth, in all the universities, in all the colleges, in all the hospitals, and in countless private laboratories where no ray of public light ever penetrates.[115]

This *ecce homo* treatment of the vivisectionist is similar in technique to Cobbe's description of the laboratory—readers are invited to look at the equipment that is used and to draw the obvious conclusion—but there is also a concomitant interest in antivivisection literature in what made the vivisectionist what he is. Ouida is very quick to pick up on the dangers of allowing what she sees as a child's natural cruelty to go unstopped.[116] She considered cruelty a progressive thing, such that once the first step had been taken, others would, of necessity, follow:

Nay, when will you do so much as remember that the coward who tortures an animal would murder a human being if he were not afraid

---

[115] *Priesthood*, 13–14.   [116] See ibid. 69.

of the gallows? When will you see that to teach the hand of a child to stretch out and smother the butterfly is to teach that hand, when a man's, to steal out and strangle an enemy?[117]

The issue here is not immediately that of pain, but the desire to inflict pain on animals is clearly seen as the initial stage in cruelty to humans and, eventually, murder.

This process of brutalization, based on the desire to inflict pain, and the concomitant insensibility to that pain, is worked through in Stevenson's *Strange Case of Dr. Jekyll and Mr. Hyde*, first published in 1886, concurrent with much antivivisection literature. As Richard Dury persuasively argues in his introduction to the *Annotated Dr Jekyll and Mr Hyde*, despite the story's seemingly allegorical nature the text has no simple basic meaning. Keys to the allegory are variously offered: 'Hyde's violence . . . [is] a reflection of Stevenson's own frustration with language';[118] the book reflects the nature of human society as Jekyll both revels in and represses Hyde's violence;[119] the book suggests the dangers of masturbation and of homosexuality;[120] Jekyll is a Promethean transgressor;[121] Hyde represents a kick-back to the savage and the evolutionarily stunted ape. All such readings may be substantiated, but none seems all-embracing. The story courts diverse readings, and as such, a reading of the book in terms of the debate over vivisection does not seem inappropriate. Indeed, that *Jekyll and Hyde* may be read in the context of antivivisection literature seems likely from internal evidence—I shall go on to discuss the fictional tropes of this genre—but it is also clear from Stevenson's essay on 'The Character of Dogs', written in 1883,[122] and from a note in Mona Caird's pamphlet *Beyond the Pale*, that Stevenson was involved in the antivivisection enterprise: his 'passionate love of animals and detestation of vivisection is well known'.[123]

[117] Quoted in Eileen Bigland, *Ouida: The Passionate Victorian* (Jarrolds, 1950) 69.
[118] *The Annotated Dr Jekyll and Mr Hyde*, ed. Richard Dury (Milan: Guerini, 1993), 26.
[119] Ibid. 28.
[120] Elaine Showalter, *Sexual Anarchy: Gender and Culture at the* Fin de Siècle (1990; Virago, 1992), 105–26.
[121] *Annotated Dr Jekyll*, ed. Dury, 28.
[122] Robert Louis Stevenson, 'The Character of Dogs', in *The Lantern-Bearers and Other Essays*, ed. Jeremy Treglown (Chatto and Windus, 1988), 183–9.
[123] *Beyond the Pale*, 42 n.

Commentators have been in the habit of ignoring the changing relationship between Jekyll and Hyde, measured by Hyde's increasing strength and ability to determine action as the story progresses. Henry James, writing two years after the publication of Stevenson's story, was disappointed in the process of transformation between the two central characters—what he saw as 'the business of the powders . . . too explicit and explanatory'[124] to be convincing. Concentrating on the process of transformation rather than its end result provides a way of re-situating Stevenson's novella in terms of its genre so that the story can usefully be read in relation to contemporaneous anti-vivisectionary novels and short stories.

Whilst Jekyll is not, of course, explicitly presented as a vivisectionist, I shall establish the ways in which the language of *Jekyll and Hyde* echoes that of the vivisection debate and deals with the issue of cruelty and the degradation of character, as well as hinting at the cruelties of vivisection/dissection. This latter consists in the inordinate amount of stress laid on the previous owner of Jekyll's house—a Dr Denham who, having nothing to do in the furtherance of the plot, used the cabinet as a dissecting room[125]—and the exterior appearance of the laboratory:

It was late in the afternoon, when Mr. Utterson found his way to Dr. Jekyll's door, where he was at once admitted by Poole, and carried down by the kitchen offices and across a yard which had once been a garden, to the building which was indifferently known as the laboratory or the dissecting rooms. The doctor had bought the house from the heirs of a celebrated surgeon; and his own tastes being rather chemical than anatomical, had changed the destination of the block at the bottom of the garden. It was the first time that the lawyer had been received in that part of his friend's quarters; and he eyed the dingy windowless structure with curiosity, and gazed round with a distasteful sense of strangeness as he crossed the theatre.[126]

Jekyll's house was explicitly based on Victor Horsley's house in Queen's Square, and, with its strange annexe and back door

---

[124] Henry James, 'Robert Louis Stevenson' (1887), in *The House of Fiction: Essays on the Novel by Henry James*, ed. Leon Edel (Rupert Hart-Davis, 1957), 114–38: 136.
[125] Robert Louis Stevenson, *Strange Case of Dr. Jekyll and Mr. Hyde* (Longmans, Green 1886), see pp. 27, 63, 95.   [126] Ibid. 44.

through which Hyde enters the laboratory, matches it point for point.[127] Horsley was probably the most notorious vivisectionist of his day, and his house was occupied by a line of vivisectionists before him. There is no doubt that Stevenson knew this as he chose the house as his model.[128]

Benjulia, in *Heart and Science*, hides his physiological experiments under the guise of chemistry, and it is chemistry from which Jekyll derives his interest. It is clearly important to the plot that Jekyll is a chemist rather than a physiologist, for this allows him to effect the change that turned him into Hyde, but descriptive aspects of the book are, nevertheless, fed into by conventional antivivisection descriptions of physiologists. The description of Benjulia's windowless laboratory and its blasted surroundings is very similar to that of Jekyll's house:

There, in the middle of a barren little field, he saw Benjulia's house—a hideous square building of yellow brick, with a slate roof. A low wall surrounded the place, having another iron gate at the entrance. The enclosure within was as barren as the field without: not even an attempt at flower-garden or kitchen-garden was visible. At a distance of some two hundred yards from the house stood a second and smaller building, with a skylight in the roof, which Ovid recognised (from description) as the famous laboratory. Behind it was the hedge which parted Benjulia's morsel of land from the land of his neighbour. Here, the trees rose again, and the fields beyond were cultivated. No dwellings, and no living creatures appeared. So near to London—and yet, in its loneliness, so far away—there was something unnatural in the solitude of the place.[129]

This emphasis on the windowless laboratory is the first of three things that define the vivisectionist in antivivisectionary fiction; allied to this is that he is found with spots of blood on his hands, and that he commits suicide, usually after committing murder. These three things can be said of Benjulia, the vivisectionist in *Heart and Science*; of the aptly named Professor Scalpelinem, who appears in a short story called 'Ratto', published in *Shafts*;[130] and of Professor Crowe, the murderous vivisectionist

---

[127] For a detailed description of Horsley's house, with public rooms at the front, and private, skylighted 'workshop' at the rear, see Stephen Paget, *Sir Victor Horsley: A Study of his Life and Work* (Constable, 1919), 142.

[128] See Lyons, *Citizen Surgeon*, 72.   [129] Collins, *Heart*, i. 261.

[130] Amos Waters, '"Ratto." A Photograph', *Shafts*, 2 (1894), 315–18, 331–4.

in *St Bernard's*; and may be said to form the template for the vivisectionist in most literary portrayals.

The laboratory with no windows, already mentioned in terms of *Jekyll and Hyde*, is conventional for obvious reasons: no vivisectionist wanted the sun shining into his laboratory and heating up his experimental animals, but it is also the case that he did not want anyone to look in and discover the nature of his work.[131] It is, however, also possible to read this structural necessity in a metaphorical manner, as many antivivisection writers chose to do. The title of Frances Power Cobbe's pamphlet *Light in Dark Places* suggests just such a metaphorical meaning and the whole pamphlet is, as already shown, structured to bring vivisectionary abuses into the public domain.

Mona Caird's suggestion of the difficulty of gaining access to the laboratory may be seen in her quotation from Amos Waters's piece in the *Agnostic Journal*:

It is extremely difficult—I believe almost impossible—for any person not favourable to the practice of vivisection to obtain admission into a physiological laboratory, when the really important experiments are going on. Mr. Amos Waters (*Agnostic Journal*, June 24, 1892), records an instance when he obtained admission, but was bound on his honour not to describe the operations that took place (itself rather a significant fact); therefore he can give no details; he can only tell us that 'he came out into the sunshine of the outer world sickened, shocked, and revolted beyond measure; the twittering of free and happy birds seemed to thrill the air with tremulous agony, and such agony so miserably meaningless and inexpressibly pitiful' was that he had left behind.[132]

The barren, unsustaining environs of the laboratory have their basis in such descriptions as Waters gives, the sunlight and birdsong of the outside world being the antithesis of the horrors of the laboratory.

In keeping with this, one of the major objections to vivisection was that better sanitation would have more effect on public health than any amount of vivisectionary knowledge. As Elsworth, the crusading, antivivisectionary doctor in *St. Bernard's*, puts it:

[131] See [Frances Power Cobbe], *Science in Excelsis* (Williams and Norgate, 1875), 7.
[132] *Beyond the Pale*, 5.

cold water and fresh air, wholesome food and temperance, want few aids from medicine for the ills of man. The wiser the physician the fewer the drugs, and by the length of your doctor's prescription you may estimate the shallowness of his pretence to wisdom.[133]

Just as light should be let in to dark places, so too should fresh air, which would blow away all vestiges of disease. The garrisoned form of the laboratory became a metaphor for the perversity of the physiologists' method of attacking disease. It is no surprise in this context, then, that Jekyll in the early stages of his experiments is described as 'shut up again in the cabinet',[134] and when trying to fight temptation, 'He was busy, he was much in the open air, he did good.'[135] As Alan Sandison points out, though in a very different context, the strange term 'cabinet' which Jekyll uses to describe his private room in the laboratory, can also mean 'the den of the beast'[136]—a significant detail in the vivisectional subtext of this story that is being uncovered here.

The second thing that defined the vivisectionist in antivivisection fiction is that he is portrayed with spots of blood on his hands which he makes no attempt either to wash off or hide. When Benjulia meets his brother in *Heart and Science*:

The spots of blood which Ovid had once seen on Benjulia's stick, were on his hands now. With unruffled composure he looked at the horrid stains, silently telling their tale of torture.

'What's the use of washing my hands, he asked, 'when I am going back to my work?'[137]

This is insensibility in one of its most blatant forms, but it is also part of a long tradition, stretching from Pontius Pilate to Lady Macbeth, and is, of course, also linked in with the saying 'to be caught red handed'. Jekyll's hands are marked out, but in a slightly different way as his predilections are overtly chemical rather than physiological. The signs of his degradation are seen not in blood-spattered hands, but in their changed appearance as he is transformed into Hyde.

---

[133] [Berdoe] *St. Bernard's*, 301.   [134] *Jekyll and Hyde*, 61.
[135] Ibid. 55.
[136] *Robert Louis Stevenson and the Appearance of Modernism* (Basingstoke and London: Macmillan, 1996), 247.
[137] Collins, *Heart*, ii. 142.

The third defining mark of the vivisectionist—suicide after murder—is clearly the case with Jekyll who, in the form of Hyde, murders Sir Danvers Carew, and then kills himself.

Such conventional similarities would be superficial, though clear, were it not for the stress laid on Hyde's desire to inflict pain.[138] He is conveyed as cruel in all aspects, but in particular as 'lusting to inflict pain'[139] and 'drinking pleasure with bestial avidity from any degree of torture to another'.[140] The terminology describing his depravity is exactly that of descriptions of callous vivisectionists in antivivisection literature: he has a 'complete moral insensibility and insensate readiness to evil',[141] and an inability to feel with his victims. Hyde's actions, when unleashed after two months' abstinence on Jekyll's part, are those of 'insensate cruelty', whilst the maid, who sees the attack on Sir Danvers Carew, typifies an expected female approach as she faints 'At the horror of these sights and sounds'.[142]

The links between Jekyll and Hyde, and the interplay between them, are of the utmost importance here. Hyde is the 'projection' of Jekyll's cruel side, whereas Jekyll, throughout, retains a mixture of good and evil—'that incongruous compound'[143]—a condition seen in the novel as the 'normal' state of humanity, though perhaps more pronounced in Jekyll than in most.

Of particular interest in respect to the brutalizing effects of inflicting pain, is the way that once Hyde is loosed through

---

[138] For Hyde's grip on popular imagination, as well as the clustering of sets of words around vivisectional and murderous cruelty, see the series of articles run in the *Pall Mall Gazette* concurrent with the Whitechapel murders of 1888. 'There certainly seems to be a tolerably realistic impersonification of Mr. Hyde at large in Whitechapel. The Savage of Civilization whom we are raising by the hundred thousand in our slums is quite as capable of bathing his hands in blood as any Sioux who ever scalped a foe' ('Another Murder and More to Follow', 8 Sept. 1888, 1). Savagery is seen to be as rampant in darkest England as it is in darkest Africa, or among any 'savage' group, a claim that was by no means unique to the *Pall Mall Gazette*. What is interesting about these articles, though, is their echoing of the terms of debate over vivisection: a possible clue to the murderer's identity comes from a Mrs Fiddymont, who sees 'a man whose rough appearance frightened her', and who has 'blood spots on the back of his right hand' ('A Possible Clue', 10 Sept. 1888, 7); the murders are carried out in 'parts of our great capital city . . . hidden from the light of day, where men are brutalized, [and] women are demonized' ('How the Poor Live', 12 Sept. 1888, 7); and the answer must come from 'pitying hearts' ('What is Wanted?', 12 Sept. 1888, 7). The language of *Jekyll and Hyde*, of the vivisection debate, and of public outrage at the Whitechapel murders here coalesces.

[139] Stevenson, *Jekyll and Hyde*, 134.

[140] Ibid. 118.   [141] Ibid. 126.   [142] Ibid. 37.   [143] Ibid. 116.

chemical agency, his nature is dependent upon Jekyll's moral feelings, though with an all-important feedback loop. Jekyll becomes inured to Hyde's brutality, and begins to enjoy his 'vicarious depravity',[144] and this deadening of sensibility allows the increase of stature—both physically and in a moral sphere—of Hyde. Jekyll protests in the early stages of experimentation that 'the moment I choose, I can be rid of Mr. Hyde',[145] or, rather more desperately, 'I swear to God I will never set eyes on him again.'[146] This proves not to be the case. The degradation of Jekyll's better self had begun, and he cannot simply give up the indulgence of Hyde and his antisocial behaviour. Hyde eventually is no longer dependent on Jekyll, but is rather the leading element in the protagonist's dual character—a fact reflected in the physical representation of Hyde. Initially, this was not the case, as Jekyll claims:

> The evil side of my nature, to which I had now transferred the stamping efficacy, was less robust and less developed than the good which I had just deposed. Again, in the course of my life, which had been, after all, nine tenths a life of effort, virtue and control, it had been much less exercised and much less exhausted. And hence, as I think, it came about that Edward Hyde was so much smaller, slighter and younger than Henry Jekyll.[147]

It is when this 'life of effort, virtue and control' is thrown over, that Hyde comes dangerously to the fore, growing in stature and in strength:

> That part of me which I had the power of projecting, had lately been much exercised and nourished; it had seemed to me of late as though the body of Edward Hyde had grown in stature, as though (when I wore that form) I were conscious of a more generous tide of blood; and I began to spy a danger that, if this were much prolonged, the balance of my nature might be permanently overthrown, the power of voluntary change be forfeited, and the character of Edward Hyde become irrevocably mine.[148]

This is exactly what happens. The 'most racking pains'[149] which accompanied the transformation between alter egos marking the

---

[144] Stevenson, *Jekyll and Hyde*, 118.   [145] Ibid. 33.   [146] Ibid. 46.
[147] Ibid. 113.   [148] Ibid. 123.
[149] Ibid. 111. See also the pains of transformation that afflict Griffin as he becomes invisible, in H. G. Wells, *The Invisible Man: A Grotesque Romance* (C.

early stages of experimentation, disappear and the change occurs 'in the confidence of slumber'.[150] Jekyll sleeps and without his consent or active will his body takes on Hyde's form. The moral is made plain when Jekyll claims: 'my virtue slumbered; my evil, kept awake by ambition, was alert and swift to seize the occasion'.[151]

Falling asleep and the state of sleeping take on similar overtones to those of looking or failing to look. Insensibility has been shown to be allied to an anaesthetized state, and the inability to feel pain finds its corollary in sleep. This is an old trope, but it is one that antivivisectionary writers liked to employ. M. S. S., in her review of *The New Priesthood*, urged women to action in just these terms:

Mothers! try to imagine the awful moral debasement, your sons must undergo, practising day by day such hellish rites as these;—men and boys in all classes, scientists and underlings, 'who have under their eyes year by year the spectacle of unceasing, and wholly unpitied, animal agony.'[152] Then the human subjects in hospitals—but the pen cannot describe the horrors many of which are hidden away in secret places. 'Would' says Ouida 'the people could awake to the uses which they, and the beasts whom they pity not, are alike put by the men of science.'[153]

Yes we echo the wish, would that they would wake up, and act; would that women especially, would wake up and act.[154]

The state of moral sleep—the insensibility to pain, for whatever reason—afflicts both the vivisectionist and the general public who refuse to face up to such behaviour and in this way abnegate their responsibility. A suitable means of opposing vivisection open to the woman confined to a limited sphere of action, and waking up to its horrors, is suggested by M. S. S.

Arthur Pearson, 1897), 162: '"But it was all horrible. I had not expected the suffering. A night of racking anguish, sickness, and fainting. I set my teeth, though my skin was presently afire, all my body afire, but I lay there like grim death. I understood now how it was the cat had howled until I chloroformed it . . . There were times when I sobbed, and groaned and talked. But I stuck to it . . . I became insensible, and woke languid in the darkness."' Passing through pain to the insensibility that renders the protagonist incapable of feeling vicarious pain and allows murder is the turning point in the plot of both *Jekyll and Hyde* and *The Invisible Man*.

[150] *Jekyll and Hyde*, 138.   [151] Ibid. 115.   [152] Ouida, *Priesthood*, 16.
[153] Ibid. 18.   [154] M. S. S., Review, 173.

at the end of her review: 'One very simple thing could be done by all women—*Ostracise from your society, from your sick room, every man who practises or encourages vivisection.*'[155] The act is, indeed, simple, but it attacks the 'dead apathetic indifference towards pain, which is seen and not felt'[156] that Ouida castigates. M. S. S. was not alone in thinking that such an approach was the only viable way of containing the vivisectional urge in men. George Bernard Shaw makes Cashel Byron, his prizefighting hero, outraged that a vivisectionist—a Frenchman who stuck 'a rat full of nails to see how much pain a rat could stand'[157]—is admitted to soirées at the home of Lydia Carew, rather than Byron himself. Non-fictional versions of direct action, or rather the desire for it, may be seen in the castigation of Baroness Burdett Coutts, one of the most influential, and certainly one of the wealthiest, antivivisectionists, who, despite her convictions, invited eminent experimental physiologists to attend a garden party held at her house.[158]

There is a very visual re-enactment in *Jekyll and Hyde* of Ouida's claim that the hand of a child which smothers a butterfly will become the hand of the murderer. Jekyll, waking from a transformative sleep, looks down at his hand:

I was still so engaged when, in one of my more wakeful moments, my eye fell upon my hand. Now the hand of Henry Jekyll . . . was professional in shape and size: it was large, firm, white and comely. But the hand which I now saw, clearly enough, in the yellow light of a mid-London morning, lying half shut on the bed clothes, was lean, corded, knuckly, of a dusky pallor and thickly shaded with a swart growth of hair. It was the hand of Edward Hyde.[159]

This is, of course, fictional, and picks up the conventions of the antivivisection novel, but Stevenson's point is that such brutalization is an everyday thing: 'Strange as my circumstances were, the terms of this debate are as old and commonplace as man; much the same inducements and alarms cast the die for any tempted and trembling sinner.'[160]

---

[155] M. S. S., Review, 173.   [156] Ouida, *Priesthood*, 69.

[157] *Cashel Byron's Profession. A Novel* (Modern Press, 1886), 96.

[158] Nicolaas Rupke, 'Introduction', in id. (ed.), *Vivisection in Historical Perspective*, 5.

[159] *Jekyll and Hyde*, 120–1.   [160] Ibid. 125.

This is important, and it is noticeable that when Jekyll succumbs to taking the phosphate that effects transformation, he says of the emergence of Hyde: 'My devil had been long caged, he came out roaring.'[161] This is the language of the preamble to the Church of England's compline service—'the devil in the shape of a roaring lion walketh about, seeking whom he may devour'—and this overtly places Jekyll's behaviour in the realms of quotidian social intercourse, rather than in the realms of fantasy. His accommodation of Hyde's behaviour, and enjoyment of it, takes its toll on his character as the two disparate forms of 'aura and effulgence of certain of the powers that made up [his] spirit'[162] begin to merge, and this is seen very clearly in the ease of transformation between the two states in the later stages of the book. The ability and, indeed, the desire to inflict pain on another that is the mark of Hyde have become a part of Jekyll as well, and it is for this reason that Jekyll no longer feels the shock and pain of transformation—he has lost the ability to feel the pain of others sympathetically, and no real transformation of character is taking place. What the reference to the Prayer Book, and the fact that Jekyll's final fall occurs when he turns to vice in his own person rather than that of Hyde, tells the reader is that Jekyll's behaviour may be seen as a metaphor for a common human condition. Degradation of character is a necessary consequence of a lost capacity to feel the pain of a suffering sentient creature vicariously, and once this brutalization has taken place there is no return. I am not suggesting that Stevenson's short story is, in any directly representational way, an antivivisection novel. Stevenson deliberately establishes a framework that allows the story to be open to interpretation, but he also uses the paraphernalia of the prevalent genre of the antivivisection novel to suggest the process of brutalization and its necessary outcome, murder. This is not a case of poorly conceived transformation, as Henry James suggests, but rather one which makes plain the contaminating danger of the infliction of pain. It is no surprise, in this context, that as Poole breaks down the door to the inner sanctum of the story's displaced vivisectionist, 'A dismal screech, as of mere animal terror, rang from the cabinet',[163] and there lies revealed

---

[161] Ibid. 126.   [162] Ibid. 110.   [163] Ibid. 82–3.

on the floor of the laboratory a figure that antivivisectionary fiction could hardly bring itself to describe: 'a body ... sorely contorted and still twitching'.[164]

George Gissing, writing *The Nether World* three years after *Jekyll and Hyde* was published, employs the same model of degeneration through the lust to inflict pain as Stevenson, and, also in a similar vein, envisages the possession of one body by another. The formerly jovial Bob Hewett is brought to conscious cruelty by his association with the vicious Clem Peckover: 'Bob would not have come to this pass—at all events not so soon— if he had been left to the dictates of his own nature; he was infected by the savagery of the woman who had taken possession of him. Her lust of cruelty crept upon him like a disease.'[165] Clem takes on the role of a savage Hyde, leading Bob deeper and deeper into degradation, until he too can no longer keep himself from violence. Pennyloaf, his luckless wife, ends up bearing the brunt of his aggression:

he leapt up and sprang on her, seized her brutally by the shoulders and flung her with all his force against the nearest wall ... With his clenched fist he dealt blow after blow at the half-prostrate woman, speaking no word, but uttering a strange sound, such as might come from some infuriate animal.[166]

The terms are very similar to those of Stevenson's story—Hyde's first attack had been carried out 'with ape-like fury ... trampling his victim under foot, and hailing down a storm of blows, under which the bones were audibly shattered'[167]—but Gissing brings the contaminating effects of such lust for pain into the working-class home.

A fear of the contaminating effects of the infliction of pain formed the core of antivivisectionary rhetoric. The terms of description are different from those of *Jekyll and Hyde*, for while Stevenson's short story worked on popular fears about the dangers of science, Ouida expressed these fears differently:

The seizure and transport of the animals, the consignment of them, first to their cages then to the holders; the capture and fixture of them in such positions as are desired, the preparation of the ovens, caul-

---

[164] *Jekyll and Hyde*, 83.   [165] *Nether World*, iii. 186.
[166] Ibid. 187–8.   [167] *Jekyll and Hyde*, 37.

drons, electrical or atmospherical machines, or other methods of torture, the cleansing and the preparation of the apparatus and of the floors and tables defiled by blood and pus, the scourging or burning of the creatures in whom portions of the brain or nerves have previously been destroyed to see if consciousness will return, all these offices are of course performed by a number of youths and men who are paid for the work, and who, year after year, have under their eyes the spectacle of unceasing, and wholly unpitied, animal agony. These men, who are of the class which gives domestics, porters, labourers, gardeners, and the like, must become entirely brutalised and hardened to such sufferings. They take from the laboratories into their homes and into the streets its teachings of a callous indifference to, and malignant diversion in, the anguish of the helpless. This result is inevitable.[168]

Ouida's language is much more explicit than that of Stevenson, or Collins, and for her vivisection was such a danger because the ability, and the desire, to inflict pain had far-reaching social implications. Such desire is almost invariably described in terms of the vivisectionist's progression through various forms of life—from the frog, through the cat and dog, and on, inevitably, to human life, in the form of the disabled, criminals, and the poor:

If the arguments of the priesthood [vivisectionists] be only followed out to their due and logical sequence, tens of thousands of men should be stretched on the torture-table beside the dog and the horse, and should be sacrificed without hesitation in the pursuit of knowledge. Indeed it would be more practical to sacrifice the idiot, the cripple, the mute, the sufferer from cutaneous or cerebral affections than to sacrifice the healthy, sound, and useful animal. Claude Bernard, Schiff,[169] and many other physiologists have candidly said that human subjects are absolutely necessary to the perfecting of science: who can doubt that in a few years' time they will be openly and successfully demanded and conceded?[170]

There are two different strands to this fear of human vivisection, and the first of them is made explicit here: man provides the best source of information about man, and if vivisection is seen as the search for knowledge and understanding of the

---

[168] *Priesthood*, 16.
[169] Moritz Schiff became Professor of Physiology at the Istituto di Studi Superiori in Florence in 1863.
[170] Ouida, *Priesthood*, 24.

human form, then the bodies of humans are undoubtedly the best source of information. The second fear is related to this: that the logic of such thinking might prove to be stronger than the 'sentimental' notions put forward to counter such logic. For antivivisectionists, such notions were particularly in danger since the humanity of physiologists suffered from the constant attrition caused by the deliberate infliction of pain. Mark Thornhill recognized this possibility, writing a pamphlet that denounced the practice of human vivisection, bringing to light abuses that were taking place largely in continental Europe.[171] As Mary Ann Elston argues, there was a very thin line between legitimate surgery and what might be described as vivisection:

The difficult and dangerous operation of ovariotomy divided doctors as much as lay commentators in the 1870s and 1880s . . . The death rates from ovariotomy were initially so high as to warrant the charge from within the profession, as well as from outside, that it was an experiment for the benefit of the surgeon not the woman.[172]

Vivisection was thought to make such abuses possible in two different, though related, ways: experimental physiologists got used to cutting up living bodies in their experiments on animals and recognized the limitation of an animal model in the resolution of human pathology; and, more important, were so brutalized in the process, that their inhibitions were removed to such an extent that a human subject, rather than an animal one, provided no additional barriers.

St. Bernard's deals with this fear explicitly, for in it Berdoe suggests the process of degradation of character that the doctor undergoes during his training, which allows him to see patients simply as material upon which he works:

[Mr Wilson] had learned how to crush out all feelings of pity that interfered with his 'work' long ago in the physiological room. He was tender, kind, and a lover of the lower animals when he began his course there, when he first obeyed the order of his teacher to slice off a piece of a living frog's eye and rub lunar caustic on the injured organ. He shuddered when the professor said: 'It won't be nice for the frog, but it will be useful to you!' But he shuddered less next time; and when he

---

[171] *Experiments*. This was read as an address at the Annual meeting of the Dover Branch of the East Kent Anti-Vivisection Society, held on 1 May 1889.
[172] Elston, 'Women and Anti-vivisection', 278.

had conquered his aversion to the torture of living dogs which licked his hands before he began, it was not difficult to do any work in the operating theatre on human beings which science might demand ... He had become so case-hardened against feeling pain in others that he could only attribute to weakness and incompetence that hesitation to cause a single unnecessary pang in any sentient being which is the unvarying qualification of all the greatest and noblest men and women of whom we know anything.[173]

The emphasis is on the operator rather than the animal, and the effects on him and his humanity rather than on the suffering he both causes and witnesses. The language Berdoe uses is strongly condemnatory—pity *interferes* with work, and the shuddering, representative of a sensibility that should be the concomitant of the recognition of pain in another, is progressively extinguished, until Wilson has reached the point of no return, and because of this is capable of murder.

The process of brutalization, and the blunting of the ability to feel, is replicated endlessly in antivivisection literature. In a closing discussion of H. G. Wells's story *The Island of Doctor Moreau*, I shall examine the ways in which Wells recognized, and pushed, the conventions of the antivivisection novel to the point of distortion. The book was almost universally disliked by its reviewers, generally on the grounds of indecency, though it was also attacked for being blasphemous—a stance Wells himself saw as a truer reading of his story. I shall be looking both at Wells's story itself and at some of its reviews, as a way of summing up the claims and counter-claims that took form in the debate over vivisection.

The plot of *The Island of Doctor Moreau* involves a vivisectionist whose goal is to mould animals in such a way that they take on human forms and attributes, and become, in fact, human through a process involving skin grafts, blood transfusion, hypnotism, and major surgery. To some extent he succeeds in his aim, and manufactures creatures who pass, for some time, as humans until the 'stubborn beast flesh'[174] resumes supremacy, and they revert to animals again. By deliberately blurring the

---

[173] *St. Bernard's*, 154–6.
[174] *The Island of Doctor Moreau* (William Heinemann, 1896), 119. Text reads 'stubborn beast flash'.

boundaries between human and animal, Wells effectively calls on the contemporary concerns of escalation to human vivisection, as well as recalling arguments over the pressing question of whether humans were wholly distinct from animals.

Dr Moreau fits easily into the conventional portrayal of the vivisectionist, though in a highly exaggerated manner. Not only are his hands covered in blood, but the whole book is blood-spattered. As Chalmers Mitchell, who reviewed the book for the *Saturday Review*, comments:

> It is blood that Mr. Wells insists upon forcing on us; blood in the sink 'brown and red,' on the floor, on the hands of the operators, on the bandages that swathe the creatures or that they have left hanging on the bushes—physically disgusting details inevitable in the most conservative surgery; but still more unworthy of restrained art.[175]

There is in this quotation the essence of the complaints that were levelled against *The Island of Doctor Moreau*, and I shall come to these shortly, but it is clear that Moreau, in keeping with the three requirements for a vivisectionist, is presented as a man with hands 'smeared red'.[176] Similarly he is a man who works in a laboratory hidden from public scrutiny, not just in a laboratory without windows, but one set up on a secluded island far from trade routes and investigative journalists, and designated 'a kind of Bluebeard's Chamber'[177] by Moreau himself. The last qualification, as detailed in the discussion of *Jekyll and Hyde*, for being a literary vivisectionist, is death by suicide, and although this is not directly the case for Wells's protagonist, he certainly meets his death at the hands of his own creature.

Chalmers Mitchell, himself a zoologist who advocated physiological techniques (and, indeed, a colleague of Wells on the *Saturday Review*), picks up on Wells's exploitation of the conventions of the antivivisection novel. Mitchell suggests that 'Dr. Moreau himself is a *cliché* from the pages of an anti-vivisection pamphlet. He has been hounded out of London because a flayed dog (you hear the shuddering ladies handing over their guineas) has been liberated from his laboratory by a spying reporter.'[178]

---

[175] Review of *The Island of Doctor Moreau* by H. G. Wells, *Saturday Review*, 11 Apr. 1896, 369.
[176] Wells, *Moreau*, 75.   [177] Ibid. 43.   [178] Review, 369.

Those 'shuddering ladies' are exactly the point, and it is clear that *The Island of Doctor Moreau* epitomizes many of the arguments that went into forming the antivivisection debate. The language of the critics who reviewed this book is telling, for it clarifies the issues that antivivisectionary writers sought to express. R. H. Hutton, reviewing the book for the *Spectator*, rather curiously, and perhaps reading what he wanted to see rather than what was written, claimed that Wells 'may, we hope, have done more to render vivisection unpopular, and that contempt for animal pain, which enthusiastic physiologists seem to feel, hideous, than all the efforts of the societies which have been organised for that wholesome and beneficent end.'[179] He goes on, however, to write: 'we do not recommend *The Island of Dr. Moreau* to readers of sensitive nerves, as it might well haunt them only too powerfully':[180] an argument fought against over and over again, as I have already suggested, in the writings of, amongst many others, Mona Caird, Ouida, and Frances Power Cobbe.

The Island of Doctor Moreau is a book full of animal pain, described as 'painful',[181] and as gripping 'the mind with painful interest and fearful curiosity'[182] by its reviewers, suggesting, again in the language of the vivisection debate, the possibilities of the transference of pain from the sufferer to the onlooker. Prendick, the shipwrecked biologist who ends up on Moreau's island, initially cannot bear to listen to the screams of the puma coming from the laboratory:

The crying sounded even louder out of doors. It was as if all the pain in the world had found a voice. Yet had I known such pain was in the next room, and had it been dumb, I believe—I have thought it since—I could have stood it well enough. It is when suffering finds a voice and sets our nerves quivering that this pity comes troubling us.[183]

The implications for the publication, in accessible forms, of physiological practice become very apparent, for if these

[179] Review of *The Island of Doctor Moreau* by H. G. Wells, *Spectator*, 11 Apr. 1896, 520.
[180] Ibid.
[181] Review of *The Island of Doctor Moreau* by H. G. Wells, *Guardian*, 3 Jun. 1896, 871.
[182] Review of *The Island of Doctor Moreau* by H. G. Wells, *Manchester Guardian*, 14 Apr. 1896, 4. [183] *Moreau*, 54.

screams were silent, then there could be no sympathetic response to them. Prendick's own response is the physical embodiment of those who found it too painful to read about vivisection: he writes, '[I] began to clench my fists, to bite my lips, and pace the room. Presently I got to stopping my ears with my fingers.'[184] But this desire not to hear is not the end of the matter. Prolonged exposure to the puma's cries of pain lead to indifference: 'So indurated was I at that time to the abomination of the place, that I heard without a touch of emotion the puma victim begin another day of torture.'[185]

This ability to withstand such demands on the sensibilities is seen by Dr Moreau as part of the process of growing up, and he goes on to fit this indifference to both sympathetic and personal pain into an evolutionary scheme:

'It is the puma,' I said, 'still alive, but so cut and mutilated as I pray I may never see living flesh again. Of all vile——'

'Never mind that,' said Moreau. 'At least spare me those youthful horrors. Montgomery used to be the same.'[186]

Sympathetic pain is the attribute of youth, and, in the process of growing up, one grows out of it. Moreau, in explaining his theories to Prendick, sticks a knife in his thigh, suggesting that

It does not hurt a pin-prick. But what does it show? The capacity for pain is not needed in the muscle, and it is not placed there; it is but little needed in the skin, and only here and there over the thigh is a spot capable of feeling pain. Pain is simply our intrinsic medical adviser to warn us and stimulate us. All living flesh is not painful, nor is all nerve, nor even sensory nerve . . . Plants do not feel pain; the lower animals as the starfish and crayfish do not feel pain. Then with men, the more intelligent they become the more intelligently they will see after their own welfare, and the less they will need the goad to keep them out of danger. I never yet heard of a useless thing that was not ground out of existence by evolution sooner or later. Did you? And pain gets needless.[187]

---

[184] *Moreau*, 53.   [185] Ibid. 157.   [186] Ibid. 108.

[187] Ibid. 114–15. That Wells's own sympathies are with Moreau is made clear in the very similar claims he makes in 'The Province of Pain', in *Early Writings in Science and Science Fiction by H. G. Wells*, ed. Robert Philmus and David Y. Hughes (Berkeley and Los Angeles: University of California Press, 1975), 194–9: 195.

It is here that one sees the reasons behind Ouida's claim that physiologists are the 'new priesthood'. Moreau takes on not only the function of the priest but also the role of the demigod, worshipped by his creatures whose litanies display their fear of their creator: '*His* is the House of Pain. *His* is the Hand that makes. *His* is the Hand that wounds.'[188] He has moved out of the realm of sympathetic response into that of objective onlooker, surveying with the impassivity of any of the physiologists whom Caird or Ouida could cite. He no longer sees suffering and, mimicking the testimony of Emanuel Klein to the First Royal Commission, can claim: 'The thing before you is no longer an animal, a fellow-creature, but a problem.'[189]

It is here, too, that the social implications of the infliction of pain for reasons of curiosity become apparent. Throughout antivivisectionary rhetoric there is the insistence that a price is to be paid for the infliction of pain, and that the debt must be repaid, usually marked out in terms of social disintegration. Caird's claim may be taken as typical:

The first indication of the dire penalty exacted of us, comes in the form of an insidious lowering of moral standards as between man and man; the check to spiritual development, the coarsening of fibre, which all go to make life for each of us more painful, more full of disillusion, more forlorn and despoiled of beauty and graciousness. This process helps to make way for the more terrifying calamities that follow in due course—the weak and the destitute being the first victims.[190]

And this is, indeed, very similar to Wells's own thinking. In an article published in the *Fortnightly Review* six months after the publication of *Doctor Moreau*, Wells seeks to explain his thinking on savagery and civilization:

in civilised man we have (1) an inherited factor, the natural man, who is the product of natural selection, the culminating ape, and a type of animal more obstinately unchangeable than any other living creature; and (2) an acquired factor, the artificial man, the highly plastic creature of tradition, suggestion, and reasoned thought. In the artificial man we have all that makes the comforts and securities of civilisation a possibility. That factor and civilisation have developed, and will develop together. And in this view, what we call Morality becomes the

---

[188] *Moreau*, 90.   [189] Ibid. 116.   [190] *Sentimental View*, 26.

padding of suggested emotional habits necessary to keep the round Palæolithic savage in the square hole of the civilised state.[191]

The civilized man is superimposed on the savage, who is kept in place only by the observance of social mores. Loosen those 'bonds of obligation'[192] and the savage is no longer held in check: Heathcliff runs wild. The social implications of the infliction of pain, which run through antivivisectionary writings, are made metaphorically clear in the collapse of Dr Moreau's experiment in society. It becomes obvious to Prendick that it is not just the explicit pain of the physiological laboratory that constitutes the suffering of the Beast-men, but rather that their society is destroyed:

Poor brutes! I began to see the viler aspect of Moreau's cruelty. I had not thought before of the pain and trouble that came to these poor victims after they had passed from Moreau's hands. I had shivered only at the days of actual torment in the enclosure. But now that seemed to be the lesser part. Before they had been beasts, their instincts fitly adapted to their surroundings, and happy as living things may be. Now they stumbled in the shackles of humanity, lived in a fear that never died, fretted by a law they could not understand; their mock-human existence began in an agony, was one long internal struggle, one long dread of Moreau.[193]

It has already been suggested in the discussion of Moreau's death that the vivisector's creatures may be read as projections of the dismemberments he inflicts, so that he is, in essence, killed by his own hand. Equally, the Beast-men can be seen as the societal results of the infliction of pain—feckless, useless, creatures who turn on one another and kill.

But it is also made plain in Wells's other nineteenth-century stories that he saw pain as the inseparable corollary to life. The Vicar, in *The Wonderful Visit*, explains the nature of the world that his Angel-guest has mysteriously fallen into: ' "Pain . . . is the warp and the woof of this life." '[194] During the course of the Angel's stay this becomes all too apparent as he not only begins to feel pain himself, brought about by a broken wing and

---

[191] 'Human Evolution, An Artificial Process', *Fortnightly Review*, NS 60 (1896), 594.
[192] Stevenson, *Jekyll and Hyde*, 112 and 131.
[193] *Moreau*, 153.   [194] *Wonderful Visit*, 158.

hunger, but he also learns the desire to inflict it on others, an emotion that had hitherto been alien to him in the 'Angelic Land'. He is initially distressed by the apparent desire of the schoolboys who throw stones at him to inflict pain for no reason, and then finds himself following suit, and almost murdering the local squire. Pain is not incidental to this plot but is its 'warp and . . . woof', much as it is seen by Wells to be the essence of humanity. Wells's debt to Thomas Huxley, whom he met when a student at the Normal School of Science in London, is visible here.[195] Huxley's 'Evolution & Ethics' (1893), suggested that pain and progress inevitably went hand in hand, and that there could be no civilized society without pain:

Where the cosmopoietic energy works through sentient beings, there arises, among its other manifestations, that which we call pain or suffering. This baleful product of evolution increases in quantity and in intensity, with advancing grades of animal organization, until it attains its highest level in man. Further, the consummation is not reached in man, the mere animal; nor in man, the whole or half savage; but only in man, the member of an organized polity. And it is a necessary consequence of his attempt to live in this way; that is, under those conditions which are essential to the full development of his noblest powers.[196]

This is the process at work in *Dr. Moreau*. The unfortunate animals, whom Moreau seeks to transform, go through the 'bath of burning pain'[197] in an attempt to reach a higher state that they are, nonetheless, never quite capable of retaining. The pain involved is seen by their creator as a necessary stage through which they must go in his speeded up process of evolution,[198] and, as such, the vivisectionary elements of the book

[195] See id., 'Professor Huxley and the Science of Biology (1884–1885)', in *Experiment in Autobiography: Discoveries and Conclusions of a Very Ordinary Brain (Since 1866)*, 2 vols. (Victor Gollancz and Cresset Press, 1934) i. 199–206. For the extent of Wells's knowledge of Huxley, see Hurley, *Gothic Body*, 55.
[196] *Evolution & Ethics: The Romanes Lecture 1893* (London and New York: Macmillan, 1893), 5.
[197] *Moreau*, 122.
[198] The same point, though in a different context, is made in H. G. Wells, *The Time Machine: An Invention* (William Heinemann, 1895). The Time Traveller, evaluating the weakness brought about by the disuse of their faculties, says of the Eloi: ' "To adorn themselves with flowers, to dance, to sing in the sunlight; so much was left of the artistic spirit, and no more. Even that would fade in the end into a contented inactivity. We are kept keen on the grindstone of pain and necessity, and,

take on a metaphorical status. Wells could not be counted as an antivivisectionist; indeed, he was a member of the Research Defence Society, and those readings, such as Hutton's, of the book which saw *Dr. Moreau* as an antivivisectionary text are surely misguided. What Wells sought to convey, using vivisection as his model, was the cruelty and randomness of the process that made civilized man what he is. The charges of blasphemy from the *Guardian* reviewer had a much firmer foundation in the text than those which suggested its antivivisectionary content.

The arguments about Moreau as demigod, and the aping of evolutionary forces, as well as the role of chance, have been rehearsed by Bernard Bergonzi in his book on the early Wells[199] and I do not wish to restate them here. What is important to my argument, however, is the way in which Wells considered pain to be an integral part of fiction, just as he saw it as an integral part of life. It was partly this novelty of conception, mixed with the desire to make the book a nerve-tingling adventure story, that made *The Island of Dr. Moreau* so unpopular with its reviewers. These two elements are conflated in such a way that the 'sensational' aspects of vivisection—those which the reader responds to physically through the process of transference—are mixed with the elements of the adventure story, where we see Prendick, alone, back to the sea with the tide rising, and the rapidly degenerating animals in front of him, exclaiming, 'There was nothing for it but courage.'[200]

In addition to this, Wells engages with the terms of the vivisection debate, giving Moreau the 'brutal directness in discussion'[201] attributed to those who performed vivisectionary experiments, epitomized by Klein's testimony to the First Royal Commission. We should recall here the many claims of antivivisectionary writers that the public only had to read what vivi-

---

it seemed to me, that here was that hateful grindstone broken at last!"' (54). When the Time Traveller realizes that the Eloi serve merely as the Morlocks's food, the necessity of the grindstone becomes apparent. For a full discussion of the role of evolution in Wells's early literary works see Jeanne and Norman MacKenzie, *H. G. Wells: A Biography* (New York: Simon and Schuster, 1973), 122 ff.

[199] *The Early H. G. Wells: A Study of the Scientific Romances* (Manchester: Manchester University Press, 1961), ch. 4.

[200] *Moreau*, 185.   [201] Ibid. 47.

sectionists wrote to find out their iniquities, for nothing was hidden. What the vivisectionist will write or say he will also do. Wells establishes the link between rhetorical structures and action, as Moreau puts into practice his desire to create, set out in his debate with Prendick, with no concern for the ethical questions that arise. What was offensive to contemporary readers was the use of such 'brutal directness' in the purveying of the philosophical aspects of the book, and the open discussion of pain. Wells 'sought out revolting details with the zeal of a sanitary inspector probing a crowded graveyard',[202] whilst calling on the stock responses of the 'shuddering ladies'— evoked by Chalmers Mitchell—as part of the adventure of the plot, and for the evocation of a frisson of horror: 'for a moment the forgotten horrors of childhood came back to my mind'.[203] The standard response to the novel may be seen in the *Speaker*'s review of *The Island of Dr. Moreau*, in which the reviewer claims that 'In the present instance [Wells] has achieved originality at the expense of decency';[204] a claim which reflects the disgust felt at the book's dual nature.

A rather more interesting review, though it claims the same moral high ground, appeared in the *Athenaeum*. It includes the denunciations of the book that came to be standard—'The horrors described by Mr. Wells in his latest book very pertinently raise the question how far it is legitimate to create feelings of disgust in a work of art'[205]—but it also raises a question that is central to the discussion of antivivisectionary writing as a whole. The writer, perhaps thinking of Hutton's *Spectator* review, complains:

It has, we observe, been suggested in some quarters that Mr. Wells was animated by a desire to expose the repulsive aspect of vivisection, but we do not believe it. At least, it is singularly ineffective from that point of view, and would be about as valuable for such a purpose as a pornological story in suppressing immorality.[206]

---

[202] Mitchell, Review, 369.   [203] Wells, *Moreau*, 27.
[204] Unsigned review of *The Island of Doctor Moreau* by H. G. Wells, *Speaker*, 18 Apr. 1896, 430.
[205] Unsigned review, '*The Island of Doctor Moreau*. By H. G. Wells. (Heinemann.)', *Athenaeum*, 9 May 1896, 615.
[206] Ibid. 616.

Here we have Mark Thornhill's dilemma over the strength of language necessary to expose vivisectionary malpractice reworded, and shifted into a slightly different sphere. Wells's text, and the reviews it prompted, embody the essential question in antivivisectionary writing: is it possible to go too far? And, if so, could it inflame the desire of readers to practise that which is so warmly denounced?

5
The Question of Shared Human Sensibility

If animal pain was discounted by vivisectionists in the face of physiological knowledge, then the pain of particular groups of humans could also be discredited and denied. This chapter deals with the ways in which the pain of individual human sufferers was read in accordance with particular preconceptions, rather than in the light of suffering endured in the body.

The first section of this chapter lays the groundwork for such discrediting of suffering as it broadly asks: what do we see when we look at pain? and how do we know that it is real? What an onlooker sees is not pain itself, but rather the body's responses to that pain which take the form of writing or rubbing. Daniel Deronda's mother, Leonora, recognizes the body's capacity for such bodily grimacing when she refuses to receive visitors under such circumstances: ' "I cannot bear to be seen when I am in pain." '[1] These signs, written on and distorting the body, are then interpreted and used to imply the presence of pain. Such 'writing', however, is not directly interpretable: the signs of suffering are there but they are open-ended and liable to misconstruction. The lack of a direct, unambiguous link between painful experience and physical expression both allows for, and extends, the disassociation between painful sign and apparent meaning introduced by novelistic convention. The second section of this chapter picks up on the terminology I have used to phrase the questions of the first—'what do *we* see? . . . how do *we* know? . . .'—asking what basis the word 'we' could have in such a context. I shall be demonstrating the fluidity of pain as a sign, and its openness to conflicting interpretation, as its basis as a shared component of human experience is variously upheld or rejected.

[1] George Eliot, *Daniel Deronda* (1876), ed. Graham Handley (Oxford: Clarendon Press, 1984), 596.

To a large extent, as I argued in Chapter 3, individuals come
to an understanding of the suffering of others through an
assumption that their pain is similar in kind if not in degree to
their own. Redrawing the dividing line between humans and
animals, Jeremy Bentham posited a question which reset the
basis for attributing values to different species: 'the question is
not, Can they *reason*? nor, Can they *talk*? but, Can they *suffer*?'[2]
The ability to suffer was seen to unify. It is no mistake that
in Frederick Gould's novel *The Agnostic Island* (1891), which
aimed at the representation of human fellowship based on
Benthamite ideas, the heroine looked for a way of finding what
was essentially human, and found it in what was presented as
brute and shareable experience: 'Can we suffer pain? Can we
feel hungry? Can we weep? Can we laugh? Can we despair? Can
we love?'[3] Gould, determined to establish the suffering of pain—
outside a scheme of atonement and redemption—as one of the
definitive ways of determining humanity, threw his net wide
including 'all men' of whatever race, creed, or social class, and
indeed women, as its members. This inclusivity, however, was
put under enormous pressure in the last two decades of the nineteenth century.

I. EVOLUTIONARY HIERARCHIES OF SUFFERING

In suggesting ways of dealing with the discrepancy between
painful state and bodily expression, the image of the earthworm—as it appeared in both scientific and literary writings—
provides a focus for the profound unease in the late nineteenth
century over the status of pain.

The way in which the worm, and its neurology, was understood, suggests the impossibility of attributing pain directly and
unambiguously to what appears to be the bodily response to
pain: the worm wriggles in what seems to be agony if cut in
half, though its neurology, and hence its place in an evolutionary scale, suggests that it feels no such thing. I shall be looking
at the ways in which scientists and theologians chose to read

[2] *An Introduction to the Principles of Morals and Legislation* (1780), ed. J. H.
Burns and H. L. A. Hart (London and New York: Methuen, 1982), 283.
[3] *The Agnostic Island* (Propagandist Press Committee, 1891), 39.

the writhings they saw in the cut worm, and considering whether what they privileged in that reading were the visual signals the worm sent out, or their previously acquired knowledge of vermicular neurology. I shall be suggesting, too, the ways in which pain itself is invisible to investigation, although it may be hinted at by particular types of behaviour and bodily expression: the furrowed brow, the clenched muscles, and so forth. Literary representations of pain allowed for the dissociation of the physical reality of suffering from the use that was made of it, and it is my aim in this chapter to suggest that not only was this true of literary constructions, but also of social ones.

I want to make it clear at the start, however, that whilst pain is elusive, those readings that discount the physical suffering of particular groups overtly refuse to acknowledge clear indications of pain. Harry Campbell, in *Headache and Other Morbid Cephalic Sensations*, makes this plain in his detailed description of 'the Visible Signs of Headache':

Headache generally gives some evidence of its presence in the facial expression. The most characteristic signs are a vertical wrinkling of the forehead just above the nose, due to contraction of the corrugatores supercilii, and a transverse wrinkling of the forehead, due to contraction of the occipitofrontalis. This brow-wrinkling is probably most apt to occur when the pain attacks the fore part of the head, and especially if the eyes are painful, or if photophobia is present.[4]

The description continues at some length: 'The temporals may be prominent', 'the pulsations of the carotids may be unusually visible', 'The complexion is apt to be sallow.'[5] But not only is a description given, but the reason for the physical signs of pain is tied firmly to physiology: this is clearly not the kind of headache that keeps Clara Middleton from the dinner table—and from Willoughby Patterne—in Meredith's *The Egoist*,[6] and nor is it the kind of pain that accompanies the death of villains, a pain superimposed on their musculature, answerable to the dictates of nemesis rather than those of pathology. It is, instead, the signal of physiological disturbance. Campbell's point is that pain can be read from bodily indicators, but as the century drew

---

[4] *Headache and Other Morbid Cephalic Sensations* (H. K. Lewis, 1894), 266.
[5] Ibid.   [6] *Egoist*, i. 270.

to a close, such an idea became less easily acceptable. Whilst the understanding of the increasing complexity of neurological organization from 'lower' to 'higher' species became more detailed, this increased knowledge of the continuum of neurological complexity specifically allowed for the dissociation of the visual prompts of pain.

Hierarchies of suffering were by no means new to a Darwinian understanding of nerves and their action, which recognized an increasing complexity of organization as the ladder of species was ascended. As G. J. Barker-Benfield argues, nerves had been held accountable for perceived differences in sensibility— between humans and animals, between the rich and the poor, between men and women—since the eighteenth century. Thomas Willis, working in the 1660s, laid the groundwork for such understanding in his recognition that 'The "nerves alone" were to be "held responsible for sensory impressions"'[7] and Newton followed, in his *Opticks* of 1675, redefining nerves as solid transmitters of vibrations, rather than Willis's hollow tubes that conveyed animal spirits. Newton himself did not, as Barker-Benfield makes clear, 'gender this scheme'[8] by suggesting that the nerves of women were of a different order from those of men, but the practice of reading sensibility against neurology and inferring neurological difference quickly followed. George Cheyne (1671–1743), whom Barker-Benfield chooses as one of the eighteenth century's pre-eminent popularizers of medical understandings of neurology, 'wished to alter the way in which people traditionally referred to such illnesses, to replace vague terms with the precise language of the physiology of the nerves'.[9] In his insistence on physiology, however, particular conceptions of nerves and their modes of functioning, unsustained by the findings of post-microscopy neurology, allowed for and indeed sustained particular ways of understanding the world. Variations of sensibility between people could be accounted for by the 'elasticity' of their nerves, by the speed at which the vibrations were enabled to pass, and by the size of particles which conveyed the vibration: the smaller and more 'delicate' the nerve, the quicker the vibration was able to pass. A link was quickly established between such 'delicacy' of nervous appa-

[7] Barker-Benfield, *Culture of Sensibility*, 3.   [8] Ibid. 5.   [9] Ibid. 7.

ratus and a delicacy of emotion, a 'refined' nerve and a refined sensibility.

Sensitivity was at one and the same time a physical and a moral attribute, and, as Barker-Benfield argues, 'Given the eighteenth-century connotations of "degree," the quality of sensibility could be seen as a badge of rank.'[10] Not only did neurology become 'gendered',—'throughout the century doctors lent their expertise to the notion that all women had more delicate nerves and, therefore, greater sensibility than men'[11]—but it also 'betokened both social and moral status',[12] and, because physiology was largely conceived of as a given, ordained by the Creator, divisions between people of supposedly differing neurological refinement were set in stone.[13] Such thinking was by no means arcane and, as Barker-Benfield argues, 'the nerve paradigm was ... widely popularized ... in large part as the result of literacy and the novel, above all, the novel of "sensibility"',[14] as Cheyne fed his conceptions to his friend Samuel Richardson, who, in turn, used them to underpin his novels of the 1740s and 1750s.

In 1858 James Samuelson wrote a book about worms and flies, entitled *Humble Creatures: The Earthworm and the Common Housefly*, the central tenet of which was that the educated man knew the workings of the relatively simple mechanisms that he owned—his penknife, for example—but had no idea about the far more complex, and more beautiful, animal and vegetable kingdom surrounding him, telling him of the glory of God. The author's attitude towards the worm and his attempt to revalue it is shown most clearly in his anthropomorphization of the animal when he tries to describe it: 'But you will perhaps be somewhat surprised to hear us speak of the "head" of a worm, for you are accustomed to connect with that idea a mouth, eyes, nose, and ears, none of which are perceptible in the worm'.[15] His attitude is endearing, and is clearly

---

[10] Ibid. 8.   [11] Ibid. 27.   [12] Ibid. 9.

[13] Some leeway existed as education of the nerves found its place, but this was largely read in terms of over-education, as the 'delicate and fine' nerves of the already sensitive were 'wasted and thinned'.

[14] *Culture of Sensibility*, 16.

[15] James Samuelson, assisted by J. Braxton Hicks, *Humble Creatures. The Earthworm and the Common Housefly. In Eight Letters* (John van Voorst, 1858), 11.

suggestive of a creature on a sensory par with the author, an attitude made explicit when he describes the nervous system of the worm:

Hence [the nerve cords] are continued, as a single nervous stem, along the whole ventral portion of the body, close to the external surface, giving out in each ring a number of branches of remarkable delicacy, which encircle the body, passing round to the creature's back, and imparting sensibility to every portion of its frame.[16]

Then in brackets he adds the motto to the emblem: '(See! what excruciating pain the angler inflicts upon the poor worm when he impales it upon his barbed hook, which he passes from one end of its body to the other!)'[17]

It is this injunction to 'See!' that I take issue with here. There is no pain actually to be seen, and if there were, neither Samuelson nor the reader, at one remove further still, could see it, for it could only be inferred from the worm's anatomy or from its behaviour. The nervous system in its 'remarkable delicacy'—redolent of eighteenth-century sensibility—is offered to us by Samuelson and laid out before us as a thing of beauty, and from it pain is deduced. Sensibility is seen as the gift of the encircling branches, and the language of description elevates the worm from its scantily developed place in nature to a place amongst human suffering, as it becomes the 'poor victim' of the angler. The title of the book, *Humble Creatures*, also serves this end with its shades of Christian humility and the elevation of the meek: it suggests a ladder of development on which the worm provides one of the lowest rungs, but which nevertheless puts the worm on a continuum of pain, the highest reach of which is human suffering. Importantly, Samuelson's argument is not that the worm does not feel pain and therefore that the angler may abuse it with impunity—the attitude of many later writers towards the worm—but rather that in recognizing its standing as a 'humble creature' the reader should learn to see its beauty and consider its ability to suffer rather than to 'kick it aside'[18] as something worthless. He suggests that despite its lowliness, the worm has rights too. This is a position that will become important in my later discussion of evolutionary scales and *Jude the Obscure*.

---

[16] Samuelson, 15.   [17] Ibid.   [18] Ibid. 4.

Twenty years later—and these were, as I suggested in the previous chapter, twenty years of intensive physiological and vivisectionary research into comparative anatomy—the anatomist's stance towards the worm had radically changed. Andrew Wilson, who published nothing under his own name, but who nevertheless represented mainstream scientific thought, provided the appendix to Charles Voysey's *Mystery of Pain*. This, despite the author's heretical position, offered the reader pain as prophylactic and pain as the means of stirring errant man to action, thus drawing him closer to God. The context here is important, for unlike Samuelson who attempts to dissuade man from hurting the humble worm through a recognition of its intricacy, Wilson denies its neurological complexity in ways similar to those of contemporaneous pro-vivisectionary writers who, in the defence of their practice, suggest the unfeeling nature of brute creation. His claim is that 'in man alone do we find the typical idea of "pain" to be represented, and his pains and sorrows may be regarded as a truly human and God-bestowed heritage; since through the exercise of his consciousness and faith, he learns through pain to know and value the pleasures and happiness of life'.[19] Humans in this way are proffered as the only creatures who can feel sensation and interpret it as pain, because they are the only ones with the intellectual strength to make use of it—their pain is the index to their humanity, the badge of their evolutionary rank.

In accordance with this, Wilson portrays the basis of the division he finds between man and worm in terms of their respective nervous systems: 'A nervous system may be defined as that which brings its possessor into relation with the world in which it lives. The more perfect the nervous system, the more intimate does the relationship between the organism and the world become.'[20] In the course of evolution the ratio of nerve endings to the outside world has increased, making humans the sensitive creatures they are. It is at this point that Wilson goes on to clarify the importance of the questions central to this chapter: what do we see when we look at pain? and how do we know that it is real?

[19] *Mystery*, 251.   [20] Ibid. 247.

A worm, cut in halves writhes, and its motions suggest to the non-physiological mind notions of extreme suffering, because the worm is being judged by the motions of the human body, or by those of a higher animal in pain. The comparative anatomist shows that the writhing of the worm, after division of its body, is due to the fact that its nervous system consists of a double nervous cord lying along the floor of its frame, so that each half possesses abundant means for exciting and controlling muscular movement. If we regard the writhings as indicative of 'pain,' then we must accord to each nerve-mass in each joint of the worm's body, functions we are unaware are performed by any nerve-masses save those comprising the brain and other nerve-centres of vertebrates—a supposition in itself absurd.[21]

The need to interpret pain neurologically is spelt out. The cut section of the worm does not have the mechanical wherewithal to suffer, only to respond reflexly to stimuli, and this is what one sees in its contortions. Samuelson's anthropomorphisms and his way of reading the worm's writhings are thus seen to be 'absurd' and a different attitude towards species deemed to be lower down an evolutionary chain is facilitated.

Voysey chose to place Wilson's paper at the end of his book to suggest the kindness of nature: to assure the reader that the animal kingdom does not suffer as we should suffer were we to be in their place.[22] It will become clear in the course of this chapter that this reading of the world, and a creature's relationships to it, may come to have pernicious social implications, as models for interpreting pain based on hierarchical structures other than purely evolutionary ones come into play, and the working classes found the validity of their physical suffering denied to them. Physiologists may have been determined to read pain in terms of purpose rather than meaning, but meaning nevertheless accrued to the neurological model, as Samuelson's theocentric readings of neurology gave place to readings which took their meaning from social level or class.

Late nineteenth-century attitudes towards the ability of such

---

[21] *Mystery*, 249.

[22] For ambivalence over the ability of invertebrates to feel, and the contrary refusal to value such suffering, see George Eliot, *The Mill on the Floss* (1860), ed. Gordon S. Haight (Oxford: Clarendon Press, 1989), 34–5: Maggie 'told Tom, however, that she should like him to put the worms on the hook for her, although she accepted his word when he assured her that worms couldn't feel (it was Tom's private opinion that it didn't much matter if they did)'.

creatures as worms to feel pain did not polarize unambiguously into those in the Wilson and those in the Samuelson camp. It is clear from Darwin—one of the leading lights in worm studies—that, despite his extensive tests on worms to check the boundaries of their sensitivity, he was still hesitant to suggest that what looked like pain, in reality was no such thing. Darwin's methods of testing worms were comprehensive, not to say exhaustive, and if anyone were to know about worms, it would surely have been he. As Desmond and Moore sum up his experiments in their biography, Darwin

experimented indoors, in the new billiard room, now turned into his study to make more space. Worms littered it, triturating through earth in glass-covered pots. Darwin stumbled around at night and flashed lights at them—candles, paraffin lamps, and even lanterns with red and blue slides. Only an intense beam brought a reflex response, when they bolted—'like a rabbit' . . .—into their burrows. Heat made little difference, even a red-hot poker held near by. Nor were they sensitive to sound. Bernard blew a whistle, Frank played his bassoon, Emma performed on the piano, and Bessy shouted, but no worms were roused.[23]

These, and many more such experiments, were performed,[24] but despite all such tests, Darwin remained uneasy. It is possible that his 1872 book, *The Expression of the Emotions in Man and Animals*, with its insistence on the ability of animals to express emotion as adequately, if not more so, than man made the dissociation of visual prompts from acquired knowledge still harder for Darwin himself to accept. He interjects an episode which suggests just this difficulty of reading visual signs, whatever the emotion involved. Darwin describes the ways in which Guillaume Duchenne—an associate of Charcot who studied human expression as portrayed in photography—'galvanized . . . certain muscles in the face of an old man'[25] and then photographed the results. Darwin showed these photographs to more than twenty (well-educated) people, both men and women, and asked them what 'emotion or feeling' was being displayed:

[23] *Darwin*, 649.
[24] See Charles Darwin, *The Formation of Vegetable Mould, through the Action of Worms, with Observations on their Habits* (John Murray, 1881), see esp. 19–34.
[25] *The Expression of the Emotions in Man and Animals. With Photographic and Other Illustrations* (John Murray, 1872), 14.

Several of the expressions were instantly recognised by almost everyone, though described in not exactly the same terms; and these may, I
think, be relied on as truthful . . . On the other hand, the most widely
different judgments were pronounced in regard to some of them. This
exhibition was of use in another way, by convincing me how easily we
may be misguided by our imagination; for when I first looked through
Dr. Duchenne's photographs, reading at the same time the text, and
thus learned what was intended, I was struck with admiration at the
truthfulness of all, with only a few exceptions. Nevertheless, if I had
examined them without any explanation, no doubt I should have been
as much perplexed, in some cases, as other persons have been.[26]

Such experimentation is, of course, deeply flawed, for the old
man's facial expressions are the result of electrical stimulation,
rather than fear or anger, so that what Darwin describes as the
'truth' of their expression stands on shaky ground: it is the construct of the viewer with no input from the man's emotions, only
from his musculature.[27] It is worth considering what it is to look
at pain in these terms, for the writhings of the worm also come
'without a word of explanation', as the worm lacks the power
of vocalization. The only 'truth' is the truth of visual perception, undercut by the dictates of comparative anatomy. Darwin
goes on, in *The Expression of the Emotions*, to suggest the
outward signs of the animal in pain:

When animals suffer from an agony of pain, they generally writhe
about with frightful contortions; and those which habitually use their
voices utter piercing cries or groans. Almost every muscle of the body
is brought into strong action. With man the mouth may be closely
compressed, or more commonly the lips are retracted, with the teeth
clenched or ground together. There is said to be 'gnashing of teeth' in
hell; and I have plainly heard the grinding of the molar teeth of a cow
which was suffering acutely from inflammation of the bowels. The
female hippopotamus in the Zoological Gardens, when she produced
her young, suffered greatly; she incessantly walked about, or rolled on
her sides, opening and closing her jaws, and clattering her teeth
together.[28] With man the eyes stare wildly as in horrified astonishment,
or the brows are heavily contracted. Perspiration bathes the body, and
drops trickle down the face.[29]

---

[26] *Expression*, 14.   [27] See Cartwright, *Screening the Body*, 60–1.
[28] Darwin's note: 'Mr. Bartlett, "Notes on the Birth of a Hippopotamus," Proc.
Zoolog. Soc. 1871, p. 255.'
[29] *Expression*, 69–70.

So Darwin describes the signs of pain in humans and animals, but despite the accurate physicality of description, the meaning of these signals is still derived from a notional understanding of them outside the physical realm: the man in pain's eyes 'stare as in horrified astonishment' (see fig. 2). We are primarily being told about what could be called the adjuncts of pain—the writhing, the sweating, the gnashing of teeth—and the emotional content of this passage—that the cow is 'suffering

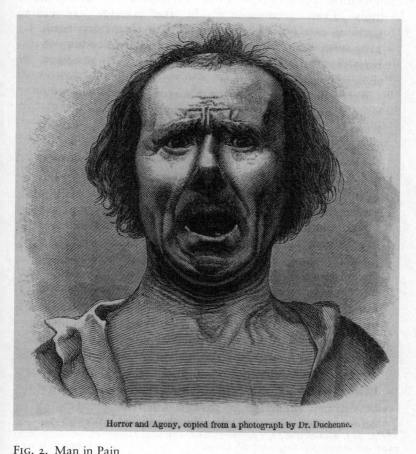

Horror and Agony, copied from a photograph by Dr. Duchenne.

Fig. 2. Man in Pain

Source: Charles Darwin, *The Expression of the Emotions in Man and Animals* (John Murray, 1872), 306.

acutely', or that the cries of an animal in pain are 'piercing'—
is in a different realm from this, or, rather, is the result of
attributing meaning to those adjuncts. In *The Expression of the
Emotions* Darwin claimed that he had initially looked for verification of empained expression in the work of painters and
sculptors, only to be disappointed. 'The reason', he writes, 'is,
that in works of art, beauty is the chief object; and strongly
contracted facial muscles destroy beauty. The story of the
composition is generally told with wonderful force and truth by
skilfully given accessories.'[30] In the passage concerning
Duchenne's experiments, Darwin made it clear how 'easily we
may be misguided by our imagination' in the reading of just
such signs or 'accessories' if explanations for what is seen are
offered to guide the mind in its hermeneutic task. It is with such
ambivalence towards the visual that Darwin wrote his later—
indeed his last and enormously popular[31]—book *On the Formation of Vegetable Mould*, which had the worm as its focus.
The profundity of Darwin's ambivalence towards the measure
of pain an injured worm feels takes shape in his observations
on the matter: 'It may be doubted whether they suffer as much
pain when injured, as they seem to express by their contortions',[32] and, later: 'But I doubt whether they were hurt, for they
are indifferent to very sharp objects, and will swallow even rose-
thorns and small splinters of glass.'[33] In the light of his certainty
over other aspects of the worm's life—its preference for green
cabbage over red, or what might be called the diet of worms—
this ambiguity over the creature's ability to feel pain is marked.
Such ambiguity is not confined exclusively to worms or, indeed,
to other small and lowly creatures, but rather is part of a much
wider difficulty where pain perception is concerned.

   Lightner Witmer, whose chapter on pain was used to ascertain the level of medical understanding of bodily suffering at the
end of the nineteenth century, is important here. A brief review
of his arguments will show the state of medical thinking on the

---

[30] *Expression*, 15. See also Bain, *Senses*, 88.
[31] See Gillian Beer, ' "The Death of the Sun": Victorian Solar Physics and Solar
Myth', in J. B. Bullen (ed.), *The Sun is God: Painting, Literature, and Mythology
in the Nineteenth Century* (Oxford: Clarendon Press, 1989), 160: 'between November 1881 and February 1884, 8,500 copies were sold and it went on outselling all
his other works'.
[32] *Vegetable Mould*, 34.   [33] Ibid. 72.

subject of pain twenty years on from Voysey, who himself wrote twenty years after Samuelson. Despite the didactic function of the chapter, Witmer's unease about the slippery nature of his subject becomes more and more apparent as the piece proceeds. He begins by saying that his chapter is written for the clinician 'for whom pain exists chiefly as a symptom of disease',[34] an adjunct that may be used as a stepping stone on the path to diagnosis. For Witmer, as for Ivan Illich, the psychological training of the clinician who meets the patient in pain is of vital importance in the reading that he makes of the situation: 'conclusions arrived at by physiologists will be largely determined by the type of psychology that happens to have impressed itself upon the advocates of these respective physiological hypotheses'.[35] The haphazard nature of psychological training becomes apparent through Witmer's sentence structures, and his insistence that the physician's whole attitude to pain, and the patient in pain, is determined by something that 'happens to have impressed itself' upon him.

The striking thing, though, about Witmer's argument is that it begins with a semblance of balance, dealing even-handedly with the clinical practices he assembles: 'traditional psychology may be said to regard pain as a feeling—*i.e.*, a purely mental state or condition, with or, more frequently, without a physical basis in the nervous system'.[36] He hints that such views may 'run riot'[37] in the works and practices of some physiologists, but it is nowhere apparent in the first half of the chapter that Witmer is profoundly in disagreement with this approach. It is only when Witmer attacks a psychologist of the school which maintains that pain is ' "subconscious, subjective, mental, without any physical basis" ',[38] and puts this belief into practice on a young woman, that Witmer is incensed into denunciation. The 19-year-old girl's pain is

described . . . as 'hysterical, subjective, mental, delusional, and not to be ascribed, therefore, as due to any physical external cause.' From a psychophysiological standpoint, serious objection may be made to this description of the pain and to the conclusion that it is not to be ascribed as due to any physical cause. The pain certainly existed as an

---

[34] 'Pain', 905.   [35] Ibid. 906.   [36] Ibid. 905–6.
[37] Ibid. 905.   [38] Ibid.

actuality in this girl's mind, and it must have had some cause, irrita-
tive or otherwise, in some part of the central nervous system. It is in
harmony with the views of the best authorities to consider this as a
pain of cortical origin.[39]

It is clear from this that there was severe professional disagreement between these two schools of thought, with equally severe
consequences for those suffering from pain, as Alice James, later
to die of a painful cancer, and repeatedly diagnosed as hysterical, discovered. There were no positive grounds for substanti-
ating or refuting the claims made for the nature of bodily pain
at the time when the encyclopedia was compiled, and this uncertainty is mirrored in the progressive sense of unease in Witmer's
writing. Scientifically, he could not know if, as accused, 'in
attempting to locate pain tracts we were pursuing a "will o' the
wisp"',[40] or whether there was, indeed, some pain centre which
would be found at a later date which would validate his belief
that all pain has a bodily origin. The only thing that the closing
argument of the chapter makes explicit is Witmer's reluctance
to commit himself. His sentences double back and regress—'it
may not be advancing too far along the road of hypothetical
speculation to suppose . . .'[41]—and such phrasing is indicative of
both a lack of absolute knowledge and a desire not to act on
supposition.

There is a curious episode in his chapter on pain when Witmer
expresses this unease as to the nature of pain very vividly. It is
an interjection of an entirely different kind from the rest of the
chapter, as Witmer tells the story of a man he has met who has
puzzled him. It is the case of

a 'professional painless man,' who . . . showed himself capable of
making himself insensible to pain whenever he wished to do so. He
had worked for some time in a dime museum as the human pin
cushion, and could be cut with a knife or stuck with pins or needles
without showing the slightest sign of pain. I have known him to hold
a red-hot half dollar in his hand without wincing until it had burnt
itself deep into the flesh. *It is impossible to say positively whether this
subject inhibited the expressive movements of pain, that is, the external signs of pain, or whether he inhibited the pain itself.* If his own
statements can be trusted, he felt pain on ordinary occasions when he

---

[39] 'Pain', 938–9.   [40] Ibid. 906.   [41] Ibid. 941.

had not made up his mind to be insensible to pain, but he reports that, when he had once decided not to feel the pain of the stimulus, the pain was no longer felt. It was not stoically endured. Moreover, there were areas of the skin which he could not render insensible to pain in this way. I am therefore inclined to believe that he inhibited the sensation of pain and not its external manifestations. [My italics][42]

Again, at the heart of this description is the worry that perhaps one cannot judge whether someone else is truly in pain by looking at her or him. Is this man suffering and just inhibiting the outward signs in a reversal of the worm's seemingly agonizing, but painless, writhings, or does he indeed feel, contrary to what might be deemed the natural course of things, no pain, unless taken by surprise?[43]

Witmer is concerned here with insensitivity based on 'freakishness', but human sensitivity was also widely perceived to be based on the evolutionary ascendancy of the well-educated upper classes. Marie Corelli, in her extraordinary first novel, *A Romance of Two Worlds* (1886), which promulgates her idea of a new 'Electric Creed', suggests both a level of physiological knowledge and a dependence on Cheyne's vision of nervous sensibility. Corelli describes nerves as 'electric wires',[44] and in so doing recognizes the electrical, rather than vibratory, nature of the nervous impulse, and suggests a nineteenth-century conception of neurology.[45] She also relies, however, on older conceptions of delicacy and refinement, as 'that intricate and delicate network of fine threads'[46] becomes, through the 'finer occupations, whose results are found in sculpture, painting,

---

[42] Ibid. 939.

[43] See Peter Melville Logan, *Nerves and Narratives: A Cultural History of Hysteria in Nineteenth-Century British Prose* (Berkeley and Los Angeles: University of California Press, 1997), 168–70, for a useful discussion of the shift from the early 19th-century, 'essentially sincere' (168) body which expresses what it feels through a 'strong connection between sign and meaning' (170) to the much more difficult to read bodily signs of e.g. George Eliot's characters.

[44] *A Romance of Two Worlds: A Novel*, 2 vols. (Richard Bentley, 1886), i. 99.

[45] As Corelli's postscript to *Two Worlds* (in Methuen popular edn., 1924, 338) suggests, however, she was convinced that science kept abreast of her knowledge, rather than the other way round: 'I may here add that the remarkable discovery of the Röntgen Ray which has astonished the world in general, has not presented itself as a novelty to me, though I have rejoiced at seeing one of the "proofs positive" of the theories I have endeavoured to inculcate made publicly and scientifically manifest.'

[46] Corelli, *Two Worlds* (1886 edn.), i. 99.

music and poetry',[47] 'more finely strung, more sensitive, more keenly alive to every passing sensation'.[48] Such nervous refinement then fixes its possessor neurologically in a hierarchical structure, as the female narrator recognizes when she claims: 'We did not create ourselves. We did not ask to be born with the over-sensitiveness, the fatal delicacy, the highly strung nervousness of the feminine nature.'[49] Grant Allen, writing slightly earlier, and with a much firmer basis in physiological science, prefigures Corelli's statements very closely. For him, the 'nervous organization'[50] is of vital importance: 'the refined . . . [have] nerves of less calibre but greater discriminativeness'[51] than the 'vulgar' whose nervous organization is necessarily 'coarse and indiscriminative'.[52] Whilst, as Barker-Benfield recognized in eighteenth-century theorists, there was the possibility of the education of the senses, this was kept firmly within trammels:

we can teach ourselves to observe every faint wave of pleasure or pain, every delicate thrill of harmony, every minute twinge of discord, which our nervous organisation renders us capable of perceiving, but we can never get beyond this natural barrier, or transcend our organic capacities.[53]

Allen, writing specifically about aesthetics, defines such coarseness or refinement of the nerves in terms of the 'bad Taste [which] is the concomitant of a coarse and indiscriminative nervous organisation',[54] and confines his remarks to this sphere, claiming that 'the vulgar', like 'children and savages', 'are pleased by great masses of colour, especially red, orange, and purple',[55] whereas those with thinner nerves 'require delicate combinations of complementaries'.[56] The aestheticizing of nervous organization is common: Svengali, the supreme musician, 'Callous as he was to the woes of others . . . was . . . a very bundle of nerves . . . especially sensitive to pain';[57] and Joseph Shorthouse's hero, John Inglesant, with 'the temperament of sensibility', 'fearful of pain, covet[ing] music . . . and

---

[47] Corelli, 112.   [48] Ibid. 112–13.   [49] Ibid. 158.
[50] *Physiological Æsthetics*, 49.   [51] Ibid. 44.
[52] Ibid. 48. See also Logan, *Nerves and Narratives*, 146. Logan discusses the link made by the doctor, Thomas Trotter, in 1805, between 'the laborer's coarse nerves' and his 'insensibility'.
[53] Allen, *Physiological Æsthetics*, 50.   [54] Ibid. 48.   [55] Ibid. 44.
[56] Ibid.   [57] du Maurier, *Trilby*, iii. 42–3.

delight[ing] in poetry and romance',[58] explicitly represents a link between musicality and physical sensitivity. These adjuncts—the ability to thrill to music—attest to the sensitivity of their possessor.[59] It is no surprise that Edward Thomas, writing of Richard Jefferies's bodily pain, sets his artistry in relation to his suffering, citing a doctor who claimed that Jefferies's portrait

'indicates the scrofulous diathesis, with its singularly impressionable temperament, its rapturous enjoyment of a delight, and its intense susceptibility to a pang.' In some way, not yet to be explained, the mortal pining of his body was related to the intense mental vivacity of his last years.[60]

Such discrimination between types of nervous organization clearly has much wider-reaching ramifications. G. H. Lewes, in *Sea-side Studies*, written in the same year as *Humble Creatures*, but utterly discarding Samuelson's theocentric logic for the 'austere necessities of science',[61] firmly sets animals and humans on the ascending scale of organization and sensitivity outlined in my discussion of worms. In so doing, he not only attributes heightened sensitivity to himself, but also moves this perception of sensitivity into the realm of action: 'I confess that my susceptibility altogether disqualifies me from witnessing, much more from performing [vivisectional] experiments accompanied with pain.'[62] His susceptibility is the fruit of his 'own organisation'[63] and the corollary of this is, of course, that those with a lower level of nervous development could, and indeed did, inflict pain. The inverse relationship between the ability to inflict pain and the inability to feel it is established here in Lewes's suggestion that his nervous organization has immediate repercussions for his actions. Lewes makes it clear that 'With lower animals the case is altogether different' from that of higher animals. 'They feel no pain'[64] and this is because of the relative simplicity of the nervous systems:

---

[58] [J. H. Shorthouse], *John Inglesant; A Romance* (Birmingham: Cornish, 1880), 331.
[59] See Barker-Benfield, *Culture of Sensibility*, 20–2 for a discussion of the link between musicality and sensitivity to pain.
[60] *Richard Jefferies: His Life and Work* (1909; Port Washington, NY and London: Kennikat Press, 1972), 172.
[61] *Sea-side Studies at Ilfracombe, Tenby, the Scilly Isles, & Jersey* (Edinburgh and London: William Blackwood, 1858), 329.
[62] Ibid. 328–9.   [63] Ibid. 329.   [64] Ibid.

Pain is only a *specialisation of that Sensibility which is common to all
animals.* It is a specialisation resulting from a high degree of differen-
tiation of the nervous system, consequently found only in the more
complex animals, and in them increasing as we ascend the scale.[65]

This ascending scale discriminates not just between species, but
also between members of the same species, so that

Even among men the difference of susceptibility is very remarkable. It
is much less in savages than in highly-civilised men, as it seems also to
be less in wild animals than in domesticated, especially petted, animals;
less in men leading an active out-of-door life than in those leading a
sedentary intellectual life; less in women than in men; less in persons
of lymphatic than in persons of nervous temperaments.[66]

The categories Lewes chooses are interesting: the sedentary male
reaches back to Cheyne's formulations,[67] whereas the claim that
sensitivity was 'less in women than in men' was widely discussed
and used in diverse ways as a political weapon.[68]

Neurological advance was widely seen in terms of an increase
in the number of nerves comprising the nervous organization.
As Wilson termed it, 'the more perfect the nervous system, the
more intimate does the relationship between the organism and
the world become'. Schemes which set such neurological
advance in terms of evolution traced 'the gradual growth of the
nervous system from the early dawn of consciousness'[69] and, in
so doing, charted a quantitative rise in neurological tissue that
allowed its increasing complexity. In an article, 'Touch and Taste
in Animals', published in *Chamber's Journal* in 1892, the author
claims that 'Man has the greatest number of sensory nerves; they
become fewer as we descend in the scale of creation, and some
of the lower invertebrates apparently have none, hence they can

---

[65] *Sea-side Studies at Ilfracombe,* 334.

[66] Ibid. 335.

[67] See Barker-Benfield, *Culture of Sensibility,* 24.

[68] See Dally, *Women under the Knife,* 81: 'In 1873, just as real progress was starting to be made in women's education and medical training, Dr Edward Clarke published his *Sex in Education.* This short book was to prove a formidable opponent
to women's advancement. Women are delicate, he insisted. Education is over-
pressure and exhaustion. Education turns women into men. Menstruation is an insu-
perable barrier to women's education. These were but common rationalisations of
old tales, but belief in them was increasing.' See Edward H. Clarke, *Sex in Education; or, A Fair Chance for Girls* (Boston: James R. Osgood, [1873]).

[69] W. J. Collins, 'Pain and its Interpretation', *Lancet,* 20 Aug. 1887, 391.

have little or no sense of pain.'[70] It is no surprise, therefore, that in Sarah Grand's *The Heavenly Twins*, published a year after the *Chamber's* article, Dr Galbraith can suggest the possibility of 'ladies . . . developing nerves'[71] when gruesome medical subjects are discussed, or that Mr Fairlie in Collins's *The Woman in White* can suggest that servants are 'persons born without nerves'.[72] This latter, of course, published in 1860 precedes the claims made in 'Touch and Taste' by some thirty years, but in claiming the lack of neurological tissue of servants, Collins marks the decided crossover between up-to-date neurological ideas and older ways of thinking about sensibility that had marked the eighteenth-century novel.

Late nineteenth-century ideas of progress and increasing complexity were to draw on such ideas as those displayed by Wilson and Wilkie Collins. The social evolutionist Herbert Spencer claimed that 'In societies, as in living bodies, increase of mass is habitually accompanied by increase of structure',[73] thus linking, in Kelly Hurley's terms, social evolution with physical evolution.[74] James Runciman, an author of nautical stories and a journalist determined to instil self-discipline into the reader of his articles, describes the evolution of society in exactly such terms of nervous organization and social complexity in his 1893 essay 'Discipline'. For Runciman, the 'Rider Haggard of ancient days'[75] who fought with mammoths left 'no indication of organization'[76] behind him, whereas those who followed left records of increasing social sophistication, until the 'most minute branchings of our complex society'[77] were evolved in a 'slow progression from savagery towards seemliness and refinement and wisdom'.[78] The terminology of neurological supremacy—refinement and organization—are mirrored in perceived structures of society, as evolutionary ideas shore up concurrent myths of racial supremacy.

[70] 'Touch and Taste in Animals', *Chamber's Journal of Popular Literature, Science, and Arts*, 5th ser. 9 (1892), 584.
[71] *The Heavenly Twins*, 3 vols. (William Heinemann, 1893), iii. 138.
[72] *Woman in White*, i. 66.
[73] *Principles of Sociology*, 3 vols. (Williams and Norgate, 1876), i. 489.
[74] Hurley, *Gothic Body*, 96.
[75] 'Discipline', in *The Ethics of Drink and Other Social Questions or, Joints in our Social Armour* (3rd edn., Hodder and Stoughton, 1893), 191.
[76] Ibid.   [77] Ibid. 193.   [78] Ibid.

Three interrelated readings of late nineteenth-century novels now follow. These are not intended to be all-inclusive, but rather suggestive of the ways in which the relationship to physical pain in a text may be used as an index to social position. I shall be looking specifically at incremental scales of sensitivity to pain, where the weight given to the capacity of an individual to suffer physically is determined by social status.

That there was a crossover between physiological and novelistic discourse, and an awareness of neurological hierarchies, based on evolutionary thought, which extended itself into a social sphere in literary writing as early as 1872, becomes clear from a reading of a short passage from Eliza Lynn Linton's *Joshua Davidson*. The self-deprecating narrator describes the difficulties Davidson has in visiting local gentry trying to find work, unsurprisingly without success, for an alcoholic burglar:

The poor were as curious specimens to [Lord X]. He never regarded them as men and women like himself and his class. He scarcely gave them credit for ordinary human feeling even; for he used to say that affections and nerves were both matters of education and refinement, and that the uneducated and unrefined neither loved nor felt as the others. Perhaps he was right. I am not physiologist enough to know much about nerves and pain and the difference of education, so far as that goes; but I think I have seen as much real affection, as much passionate self-abandoning, self-sacrificing love among the poor as there is among the rich.[79]

The blurring of categories in this passage is important. It looks at first as though Lord X, firmly ensconced in the nobility and as reported by the narrator, takes a standard aristocratic line: he treats the poor as 'specimens' who are the object of his regard, and denies their capacity for feeling. This suggests his own sensibility, born of class and, as he suggests, of education and refinement. But John, the narrator, problematizes the easy assumption of the nature of feeling and sensibility, using the same vocabulary, but putting it firmly in the field of neurology, reinterpreting as he does so the basis of refined sensibility. From aligning nerves with affections as Lord X does, suggesting a metaphorical nervous system reverberating with refined

[79] *The True History of Joshua Davidson* (Strahan, 1872), 194–5.

emotion, John puts these nerves into a new partnership with a physiologically grounded 'pain'. Lord X's claim that the poor 'neither loved nor felt' as he does is seen to be double-edged, for the feeling involved is not mental perception as he understands it, but rather involves their physical facility to feel: in short, the evolutionary status of their nervous system.

Using this idea of evolutionary scales of pain at work even within humankind, marking off the savage from the civilized, and the poor from the rich, I now move into a discussion of a passage from Hardy's *Jude the Obscure* (1894). In this, I shall be looking at the metaphoric power of the image of the worm, and its implications for the neurological elitism that offers a vision of the world with a progressive scale from non-pain to pain perception, with the worm firmly at the lower end.[80]

The image of the worm provided a potent image of the powerless for the Victorian reader, though its status as sentient or insentient was by no means firmly established. Heathcliff's pleasure is derived from his ability to hurt, as he exclaims: ' "I have no pity! The worms writhe, the more I yearn to crush out their entrails! It is a moral teething, and I grind with greater energy, in proportion to the increase of pain." '[81] Mrs Tenbruggen, however, the masseuse of Wilkie Collins's *The Legacy of Cain*, approaches the worm from the other end, recognizing both the ability to place individuals according to their class and to attribute powerlessness to those considered metaphorically to be worms. Her object, then, is to dissociate herself from the image, and in doing so she makes plain a level of social aspiration:

Some of their ... medical newspapers ... declare that my fees are exorbitant; and there is a tendency among the patients—I mean the patients who are rolling in riches—to follow the lead of the newspapers. I am no worm to be trodden on, in that way. The London people shall wait for me, until they miss me—and when I do go back, they will find the fees increased.[82]

---

[80] For a very different reading of Jude's relationship to worms, see James R. Kincaid, 'Girl-Watching, Child-Beating, and Other Exercises for Readers of *Jude the Obscure*', in *Annoying the Victorians* (New York and London: Routledge, 1995), 233–47. For a reading of Jude's sensitivity see also Lansbury, *Old Brown Dog*, 38.

[81] Emily Brontë, *Wuthering Heights*, 186.   [82] *Cain*, iii. 54.

The worm for Mrs Tenbruggen, whether sentient or not, is powerless and as such is there to be trodden on, and she refuses similarity to it.

Not only worms, with their associations with Christian humility, could be used as neurological and social markers in this way, but the slug could also provide a measure of sentience. Robert Hichens in *The Green Carnation* (1894) sets up a conversation between Mrs Windsor, and the book's Lord Alfred Douglas character, Reggie Hastings. Hichens satirizes the tendencies of aestheticism, whilst also suggesting a widespread knowledge of the nervous basis of sensation:

'I have found several slugs,' [Mrs. Windsor] answered triumphantly, 'but I can't kill them. They move so fast, at least when they are frightened. You would never believe it. I came upon one under a leaf just now, and it started just like a person disturbed in a nap . . .'

'I suppose slugs have nerves, then,' Reggie said, getting up out of his hammock, 'and get strung up like people who over-work. Just think of a strung-up slug! There is something weird in the idea. A slug that started at its own shadow. Here is tea!'[83]

The projection of mental categories—here the belief in a sensitive nervous organization—onto the lowly slug clearly suggests a tendency to read the sensitivity of animals in accordance with human frames of reference. The obscurity of Jude, as I shall argue, has much to do with his ready association with the worm.

The vermicular passage in *Jude* comes from the beginning of the novel when Farmer Troutham has given Jude the sack for his inadequate bird-scaring technique. The boy, unwilling to face the villagers, instead of taking the direct route home, walks back across the wet fields, finding in his way 'scores of coupled earthworms lying half their length on the surface of the damp ground'. The narrator tells us:

Though Farmer Troutham had just hurt him, he was a boy who could not himself bear to hurt anything. He had never brought home a nest of young birds without lying awake in misery half the night after . . . He could scarcely bear to see trees cut down or lopped, from a fancy that it hurt them; and late pruning, when the sap was up and the tree bled profusely, had been a positive grief to him in his infancy. This weakness of character, as it may be called, suggested that he was the sort of man who was born to ache a good deal before the fall of the curtain upon his unnecessary life should signify that all was well with him again. He carefully picked his way on tiptoe among the earthworms, without killing a single one.[84]

The mental framework that this implies deserves consideration. Jude, and indeed the reader, may not know explicitly that worms cannot feel pain (though Hichens's novel, written two years before Hardy's, suggests that the readership would); rather he accepts the idea of a creation suffused with sentience.[85] Reggie Hastings lifted the slug to the level of the overworked middle classes, whereas Jude takes an opposite line, and attributes sentience to the lowly and in so doing validates their suffering, as well as his own. Swung round by the angry Farmer Troutham, Jude finds himself compared to 'a hooked fish',[86] one step up from Samuelson's hooked worm. Whilst Hardy's simile suggests the 'centrifugal tendency of his person',[87] it also very deliberately links him to a supposedly insensate lower creation, but in ways which suggest its sensitivity. His similarity to the lower orders of animal creation makes him not only reluctant to hurt unhurtable worms, but he also cries in anguish at the seeming distress of cut trees that weep sap. A hierarchical structure of those things which feel pain, and those which do not, is in place, but the cut-off point between sensitivity and insensitivity is by no means clear, or at least is not in line with contemporary scientific thought.

The assessment of Jude here is unequivocal: he is born to suffer not just because it is part of the human condition to suffer, but because of his ability to feel with the seeming sufferings of lower creation. His 'fellow-feeling united his own life with theirs',[88] and the reader is presented with his deliberate

---

[84] *Jude the Obscure* (Osgood, McIlvaine, 1896), 13.
[85] See also Samuel Butler, *The Notebooks of Samuel Butler* (1912), ed. Henry Festing Jones (Hogarth Press, 1985). Butler argues for a similar sentience, not necessarily based on neurology, suffused throughout creation: 'It is generally held that animals feel; it will soon be generally held that plants feel; after that it will be held that stones also can feel. For, as no matter is so organic that there is not some of the inorganic in it, so, also, no matter is so inorganic that there is not some of the organic in it. We know that we have nerves and that we feel, it does not follow that other things do not feel because they have no nerves—it only follows that they do not feel as we do', 79–80.
[86] *Jude the Obscure*, 12.   [87] Ibid.   [88] Ibid. 11.

avoidance of the infliction of pain. This is not just a minor character trait of Jude's, but rather a way of positioning him in the universe, and of suggesting the nature of his relationship both with the world and with Sue. So much so that after Aunt Drusilla's funeral, when Sue has left Phillotson, both Jude and Sue, sleeping in separate houses, are awakened by the cries of a rabbit caught in a trap. Sue, waiting at the window, realizes that Jude has gone to put the rabbit out of its misery and pain, and eventually they meet in a highly charged moonlit scene where she indicates the sexual horrors of her marriage and he makes plain his love. That Jude's sensitivity is double-edged is very apparent: it is their shared reaction to the rabbit's cry of pain that brings Sue and Jude together, but which also is part of the inherent pain of their relationship. It is at the time that Jude so resolutely avoids hurting the coupling worms that Aunt Drusilla advises him, ' "Jude, my chile, don't *you* ever marry" ',[89] and it is to this that we are referred when the possibility of his second marriage comes into play. The adult Jude, who cannot bear to hear the audible expression of the rabbit's pain, is deliberately linked back to his younger self: 'He who in his childhood had saved the lives of the earthworms now began to picture the agonies of the rabbit from its lacerated leg.'[90] We are thrown back to Samuelson's fully sentient creation and his injunction to 'see' the pain of the hooked worm, as Jude not only hears the rabbit's cry, but also gives it a bodily form from which he infers its pain. But how can one 'picture agonies'? It is, as I have discussed in relation to Darwin and Witmer, the contention of this chapter to suggest that there is nothing innate to picture: there is no essence of pain to be found. As I argued in Chapter 3, this emptiness at the centre of pain prompts its referential reading, and allows the possibility of the denial of suffering in others according to the chosen embodiment of pain.

There is an obvious connection between the protagonist's own lowly position with regard to the Christminster colleges, and the position of the worms he deliberately chooses not to hurt. In recognizing the sensitivity of creatures not highly developed in evolutionary terms, he affirms his own sensitivity, and his right to aspire to education. The boy who recognized 'the thwarted

[89] *Jude the Obscure*, 9.   [90] Ibid. 268.

desires'[91] of the birds he is meant to be scaring off is not an unfeeling mass, but has legitimate desires of his own. Charles Voysey, defending God and his modus operandi, employs a parallel terminology:

To be wantonly or even unmindfully cruel would be to be *below* men's thoughts and ways. To give life, when it could be withheld, only to be spent in fruitless misery would be a crime against even an aphis or a worm. To create longings, desires and aspirations—even in the heart of a grub—and not to gratify them is an act of unvarnished cruelty.[92]

It is clear from this comment how such evolutionary scales could be manipulated and politicized. In choosing to deny the sensitivity of worms it is possible to mistreat them with impunity. What would they care since a benign God has not given them the capacity to suffer? Runciman suggests an analogue to Jude's position in his essay 'Discipline' when he becomes enraged by Carlyle's essay valorizing Friedrich Wilhelm, whom Runciman designates 'The unfeeling old king [who] used to go about thumping people in the streets with a big cudgel.'[93] Runciman suggests that Carlyle's response to such institutionalized abuse of power would be 'that the world would not have been much the worse off if a stray literary man here and there could have been bludgeoned'.[94] This is about autocratic power, but where it sheds light on Jude's predicament is in Runciman's attacks on Carlyle's own pedigree:

Carlyle, who was a Scotch peasant by birth, raised himself until he was deservedly regarded as the greatest man of his day, and he did this by means of literature; yet he coolly sets an ignorant, cruel, crowned drill-serjeant high above the men of the literary calling. It is a little too much! Suppose that Carlyle had been flogged back to the plough-tail by some potentate when he first went to the University[95]

The language here is that of intellectual, rather than social, ascendancy, but again images of height are invoked as Friedrich Wilhelm is placed at the top of the social pile and given carte blanche to beat those below. Such actions, of course, have nothing to do with neurological hierarchies, and this is exactly the point. Social convention which would allow Carlyle to be

---

[91] Ibid. 11.   [92] *Mystery of Pain, Death and Sin*, 34.
[93] 'Discipline', 193.   [94] Ibid. 193–4.   [95] Ibid. 194.

'flogged back to the plough-tail' has nothing whatever to do with an unchangeable nervous organization. Indeed, Carlyle, in Runciman's portrayal, provides the image of the 'Scotch peasant'—figured in neurological terms, as having 'coarse' nerves—breaking the bounds of education enabled by such a neurological organization. What this story makes clear is that hierarchical visions are sustained by those with power, and, as such, it reflects on the neurological hierarchy that sustained late Victorian social relations and suggests the fallacy of such hierarchical visions.

Jude, like Carlyle, longs to ascend the hierarchical structures of society, but unlike Carlyle, he fails. He is placed in the ambivalent position of being the one worm that has been given 'longings, desires and aspirations' all of which are most assiduously disappointed. Cutting across this, is Hardy's own assertion, cited by John Carey in *The Intellectuals and the Masses*, that

You may regard a throng of people as containing a certain small minority who have sensitive souls; these, and the aspects of these, being what is worth observing. So you divide them into the mentally unquickened, mechanical, soulless; and the living, throbbing, suffering, vital, in other words into souls and machines, ether and clay.[96]

Hardy takes up the same high ground of regard as that occupied by Lord X in *Joshua Davidson*. Indeed, Carey, in introducing this passage, mentions him as a 'highbrow looking across the gulf' at the masses in the dichotomy that provides the dynamic for his book. The choice between 'souls and machines, ether and clay' is being made on aesthetic grounds: the reader is offered the 'sensitive souls' and their 'aspects'—what I have called their adjuncts, and Darwin their accessories—as the objects of observation and fitting subjects of the novel, and the hierarchies established here are as discriminatory as those offered by Lord X's social position and perspective.

Shifting ground slightly, I move now from Jude's identification with the pain of worms to the experience of pain portrayed in George Moore's novel *Esther Waters*. Hardy, in the quota-

---

[96] *The Intellectuals and the Masses: Pride and Prejudice among the Literary Intelligentsia, 1880–1939* (Faber, 1992), 10. Carey cites Michael Milgate (ed.), *The Life and Works of Thomas Hardy* (Macmillan, 1984), 192.

tion just discussed, makes possible the isolation of the individual who feels acutely, and in so doing provides theoretical leverage for those wishing to politicize the perception of pain. In his realist enterprise, Moore allows Esther, his working-class heroine, to feel pain in a manner generally denied to the working classes. Esther, in the face of John Conquest's observation that the working classes felt no pain in giving birth, suffers greatly, and as such gives readers a way of understanding the heroine's place in society through a recognition of her bodily experience.

The narrative concerning Esther and William's lovemaking is very blurred—not only because he has got her drunk—and it is not easy to discern exactly what is going on. The reader is simply told that

The wheat stacks were thatching, and in the . . . warm valleys, listening to the sheep bells tinkling, they often lay together talking of love and marriage, till one evening, putting his pipe aside, William threw his arm round her, whispering that she was his wife. The words were delicious in her fainting ears. She could not put him away, nor could she struggle with him, though she knew that her fate depended upon her resistance, and swooning away she awakened in pain, powerless to free herself[97]

The only thing of any solidity here is her awakening in and, indeed, through pain. Moore expresses the pain of the loss of virginity as well as the pain of childbirth itself, about which he is surprisingly forthcoming, writing: 'it seemed to her that she was being torn asunder',[98] and, later, 'Esther was clinging to the table . . . with pain so vivid on her face that Mrs. Jones laid aside the sausages she was cooking.'[99] There is a serious point here: the emphasis on the sausages may seem trivial, but her pain is never treated as comic despite its very domestic setting, nor is it ever passed over as was the norm in Victorian fiction. Elizabeth Gaskell's *Ruth* provides a fitting model of Victorian fictional parturition, as her pain is displaced into grief—her

[97] *Esther Waters* (1894, rev. 1899; Oxford: Oxford University Press, 1991), 73. I am using David Skilton's World's Classics edition of *Esther Waters*, based on the 1931 text 'which incorporates all [Moore's] emendations, and presents the novel as he eventually left it' (p. xxiv), because of the difficulty of obtaining the revised editions.
[98] Ibid. 124–5.   [99] Ibid. 121.

'dreamy eyes fill[ing] with glittering tears'[100]—and the birth itself is presented as an accomplished fact, rather than as the result of labour: 'The earth was still "hiding her guilty front with innocent snow," when a little baby was laid by the side of the pale white mother.'[101] Her paleness suggests the process of giving birth, but that process itself is forced off-stage. As Tess Cosslett suggests,

Childbirth, as an experience belonging to the private sphere of womanhood, has long been marginalised as a subject for public representation . . . Before the twentieth century, childbirth did not often appear in fiction, and when it did it was nearly always seen from an audience point of view—the father's, the attendants'.[102]

The pain of childbirth did not, as a matter of course, find a place in fiction, though by the latter third of the century examples of painful birth began to appear: Collins's Anne Silvester, 'with her handkerchief twisted between her set teeth, and her tortured face terrible to look at',[103] gives birth to an illegitimate—and dead—child, and Catherine Elsmere, in an extraordinary fashion, rails against the pains of parturition: ' "It seems . . . to take the joy even out of our love—and the child. I feel ashamed almost that mere physical pain should have laid such hold on me." '[104]

Moore's heroine, however, stands out because she is one of the working classes, and the question to be asked in the light of the issues raised in this chapter is, who can afford to feel the pain of the loss of virginity, or, indeed, of childbirth? Mrs Saunders, Esther's mother, claims that the pain of the working-class woman lies in the number of children she has, and the way she is beaten by her husband: the quotidian grind of working-class life. Pain in childbirth, as I argued in the previous chapter, was not seen as a universal condition, but rather as the fruit of

---

[100] *Ruth: A Novel* (1853; Chapman and Hall, 1855), 112.
[101] Ibid.
[102] *Women Writing Childbirth: Modern Discourses of Motherhood* (Manchester: Manchester University Press, 1994), 1.
[103] *Man and Wife: A Novel*, 3 vols. (F. S. Ellis, 1870), ii. 171.
[104] Mrs Humphry Ward, *Robert Elsmere*, 3 vols. (Smith, Elder, 1888), ii. 145. For discussions of this passage in terms of Ward's own response to the pain of childbirth and its social consequences, see Elaine Showalter, *A Literature of their Own: From Charlotte Brontë to Doris Lessing* (1978; rev. edn., Virago, 1993), 230–1, and Anne Fremantle, *Three-Cornered Heart* (Collins, 1971), 67.

a luxurious lifestyle—the province of the civilized rich. As Conquest argued, the ability to suffer marked off the civilized from the savage. It is also clear that Conquest held servant girls to be in the same unfeeling category as the women of Asia, Africa, and the West Indies whom he termed savages:

Still further to establish the assertion that human parturition is not necessarily a process of danger, we know that in this country servant girls who become illegitimately pregnant, very often absent themselves for an hour or two, and after giving birth to a child, return to the discharge of their household duties immediately.[105]

This is just Esther's case, but her story is very different. Moore's book is radical not just in using a servant as the heroine, but in allowing this kind of overthrow of cultural expectation. He allows her the body and the physical suffering of those considered to be her social superiors, and he uses her ability to suffer to point to her heightened sensibilities.

Moore offers the pains Esther suffers as a doorway to heightened consciousness, using the language of the Magnificat to underpin such sensations: 'it was in this death of active memory that something awoke within her, something that seemed to her like a flutter of wings'.[106] What awakes within her when memory is inactivated in this way is not just her child, but also a new consciousness of her surroundings, and what Moore sees as a heroic self. Recognizing the class of his heroine, Moore feels the need to elaborate on this point:

Hers is a heroic adventure if one considers it—a mother's fight for the life of her child against all the forces that civilisation arrays against the lowly and the illegitimate. She is in a situation to-day, but on what security does she hold it? She is strangely dependent on her own health, and still more upon the fortunes and the personal caprice of her employers; and she realised the perils of her life when an outcast mother at the corner of the street, stretching out of her rags a brown hand and arm, asked alms for the sake of the little children. For three months out of a situation and she, too, would be on the street as a flower-seller, match-seller, or—[107]

Her heroism depends not just on this overcoming of adversity, but on the ways that she begins to respond to the people and

---

[105] *Letters*, 48.   [106] *Waters*, 85.   [107] Ibid. 172.

objects around her. This change in her perceptual level is no surprise for the book is one of constant social flux: fortunes are made and lost in gambling, and the rich of the previous generation are the servants of the next, whilst Esther's staunch, though sexualized, Protestantism allows for a further recognition of the identity between classes. She says of Peggy, the daughter of her mistress, who has 'stolen' William from her: 'But they were all of the same flesh and blood. Peggy wore a fine dress, but she was no better; take off her dress and they were the same, woman to woman.'[108] This is the beginning of a strangely mystical scene, where Esther, despite her recurrent fits of vagueness, moves from below stairs—the realm of the servant—up to the richness and profusion of the upper part of the house:

> She pushed through the door and walked down the passage. A few steps brought her to the foot of a polished oak staircase, lit by a large window in coloured glass, on either side of which there were statues. The staircase sloped slowly to an imposing landing set out with columns and blue vases and embroidered curtains. The girl saw these things vaguely, and she was conscious of a profusion of rugs, matting, and bright doors, and her inability to decide which door was the drawing-room of which she had heard so much, and where even now, amid gold furniture and flower-scented air, William listened to the wicked woman who had tempted him away from her.[109]

She is unfamiliar with the world above stairs, but at the same time, she becomes 'conscious' of it in ways other than those of a servant, of its colour and its scent. It is clear that she is not concerned that the oak staircase needs to be endlessly polished, but rather that it is a thing of beauty in itself, as well as being the metaphorical means of ascent into a world of heightened sensitivity. The recognition of her physical pain allows her to ascend the ladder of sensibility, and to gain 'refinement'. In Moore's refusal to accept conventional strictures as to who can and who cannot feel pain, and his insistence that Esther's suffering is serious rather than comic, he attacks the claims of neurological elitism and offers in its place a more flexible framework.

Hierarchies of suffering and the difficulties of attributing a specific place on a hierarchical ladder to an individual sufferer

---

[108] *Waters*, 80.   [109] Ibid.

have been at the centre of this section. In establishing the factors that go towards underpinning the perceived ladders of sensitivity, I have suggested that neurology, broader ideas of social progress, and an older scheme of refined sensibility, often coincided in such a way as to work together for the desensitizing of the working classes. Francis Newman cites the Catholic doctrine of soulless animals as an invidious means of institutionalizing the abuse of those creatures considered lower down the ladder. Newman claims that

An eminent priest in Rome has preached with contempt of those who object to the torture of brute animals. Men (says he) must not be tortured; *for*, they hav immortal souls. Other animals ar not immortal; *therefor*, they hav no rights that man needs to respect. They may be tortured at his pleasure.—Now if this were the doctrin of one man, it might be passed by as an eccentric insanity. But I learn that it is really Catholic doctrin, and that historically it has leavened the vulgar Italians with dire callousness to the sufferings of the lower races.[110]

This argument, to a large extent, is matter for the previous, vivisectional, chapter, but in designating animals 'the lower races' Newman calls on a terminology of human relationships and his annoyance at the ability to ignore 'these inferior races [who] *hav nerves as sensitiv as the human*'[111] questions the lines of demarcation that G. H. Lewes was trying to set up and which Darwin found so problematic. In attributing the ability to feel pain to the relative complexity of neurological organization, and fitting this ability into an ascending scale of sensitivity, some degree of leeway was given to the individual sufferer, who at least had the possibility of ascending the ladder. What Newman despised here is the thinking to be discussed in Section II: the idea that there is a definite cut-off point between 'the lower races' and the 'higher'. Humans with souls can suffer; animals without simply cannot, and an uncrossable chasm exists between them.

II. EXCLUDING THE DEVIANT

If Jude looked at bodily sensitivity from the lower steps of an evolutionary ladder, then the perspective from the top was very

---

[110] *Life After Death? Palinōdia* (Trübner, 1886), 21–2. Spelling as original.
[111] Ibid. 22. Spelling as original.

different. Victorian, white, sane, civilized, law-abiding, European Christians were able to construct a sense of self by saying, I feel pain therefore I am not a savage. I feel pain therefore I am not hysterical, not a physiological anomaly, not an animal, dead or dying, nor am I a criminal. In this way they could define what they were by what they were not. Medical and criminological textbooks sought to exclude the idiot, the lunatic, and the instinctive criminal from what would be deemed normal sensation, whilst freak shows pushed to the fore Tomasso, the Human Pincushion; Alfonso, the man capable of eating fishhooks and glass; and Rob Roy the Albino and Dislocationist, who 'has the power . . . to put every joint in his body out . . . painlessly',[112] as a way of forcing such performers to stake out their difference. As Alison Hennegan argues, the definition of the normal by exclusion of the deviant was by no means confined to bodily pain, but was part of a much broader cultural phenomenon:

During the second half of the nineteenth century, all over Europe, practitioners of newly developing disciplines and sciences were busily codifying humanity: Charcot in France; Krafft-Ebing in Germany; Lombroso in Italy; Tarnowsy . . . in Russia; Havelock Ellis in England; and . . . Freud in Vienna. They and many others were intent on identifying, describing, classifying and explaining the many variations in human physiology, psychology and sexuality.

Ostensibly their purpose was benign: arguably their impact has been unfortunate. Underlying this vast examination of human diversity was a strong belief in a human norm against which 'variations' were to be judged and found wanting. The 'variant' rapidly became the 'deviant' or 'pervert', in need of punishment, or treatment, or eradication. Forms of human behaviour hitherto deemed normal were now declared pathological.[113]

Much as antivivisectionists could be deemed 'zoophilpsychotics' and thus disregarded as oversensitive, so too, in a parallel though opposite way, could those defined as criminals be pushed to the side as insensate. The ability to feel pain was

---

[112] Clarence L. Dean, *The Official Guide. Book of Marvels in the Barnum & Bailey Greatest Show on Earth. With Full Descriptions of the Human Prodigies and Rare Animals* (Barnum and Bailey, 1899), 15.

[113] 'Personalities and Principles: Aspects of Literature and Life in *Fin-de-Siècle* England', in Mikuláš Teich and Roy Porter (eds.), *Fin de Siècle and its Legacy* (1990; Cambridge: Cambridge University Press, 1993), 202.

polarized, and the two poles of sensitivity and insensitivity were deemed to have an almost impassable gulf between them, allowing a smug safeness to come with the ability to be hurt.

This segregation of people, which I have figured as an uncrossable gulf, was also commonly represented as a 'line' drawn between different groups: a metaphor that flirted with the danger of the situation. For whilst a gulf physically could not be crossed, a line drawn involves no such physical barrier.[114] Rhoda Broughton's Sarah Churchill humorously makes the point that lines of division are drawn between social classes: ' "It is a liberal age," says Sarah philosophically, "but one must draw the line somewhere. I draw the line at artificial manure!" '[115] Whilst *Belinda* is a story about marriage, Joshua Davidson (still hunting for a sponsor for his alcoholic burglar) finds division much more firmly marked by Mr C who 'drew a line hard and fast where Joshua did not. His line was respectability. He distinctly refused to aid those who were helpless paupers, or those of bad repute.'[116] As David Garland argues, the model of a line dividing classes was firmly established in the social structures of late Victorian Britain, as its disciplinary institutions 'successfully concentrated criminality into the lowest sections of the population and produced a definite social division between these groups and their more "respectable" peers'.[117] Division was not simply seen as the segregation of similar, though differently circumstanced, people, but rather as the marker of difference. Alison Hennegan, discussing Nordau's *Degeneration*, suggests the way in which the word 'Degenerate, once solely an adjective, had become a noun: people could be "degenerates".'[118] Not only this, but

---

[114] Antivivisectionary writers exploited the insubstantiality of such a line in their vision of the inescapable escalation from animal vivisection to human vivisection. See Lewis Carroll, *Some Popular Fallacies About Vivisection* (Oxford: privately printed, 1875). Carroll writes with heavy irony 'that while science arrogates to herself the right of torturing at her pleasure the whole sentient creation up to man himself, some inscrutable boundary line is there drawn, over which she will never venture to pass', 14. Mona Caird reverses the irony by calling her pamphlet *Beyond the Pale*. In so doing she pushes vivisectionists and their practices across a firmly designated marker and dissociates them from those of sensibility.

[115] *Belinda*, 40.   [116] [Linton], *True History*, 72.

[117] *Punishment and Welfare: A History of Penal Strategies* (Aldershot: Gower, 1985), 38.

[118] 'Personalities and Principles', 189.

Other adjectives—socialist, communist, anarchist, homosexual and criminal, for example—gained an additional resonance when used as nouns. 'Criminals' are those whose total human identity is deemed to consist of their criminality. It is a way of thinking tailored for those who seek scapegoats, who require always to be allowed to believe that danger can be kept out, 'over there', outside and beyond one's own self or circle.[119]

But in the face of theoretically laid out distinctions these fiercely demarcated boundaries were breached in practice rather than in principle as the evidence of anthropology undercut the claims of criminology, and as humans refused to fit into the categories designated for them.

In the first instance I shall be looking at the phenomenon of fire-walking which was becoming a particularly hot issue in the 1890s. In this practice it seemed that only a sacred few, drawn from the ranks of those deemed insensate savages, were exempt from the pain of burning, as a black/white dichotomy of the initiated and uninitiated was worked out on the red-hot coals. From here, I shall move on to discuss the related pain of tattooing, which proved to be a much more difficult problem, as the supposed insensitivity of criminals as a group got caught up in the painful process of coal dust and needles, and the royal families of Europe further complicated the theoretically sharp edges of criminological utterance by delighting and engaging in the supposedly savage process.

But first fire-walking. The phenomenon is best approached by looking at a mixture of first-hand accounts of the 'Te Umu-Ti' or Polynesian fire-walking ceremony as represented in anthropological journals of the 1890s, along with the more sceptical account given by Andrew Lang in *Modern Mythology* (1897). In the first-hand accounts of Miss Teuira Henry, Mr Hastwell (whose narrative is appended to that of Henry), and Colonel Gudgeon, the third of whom walked across the red-hot coals himself, there is no sense of trickery: the walk can only be accomplished because of the nature of the walker. Henry claims that 'only two individuals (Tupua and Taero), both descendants of priests'[120] can now walk through flames without suffering

---

[119] 'Personalities and Principles', 189.
[120] 'Te Umu-Ti, A Raiatean Ceremony', *Journal of the Polynesian Society Containing the Transactions and Proceedings of the Society*, 2 (1893), 106.

either pain or physical damage, and Hastwell describes the scene:

When I witnessed it, on the second day, the flames were pouring up through the interstices of the rocks, which were heated to a red and white heat. When everything was in readiness, and the furnace still pouring out its intense heat, the natives marched up, with bare feet, to the edge of the furnace, where they halted for a moment, and after a few passes of the wand made of the branches of the *ti*-plant by the leader, who repeated a few words in the native language, they stepped down on the rocks, and walked leisurely across to the other side, stepping from stone to stone. This was repeated five times, without any preparation whatever on their feet, and without injury or discomfort from the heated stones. There was not even the smell of fire on their garments.[121]

This description provides a strange conjunction of languages and terms of reference, as Hastwell swings between a sense of otherness and of similarity, and of scientific accuracy and pseudo-magical deception. For whilst he claims to bear witness to a seeming religious truth, he also measures this truth by the accuracy of his language—he speaks of 'interstices' rather than 'gaps' between the rocks, and of the scientific fivefold repetition of the experiment, though this, in itself, replicates ritualistic repetition. This established, he goes on to describe the rites of the Maori priest as the mere repetition of a few words accompanied by a few passes of the wand: hardly a determined attempt to understand the nature of what was going on in front of his eyes. The ambivalence deepens as he notes that the natives march up, and then halt, for the terms of description are clearly military—and, indeed, many of the onlookers were French soldiers—and yet the natives march in 'bare feet' and in this way are characterized as distinctly savage.[122] Then the metaphor changes, and the savages 'walked leisurely across to the other side' as though they are ambling in the park, yet the language of safety—they are 'stepping from stone to stone'—calls on safe

---

[121] Ibid. 108.

[122] See Rudyard Kipling, *Kim* (Macmillan, 1901), 153, 167, 178 where Kim's ambivalence about wearing boots clearly marks his cultural ambivalence. For a discussion of Kim's cultural transvestism see also Anne McClintock, *Imperial Leather: Race, Gender and Sexuality in the Colonial Contest* (New York and London: Routledge, 1995), 70.

footholds above a torrent of water or through a mire, whilst in reality these stones are 'heated to a red and white heat'. In the normal course of events, such stepping stones, instead of saving or sustaining as they do here, would burn and cause great pain. And yet the lack of pain is the thing of importance about this ritual and what makes it worthy of description: the two men should have run screaming from the stones. In his attempt to render the experience truthfully and to rid the reader of any idea of trickery, Hastwell has underplayed the element that makes the display important: any fire-walker failing to cross safely would, no doubt, feel more than the 'discomfort' he mentions. Whilst unable to proffer any explanation for this display of fire-walking, Hastwell finds solace in scientific enquiry. He writes: 'No one has yet been able to solve the mystery of this surprising feat, but it is hoped that scientists will endeavour to do so while those men who practise it still live.'[123]

The case is, however, slightly different with Colonel Gudgeon, for he accomplishes the feat himself, but believes this to be the case only because the *tohunga*, or priest in charge, one of a line of 'hereditary fire-walkers',[124] has handed over his power, or *mana*, to the English men that they might walk through the flames in safety: 'A man must have *mana* to do it; if he has not, it will be too late when he is on the hot stone of Tama-ahi-roa.'[125]

Indeed, one of the party of Europeans who attempted the crossing on this occasion was badly burned because he 'was spoken to, but like Lot's wife [l]ooked behind him—a thing against all rules'.[126] This burnt man raises pertinent questions of who does and who does not feel pain. Gudgeon describes his own experience in terms of the sensations he anticipated:

I walked with bare feet . . . I did not walk quickly across the oven, but with deliberation, because I feared that I should tread on a sharp point of the stones and fall. My feet also were very tender. I did not mention the fact, but my impression as I crossed the oven was that the skin would peel off my feet. Yet all I really felt when the task was accomplished was a tingling sensation not unlike slight electric shocks on the

[123] Henry, 'Te Umi-Ti', 106.
[124] Gudgeon, 'Te Umu-Ti, or Fire-walking Ceremony', *Journal of the Polynesian Society*, 8 (1899), 60.
[125] Ibid. 59.   [126] Ibid.

soles of my feet, and this continued for seven hours or more. The really funny thing is that, though the stones were hot enough an hour afterward to burn up green branches of the *ti*, the very tender skin of my feet was not even hardened by the fire.[127]

This description is about the anticipation of pain and the non-fulfilment of such anticipation for whatever reasons, and this is the framework in which Gudgeon reads the experience. As a European, civilized Christian rather than a Polynesian savage, pain could be expected to fall to his lot. As he is careful to point out his feet are particularly tender, suggesting his European sensitivity, and his vulnerability is suggested by the failure of his compatriot who is, indeed, badly burned. Likewise his public-school stoicism—he 'did not mention' the tenderness of his feet—suggests a tradition of painful experience with concomitant repression of its expression.

Gudgeon's uneasiness as to what he felt, and what he expected to feel, or should have felt, is written throughout this paragraph, and what Hastwell describes as a 'surprising feat' is seen in terms of his own 'surprising feet' which behave in an entirely unexpected manner. He calls the walk across the red-hot coals a 'task' and yet it is hard to see how this act, albeit brave, of anthropological fieldwork could be seen as something that had to be done, unless in terms—as already suggested—of a misplaced stoicism: believing that the skin would peel from his feet, he chooses to walk the hot coals as a means of understanding the phenomenon. Likewise it becomes clear that despite his expectations, what he 'really' felt was nothing like pain, only a 'tingling sensation' lasting for some hours. And this experience can only be described as 'funny', curious, surprising, for there is no rational explanation: 'I can only tell you it is *mana—mana tangata* and *mana atua*.'[128]

This is, however, a deeply ambivalent situation, for Gudgeon could be expected to fit in with contemporary European thought in believing that savages did not feel anything in any case, and indeed, in writing about the Maoris he was concerned with the same group of natives that I shall be discussing in terms of tattooing: a group of people who were contemporaneously clearly stereotyped as being insensitive to pain. But fire-walking does

---

[127] Ibid. 59–60.   [128] Ibid. 60.

not lean on the assumption that savages do not feel, but rather suggests that it is a miracle that they do not in this context. Gudgeon, in fire-walking himself, is perplexed at his success, but instead of falling back on a naturalistic explanation, that he walked at such a speed that no damage could be done by the flames,[129] he chooses to fit in with the explanation of the Maoris, that the power to walk could be handed over to him by a priest. But again his reaction is ambivalent, for at the same time as accepting that his success is miraculous, he stresses the unique sensitivity of his own feet as distinct from those of the Maoris: a miracle has been performed, but it is one of particular efficacy where he is concerned.

Andrew Lang, too, is concerned—as he suggests in recording the words of Basil Thomson's *South Sea Yarns*[130]—with the sensitivity of feet, both as an index to civilization and as a thing which may suffer or not according to its physical state:

We caught four or five of the performers as they came out, and closely examined their feet. They were cool, and showed no trace of scorching, nor were their anklets of dried tree-fern leaf burnt. This, Jonathan explained, is part of the miracle; for dried tree-fern is as combustible as tinder, and there were flames shooting out among the stones. Sceptics had affirmed that the skin of a Fijian's foot being a quarter of an inch thick, he would not feel a burn. Whether this be true or not of the ball and heel, the instep is covered with skin no thicker than our own, and we saw the men plant their insteps fairly on the stone.[131]

Again the question arises of how the 'we' of this assertion is constructed. Physical difference shows itself on the feet as hardened skin—the result of going barefoot—but this is not enough to account for the difference in pain thresholds, or, indeed, for the non-combustion of the tree fern. It is clear from such description that Thomson is baffled by the proceeding, and by

---

[129] See also Edward Tregear, 'The Maoris of New Zealand', *Journal of the Anthropological Institute of Great Britain and Ireland*, 19 (1890), 97–123. For a modern appraisal of such phenomena as fire-walking and hook-hanging, see Doreen R. G. Browne, 'Ritual and Pain', in Ronald D. Mann (ed.), *The History of the Management of Pain: From Early Principles to Present Practice* (Carnforth, Lancs and Park Ridge, NJ: Parthenon, 1988), 31–49.

[130] 'The Fiery Furnace', in *South Sea Yarns* (Edinburgh: William Blackwood, 1894), 195.

[131] Lang, *Modern Mythology* (Longmans, Green, 1897), 158. Thomson, 'Fiery Furnace', 205.

the difference from himself of the Fijians: the barefoot savages who need to be 'caught' as they come up out of the pit, but who do not feel the pain of burning. Part of this bafflement seems to arise from the similarities between the Europeans and the Fijians—'the instep is covered with skin no thicker than our own'—for it is not clear, if this is the case, and there is no physiological explanation, in what the difference inheres. Jonathan, the leader of the Fijians, suggests a miraculous explanation, whilst Thomson turns more immediately to confusion and then to the language of Christian religion. He makes clear in his terminology of pits, infernos, and fiends—'the pit turns into the mouth of an Inferno, filled with dusky frenzied fiends, half seen through the dense volume that rolls up to heaven and darkens the sunlight'[132]—where his allegiances lie. In not feeling pain, the 'savages' refuse the ordinance of God who, in Christian eyes, inflicts pain for the good of mankind. It is no surprise, either, that Hastwell should describe the pit walked across as the 'Fiery Furnace'—the language of hell and eternal damnation—for this image of fire, though wearing thin by the 1890s, became the ultimate Victorian ideal of extreme pain. The priesthood of the two men capable of traversing the flames, who are able to step aside from pain, is invoked as a counterpoise to a Christian framework.

And this, I think, leaves the anthropologist of the 1890s and his voyeuristic impulses—'the cameras snap, the crowd surges forward'[133]—in a strange position. For the absolute given of pain caused by burning is no longer an absolute given, and where this is the case there is no viable explanation. Andrew Lang, disbelieving what he hears of fire-walking, attempts to shift it into the realms of trickery—'the miracle of passing through the fire uninjured is apparently feigned with considerable skill, or is performed by the aid of some secret of Nature not known to modern chemistry'.[134] Whatever the explanation, the meaning of pain has become slippery, not least because it seems that the 'power' to fire-walk can be handed from the savage to the civilized man, and this immunity from pain, whilst being a touchstone of race, begins to blur the edges.

---

[132] Lang, *Mythology*, 158. Thomson, 'Fiery Furnace', 204.
[133] Lang, *Mythology*, 157. Thomson, 'Fiery Furnace', 203–4.
[134] *Mythology*, 154.

Tattooing, though surprisingly popular in the late nineteenth century, had a fraught relationship with the experience of pain and who was thought to suffer it. I shall be discussing various records of the kinds of people who were being tattooed as they appeared in anthropological and criminological works, as well as in the periodical press and in novels. Tattoos spread from sailors and the freak show where they were unthreatening—it was, after all, recommended to sailors that they gain distinctive tattoos as identifying marks in case of drowning at sea—to (though to a limited extent) the general populace. By the 1890s the urge to be tattooed was deemed a 'craze' among the upper classes, and it is no surprise that a poem about tattooing, 'Art's Martyr', appeared in Andrew Lang's 1885 book *Rhymes à la Mode* which also takes on such topical issues as the 'Girton Girl' and Railway Novels.[135]

Havelock Ellis's 1889 book *The Criminal* deals with what was perceived as the other end of the social scale, and the group designated criminals. Ellis sought to synthesize the work of continental researchers in the field of criminal anthropology, and to mark out the ways in which the instinctive criminal, rather than he who committed a crime of passion, differed from the norm. There were many ways—detailed by Ellis in his book—that the criminal was marked out as different from the law-abiding citizen, but one of the primary ways was his physical and psychological insensitivity. For Ellis the practice of tattooing allowed him the means of excluding from sentience a group designated criminals. As Ellis wrote, closely following the Italian criminologist Cesare Lombroso:

The extent to which tattooing is carried out among criminals, sometimes not sparing parts so sensitive as the sexual organs, which are rarely touched even in extensive tattooing among barbarous races, serves to show the deficient sensibility of criminals to pain. The physical insensibility of criminals has indeed been observed by every one

---

[135] 'Art's Martyr', in *Rhymes à la Mode* (Kegan, Paul, French, 1885), 94–6. The poem, which ends tragically, nevertheless begins happily enough, and the first verse serves as an index to the popularity of tattooing among the aesthetically fashion-conscious: 'He said, the china on the shelf | Is very fair to view, | And wherefore should mine outer self, | Not correspond thereto? | In blue | My frame I must tattoo.' Sadly this self-decoration goes wrong when the Burmese tattoo the narrator in vulgar colours and he ends up looking like a cheap Christmas card.

who is familiar with prisons. In this respect the instinctive criminal resembles the idiot to whom, as Galton remarks, pain is 'a welcome surprise.'[136] He may even be compared with many lower races, such as those Maoris who did not hesitate to chop off a toe or two, in order to be able to wear European boots.[137]

Much as, in the previous chapter, we saw vegetarians, antivivisectionists, and feminists grouped together in order to discredit them, there is here a similar pulling together of types of people who supposedly cannot feel: the idiot, the criminal, and the savage. Their insensibility is immediately discernible: 'Everyone who is familiar with prison' will have noticed it, and what is more, it is the case with *all* instinctive criminals. Perhaps the most striking thing to arise from such comment is the level of proof required to suggest physical insensibility: tattooing of the genitals can *only* mean a 'deficient sensibility of criminals to pain', and there is no suggestion of possible motivations for such actions.

What is particularly worrying is the inbuilt circularity of such arguments, for if the a priori assumption is that criminals cannot feel pain because they take pleasure in inflicting it, or because they have tattoos which no right-thinking person would endure, then all of their behaviour is read in this light. This kind of thinking is at its most disturbing when Ellis cites the amount of self-mutilation in prisons: 'At Chatham in 1871–72, 841 voluntary wounds or contusions are recorded; 27 prisoners voluntarily fractured a limb . . . ; 62 tried to mutilate themselves, and 101 produced wounds by means of corrosive substances.'[138] This is seen not as the consequence of incarceration, but rather as the action of a trickster aiming to attain some trivial end and who does not feel the pain he inflicts on himself. Here, too, the criminal is seen as an object of observation, and as such a counter in a game of physiological positioning. The average European—the owner of the boots, a sign of the march of

---

[136] Galton, *Inquiries*, 28. Galton goes on to suggest: 'I also saw a boy with the scar of a severe wound on his wrist; the story being that he had first burned himself slightly by accident, and, liking the keenness of the new sensation, he took the next opportunity of repeating the experience, but, idiot-like, he overdid it', 29.

[137] Havelock Ellis, *The Criminal* (1889; Walter Scott, 1890), 112.

[138] Ibid. 115.

progress, which the unfeeling Maori covets—is on one side of
the great sensibility divide, whilst far away on the other side are
the idiot, the criminal, and the savage. Ellis sees the perceptual
scheme of the white, civilized, sane, boot-wearing Christian
as the pinnacle of evolutionary achievement, but rejects the
hierarchical structure that this implies: criminals do not
have degrees of sensitivity, rather they just do not feel, they are
'deficient'.

It is, of course, impossible for Ellis to maintain this position,
because it is blatantly not the case. So whilst he makes broad
generalizations about the insensitivity of criminals, there are
also currents in the book that suggest that they can—and do—
feel, at least to some extent. Whilst much of Ellis's evidence
depended on the hearsay evidence of the pregnant woman,
giving herself a supposedly painless Caesarean section with a
kitchen knife, only to murder the baby when it emerged,[139] or
on the evidence of a surgeon who claims to 'have extirpated
tumours . . . of considerable size . . . without the necessity of
producing anæsthesia',[140] he also drew on the experience and
experimental data of continental scientists deemed to be experts
in the field:

Working with Du-Bois Reymond's electrical apparatus, in conjunction
with Marro, [Lombroso] found the sensibility of the criminals much
inferior to that of the normal persons examined. Swindlers possessed
much greater sensibility than murderers and thieves. Marro found sensibility, measured by an esthesiometer, most obtuse in murderers and
incendiaries.[141] Similar results were obtained by Ramlot, in reference
to tactile sensibility; he examined 103 criminals and 27 normal
persons, and found obtusity in 44 per cent. of the former, and in only
29 per cent. of the latter.[142]

---

[139] Ellis, 114.

[140] Ibid. 113. The scandal over the number of painful operations performed on
the impoverished patients at the Chelsea Hospital for Women (discussed in the previous chapter) strongly suggests that such examples should be discounted as evidence of the women's insensitivity.

[141] For descriptions of Du-Bois Reymond's electrical algometer and Weber's esthesiometer see Gina Lombroso Ferrero, *Criminal Man according to the Classification
of Cesare Lombroso. Briefly Summarised by his Daughter* (Knickerbocker Press,
1911), 245–7.

[142] Ellis, *Criminal*, 115.

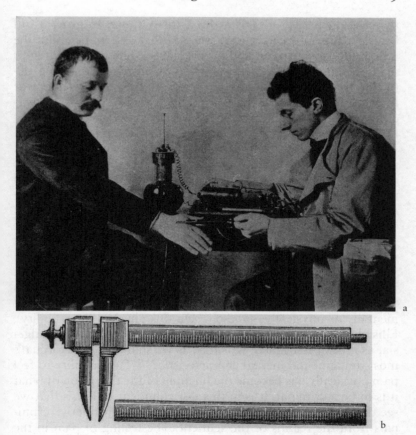

FIG. 3. *a* Du-Bois Reymond's Electrical Algometer *b* Weber's Esthesiometer

Source: Gina Lombroso Ferrero, *Criminal Man According to the Classification of Cesare Lombroso. Briefly Summarised by his Daughter* (Knickerbocker Press, 1911), figs 35 (7a) and 34 (7b).

The value of the results of such experimentation is dubious, not least because of the disproportion in the numbers tested, but it should also be borne in mind that experimental evidence showed instinctive criminals to have better eyesight, worse hearing and sense of smell, virtually no ability to blush, and in the case of male criminals at least the inability to grow a full beard.[143] It is in the light of these data that assertions about the non-ability to feel pain should be placed. There is no attempt made to contextualize the response of criminals to being deliberately hurt, and there is no suggestion that an element of bravado might modify their response. This is strange as it was clear from the well-documented tales of sailors that whilst they found tattooing painful, the proven ability to endure such pain was part of what made tattoos attractive to them for it showed their fortitude.[144] There is no reason to doubt that criminals exposed to such experimentally inflicted, deliberate pain would not react in a similar fashion. The desire on the part of criminologists to push the criminal out of the realms of the 'normal', shown also in their tendency to classify criminals with other supposedly insensate groups, allowed for such short-sightedness in interpreting experimental evidence.

The crux of the matter, as Ellis makes clear later in the book, is the perceived direct link between the ability to hurt others through criminal activity and the inability to feel things—mentally or physically—oneself. 'On this physical insensibility', Ellis claims, 'rests that moral insensibility, or psychical analgesia, as it has been called, which is, as we shall see, the criminal's most fundamental mental characteristic.'[145] The inability to feel pain physically has become the linchpin of the definition of what it is to be a criminal. It is in this last comment of Ellis's that we see the rationale behind the desire to exclude instinctive criminals from the realms of the sentient. The feeling of pain in the law-abiding shores up the sense of not being criminal, and it is this that makes it almost impossible for them to commit violent crime. It is, I would suggest, this desire to exclude deviant elements of society that leads to the blind spot of criminologists in recognizing the sense of pain in those whom they studied.

[143] See Stephen Jay Gould, *The Mismeasure of Man* (1981; Penguin, 1992), 130. Gould demonstrates the falsity of Lombroso's statistics using the argument that criminals have smaller brains than non-criminals, and disproves the claims made by using the criminologist's own data. Ellis, who used Lombroso as the source of much of his information, inherited these deficient data.

[144] Hanns Ebensten, *Pierced Hearts and True Love: An Illustrated History of the Origin and Development of European Tattooing and a Survey of its Present State* (Derek Verschoyle, 1953), 22.

[145] *Criminal*, 123.

Tattooing can also be profitably approached from a slightly different angle by looking at some of the ways in which it became so firmly attached to criminality. Up until 1879 the letters D for 'deserter', and BC for 'bad character' were tattooed onto the bodies of offending British soldiers,[146] whilst any other tattoos they might have could be recorded as characteristic marks kept by the police.[147] Novelists were quick to associate criminality and tattooing, as such titles as Major Arthur Griffiths's *The Brand of the Broad Arrow* (1886) make clear in their association of the brand or tattoo and the sign of the criminal. Count Fosco's tattoo, called a brand and probably made by igniting a mixture of gunpowder and ink on the skin, indelibly associated the tattoo with the secret society, and indeed in this case with the traitor, as the initial 'T' of *traditore* was superimposed on the tattoo, linking the criminal act with the tattoo itself. Similarly, Fergus Hume's *Tracked by a Tattoo* (1896) follows very closely in Collins's footsteps, using the established trope of the tattoo as the mark of a secret society as a decoy for the inheritance plot that is really under way. It is in this novel, as in Hardy's *A Laodicean* (1881), that the tattoo is used as a kind of birthmark, liable to being faked.[148] It is no surprise in Hume's novel that the pretender to an estate is murdered by the process of tattooing itself—the needle used to pierce the skin is filled with a deadly poison—as he attempts to prove himself the heir by gaining the required mark, and in so doing the link between criminality and the tattoo is firmly forged. Hardy's treatment of Dare—the bastard son of a dispossessed aristocrat—is more sophisticated. In a book where familial likeness is seen in the family portraits and the De Stancey face is more continuous than the possession of the family seat, where the photographic likeness of Somerset may be distorted warping him into the semblance of a drunken sot, and Uncle Abner is marked for life in

[146] Ebensten, *Pierced Hearts*, 20. See also Jeff Jaguer, 'My Trade is Tattooing', in *The Tattoo: A Pictorial History* (Horndean: Milestone, 1990), first of section of unnumbered pages. Jaguer tells the story of sailors who, considering themselves in danger of a flogging, would tattoo a large crucifix reaching across their shoulders and down the length of their back to make such corporal punishment seem sacrilegious.

[147] Ebensten, *Pierced Hearts*, 33.

[148] See also Haggard, *Solomon's Mines*, 154. The snake tattooed around Infadoos proclaims him king, but also determines his status as a savage.

the redness of his face in the perpetration of a crime, it becomes clear that virtue is open and fluid, liable to misrepresentation, whilst criminality seeks to fix a single meaning—Dare has the words 'De Stancy' tattooed across his chest in an attempt to secure an inheritance that is not his—or is fixed in the moment of a criminal act—in Abner Power's case the explosion of the bomb of which he was trying to dispose. In both cases, the men force themselves into the possession of recordable criminal characteristics.[149] Criminality is hidden, just as the tattoo is hidden, under the clothes, but as Lombroso claims, the man with the tattoo who has not committed a murder (Dare pulls a gun on both Havill and Abner Power) has died too young—one might want to ask for whom. It is this spirit that Stevenson invokes in his description of Billy Bones's tattoos in *Treasure Island*. For amongst such phrases as ' "A Fair Wind," ' and ' "Here's luck," ' Bones has 'up near the shoulder . . . a sketch of a gallows and a man hanging from it—done . . . with great spirit'—a mark which the doctor examining him describes as '[p]rophetic'.[150] It is just after this that the black spot marking the doom of this violent buccaneer is delivered. Such tattoos as this were not rare on the bodies of real criminals as Lacassagne, the French criminologist, claimed, and such phrases as 'born under an evil star' or 'the galleys await me' could be found on the bodies of the criminals whom he studied.[151] Not only this, but as Fletcher suggests, the tattoos a criminal bore could not only alert a potential victim of his criminality, but also provided a way of describing him to the police.[152] The first statistics to be published on

---

[149] See Joseph Conrad, *The Secret Agent: A Simple Tale* (Methuen, 1907). The views voiced by Conrad's Karl Yundt—for whom ' "Lombroso is an ass" '—refuse the suggestion that criminality marks the criminal, but argue instead that society marks him out. ' "And what about the law that marks him still better—the pretty branding instrument invented by the overfed to protect themselves against the hungry? Red-hot applications on their vile skins . . . That's how criminals are made for your Lombrosos to write their silly stuff about" ' 65.

[150] *Treasure Island* (London, Paris, and New York: Cassell, 1883), 17.

[151] See Robert Fletcher, *Tattooing Among Civilized People. Read Before the Anthropological Society of Washington, December 19, 1882* (Washington: Judd and Detweiler, 1883), 13.

[152] See ibid. 13–14: 'The sentence *Né sous mauvaise étoile*—born under an evil star—was tattooed upon the arm of Philippe the strangler of prostitutes, and aided in his conviction. One of his intended victims related at his trial how she had one evening taken a man to her room, but becoming alarmed at his savage looks and at the tattooing on his arm, she contrived to make her escape. It was not the ill-

tattooing were derived from men collected together in one place, that is to say, in prison,[153] and it is therefore no surprise that the linkage between decorating the skin and criminality became such a strong one.

But the founding reason for Lombroso at least, and for Ellis who followed him, why criminals, above all others, were covered in tattoos was because, as a modern-day throwback to the savage state, they were incapable of feeling physical pain: the 'multiplicity of figures' sported by criminals 'proves also that criminals, like savages, are very little sensitive to pain'.[154] Lombroso, by claiming that tattooing was an atavistic instinct acted on by criminals, linked the criminal with the savage and invoked the old syllogistic logic, standard in discussing the savage: the process of tattooing is painful; savages have tattoos; therefore savages do not feel pain. But there is no real logic here, for the premiss of the syllogism is that savages do not feel pain. There is no question, for Lombroso at least, that the savage is stoically bearing such pain in the name of religious duty, or, indeed, for any other purpose. He cites a criminal talking about his own tattoos being 'for us thieves what the black dress coat and the decorated vest is to society. The more we are tattooed the greater is our esteem for one another; the more an individual is tattooed, the more authority he has over his companions.'[155] Even in the face of this direct claim that social ascendency is more important than the pain of the procedure, Lombroso failed to recognize the validity of social factors in the acquisition of tattoos. Despite clear evidence to the contrary, groups of people—primarily criminals, but others too—were categorized as insentient.

Lombroso's 1896 article in the *Popular Science Monthly* is fascinating in this respect, and by using it, it is possible to

augury of the sentiment of the inscription which frightened her so much as the belief that it indicated an escaped convict. She identified him by face and by tattooing. During the period from 1864 to 1866 over a dozen murders of prostitutes living in their own apartments were committed by this man. The guillotine duly fulfilled the ominous inscription on his arm.'

[153] Ebensten, *Pierced Hearts*, 21, 33.

[154] Cesare Lombroso, 'The Savage Origin of Tattooing', *Popular Science Monthly* (Apr. 1896), 798.

[155] 'Illustrative Studies in Criminal Anthropology', 3 pts., *Monist*, 1 (1891), 177–85, 186–96, 336–43: 195.

establish some of the ambivalence that grew up around the practice of tattooing towards the turn of the century, which was,
despite Lombroso's insistence, becoming popular amongst all
classes of people. Prosperous businessmen, for example, were
said to favour a design picturing three naked women bearing
the words 'Wealth, Industry, Prosperity', a bishop apparently
chose a serpent coiled round a cross for his arm,[156] and a young
woman celebrated Victoria's jubilee on her chest with the
queen's portrait flanked by the words 'Peace' and 'Unity'.[157]
Lombroso flying in the face of such popularity, began his article:

> I have been told that the fashion of tattooing the arm exists among
> women of prominence in London society. The taste for this style is not
> a good indication of the refinement and delicacy of the English ladies:
> first, it indicates an inferior sensitiveness, for one has to be obtuse to
> pain to submit to this wholly savage operation without any other
> object than the gratification of vanity; and it is contrary to progress,
> for all exaggerations of dress are atavistic.[158]

Whilst Lombroso is right about the growing popularity of the
practice among 'English ladies', there is no doubt in Lombroso's
mind about the relationship of pain to tattooing: if the person
in question had the ability to feel pain they would not go
through with the operation. The savageness of the process is
reflected by the savage insensibility of the tattooed woman. But
the meaning of tattooing, of course, was much more problematic than this, for savages did feel the pain of tattooing, as
well as pain in all its other forms, and it is hard to believe at
such times that Lombroso was not studiously suppressing
accounts of the pain that such so-called savages endured.

Herman Melville in *Typee* (1846) had fictionally recounted
the pain of the process,[159] and the anthropological work done
in this field, throughout the century and gathered together in,
amongst other works, Major-General Robley's *Moko; or Maori
Tattooing*, suggested beyond the shadow of a doubt that the
process caused intense pain to those under the shark's tooth.
Similarly Tighe Hopkins, writing two articles for the *Leisure*

---

[156] Ebensten, *Pierced Hearts*, 26.   [157] Jaguer, *Tattoo*, 52.
[158] 'Savage Origin', 793.
[159] *Typee; or, a Narrative of a Four Months' Residence among the Natives of a
Valley of the Marquesas Islands; or, A Peep at Polynesian Life* (1846; John Murray,
1847), 240.

Hour in 1895, brought savage tattooing to a non-specialist audience, as he celebrated the stoicism of those being tattooed: 'As to the sufferings endured (usually with a fine heroism) by savages under the hands of the tattooer we have the testimony of innumerable travellers.'[160] It is in such comments that the problem of tattooing really comes to the fore, for they undercut the exclusivity in pain sensation aimed at by the civilized.

The *Boy's Own Paper* could attempt to treat the tattooed chief of the South Seas with irony by delineating him next to his canoe with the legend 'Gentleman of the Marquesas in rowing costume', but such cheap jibes were seriously undercut by the 'fine heroism' of which Hopkins speaks. For whilst the *Boy's Own* was attempting to show boys the foolishness of tattooing—it 'is not an enviable practice, nor one it is desirable to encourage' because its end is 'the disfigurement of fair human flesh'[161]—the tattooed savage also displayed the 'fine heroism' in facing pain which, it was hoped, was being inculcated in the boys. There is a great deal at stake in that phrase 'fair human flesh' and it is no mistake that flesh that can be disfigured is fair or pale. The author of the *Boy's Own* article on tattooing goes on to say: 'Dark-skinned people are often much alike, and, in default of clothes, characteristic tattoo patterns were, it is probable, of great service as distinguishing marks.'[162] Archbishop Whately, lecturing in 1855, had used a similar argument, twisting it slightly to suggest that the savage was deliberately bent on self-mutilation:

Most . . . [savages] not only paint their skins with a variety of fantastic colours, but tattoo them, or decorate their bodies . . . with rows of large artificial scars . . . Some of them wear a long ornament of bone thrust through the middle cartilage of the nose, so as to make the speech indistinct. . . . And some tribes, again, artificially flatten, by pressure, the forehead of their infants, so as to bring the head even nearer than nature has formed it, to a resemblance to that of a brute.[163]

---

[160] 'The Art and Mystery of Tattooing', *Leisure Hour*, 44 (1895), 696.
[161] 'Tattooing', *Boy's Own Paper*, 29 Mar. 1884, 412.
[162] Ibid. 413.
[163] 'On the Origin of Civilisation. A Lecture by His Grace the Archbishop of Dublin. To the Young Men's Christian Association', in *Lectures Delivered before the Young Men's Christian Association, in Exeter Hall, From November 1854, to February 1855* (James Nisbet, 1855), 8–9. For the background to the classification of the negro as a separate species and Whately's role in this, see Margaret T. Hodgen,

The important part of such an assertion is that savages decorate themselves in these ways *so as* to distort and disfigure themselves: it is a deliberate act of degradation, although in doing so
they are acting in accordance with their savage nature. Whately
claims that 'at first [one is] inclined to doubt whether they can
all belong to the same Species'[164] as the civilized European, and
this process of setting up boundaries that cannot be crossed
is similar in type, if not degree, to the pushing outside the pale
of the criminal who likewise chooses to disfigure his flesh
with tattoos and to fall away, in his criminality, from the high
standards set by civilization.

Tommo, the hero of Melville's *Typee*, when faced with
enforced facial tattooing by the savages who hold him captive—
a story that was told and retold by the tattooed men and women
who put themselves on display in freak shows—is appalled at
the idea that he 'should be disfigured in such a manner as never
more to have the *face* to return to [his] countrymen'.[165] It is a
poor joke, perhaps, but it does suggest something about the
status of tattoos and the way they would have been interpreted
by late nineteenth-century viewers. There is a strange paragraph
in *Daniel Deronda* where Leonora defends herself for cutting
Daniel off from his Jewish heritage:

'You say it was a shame to me, then, that I used that secrecy,' said his
mother, with a flash of new anger. 'There is no shame attaching to me.
I have no reason to be ashamed. I rid myself of the Jewish tatters and
gibberish that make people nudge each other at sight of us, as if we
were tattooed under our clothes, though our faces are as whole as
theirs. I delivered you from the pelting contempt that pursues Jewish
separateness.'[166]

Shame and the tattoo are inextricably linked here, not least
because those people tattooed under their clothes were widely
considered to be prostitutes.[167] Leonora in her role as a famous

Early Anthropology in the Sixteenth and Seventeenth Centuries (Philadelphia,
University of Pennsylvania Press, 1964), 380–2.

[164] 'On the Origin', 4.   [165] *Typee*, 242.   [166] *Deronda*, 592.
[167] See Fletcher, *Tattooing*, 18–19: 'Tattooing among women in civilized life is
almost confined to prostitutes . . . Parent-Duchatelet, in his classic work on prostitution, states that the women who came under his observation were never tattooed
upon parts of the body habitually exposed, or which were easily uncovered in ordinary life, as the arms, but the upper part of the arm or shoulder, the space beneath
the breasts, and especially the chest, were the spots chosen.'

singer is mirrored by Mirah with her enforced stage appearances and near prostitution, and by invoking the image of the tattoo, Eliot draws together a collection of disparate ideas—of shame, of prostitution and criminality, and of otherness—and feeds these back into her negative image of what it is to be Jewish. Written in 1876, *Daniel Deronda* pre-dates the tattoo craze, but it becomes more and more obvious as the century progressed that people *could* 'face' the world with tattoos, and indeed revelled in doing so. Britain's first professional tattooist—D. W. Purdy—set up in London in 1870, and in 1881 George V, or the Duke of York as he then was, was tattooed along with his brother the Duke of Clarence, as were many of the male members of European royal families at about the same time.[168] The year 1881 was an important one for tattooing in Britain for it was the year when the famous Prince Constantine, the first of the fairground tattooed men, was shown at the Westminster Aquarium in a double bill with 'The Leopard Boy' who was, it seems, a grave disappointment. There is an amusing review of this spectacle in *Punch* where the reader is again given the story that Constantine (as so very nearly happened to Melville's Tommo) was forcibly tattooed at the hands of Chinese Tartars. It is here that the pre-established meaning of tattooing begins to be put under pressure, for it was clearly in Constantine's interests to affirm the painfulness of the acquisition of his seven million punctures. His claim that ' "I alone of all men have survived the torture of tattooing, and I am the only human being of my kind in all the wide world" ',[169] though wildly exaggerated by the 1880s, was responsible for the inordinate amount of money he earned: in America in the 1870s he was earning $1,000 a week.[170]

The pain of tattooing was, throughout the last three decades of the century, very much the slave of categorization, for whilst criminologists chose to simplify and emphasize its painlessness—nobody other than an insensate criminal would have such a thing done—fairground attractions went to the other extreme

---

[168] Jaguer, *Tattoo*, 112.

[169] 'Farini's Foreigners', *Punch*, 81 (3 Dec. 1881), 264.

[170] R. W. B. Scutt and Christopher Gotch, *Art, Sex and Symbol: The Mystery of Tattooing* (1974; 2nd edn. rev., New York and London: Cornwall Books, 1986), 154.

to suggest the enforced and insufferable torment they withstood, setting themselves up as much-maligned victims. Their position, if seen to have chosen whole-body tattooing and the deliberate distortion of features that it involved, would have been untenable, and their ability to feel pain questionable. As time passed, however, tattooed men and particularly women—no doubt partly because of the unusual amounts of naked flesh on display[171]—became enormously popular as fairground attractions, relying on the peculiarity of their appearance and the intense pain involved in obtaining it. Indeed, tattooing became so popular that the standard freak show exhibits—the dwarf and the fat lady—were not enough of a draw on their own account but were obliged to have themselves tattooed if they were to continue in popularity.[172] Some, however, were not prepared to undergo the pain of the process, and many supposedly tattooed men and women—as happens in W. L. Alden's *Among*

---

[171] Rider Haggard makes clear the illicit sexual charge of tattoos displayed on the female body in *Mr. Meeson's Will* (Spencer Blackett, 1888). The heroine of the novel, Augusta Smithers, finds herself marooned on a desert island with her future husband's uncle, the Mr Meeson of the title. Meeson has disinherited his nephew but wants to reinstate him as his heir, and, having no paper on the island, he has the new will tattooed on Augusta's back using the ink from a cuttle fish and a sharpened fish bone. Not only does Augusta recognize her neck as one of her most charming body parts—'Augusta bit her lip, and the tears came into her eyes. She was only a woman, and had a woman's little weaknesses; and, though she had never appeared in a low dress in her life, she knew that her neck was one of her greatest beauties'— but to display it, as she is forced to do in the final court scenes of the novel, she also needs to be in a state of undress. To prepare for the tattooing she is 'dressed, or rather undressed, for the sacrifice' (136), and by the time she enters the legal process the sexual nature of her tattooing becomes very apparent, as does her openness to inspection. The nervous lawyer who validates the will is horrified, though attracted, by the idea of viewing the will, and finds as he looks at it that all is in order, except that it remains undated. Her bare shoulders are open to his inspection already, but his next comment makes clear the tantalizing nature of the tattoo: ' "Signed and attested, but not dated. Ah! unless," he added, "the date is lower down" ' (212). Augusta, in her capacity as an official document, claims that she is ' "public property now" ' (213), but this description of herself equally calls on the association of female tattooing with prostitution, and Augusta, who becomes the cynosure of the courtroom, finds 'hundreds of eager eyes . . . fixed upon her unfortunate neck' (251), and the photograph of herself, taken for legal reasons, being sold freely in the streets. For further discussion of Haggard's book, see Garrett Stewart, 'Reading Figures: The Legible Image of Victorian Textuality', in Carol T. Christ and John O. Jordan (eds.), *Victorian Literature and the Victorian Visual Imagination* (Berkeley and Los Angeles: University of California Press, 1995), 352–4.

[172] Ebensten, *Pierced Hearts*, 18.

the Freaks (1896)—repeatedly had their designs stencilled on instead.[173]

Barnum's guide, produced when the Greatest Show on Earth came to Olympia in 1898, provides an interesting case study of the genuine article, for in it Miss Annie Howard, the Tattooed Woman, is described as 'a "freak" of art, and not of nature'.[174] The phrase is intensely revealing, for whilst she is catalogued alongside Tomasso the Human Pincushion, whose act involves 'thrusting pins, needles, and even hat pins through his arms, lips and ears',[175] she repudiates his unusual physiology and holds out for her own ability to suffer. He, it seems, is a real 'freak', a physiological anomaly, who cannot feel anything, whereas for Annie Howard, 'the "freak" of art', it 'took eighteen months of excruciating torture'[176] to procure the 590 designs in red, blue, and brown that adorn her body. It becomes clear from this, as with the sailors who would tattoo a ship in full sail on the intensely painful region of the chest, that part of the meaning of the tattooed man or woman, was the amount of pain they had withstood in getting it done. It is revealing, too, that Barnum's guide, originally called *The Wonder Book of Freaks and Animals*, became, for the second edition, *The Book of Marvels*, professedly dealing with 'human prodigies' rather than freaks, under the billing 'Strangest Human Beings on Earth. Yet in their Feelings and Affections the Prodigies are "Even as You and I." '[177] And this, particularly in the case of Annie Howard, allows her to become the epitome of the non-criminal tattooed person of the 1890s, for whilst her case is extreme—she 'conceived the idea of being tattooed all over and going on show as her brother had done before her'—yet she felt the agony of the process 'Even as You and I'.

For the British general public, widely cognizant of the practice by the 1890s, there was a deep-seated ambivalence about the possible meanings of the pain of tattooing. There is no doubt

[173] See *Among the Freaks* (London, New York, Bombay: Longmans, Green, 1896), 6.
[174] Clarence L. Dean, *The Wonder Book of Freaks and Animals* (Barnum and Bailey, 1898), 21.
[175] Id., *The Official Guide. Book of Marvels in the Barnum & Bailey Greatest Show on Earth. With Full Descriptions of the Human Prodigies and Rare Animals* (Barnum and Bailey, 1899), 15.
[176] Id., *Wonder Book*, 21.   [177] Id., *Official Guide*, 7.

about the widespread nature and popularity of the phenomenon as tattooing spread from the freak show to the general
public. Burne-Jones, visiting a freak show sometime in the
1880s, saw a woman who had the Last Supper tattooed across
her shoulders. He was so delighted by the display that ten years
later, when he saw her show advertised once again, he returned,
only to be horrified by the fact that she had grown enormously
fat causing the apostles to grin inanely.[178] This story suggests the
widespread appeal of tattooing albeit in terms of the onlooker's
admiration rather than personal participation. Similarly, in
1884 the heavily tattooed Maori chief-of-chiefs, King Tawhiao,
came to Britain to petition Queen Victoria. She refused to see
him, but, despite this setback, a 'special display of fireworks,
which included a pyrotechnical representation of his face'[179] was
put on at the Crystal Palace, emphasizing his otherness but, in
a strange way, valorizing his fortitude. In so doing, a strange
tension was established between the savage, the prototype tat-
tooee, as an unfeeling lump of meat, who could carve his own
flesh without pain and who could therefore wickedly capture
European travellers and tattoo them because incapable of suffering vicariously, and this real figure of King Tawhiao who
wore a white hat and claimed rather touchingly that 'for a fortnight when his lips were being done he had to be fed most
tenderly'.[180]

From this widespread knowledge of the tattooing of savages
and 'freaks', and, indeed, of sailors, it is not hard to see that the
practice would spread to certain members, at least, of the public
at large, completely overriding the claim that only criminals or
prostitutes were tattooed. As Gambier Bolton, who himself had
a snake tattooed around his neck, was to write in the *Strand* in
1897: 'suffice it to say that Royal Princes and Dukes, the
members of our nobility and thousands of humbler folk, bear
to-day on their bodies clever, humorous, and artistic designs the
work of . . . Macdonald, of Jermyn Street',[181] one of a number
of tattooists working in London in the late nineteenth century.

[178] Scutt and Gotch, *Art, Sex and Symbol*, 154–5.
[179] [H. G.] Robley, *Moko; or Maori Tattooing* (Chapman and Hall, 1896), 113.
[180] Ibid. 112–13.
[181] 'Pictures on the Human Skin', *Strand Magazine: An Illustrated Monthly*, 13
(1897), 434.

Lombroso's 1896 *Popular Science* article brings to the fore the disparity between criminological statements about tattooing and the practice itself, with a deep-seated ambivalence which the author steadfastly refused to acknowledge. For whilst the reader is told that criminals are tattooed in jail because 'Inaction is even harder to endure than pain',[182] this kind of motivation entirely drops out of his thinking in his confirmed belief that tattooing is atavistic, and that those who are tattooed necessarily have 'a blunted sensibility'.[183] Lombroso's arguments refused to accept any explanation outside his own system, and the evidence evinced for his propositions relies on the strength of his own assertion rather than on empirical data:

After this study, it appears to me to be proved that this custom is a completely savage one, which is found only rarely among some persons who have fallen from our honest classes, and which does not prevail extensively except among criminals . . . To us [tattoos] serve a psychological purpose, in enabling us to discern the obscurer sides of the criminal's soul, his remarkable vanity, his thirst for vengeance, and his atavistic character.[184]

Built into this comment is Lombroso's belief that the criminal is insensate as he makes clear in the statement that tattooing is atavistic and 'completely savage'. His conclusions rest on the central assumption that savages do not feel pain, and his belief in this is such that, for him, it validates all inferences. As Stephen Jay Gould makes clear, Lombroso's contemporaries did not fail to recognize his 'lawyerly, rather than scientific approach',[185] and Gould cites Paul Topinard's condemnatory comment of 1887 to clinch his point:

[Lombroso] did not say: here is a fact which suggests an induction to me, let's see if I am mistaken, let's proceed rigorously, let us collect and add other facts . . . The conclusion is fashioned in advance; he seeks proof, he defends his thesis like an advocate who ends up by persuading himself . . . [Lombroso] is too convinced.[186]

Lombroso's argument for painless criminality, then, follows in a recognized pattern and is, in the end, entirely circular. The

---

[182] 'Savage Origin', 800.   [183] Ibid. 802.   [184] Ibid. 803.
[185] *Mismeasure of Man*, 132.
[186] Cited ibid. 132–4. See also Hurley, Gothic Body, 94 n., for the contemporary reception of Lombroso's ideas on atavism.

savage does not feel pain. The savage has tattoos. The criminal has tattoos. Therefore the criminal does not feel pain. Ellis adds to this by asking how can the criminal feel pain when he inflicts it on others, bringing his supposed physical responses into line with his moral ones. Here, the criminal enters a second loop as he is compared in his moral idiocy to the clinical idiot who is deemed unfeeling.[187] The base of this pyramid is the assumed insensitivity of the savage, whose widely documented, tattoo-induced sufferings are completely ignored in the face of popular belief. In much the same way, the painlessness of criminals in the hands of criminologists became a commonplace, and was no longer open to question. Stefan Richter in *Tattoo* argues that the only possible explanation for Lombroso's detestation and horror of tattoos is conspiracy, and claims that 'The middle class', headed by Lombroso himself, 'led a bitter fight against tattooing because they, not mistakenly, saw it as a sign of rebellion against the middle-class ideals of conformity and inconspicuousness.'[188] Richter himself has an axe to grind, casting himself as the tattooed rebel standing firm in the face of middle-class oppression, and believing that 'This is a generalized prejudice which since then has been diligently nourished by criminologists . . . and is still widespread today.'[189] Such a view seems too strong, but it is clear that criminologists, for whatever reason, clung determinedly to the category of criminal and staunchly held on to prejudice in the face of experience, pushing the instinctive criminal outside the parameters of 'normal' sensibility and excluding him from a group that could define themselves in terms of their ability to feel pain. This is not far from the pronounced racism of Archbishop Whately's claim that savages are of another species.

III. CLASS AND THE INFLICTION OF PAIN

In this final section I shall be making clear the implications of class for the ability to inflict pain rather than to suffer it.

---

[187] See e.g. Galton, *Inquiries*, 28–9; Paul Sollier, 'Idiocy', in Stedman (ed.), *Twentieth Century Practice*, xii. 294–5; William W. Ireland, *On Idiocy and Imbecility* (J. & A. Churchill, 1877), 254–7.
[188] *Tattoo* (London, Melbourne, New York: Quartet Books, 1985), 12–13.
[189] Ibid. 13.

Looking at the ways in which Robert Louis Stevenson and Lloyd Osbourne provided models of the chasm between the sentient and the insentient in *The Ebb-Tide* (1894) it becomes clear that the working classes—to a certain extent because of the language they used—were projected to the opposite side of the abyss from the sensitive upper classes, where—in a corollary to Ellis's association of physical and moral insensibility—they were then at liberty to inflict pain.

John Henry Newman, in *The Idea of a University*, expressly connected class and level of education with a sympathetic response to pain, claiming that 'it is almost a definition of a gentleman, to say he is one who never inflicts pain'.[190] In discussing Stevenson's *The Ebb-Tide: A Trio and Quartette*, written in association with Lloyd Osbourne, I shall be drawing out some of the implications of Newman's statement,[191] which embodied much late nineteenth-century thought on the infliction of pain. Much as Havelock Ellis argued for the analogy of moral and physical insensibility, Newman, too, made it plain that the response to pain is part of a complete way of life, and that the desire not to inflict pain physically is reflected in an equivalent desire not to inflict mental pain in day-to-day interactions. 'If he [the gentleman] engages in controversy of any kind, his disciplined intellect preserves him from the blundering discourtesy of better, though less educated minds, who, like blunt weapons, tear and hack instead of cutting clean.'[192] It is this 'tear[ing] and hack[ing]' that Stevenson takes up in his story, making the infliction of pain, by the throwing of vitriol, the touchstone of class, civilization, and gentlemanliness.

Vitriol-throwing, like tattooing, was a craze of the 1880s. As Ruth Harris argues, the Comtesse de Létil, who threw vitriol in the face of her adulterous husband's mistress, 'started off the vogue for vitriol-throwing'[193] in 1880. The Comtesse was

---

[190] *Discourses on the Scope and Nature of University Education. Addressed to the Catholics of Dublin* (Dublin: James Duffy, 1852), 372.

[191] For the complexities of Newman's discussion—the tension between the Christian and the gentleman—see Robin Gilmour, *The Idea of the Gentleman in the Victorian Novel* (George Allen & Unwin, 1981), 88–92.

[192] Newman, *Discourses*, 329.

[193] *Murders and Madness: Medicine, Law, and Society in the* Fin de Siècle (Oxford: Clarendon Press, 1989), 239. See also Arthur Conan Doyle, 'The Illustrious Client', in *The Case-book of Sherlock Holmes* (John Murray: 1927), 11–46. Kitty Winter, ruined by the notorious Baron Adelbert Gruner, throws vitriol in his

brought to trial but acquitted because her motives were seen to be pure, and her crime one of passion rather than deliberate intent. The acquittal was to have implications for later vitriol-throwers, who pleaded her precedent and although, as Harris claims, the crime was 'perceived as a premeditated act of brutality and cruelty, the familiar representation of honourable motives meant that even the *vitrioleuse* was often acquitted'.[194] The judgement again shows the workings of class as the violence of the deed is occluded by the elevated social position of the *vitrioleuse*. For the working-class criminals of Lombroso and William Ferrero's *The Female Offender* the case is far different, as the violence of the act marks out the instinctive criminal rather than one worked upon by passion:

The use of vitriol . . . is opposed by its insidiousness and inhumanity to the nature of the true crime of passion. The refinement of cruelty in the method, and the coolness necessary to its employment (for the fluid must be well aimed), are contrary to the supposition that the woman is very much excited at the moment of execution.[195]

Lombroso and Ferrero are out to prove that the 'terrible point of superiority in the female born criminal over the male lies in the refined, diabolical cruelty with which she accomplishes her crime'[196] and vitriol—again, as with tattooing—managed to cover both ends of the social scale and acquire a different meaning at each end. For working-class, born criminals it was the expression of their innate desire to inflict pain—'Da . . . , asked why she had not stabbed her lover instead of throwing vitriol at him, answered in the words of the Roman Tyrant, "*Because I wished him to feel the bitterness of death!*"'[197]— whilst for the aristocracy it was the sign of a sufferer pushed beyond endurance into action.

Stevenson's story, which includes a vitriol attack, rests not just on the infliction of pain, but also insists on pain as a shared part

---

face: 'Extenuating circumstances came out in her trial that the sentence . . . was the lowest possible for such an offence' (46). Neither Holmes nor Watson, though appalled by the act, can find any sympathy for the victim. Watson sees 'the vile life which had led up to so hideous a change' (43), whilst Holmes reads the destroyed faces as 'the wages of sin' (44).

[194] *Murders and Madness*, 239.
[195] *The Female Offender* (T. Fisher Unwin, 1895), 259.
[196] Ibid. 148.   [197] Ibid.

of life. Just as Newman's gentleman 'submits to pain, because it is inevitable',[198] the characters of *The Ebb-Tide* find themselves in a world of pain. Pain, particularly toothache, is established early on in the novel as the ground of metaphors, a universal condition, and as such one of the few things which links the three wildly disparate characters who form the 'trio' of the title. Herrick finds himself raging 'against himself, as a man bites on a sore tooth';[199] his spirits are jarred 'like a file on a man's teeth';[200] and later 'instinctively, as one shields himself from pain, [he] made haste to interrupt'.[201] These are not metaphors of physical pain that mirror the mental pain of an inner life, though Stevenson does call on these since images of the rack and crucifixion reflect tortured mental states, but rather they rely on the behaviour aroused by painful sensations. As such, these metaphors form the groundwork for the climax of the novel. Whilst the ability to suffer is deemed universal by Stevenson, the ability to inflict pain is quite a different matter, as the plot revolves round the murder of Attwater, the man in charge of the island on which they land. Davis, the drunken sea captain, and Huish, the Cockney clerk, must choose between murder and starvation. The difficulty lies not in the murder itself, but in the means of murder, Davis preferring a bullet, whilst Huish intends to throw vitriol into Attwater's face. The problem that the former captain has is made clear by their conversation:

'We'n you're back's at the wall, you do the best you can, don't you?' began the clerk. 'I s'y that, because I 'appen to know there's a prejudice against it; it's considered vulgar, awf'ly vulgar.' He unrolled the handkerchief and showed a four-ounce jar. 'This 'ere's vitriol, this is,' said he.

The captain stared upon him with a whitening face.

'This is the stuff!' he pursued, holding it up. 'This'll burn to the bone; you'll see it smoke upon 'im like 'ell fire! One drop upon 'is bloomin' heyesight, and I'll trouble you for Attwater!'

'No, no, by God!' exclaimed the captain . . .

---

[198] *Discourses*, 329.
[199] Robert Louis Stevenson and Lloyd Osbourne, *The Ebb-Tide: A Trio and Quartette* (William Heinemann, 1894), 40.
[200] Ibid. 73.   [201] Ibid. 130.

'Fust thing you know, you'll see him running round and 'owling like a good un. . . .'

'Don't!' said Davis. 'Don't talk of it!'

'Well, you *are* a juggins!' exclaimed Huish. 'What did you want? You wanted to kill him, and tried to last night . . . and 'ere I show you 'ow; and because there's some medicine in a bottle you kick up this fuss!' . . .

'I don't know what it is,' cried Davis, pacing the floor; 'it's there! I draw the line at it. I can't put a finger to no such piggishness. It's too damned hateful!'

'And I suppose it's all your fancy pynted it,' said Huish, 'w'en you take a pistol and a bit o' lead, and copse a man's brains all over him? No accountin' for tystes.'[202]

The way in which Stevenson creates class identity for Huish is clear in this passage: he is 'awf'ly vulgar' not just in the way that he speaks which indicates his social standing, but also in his desire to inflict pain: the two are intimately related. An unsigned review appearing in the *Speaker* shortly after the book's publication links Huish's speech patterns with his anti-social behaviour:

He is a Cockney born and bred, with the little narrownesses and vulgarities of his class, and that terrible sharpness of intuition which sometimes disconcerts the wisest. He talks the slang of Whitechapel, and knows the latest of music-hall ditties . . . Of conscience, honour, loyalty, he knows less than the beasts that perish.[203]

Whilst this review also suggests that the three main characters have 'fall[en] away from civilisation',[204] it is clear that this is not the determining factor in Huish's behaviour: Herrick, 'the University man, who carries his tattered Virgil in his pocket to remind him of what he once was'[205] does not fall to such depths, and nor does Davis the ruined sea captain. What seems to be decisive about Huish is 'the little narrownesses and vulgarities of his class': it is the 'terrible sharpness of [his] intuition' that is fatally transmuted into the 'terrible sharpness' of murder.

Davis, equally guilty of the desire to murder, does not sink so low, and the reason for this lies in his revulsion at Huish's

---

[202] Stevenson, *Ebb-Tide* 210–12.

[203] Review of *The Ebb-Tide* by Robert Louis Stevenson, *Speaker*, 29 Sept. 1894, 362.

[204] Ibid.   [205] Ibid.

cruelty. Much as Hyde in *Jekyll and Hyde* is described as 'lusting to inflict pain', Huish seems to delight in vitriol-throwing: Davis is horrified to realize that Huish has done it before. But Davis's reaction to Huish is telling, for he deems him 'piggish' and claims 'I just draw the line' at his behaviour. Whilst the drawing of such a line might seem just a petulant refusal to fall in with Huish's logic, it also calls on Lombrosian thinking. The nomenclature is decisive, for it firmly pushes Huish into the realm of the brutish, and then 'draw[s] the line' between him and the supposedly more civilized Davis. As Huish walks towards Attwater, the former's 'unhappy physical endowments' are picked up, his ape-like 'disproportionately long and broad' hands,'[206] the description of which determines his place in an evolutionary scale. This seems to be Lombroso's argument, in that the criminal has passed a specific point beyond which pain is felt neither physically nor vicariously. Stevenson's approach, however, is more complex for as the vitriol explodes in Huish's own face he feels 'hell's agonies',[207] the suffering of which would be denied to Lombroso's insensate criminals.

It becomes clear from Stevenson's calling on images of markers of division that, for him, as for many of his contemporaries, class was thought of as defining in the relationship of an individual to the infliction of pain. Huish is insistent that Davis wants to murder 'in kid gloves',[208] a stock phrase denoting both wealth and status, but one which is doubled-edged, for it suggests in the animality of the gloves the desire to draw on and then to discard brutishness.[209] This is not, however, possible, as Huish makes clear when he states that 'Murder ain't genteel':[210] the kid gloves are either on or off, the line is drawn and cannot be crossed. As with *Jekyll and Hyde*, Hyde's murderous hands cannot be contained within the white,

---

[206] Stevenson and Osbourne, *Ebb-Tide*, 225.
[207] Ibid. 229.   [208] Ibid. 213.
[209] George Bernard Shaw uses similar images of the gloved hand in *Cashel Byron's Profession*. In this novel about amateur and professional boxing, Shaw suggests that the donning of boxing gloves is the mark of amateurism rather than professionalism, and as such suggests that such fighting is about athleticism rather than a desire to inflict pain: the two types of fighters are kept clearly apart—a line is drawn between them—by the assumption of gloves. It is, however, the aim of the novel to suggest that this line is by no means a clean one.
[210] Stevenson and Osbourne, *Ebb-Tide*, 213.

professional, moneyed hands of Jekyll, but break through when he is sleeping. Stevenson seems to veer between a reading of Huish that suggests his readiness to inflict pain is a result of his innate savagery, his animal qualities, and a reading that relies much more heavily on his class.

In this chapter I have aimed not to provide a definitive outline of the ways in which pain was read after the framework of religious rationalizations began to buckle, but rather to suggest that such a definitive outline would be worthless in its crass simplification. I have suggested that two models of painful suffering, seemingly contradictory, could lie alongside each other without affecting the viability of the other, and that each had a particular role to play in attributing meaning to pain. I further argue that the infliction of pain, supposedly resting on an inability to feel personally, was capable of distortion, and could be pulled in different directions according to class. Whilst I showed the ways in which exponents of Christianity gathered arguments eclectically from various discourses in an attempt to shore up the viability of Christian representations of the purpose of pain, class represented a much more mutable category than most used to define the relationship to pain. Whilst Stevenson incarnates the urge to inflict pain in a Cockney clerk in *The Ebb-Tide*, Wilkie Collins uses Betteridge, the butler in *The Moonstone*, to attribute the infliction of pain to the other end of a social scale. Speaking of what he terms 'gentlefolk' he suggests that,

Their lives being, for the most part, passed in looking about them for something to do, it is curious to see—especially when their tastes are of what is called the intellectual sort—how often they drift blindfold into some nasty pursuit. Nine times out of ten they take to torturing something, or to spoiling something—and they firmly believe they are improving their minds, when the plain truth is, they are only making a mess in the house.[211]

Sticking pins into or cutting up frogs, newts, and beetles, 'without a pang of remorse',[212] is not 'cruel nastiness',[213] but rather is redefined as 'a taste . . . for natural history'.[214] Attributing the happy infliction of pain to the rich rather than the poor,

---

[211] *The Moonstone. A Romance*, 3 vols. (Tinsley, 1868), i. 99.
[212] Ibid.   [213] Ibid.   [214] Ibid.

far from destroying the arguments of this chapter, simply suggests that the apprehension of the meaning of pain was far from simple. My aim has not been to be definitive, but rather to suggest some of the widely held, if contradictory, strategies and blindnesses of those who took the shaping of the meaning of pain into their own hands. In so doing, it has become clear that pain has no innate meaning, but rather is subject to the diverse social and political aims of those who chose to interpret it.

6

The Pleasures and Pains of Flogging

Up until this point this book has dealt with pain as an evil;
something, as Alexander Bain wrote, that 'we avoid, repel, flee
from'.[1] Largely organically generated rather than externally
inflicted, the pains discussed have required an explanation, an
attribution of meaning, to make them make sense, or indeed
become bearable to those who suffered or to those who com-
passionated such suffering. Deliberately inflicted beating, in the
many forms that it took during the nineteenth century, once
again brought the question of the meaning and purpose of pain
into the foreground. Since it clearly did not have to be inflicted,
it became a pronounced marker of the moral efficacy attributed to corporeal suffering. Those who found themselves being
beaten had no chance of either avoiding or fleeing from it since
they were restrained, either by the social conventions of silence
in the face of physical suffering, or, perhaps more effectively, by
the straps and constraints of the flogging block. The deliberate infliction of pain was seen as an effective means of social
control. Much as organically generated pain could be said to be
the Hand of God at work chastising and chastening humankind,
the flogging of criminals or the birching of children in schools
could be given a parallel rationale. As Ian Gibson claims in his
book on flogging, *The English Vice*, 'Upper- and middle-class
Victorian fathers . . . could and did see themselves as created in
the image of a punitive flagellant God . . . The evidence is that,
in these social groups, there was endemic beating in the home
in the nineteenth century.'[2] Such punishment was not, however,
restricted to the home, but spilled over into schools and penal
structures. During the 1870s, as Gibson argues, 'a spate of
beating scandals at the public schools'[3] broke out, when boys

---

[1] *Senses*, 89.
[2] *The English Vice: Beating, Sex and Shame in Victorian England and After*
(1978; Duckworth, 1992), 52.
[3] Ibid. 71–2.

were dangerously hurt by the floggings they received. It is clear from the public concern aroused by such incidents, and indeed from the nostalgic way in which a number of writers looked back to the good old days of flogging in the early nineteenth century, that flogging was falling out of favour in a way coterminous with the decline of belief in a physical hell and divinely inflicted suffering in general.

The same was true of beatings in prison. Penal punishment in the nineteenth century has been discussed in recent years by Martin Wiener and David Garland, both of whom notice the marked decline in physical punishment over the course of the century. Garland traces the legislation that progressively brought an end to the corporal punishment of adults by the 1880s, effectively starting with the Whipping Act of 1861,[4] whilst Wiener, arguing that anaesthetics and the decline in religious thinking eroded a belief in the usefulness of physical pain, recognizes the shift towards measuring the pain of prisons in terms of deprivation, rather than physical pain—an approach surely sustained by the figures that he cites:

Prisoners receiving corporal punishment in local prisons, as a percentage of average daily population, fell slowly from an average of 1.08 percent in the period from 1868 to 1877 to .80 percent from 1892 to 1893, and then rapidly to .50 percent from 1894 to 1895.[5]

This final chapter revisits the subject of the first: the relationship of inflicted pain to punishment. It became apparent that Christians persistently tried to read pain as the work and desire of a caring God who wanted the best for humankind and saved them from wrongdoing by the sharp infliction of pain. With the logic of Charles Voysey advocating a good whipping for intransigent children, George Venables, Honorary Canon of Norwich, was, in 1900, still able to give a sermon—*A Stinging Rod for a Sinning Nation*—in which he read the defeats and humiliations of the British army in South Africa as the work of the Lord:

This rod is laying upon us, at this time, *sharp, severe, stinging stripes*, administered to this great and mighty nation by a people not numbering one million, and with an annual revenue of about half the sum

[4] Garland, *Punishment and Welfare*, 6.
[5] *Reconstructing the Criminal: Culture, Law, and Policy in England, 1830–1914* (1990; Cambridge: Cambridge University Press, 1994), 335.

already spent by us in our efforts to force them to do what is right. And this '*rod*' is, I feel certain, '*appointed*' by God.[6]

This logic of beneficently inflicted pain, shored up by biblical quotation, became the rationale of those determined to cure the ills of others through the infliction of pain, usually in the form of flogging. Whilst Venables's rod is clearly metaphorical, for much of the nineteenth century it was all too physical. As the Tory MP Sir Charles Adderley was to claim in his pamphlet *A Few Thoughts on National Education and Punishments* (1874), 'It is essential to the curative function of punishment that it should be painful',[7] or as Thomas Hughes was to urge in the case of a fictional school bully in *Tom Brown's School Days* (1857), 'severe physical pain is the only way to deal with such a case'.[8] Whilst Hughes has punishment in mind its purpose is clearly meant to be improving. As the narrator of the story adds, one former bully beaten in this way, 'sought out Holmes', who did the beating, 'and thanked him, saying it had been the kindest act which had ever been done upon him, and the turning point in his character; and a very good fellow he became, and a credit to his School'.[9]

This notion of the formation of character is of vital importance to the question of flogging in schools, for the way in which a flogging was received was thought to speak volumes about the boy being flogged. The caning given to the cowardly bully Brigson in Frederick Farrar's famous and genre-setting school story, *Eric; or, Little by Little* (1858) proves that the boy is no good. Instead of taking his flogging in silence and like a gentleman, Brigson 'los[es] every particle of self-control'[10] and roars in pain:

---

[6] *A Stinging Rod for a Sinning Nation. A Sermon Preached in Burgh Castle Church, (Suffolk) After Reading the Queen's Letter for the Army in South Africa and Sufferers by the War, Sunday Morning, Jan 7th, 1900* (Norwich: Agas H. Goose, 1900), 1.

[7] *A Few Thoughts on National Education and Punishments* (Longmans, Green, 1874), 49.

[8] *Tom Brown's School Days. By an Old Boy* (Cambridge: Macmillan, 1857), 233.

[9] Ibid.

[10] *Eric; or, Little by Little. A Tale of Roslyn School* (Edinburgh: Adam and Charles Black, 1858), 254.

At the first stroke he writhed and yelled; at the second he retreated, twisting like a serpent, and blubbering like a baby; at the third he flung himself on his knees, and, as the strokes fell fast, clasped Mr. Rose's arm, and implored and besought for mercy.[11]

His degeneracy becomes all the more apparent in the face of the behaviour of the other boys beaten at the same time, since 'No other boy cried, or even winced.'[12] 'Looks of the most unmitigated disgust and contempt were darted'[13] at Brigson, and this contemptible behaviour means that the other boys begin to 'loathe and nauseate'[14] him in accordance with his newly revealed character. The stress on not crying out when beaten, allied to the more general conventions of silence in the face of pain, is paramount in Victorian fiction and literature of all kinds that dealt with flogging. Swinburne, the epicure of flagellation, was to make one of the many flogged schoolchildren in his anonymous poems pithily express this point of honour: 'Each time the twigs bend round across my Bum | Pain bids "Cry out," but Honour bids, "Be dumb." '[15] It falls to Reggie, the boy in Swinburne's posthumously published novel *Lesbia Brandon*, to make it clear just how difficult it was to keep silent in the face of such pain. 'The boy sobbed and flinched at each cut'[16] inflicted on him by his teacher, but found strategies for staying silent, 'brac[ing] his muscles and harden[ing] his flesh into rigid resistance'.[17] As the birch descended, 'the cuts stung like fire, and burning with shame and pain alike, he pressed his hot wet face down on his hands, bit his sleeve, his fingers, anything; his teeth drew blood as well as the birch; he chewed the flesh of his hands rather than cry out'.[18] It is the class of the person being beaten that is of the greatest importance, and it is this that distinguishes Reggie's suffering from Brigson's ungentlemanly failure in the face of a flogging.

---

[11] Ibid.   [12] Ibid. 255.   [13] Ibid.   [14] Ibid. 255–6.

[15] 'The Flogging Block: An Heroic Poem. By Rufus Rodworthy, Esq. With Annotations by Barebum Birchingham, Esq., . . .', British Library, Ashley MS 5256, prologue.

[16] *Lesbia Brandon: An historical and critical commentary being largely a study (and elevation) of Swinburne as a novelist*, ed. Randolph Hughes (Falcon Press, 1952), 32.

[17] Ibid. 33.   [18] Ibid.

This chapter will deal more fully with the question of class and the ability to sustain a beating with honour, but this in itself raises the question of whether such beatings should be endured at all. The arguments over flogging in schools that were rehearsed across the country towards the end of the century were deliberately parodied by William Stewart Ross—the editor of the *Secular Review*,[19] and trainee-priest turned atheist—who published under the pseudonym 'Saladin'. Ross was, perhaps, less concerned with the pain deliberately inflicted on small boys than he was with the beating of children as a model and metaphor for the dealings of God with man, though this does not invalidate his horrified response to the beating itself. In the title of one of his short stories, *A Fearful Flogging, by One Who Endured it*,[20] Ross deliberately parodies the manner in which the advocates of flogging chose to sign their correspondence in the press, using such designations as 'One who was Flogged in his Youth, and Has Never Regretted It'.[21] In so doing Ross held up those who advocated the beating of children to public scrutiny and rendered the effects of severe physical beating painfully obvious. It becomes clear from Ross's own descriptions of being beaten with a tawse at school that such infliction of pain was by no means trivial:

I held out my hand to receive the stripes till every finger became a hell of suffering, and every nerve in my body tingled in agony. In desperation I refused to hold out my bleeding hands any longer; but the stubbornness of desperation did not avail me. With all the writhing fury of the snakes on the head of Megæra, the *tawse* descended on my naked feet and ankles, till the blood stained the dusty boards of the floor. Come death, come life, I could stand this no longer.[22]

The viciousness of this flogging, recalled from Ross's youth, is borne out by numerous accounts of school life—particularly public school life—written during the Victorian period. The Revd C. Allix Wilkinson, writing in *Reminiscences of Eton* (1888), looks back to his time at Eton in the 1840s under the

---

[19] Jointly with Charles Watts in 1883, and solely from 1884.
[20] *A Fearful Flogging, by One Who Endured it. Based upon a ms. in the Possession of Saladin* (W. Stewart, 1894).
[21] *Notes and Queries*, 18 Oct. 1862, 312.
[22] Richard B. Hithersay and George Ernest, *Sketch of the Life of Saladin (W. Stewart Ross.) Freethinker and Journalist* (W. Stewart, [1887]), 48.

notorious flogging headmaster Dr Keate and takes an evident delight in the infliction of pain. For him 'Flogging was the head and front, or perhaps I may say the head and tail, of the system',[23] and the cheap joke embodied in this claim—one that is repeated in Ross's short story—suggests the inexplicable fondness with which flogging in schools was remembered in later life by those who endured it. Not only did Wilkinson remember the process with pleasure, but he also, as did all of those who wielded the whip, shored up his sense of its rightness and inevitability by using biblical quotation: 'A rod is for the back of him that is void of understanding' (Prov. 10: 12); 'He that spareth the rod hateth his son: but he that loveth him chasteneth him betimes' (Prov. 13: 24); 'The rod and reproof give wisdom: but a child left to himself bringeth his mother to shame' (Prov. 29: 15).[24] Wilkinson, in a manner that again recalls the debates over vivisection, sets duty against sentiment, and inveighs against sentimentality using a pseudo-biblical register to refer to his collection of biblical justifications of flogging:

Hear ye this, ye squeamish mothers: here is authority ye cannot gainsay. The spade is called a spade. Turn and twist the words as you will, in your tender-hearted and bashful leniency, old Keate *had* a good foundation for his discipline. 'Spare the rod, spoil the child,' was certainly the motto on the college arms in his time.[25]

It is ironic, in ways that William Stewart Ross would doubtless have enjoyed, that this final justification—'spare the rod and spoil the child'—is, in fact, from Samuel Butler's *Hudibras* (II. i. 884) in which, as Henry Salt, the editor of *The Humanitarian* and staunch opponent to corporal punishment, was to put it in his own *Memories of Bygone Eton*, 'a certain too outspoken Lady . . . is persuading the amorous Knight, Sir Hudibras, to undergo a whipping'.[26] For Salt, 'It is significant that a comic writer, who frankly treats the subject as what it is, an indecent one, should have provided many generations of respectable parents and pedagogues with a supposed text from the Bible.'[27]

It is against this backdrop of beating and of biblical justification for beating that Ross's story needs to be read. The outline

---

[23] *Reminiscences of Eton (Keate's Time)* (Hurst and Blackett, 1888), 17.
[24] Ibid. 17–18.   [25] Ibid. 18.
[26] *Memories of Bygone Eton* (Hutchinson, [1928]), 73.   [27] Ibid.

of *A Fearful Flogging* is this: that Donald, a teenage boy, is viciously flogged and expelled from school for breaking bounds to be with a milkmaid. The schoolmaster, Dr Fergusson, leaves the boy's buttocks covered in lacerations and bruises, and the story provides an obsessive exploration of what these physical marks might mean and what can be inferred from them. In doing this, Ross provides a forceful critique of the belief that such infliction is meaningful; that God inflicts pain lovingly on humankind for its own good. Donald, at times, sees the marks as a reminder of Jenny, the milkmaid, whilst his father sees 'a representation of the American flag, the glorious gonfalon of the stripes and stars',[28] a reading suggestive of meaning, but in reality devoid of it since it refers only to the physical marks of the beating, rather than having a national or patriotic significance. The overwhelming hermeneutic drive of the story is, however, to read the infliction of pain by the teacher as a means of undercutting the validity of a theological reading of pain as given by God to chasten in the cause of salvation. Ross was satirizing a particular kind of theological text, and perhaps the most apposite of these to this argument is Frederick Gant's *The Mystery of Suffering, Human and Theological*, in which a Christian apologist and long-standing surgeon at London's Royal Free hospital, sets out his thinking about the rationale of pain:

Mysterious as may be the element of suffering in human-life history at first sight, its mysticism would disappear in the discovery of a purpose or of purposes to which it is subservient; and if the design be beneficent for the sufferer's physical and moral well-being, the otherwise intolerable becomes endurable, possibly even a welcome companion in life's rough journey.[29]

Gant is claiming that the purpose to which pain is subservient is the didactic aim of the Deity—what Christian theology sees as God's desire to improve man morally through bodily suffering: as he writes, 'Pain is . . . *teacher* and . . . *chastiser*.'[30] It is this characterization of God-inflicted pain as teacher that Ross employs in *A Fearful Flogging* to cut the ground from under it.

---

[28] *Fearful Flogging*, 17.
[29] *The Mystery of Suffering, Human and Theological* (Elliot Stock, 1900) 10.
[30] Ibid. 12.

The Mystery of Suffering is interesting, if appalling, because of its insistence that one must move beyond pain itself, beyond the level of mystery, into interpretation and meaning. As Gant argues, 'No observing and reflecting mind can have been thus led to the study of human nature ... without seeking to interpret the purpose ... of all the misery and woe to which man alone is ever subject.'[31] The end of this process, for Gant, is the finding of God at the heart of pain, and the concomitant acceptance of physical and mental suffering as a needed gift. Neither Gant nor Ross, in a way typical of much writing about pain, will accept pain simply as a phenomenon, but feel the need to move beyond it, and to establish a meaning for it derived from something other than bodily malfunction. In Ross's case, however, the stated desire to read pain as something wisely and divinely inflicted collapses into a welter of private meanings, as his satirical and anti-theological purpose is worked out.

Ross's story is sharply satirical, and veers between establishing a direct connection between the wisdom and justice of Dr Fergusson and the wisdom and justice of God, and a denunciation of the schoolmaster's techniques and purposes, his pomposity and his cruelty. In so doing Ross lays bear the basis of his denunciation of Christianity, and his intense dislike of the place that physical pain plays in its interaction with the world.

Ross deliberately sets the school with its brutal floggings in his chosen theological framework by calling it Angel Turret. Immediately, however, he undercuts this by implying that this appellation is just a name—Donald's father renames it the Devil's Turret when his son is sent home to him badly injured—and in this somewhat facile exchange of titles, Ross clearly points out that a bad thing is not necessarily good because it has been called good. In this way, he gives himself the leeway to suggest that the pain inflicted by God need not—and indeed must not—be seen to have a remedial function. In *The Flagellants* (1890), another of his pamphlets, this time more directly addressed to the problem of pain and its relationship to God, Ross is at pains to suggest that people choose to read and interpret their bodily sufferings in particular ways. It is the folly of submitting to pain, and indeed inflicting it upon oneself for the

---

[31] Ibid. 9.

supposed glory of God, that he inveighs against so heavily, claiming that

backs always will be flogged, and noses ever will be held to the grind-stone, till he with the back and he with the nose takes the trouble to cultivate his brain, and dares to confront, eagle-eyed, the authorities that would make him a chattel and a poor mad catspaw in the hands of priest and tyrant.[32]

The desire to claim pain back from its long-established place as the outward sign of God's mercy is of vital importance: it is, Ross argues, liberating to see pain as arbitrary and open to interpretation.

Ross uses the language of Christian theology throughout *A Fearful Flogging* to suggest that right is on the side of the beater. Donald is told that he will be 'beaten with many stripes in vindication of the outraged reputation of this seat of learning'[33]— pain here is retributive, but it is also established as the prompt to spiritual regeneration. In a much-repeated phrase, Donald 'meditate[d] upon the many stripes on my person, the outward and visible signs of an inward grace which I fear I did not possess'[34] and claims that he '*must* behold these stripes by which the honour of Angel Turret had been vindicated and my own moral redemption secured'.[35] Pain is offered to us here as a sacrament, 'the outward and visible sign of an inward grace', and the stripes as the personal corollary of the redemptive stripes of Christ through which the sinner is healed.[36] The plot of Ross's story revolves around the decoding of these stripes— the reading of their meaning. Donald is given the standard pain rhetoric reproduced in many descriptions of the infliction of pain when he claims that he will 'let the curtain fall over the sickening details of how I was stripped, strapped, and flogged till I fainted'[37]—the claim being the familiar one that the infliction of such pain was too painful to read about. But it is also the language of allegory, and this is an aspect Ross is keen to exploit since it gives a way of approaching the mystery beyond the veil—the meaning of the pain demanded by God. Donald is

---

[32] *The Flagellants* new edn. by Saladin (W. Stewart, 1890), 3.
[33] *Fearful Flogging*, 15.   [34] Ibid. 17.   [35] Ibid.
[36] Isa. 53: 5; 1 Pet. 2: 24.   [37] *Fearful Flogging*, 15.

left with the visible signs of his pain—as well as a residual sore-
ness—and it is through these that he desires to come to an
understanding of what the infliction of pain means: if he cannot
reconcile the infliction of pain with goodness, he is forced to
accept his father's estimate of such pain as meaningless and
wicked. In the course of his exegetical frenzy he is made to
express his

wild and all-absorbing desire to read the primitive hieroglyphy which
Dr. Fergusson and his principal assistant, a B.A. of Oxford, had written
upon me with rods. They were two learned men. I *must* see what, in
their wisdom, they had written with sticks, using my skin for parch-
ment. The result of their labour, I determined, should not be lost to
the world.[38]

The absurdity of such claims is manifest, but it is an absurdity
which recoils on the idea of a kind God inflicting pain for the
good of man, and makes risible the idea that suffering can be
learnt from. An appalling tale then follows of how Donald sits
on a tray of salt 'that [he] might learn and note from the spasms
and yanks of pain the particular directions and crossings and
re-crossings and notches and stars and scars of the stripes
with which my morals had been so learnedly, if not humanely,
healed'.[39] There is concentrated in this passage some of the
ambivalence of the story as a whole, for when the phrase
'learnedly, if not humanely' is redirected to God's purposes in
inflicting pain rather than just to the schoolmaster who is acting
as his stand-in, the similarity between a loving God and an
inflexible sadist becomes apparent. Ross also makes it clear at
this juncture that pain is a part of human life, and is suffered
as part of daily existence. The supposed manuscript records
Donald saying:

I uttered a savage yell, and ran tearing across the floor as if all the
fiends had been behind me. I had had my arm broken, my skull fractured, and my two teeth kicked down my throat [in a milking acci-
dent]; but, in insufferable pain, this salt experiment beat all my
previous experiences hollow.[40]

Ross uses the 'as if . . .' structure that Elaine Scarry recognizes
in *The Body in Pain*—Donald runs 'as if all the fiends had been

---

[38] Ibid. 22.   [39] Ibid.   [40] Ibid.

behind me'—but in a way which again falls outside Scarry's 'two and only two' categories of pain description. Being pursued by fiends does not suggest the physical dissolution Scarry suggests and it is clear that Ross is using this as a weapon against a hijacked, God-based meaning for pain. In suggesting the metaphorical status of pain description, Ross undercuts the validity of a divine explanation, as well as suggesting through the salt experiment that pain can also be in one's own hands. It is a *savage* yell that Donald gives—the direct antithesis of a civilized and Christian one—and readers are offered other experiences of pain to which he does not seek to give meaning: the broken arm and the fractured skull. A curtain is drawn over the pain of flogging, but physical suffering is displaced to other parts of the story, and in this way Ross offers other frameworks for, and other levels of importance to attribute to, pain. It is this move towards other interpretations that so forcibly undercuts a God-based meaning for pain. For bubbling up throughout the text are alternative, and indubitably viable, meanings for and explanations of physical suffering. This is, perhaps, seen most clearly in the enlightening story of how Donald's mother prevents her husband from murdering the schoolmaster by pouring a kettle full of hot water over his feet. Donald's father 'uttered a roar of pain, and, without opening the glass door, crashed through it . . . he swore like a fiend and jumped mountain high with agony'.[41] This is what we are told is behind the curtain— the pain that is too painful to tell, which is also the pain of a loving God. It is clear here, however, that the pain is inflicted by Donald's mother, who reads pain as part of a hierarchical and worldly structure, and her husband's physical suffering— vividly evoked—prevents his murdering Dr Fergusson. Pain is deliberately set against something else and its relative value assessed. In this case, pain is preferable to murder: it is not a given, but something the relativism of which may be exploited.

After the failure with the salt, Donald becomes desperate to read and interpret the marks left by Dr Fergusson, and in the end comes on the idea of getting the gardener to draw a facsimile of his cuts and bruises, and this drawing—a mess of hieroglyphics and squiggles—is included in the body of the text and

[41] *Fearful Flogging*, 16.

as the front cover of the story. Donald is horrified when he sees it for it is, of course, 'utterly incomprehensible',[42] just 'scribble'.[43] It is clear to the reader that this is all it is, that there is no divine meaning to be drawn from the visible signs of pain. In calling it 'mystic scribble', however, Donald seems to accept the curtain of allegory and the idea that pain apparently without meaning can be profoundly meaningful, although man's intellect is insufficient to decipher it:

in that mystic scribble, which had been subsequently retraced by the flame-pen of the salt, lurked the key to unlock that problem in ontology, the Origin of Evil, and the sword with which to cut the Gordian Knot of Evil's Final Eradication. I gazed on the map-document with that absorbing dream worship with which we regard that which at once awes our senses and baffles our reason.[44]

The claims made here for deciphered pain are clearly both enormous and ludicrous, unless the author of them is indeed omniscient. But Ross, throughout the story, is at pains to undercut the authority of the pedagogue through a deep-seated ambivalence, both in his use of oxymoronic phrases, such as 'mystic scribble', and in Dr Ferguson's patterns of speech. He is presented at once as a 'snuffy old rascal'[45] and the fount of all wisdom, and his speech, whilst claiming the privilege of wisdom, is pompous and absurd. About to beat the boy, he instructs him to 'Divest [himself] of the garment that envelopes that part of [his] somatic entity upon which, from time immemorial, flagellation has been conventionally laid.'[46] This is the language of authority and power, but it is also manifestly ridiculous. The 'writing with the stick'[47] which Donald eventually sends to a learned cleric to decipher is both arcane and inane, the deciphered 'cryptogram'[48] reading in part and typically: 'Wo, wo, son of Pomponius Mela, with the iron in the groin and the foundations beaten like an anvil of Mulciber.'[49] This is the translation with which Donald is presented, and at which he is appalled and disappointed, exclaiming, 'No wonder the thrashing did me no good! No wonder that I felt quite as wicked as ever!'[50] Even those within the veil of allegory, after

[42] Ibid. 24.   [43] Ibid.   [44] Ibid.   [45] Ibid. 15.   [46] Ibid.
[47] Ibid. 23.   [48] Ibid. 25.   [49] Ibid. 27.   [50] Ibid. 28.

'prayerful reading and . . . philological synthesis'[51] cannot make sense of the infliction of pain, for it is, in fact, meaningless, cruel, and arbitrarily meted out. Ross, with a series of cheap jokes on the subject of whipped buttocks built into the text—'I would be at the bottom of all this',[52] 'I had the stick-writing of a great seat of learning unrolled before me'[53]—seriously undermines the claim that good will come of this beating, for before the idea has a chance to establish itself, he sniggers at it on a stylistic level, as well as making it a subject for ridicule in the subject matter of his story.

Ross's insistence on the marks left on the body as a form of writing is by no means unusual in writing about flagellation towards the end of the nineteenth century. The Revd Wilkinson's insistence on the college motto—'Spare the rod, spoil the child'—is twisted further when he makes it plain that boys who were beaten at Eton had 'the "college arms" . . . stamped upon them'[54] by the birch. What becomes evident from this is the sense of the class of the boy being beaten, for each time this happened the mark of the public school was fixed on his body. It was an idea with which Algernon Charles Swinburne was obsessed, and one that worked itself out both in his letters to his close friend, Richard Monckton Milnes, and in his unsigned contribution to *The Whippingham Papers*, a collection of flagellatory writings published privately in 1888. There is the same insistence in Swinburne's 'Arthur's Flogging' on the writing of the birch that is found in Ross's *Fearful Flogging*, but not the same desire to render the beating that left it there unacceptable. In stanzas typical of much flagellatory verse, Swinburne describes the process of 'Arthur's Flogging':

> He clapped his hands behind—the birch twigs caught 'em
>   Across, and made them tingle too and bleed;
> And harder still the birch fell on his bottom,
>   And left some fresh red letters there to read;
> Weeks passed before the part inscribed forgot 'em,
>   The fleshy tablets, where the master's creed
> Is written on boy's skin with birchen pen,
> At each re-issue copied fair again.

---

[51] *Fearful Flogging*, 26.   [52] Ibid. 25.
[53] Ibid. 24.   [54] *Reminiscences*, 41.

This was the third edition, not the first,
    Printed on Arthur's bottom in red text
That very week, with comments interspersed,
    And cuts that left the student's eye perplexed,
Though in the love of flagellation versed,
    You hardly could tell one cut from the next;
All the smooth creamy paper, white and pink,
Was crossed and scored and blotted with red ink.

The fair full page of white and warm young flesh
    Was ruled across with long thick lines of red,
And lettered on the engraved backside with fresh
    Large characters, by all boys to be read,
In hieroglyphs fine as a spider's mesh,
    With copious coloured cuts illustrated,
Warm from the hand of the artist that begot 'em,
To adorn the bare blank page of Arthur's bottom.[55]

The emphasis is strikingly different from Ross's, but the vocabulary is the same since a religious terminology is deliberately
employed and subverted. The schoolmaster's power is conflated
with that of God as 'the master's creed | Is written on boy's skin'
and the boy's buttocks become 'fleshy tablets' on which the law
is laid down, just as in a subsequent stanza the boy is forced to
'plead for mercy'.[56] There is the same insistence on the interpretation of the 'hieroglyphs' left by the birch, but the super-
abundance of such references leads not to satire as it does with
Ross, but to an enthralled relishing of the event. The marks are
done in 'red text' to mark the importance of this occasion, and
blood becomes nothing other than 'red ink' that blots the page,
whilst the 'cuts' of the birch become the woodcuts or illustrations that colour the book.

But what in the end is written on the bodies of these boys is
not the meaningless hieroglyphics of Ross's short story, but a
way of identifying their class, for these are, above all else, public
school boys who are being beaten—boys from families with
enough money and social status to require them to enter into
this tradition and to be forced to show their fortitude on the
flogging block. The 'college arms' of which Wilkinson writes are

---

[55] *The Whippingham Papers: A Collection of Contributions in Prose and Verse,
Chiefly by the Author of the 'Romance of Chastisement'* (privately printed, 1888),
10–11.   [56] Ibid. 13.

endlessly put on display in Swinburne's poem as the boys' buttocks become 'a fair field'[57]—a heraldic term—on which their
coats of arms are engraved:

> But crests and arms and quarterings and supporters,
>   And all emblazoned flourishes her field,
> Are no defence for a boy's hinder quarter[s],[58]
>   Nor will he find his coat of arms a shield
> For his bare bottom . . .
> His coat is birch *per fesse*, and total gules,
>   Poor fellow! 'tis an ancient coat, and good;
> And, from of old, was borne in all boys' schools
>   Since the first flogging block was made of wood;[59]

The strokes of the birch mean that the 'total gules', the colour
of white ermine dyed red, in this case by the flogging, is *'per
fesse'*, between the lines that mark out the edge of the heraldic
field. The 'quarterings' denote both heraldic significance and an
extreme bodily punishment—it is no surprise that the flogging
is carried out on a 'block' and is known as an 'execution'—
whilst the 'supporters' can be either the heraldic beasts who
hold up the shield or the two boys designated 'holders down'[60]
who flank the boy being beaten. Instead of being a protection,
however, this coat of arms cannot 'shield' the sufferer, but
instead becomes the embodiment of his suffering. The point that
Swinburne insists on is that this is part of a long tradition, and
one that 'from of old, was *borne* in all boys' schools'. The coat
of arms marks out these boys not just because it belongs to
them, but because it is also suffered by them and renders them
worthy of being beaten. The narratorial voice of 'Arthur's
Flogging' claims that 'on the flogging block, I've often wished |
To be a boy that drives a plough or cart'[61] since such boys are
supposedly physically incapable of the acute sensation allowed
to the upper classes. Swinburne was to put it more bluntly in
one of his letters to Monckton Milnes, a fellow old Etonian to

---

[57] *Whippingham Papers*, 6.
[58] 'Pencil corrections, possibly by [Henry Spencer] Ashbee' (note in British
Library Copy).
[59] *Whippingham Papers*, 5–6.
[60] James Brinsley-Richards, *Seven Years at Eton, 1857–1864* (Richard Bentley,
1883), 71.
[61] *Whippingham Papers*, 5.

whom Swinburne was writing about the latter's attempt at flagellatory fiction:

I am surprised that a man of refinement, whom I had taken to be an
educational aristocrat of the purest water—and blood, should have
mixed the bitter-sweet fountain of Heliconian brine, the pure salt
Hippocrene of boys' tears and birchen pickle, with the obscene puddle
of corduroy bourgeoisie. Is a 'greasy grasp' to pollute by its distract-
ing and nauseous contact the skin of a boy's hands while the skin of
his bottom is reddening with the voluptuous blush of a most delicate
agony? Is a butcher's blood to tingle, a tailor's flesh to wince, from the
discipline of nobles, the correction of a prince?[62]

Swinburne repeatedly draws on the language of inability and
class-inflected sensibility—Monckton Milnes is 'a man of refinement', one with a refined and sensitive neurological organization—whilst the boy is capable of 'a most delicate agony' of
which the butcher's lad could only dream. Flogging is 'the correction of a prince' and is, in effect, wasted on the lower classes
who both do not know how to endure suffering and who cannot
feel it as acutely as their aristocratic counterparts: it is, as the
narrator of 'Arthur's Flogging' puts it, a way of making 'high-
born bottoms "blush with noble blood"'.[63]

The metaphor of flesh as paper to be marked, and the insistent punning that goes with this, is continued to such an extent
that this body in pain becomes something to be looked at and
enjoyed rather than to be horrified at. James Brinsley-Richards's
Seven Years at Eton (1883) bears witness both to the voyeurism
involved in public school floggings and the pleasure of the staff
and boys in the process. In anticipation of one such flogging in
the Lower School, the first that Brinsley-Richards was to see in
his time at Eton, the author describes the 'front place'[64] that he
himself attained at the event and the way in which 'Several
dozens of fellows clambered upon forms and desks'[65] to get the
best view. His comment on flogging once again draws together
antivivisectionary and anti-flogging rhetoric, for the reader is
unequivocally told that watching such sights brutalizes since the

---

[62] *The Swinburne Letters*, ed. Cecil Y. Lang 6 vols. (New Haven: Yale University
Press, 1959), i. 74–5: 'To Richard Monckton Milnes, Fontmel Lodge, February 3
[1863]'.
[63] *Whippingham Papers*, 5.
[64] *Seven Years at Eton*, 71.   [65] Ibid.

infliction of pain starts to be seen as a pleasure: 'It is quite true
that the eyes and nerves soon get accustomed to cruel sights. I
gradually came to witness the execution in the Lower School
not only with indifference, but with amusement.'[66] It is here that
the reader is returned to Swinburne's 'Arthur's Flogging' with
its vision of the sadistic schoolmaster:

> So Arthur's bottom seems, between the cuts,
> To vibrate under his tormentor's hands,
> Who, gloating on it, as he flogs it, gluts
> His eyes with the full prospect, while these great
> Red cheeks contract at each cut, and dilate.[67]

The boy is given all the attributes of acute sensitivity denied to
the 'boy that drives a plough or cart', with his body represented
as a musical instrument which 'vibrate[s]', set against the sadis-
tic and vampiric pleasures of the schoolmaster who 'gluts | His
eyes' on the blood-spattered nakedness that he creates.

It is here that Swinburne gets closest to admitting the pleasure of those who did the beating: a phenomenon that persistently gets pushed to the margins in many flagellatory writings,
but which comes to the fore in the privately printed flagellatory
pornography that came to a head in the late nineteenth century.
As Steven Marcus argues in *The Other Victorians*, vast quan-
tities of flagellatory pornography were published during the
Victorian period,[68] and although Marcus's particular area of
interest is the middle of the century the same was certainly true
during the 1880s and 1890s. A case in point is the volume, supposedly by a Mrs Martinet, called *The Quintessence of Birch
Discipline* (1870). This fits with Marcus's description of such
writings in that it 'assumes that its audience had both interest
in and connection with the higher gentry and the nobility',[69] and
'further assumes that its audience had the common experience
of education at a public school'.[70] Mrs Martinet is a school-
teacher who relies on the birch to keep discipline amongst her
pupils, but who takes her summer holidays in Scarborough
where she sets up a flagellation establishment, frequented pri-

---

[66] Brinsley-Richards, 72.   [67] *Whippingham Papers*, 12.
[68] *The Other Victorians: A Study of Sexuality and Pornography in Mid-
Nineteenth-Century England* (1964; Corgi, 1969). See ch. 6, 'A Child is Being
Beaten'.
[69] Ibid. 256.   [70] Ibid.

marily by the lascivious, and, of course, upper-class, Sir
Frederick Flaybum. Where this book is interesting is not in the
supposed sexual pleasure of the young girls being beaten—'the
pain of the birching seemed lost upon them, and it was most
delightful to watch the lascivious expressions of their juvenile
faces, as they moaned with . . . pleasurable emotions'[71]—which
is criminally absurd, but in the way it makes manifest the lustful
pleasure of those who wielded the whip. Mrs Martinet, whilst
flogging a 9-year-old girl, finds that the event 'warmed [her]
blood in a surprising way'[72] and 'an indescribably voluptuous
feeling'—and here we are back to Swinburne's vocabulary in his
letter to Monckton Milnes—'came all over [her], and [she] actually emitted with an excess of pleasure far beyond any [she] had
ever experienced in the arms of a lover'.[73] The story embodies
the clinical terminology set by Krafft-Ebing in *Psychopathia
Sexualis*, his discussion of sadism and masochism which first
appeared in an English translation in 1892. The two girls, like
Krafft-Ebing's masochist, find that 'the person in a state of
masochistic ecstasy feels no pain'[74] and Mrs Martinet, in the
manner of many of the case studies in *Psychopathia Sexualis*,
'found great sexual pleasure'[75] in the act of beating these children. There is no question—and nor is there meant to be—that
this is a sexually motivated flogging, but where *The Quintessence of Birch Discipline* acts as an interesting gloss on much
of the literature that arose from the flagellation debate is in its
use of the language of correction that the teacher in William
Stuart Ross's *Fearful Flogging* used. Sir Frederick, urging Mrs
Martinet on to further flogging, defers to her as teacher and
legitimate chastiser:

'I am so sorry you should have such troublesome children to coreect
[*sic*] for me . . . They will quite spoil your visit, my dear Madame,
but such obstinacy must be overcome now, or they will be spoilt for
life . . .'[76]

---

[71] *The Quintessence of Birch Discipline. A Sequence to the Romance of Chastisement* (privately printed, 1870), 23.
[72] Ibid. 10.   [73] Ibid.
[74] *Psychopathia Sexualis, with especial reference to Contrary Sexual Instinct: A
Medico-Legal Study*, authorized trans. of the 7th enlarged and rev. German edn. by
Charles Gilbert Chaddock (Philadelphia and London: F. A. Davis, 1892), 148.
[75] Ibid. 83.   [76] *Quintessence*, 11–12.

It is the old 'spare the rod, spoil the child' vocabulary that marks so much of the late Victorian debate over the corporal punishment of children, but which here is seen to be the hollow sham that it so often was.

It is in flogging narratives derived from the army and navy that the issues of the enjoyment of the flogger as well as the class of the victim came clearly into focus. The legal flogging of members of the armed forces became a pressing issue towards the end of the century since soldiers and sailors could be legally and brutally beaten in ways that were impossible for the civilian, and, indeed, the case for the court-martialled soldier or sailor was worse still. Narratives of actual floggings in the services abound in a variety of literary forms, written for widely divergent reasons, throughout the nineteenth century. William Stables recounts his experiences of watching floggings in his capacity as a doctor in *Medical Life in the Navy*[77] (1868); Archibald Forbes, a journalist for the *Evening Star* and *Daily News*, tells of his own flogging in the army in *Soldiering and Scribbling*[78] (1872); William Cooper in *A History of the Rod*[79] (1869) gathers together a collection of flogging narratives in chapters on the army and navy in a book that purports to be a serious historical text; and perhaps rather less disingenuously, texts such as *Experiences of Flagellation . . . Compiled by an Amateur Flagellant* (1885) gather together tales of flagellation, along the lines of Mrs Martinet's *Birch Discipline*, of both schoolgirls and sailors, clearly intended to titillate the flagellatory fantasies of the reader.[80]

Whatever the purpose of the text, the narrative is always the same in outline. In much the same way that Steven Marcus sees the formulaic nature of flagellatory pornography, in which a 'fantasy is presented in an astonishing variety of forms, all of which repeat the same unvarying idea',[81] so too did those who

---

[77] *Medical Life in the Navy* (Robert Hardwicke, 1868), 94–9.

[78] *Soldiering and Scribbling: A Series of Sketches* (Henry S. King, 1872), 82–90.

[79] *A History of the Rod in All Countries from the Earliest Period to the Present Time* (new edn., William Reeves, [1869]), 347–72.

[80] *Experiences of Flagellation. A Series of Remarkable Instances of Whipping Inflicted on Both Sexes, with Curious Anecdotes of Ladies Fond of Administering Birch Discipline. Compiled by an Amateur Flagellant* (printed for private circulation, 1885).

[81] *Other Victorians*, 255.

wrote about flogging in the armed forces seem to follow a pre-
scribed set of rules. Archibald Forbes's description of his own
flogging is a case in point, for first of all he sees this flogging in
terms of 'suffer[ing] . . . ignominy'[82] rather than of suffering
pain and immediately the paradigm is established. One of the
primary reasons why flogging was fought against was precisely
because it was thought to degrade those who felt the touch of
the cat and nine tails on their naked shoulders rather than
because it hurt. Next, the man about to be flogged is offered
alcohol to assuage the oncoming pain, either by the surgeon
who presides over the flogging or by one of his friends, but this
is scornfully rejected. As Forbes claims, 'I could not bring myself
to use his recipe for Dutch courage, it would have been more
degrading than the lash itself.'[83] In this refusal, the manliness
and stoicism of the man about to suffer is brought to the fore.
Next comes the ceremony of undressing—'All I had to do was
to take my stock and braces off, buckle on a waiststrap, give
my cloak to one of the escort to throw over my shoulders after
the butchery was over, and then I was ready'[84]—a ritual repeated
in descriptions of flagellation, and dwelt on endlessly in flagellatory pornography. Finally comes the description of the
flogging itself, and once again Forbes's narrative serves as an
exemplar:

my wrists were securely lashed to the triangles, and the colonel's stern
voice gave the word 'Begin.' At last down came the thongs, with an
angry whizz, straight and fair on the back, and every nerve in my body
gave a bound from my brain to my toes. The actual pain of the lacerated flesh, agony as it was, was nothing compared with the horrible
crashing jar on the nerves, and it was this which so taxed my resolution to repress any sign of feeling. Every atom of my whole body
seemed imbued with a separate palpitating, throbbing existence—the
whole muscular system thrilled and vibrated with a convulsive agony.
Another blow higher up, and every nerve gave a fresh stab and shoot,
as if it would crack. 'Three!'—still a wilder quiver shot through me,
and I had to clench my lower lip desperately between my teeth, or I
could not have restrained the convulsive impulse to call out.[85]

What Forbes is emphasizing here is the acutely sensitive neurological and muscular organization of the body being flogged.

[82] *Soldiering and Scribbling*, 87.   [83] Ibid.   [84] Ibid.   [85] Ibid. 88.

The language, once again, is that of sensibility as his 'palpi-tating, throbbing' body 'thrilled', 'vibrated', and 'quiver[ed]' in response to the laying on of the lash. The description is filled with such words associated with heightened sensibility, but these come into sharp conflict with the 'crashing' of the lash and the 'lacerated flesh' that it flogs into being. As I suggested in the previous chapter, variations of sensibility between people could be accounted for by the speed at which vibrations were able to pass along the sufferer's nerves: the smaller and more delicate the nerve, the quicker the vibration was able to pass, and the more acutely the sensation was felt. Here the soldier's reactions to pain are unnervingly fast: this is clearly not the slow and unresponsive body supposed to exist by Lombroso and other criminal anthropologists of his kind. Pain 'stab[s]' and 'shoot[s]' and the whole of Forbes's nervous system, 'from my brain to my toes', is drawn in as it responds sympathetically to the pain inflicted on the back itself. Such sympathy in suffering, quiverings, and throbbings were usually associated with women rather than men, and indeed Forbes, in his suffering, is once more implicitly connected to a female sensitivity when he only 'just managed to reach the hospital before [he] fainted'.[86] This language of sensibility, however, comes into conflict with a determinedly masculine vocabulary of public school stoicism, shown in the 'resolution to repress any sign of feeling': the body suffers and yet the real man refuses to express such suffering even if it means that he must bite back his screams.

What Forbes remembered in after years is not the pain of the flogging, but the 'burning sense of wrong and injury',[87] the shame of being 'beaten like a hound',[88] and this sense of the ignominy of being flogged is the thing that comes across most firmly in flogging narratives. The 'hardy, bold, and wiry'[89] British marine who is flogged in Stables's *Medical Life in the Navy* finds that he can bear the pain of the flogging, but what he finds intolerable is the shame of it, saying to the doctor who examines him: 'it's my feelings they'll hurt. I've a little girl at home that loves me, and—bless you, sir, I won't look her in the face again no-how.'[90] Worse than this, however, is the way in

---

[86] *Soldiering and Scribbling*, 90.   [87] Ibid. 83.   [88] Ibid. 90.
[89] Stables, *Medical Life*, 95.   [90] Ibid.

which it 'brutalised the man and turned him hopelessly upon society',[91] forcing the once worthwhile citizen out to the margins, and effectively criminalizing him.

E. Livingstone Prescott's[92] novel *Scarlet and Steel* deals in graphic detail with the moral and physical effects of flogging in the army, and this brutalization of the man being flogged. Written in 1897, sixteen years after flogging had supposedly been abolished in the army, Prescott's book deals with the exception to the rule: it was still possible to flog offenders in military prisons,[93] though officers were exempt from this punishment.[94] What is interesting about Prescott's novel, and where she displays her sense of the relationship between class and the ability to suffer physically, is in its dealing with a gentleman who is, however, no longer an officer, but falls into the ranks, and therefore eludes the legislation that was put in place to protect him. Her 'novel with a purpose'[95] is the story of Sholto Mauleverer and his fall from grace. After being tricked into losing the family fortune, Sholto enlists in the ranks in the army, where his upperclass disposition and tendency to hit people lands him in a prison gaol, where he is flogged and birched on three separate occasions.

The ambiguities in Prescott's writing find shape in the clash between Sholto's 'red and purple weals'[96] and the pain that he feels as a gentleman. One of the first things readers hear about Sholto is that he has been sent down from Oxford University for hitting someone, and this gives a fair indication of the course of the book. It is, however, when he beats his groom that there is a collision of variant meanings as to the nature of the infliction of pain, which forms itself in Sholto's subsequent conversation with his father:

He was again inclined to be ashamed of his violence; not because he thought it wrong, but that, in his view, much worse thing, ungentlemanly.

---

[91] Alfred Kinnear, *Across Many Seas: A Story of Action from Crimea to Coronation* (Bristol and London: J. W. Arrowsmith, 1902), 24.

[92] A pseudonym for Edith Catherine Spicer Jay.

[93] See Gibson, *English Vice*, 171.   [94] Ibid. 176.

[95] E. Livingstone Prescott (pseud.), *Flogging NOT Abolished*... (Clapham: A. Bachhoffner, 1897), 1.

[96] Edd., *Scarlet and Steel: Some Modern Military Episodes* (Hutchinson, 1897), 262.

'I suppose I oughtn't to have done it, sir.'

'Why not?' asked his father coldly. 'Why shouldn't you thrash your own servant? These fellows don't feel, you know.'

'Well, not as we should, I suppose,' said Sholto. 'My temper got the better of me.'[97]

Sholto's father, firmly entrenched in his aristocratic position, takes up the line taken with criminals and the working classes spelt out in previous chapters. He can thrash servants because they simply do not feel it. The dubious logic of this becomes apparent in the course of this novel, not least because the motives of someone beating a servant for his own pleasure rather than the servant's moral edification suggest the thinking of a Mrs Martinet or a Sir Frederick Flaybum. Sholto's ambivalent answer—that servants feel 'not as we should, I suppose'—suggests both a grudging acceptance of his father's reading and an admission that this is not how one should behave. In other terms, Sholto is quite right when he says 'I oughtn't to have done it' when he talks about the unthinking infliction of pain, for it is this incident that brings about his downfall and degradation, as Boucher, the man whom Sholto thrashes, in turn flogs him in the prison gaol, taking a sadistic pleasure by 'a little too obviously put[ting] his heart into his work'.[98]

Prescott is concerned with the differing ways in which people feel, and Sholto, like Archibald Forbes, is persistently represented as a man of great sensitivity, with 'quivering nerves'[99] and 'skin like a lady's'.[100] His problem is precisely that he is a gentleman and feels with an exquisite sensitivity. In a series of chapters strangely and indecorously called 'A Tune on the Triangles'—alluding to the frame onto which the soldier was tied—and 'A Cat-astrophe', Prescott's punning titles belie the serious nature of the infliction laid on her hero. In a form very similar to that of Forbes's narrative, the description of the stripping, strapping down, and flogging of Sholto takes its course, with a similar conflict between the language of sensitivity—'Sholto's whole soul and body felt like one raw palpitating nerve'[101]—and the language of degradation, as he is repeatedly 'flogged like a yelping cur'.[102]

---

[97] Prescott, *Scarlet* 21.   [98] Ibid. 284.   [99] Ibid. 252.
[100] Ibid. 263.   [101] Ibid. 287.   [102] Ibid. 288.

Prescott eventually resolves the novel and redeems Sholto from shame by making her hero recognize his affinity with Christ who also suffered a flogging. Sholto sees a picture of the flagellation of Christ with its legend, 'With His stripes we are healed',[103] and is drawn to a belief in God: 'At last, out of the silence and the darkness, actual and spiritual, broke faintly this declaration of faith: "My Brother—and my God!"'[104] His sufferings are redeemed in ways that William Stuart Ross so resolutely satirized in *A Fearful Flogging*.

Whatever Prescott's avowed aim in writing the novel, and the concomitant pamphlet *Flogging* NOT *Abolished in the British Army* (1897), it was not simply the total abolition of flogging in the army that she required, but the flogging of *gentlemen* who could not sustain such treatment. Sholto repeatedly appeals to the officials who observe his floggings in these terms: 'You're a gentleman. I was, once. Help me!'[105] as if this link between them renders his present predicament impossible to sustain. Indeed, Prescott's final appeal in this matter is not that flogging degrades everybody, but that 'the man who feels it most morally, is he who least deserves it',[106] a position acknowledged in the 1881 legislation that made the flogging of officers in military prisons illegal. It is the opposite side of the coin from Havelock Ellis's morally and physically insensate criminal who commits crimes because he cannot feel pain vicariously. Sholto, for Prescott, should be allowed the peccadilloes of his class—the inability to refrain from punching people—since his physical sensitivity renders physical punishment too horrifying to contemplate. Boucher's cruelty lies not just in his over-exuberance in flogging his former employer, but also in the aspersions that he casts over Sholto's class. In words which echo Forbes's and which reverberate throughout flogging narratives, 'for all his resolution, [Sholto] could not repress a cry'.[107] Prescott's insistence on the horrors of the punishment allows the thrashed groom to taunt Sholto with his inability to take a flogging in silence, and jeer: '"Old Barnes used to say 'blood tells.' Why, you made more noise than a little shrimp of an East-End larrikin as I helped to tie up! But there—you're only a half-bred one, after all."'[108]

[103] Ibid. 348.   [104] Ibid.   [105] Ibid. 261.
[106] Ibid. 312.   [107] Ibid. 283.   [108] Ibid. 277.

Sholto is declared illegitimate at the beginning of the novel, and
this is, indeed, how his inheritance and his status as a gentleman is taken from him, but it is, in fact, not the case: his inability not to scream out in agony is a sign of the severity of the
infliction and his own sensitivity rather than his lack of fortitude. Once again, however, what matters is not so much the
physical suffering involved as the degradation of character that
comes with being publicly beaten:

Sholto left behind him, driven out by the reforming (?) rod, such poor
remnants of honour, decency, belief in God or man, as he had struggled to maintain till now. Morbid shame, sick terror, a lower deep
of despairing hatred to all, took their place. His physical self showed
it—he never squared his shoulders, nor swaggered with his old easy,
graceful swagger, more, and though he still sneered and swore, and
did worse, all was in a melancholy, lifeless whisper. He adopted, with
strange facility, from that hour, the prison manners of the 'old hands'
there, and no longer flushed indignantly at Boucher's coarse and fre-
quent comments on the results of his three scourgings; but took
humiliation as a matter of course in all things, and slunk about, like
a stray dog expecting a kick, at the bidding of anything in blue cloth
and bright buttons.[109]

As Walter Spens, one of the Sheriff-Substitutes of Lanarkshire
during the 1870s, claimed more than twenty years before
Prescott's book was written, 'The lash was abolished in the
army, one chief reason for which was the loss of self-respect
which it caused in many who suffered under it.'[110] Prescott's
Sholto could stand as the degraded type whose creation Spens
acknowledged and feared, since the system of disciplinary,
indeed retributive, flogging, for Spens, was 'not a rule which
commends itself to . . . refined and educated people'.[111] Again,
in this, there is the appeal to the 'refined'—those who feel
acutely and sensitively—and the linking of this to the 'many'—
by no means all—of those who were flogged and consequently
degraded. Lord Courtallen, one of *Scarlet and Steel*'s minor

[109] *Scarlet*, 312.
[110] *Jurisdiction and Punishments of Summary Criminal Courts (With Special Reference to the Lash); Being Answers to the Home Secretary's Queries to English and
Scotch Magistrates* (Edinburgh: T. & T. Clark, 1875), 68.
[111] Ibid.

characters, suggests to his brother, who has served time in a military gaol alongside Sholto, that only the 'offscourings of the army'[112] are flogged, but it is clear from the description of Sholto's degradation that Prescott is keen to show the process by which a gentleman can be turned into such an 'offscouring'. She does, however, allow the assumption to ride that flogging the dregs of society is acceptable, whilst flogging a gentleman is not. Lord Courtallen is led to accept that there are in military prisons men 'with the same nerves to shrink from pain'[113] as himself, and that for these such a deliberate infliction of pain is an outrageous scandal.

Sholto's tormentor, Boucher, is presented as one who takes great pleasure in the infliction of pain as a form of retribution, but there is no sense of sexual pleasure in his response, and Prescott, in this respect, is in the vast majority in failing to recognize, or at least to articulate, this possibility. But for George Bernard Shaw, one of the most outspoken amongst the anti-floggers, this was the dangerous undercurrent to flogging that needed to be acknowledged and stopped. What Shaw terms a 'flagellation neurosis', pushing the desire to hurt into the realms of the pathological, becomes 'a horrible passional ecstasy in the spectacle of laceration and suffering from which even the most self-restrained and secretive person who can prevail on himself to be present will not be wholly free'.[114] To watch a flogging was to be infected by it, to be brutalized, as those who performed vivisectional operations were brutalized by the process. If Swinburne recognized with pleasure the schoolmaster's ability to 'gloat' over the sufferings of the child he was beating, then Henry Salt, the editor of the journal the *Humanitarian* and like Swinburne a former Etonian, saw the dangers, and the horrors, of it in his 'Hymn of the Flagellomaniacs':

> As the miser craves for treasure,
>   As the drunkard craves for grog,
> So we crave for morbid pleasure—
>   Something sentient to flog!

---

[112] Prescott, *Scarlet*, 352.
[113] Ibid. 350.
[114] George Bernard Shaw, Letter to *Saturday Review*, 28 Aug. 1897, 224.

Give us juvenile offender,
    Truant oft from school or church,
Yet for prison cell too tender:—
    Ah! to brand him with the birch!

Give us gaol-bird past repentance,
    Brutalised too deep for that:—
Ah! to wreak on him the sentence
    Of the sanguinary 'cat'!

All the tortures—hanging, burning,
    Cropping, thumbscrew, boot, and rack—
Pale before our fevered yearning
    For the bare and bleeding back.

As the miser o'er his treasure,
    As the drunkard o'er his grog,
So we gloat with maniac pleasure
    O'er our joy of joys—to flog![115]

For Salt, flogging, despite the endless biblical and penal justifications, had nothing to do with the efficacy of the act itself as
a deterrent or punishment, but was predicated on the active,
gloating enjoyment of the man wielding the whip and the
institution that allowed it. The feverish, maniacal pleasure, the
drunken yearning desire of the flogger, pushed flogging out of
the realms of the rational and into the realm of 'passional
ecstasy' Shaw so greatly feared.

In a parallel manner, what had started off in such journals
as the *Family Herald*, the *Queen*, and the *Englishwoman's
Domestic Magazine* as part of a legitimate debate about the
efficacy of beating children slipped into a forum for pornographic flagellatory fantasy.[116] A mother's belief that 'a girl
can be made to feel the birch with her drawers on'[117] becomes
something rather different in the hands of a different kind of
writer, as the procedures of inflicting a beating are described at

---

[115] *Consolations of a Faddist: Verses Reprinted from 'The Humanitarian'* (A. C.
Firfield, 1906), 28.

[116] For contemporary discussion of this series of letters to popular journals, see
Cooper, *History*, 462–77: chs. 44 'Birch According to the "Family Herald"' and 45
'Birch in the Boudoir'; for a more recent perspective see Gibson, *English Vice*,
194–232: ch. 5 'The Flagellant Correspondence Column in Nineteenth-century
England'.

[117] *Indecent Whipping* [London, 1880?], 6. This is a collection of letters reprinted
from the *Englishwoman's Domestic Magazine*.

considerable length. 'A Parent' writes of the treatment of her daughter:

She was taken upstairs and arrayed in a punishment dress—*i.e.*, a long calico garment, resembling a night-dress;—conducted to the dining-hall, and then and there stripped naked in the presence of the whole school, and flogged by the gardener, being held meanwhile by two of the day-masters. The poor child's shrieks and prayers for mercy were disregarded, and the most brutal punishment administered by a man's strong right hand, with a birch-rod, continued. Several eye-witnesses state that when she was released, after receiving between fifteen and twenty cuts, she would have fallen to the floor fainting almost, but was caught in the arms of a bystander. Needless to say, on this outrage reaching my ears, I had her immediately removed, and only my dread of seeing the thing reported in the public newspapers prevented my immediately instituting legal proceedings.[118]

It is a cruel story if it is true, but certainly by the 1880s, when this collection of letters was gathered together, considerable doubt had been thrown on the motives of those who wrote and those who read such letters. There is no question that Swinburne took particular delight in the flagellatory correspondence in the press[119] and, as William Cooper suggests in his own book on flogging, the editors of the journals involved in the debate were also clearly doubtful of the veracity of the letters sent to them. As Cooper points out, 'When the controversy carried on in the *Family Herald* begins to flag it is stimulated by some such letter as that of Miss Birch', an advocate of flogging in girls' schools whose pseudonym clearly fits easily alongside those of Lady Gay Spanker, author of the overtly pornographic *Tales of Fun and Flagellation*[120] or Lady Termagant Flaybum, responsible for a collection called *Sublime of Flagellation*, addressed to Lady Harriet Tickletail, of Bumfiddle-Hall.[121] Then Cooper adds:

We gather from his remarks that the editor is evidently very suspicious of his correspondents. In many of the answers he conveys the idea that he is dealing with some one who is not what he (or she) implies by the

---

[118] Ibid. 3.   [119] See Gibson, *English Vice*, 58.
[120] *Tales of Fun and Flagellation* (privately printed, 1896).
[121] *Sublime of Flagellation: in Letters from Lady Termagant Flaybum, of Birch-Grove, to Lady Harriet Tickletail, of Bumfiddle-Hall. In which are Introduced the Beautiful Tale of La Coquette Chatie, in French and English; and the Boarding-School Bumbrusher; or, the Distresses of Laura* (George Peacock, n.d.).

signature attached to the letter. In other words, we gather from some of the communications that men are engaging in the correspondence from prurient or, at least, questionable motives. Many of the writers desire strongly to have particulars of the *modus operandi*—that is, whether the culprit is put over the knee, mounted on some person's back, laid over a chair, tied down on an ottoman, whipt in bed, or how the necessary chastisement is administered, also what amount of whipping is given for different offences. Some of the correspondents are very stupid, others not very truthful or inventive, for we find the whipping letters of early numbers repeated in late numbers, and so on, with accounts of schools which evidently never were in existence.[122]

The detailed description of flogging has become a recognized source of readerly pleasure. But if here, in the periodical press, it remains submerged, in the decadent writings of the 1890s it was to come into its own. Not only did the decadent of the 1890s deliberately seek out sensation in a variety of ways—particularly in this instance both by wielding and by yielding to the whip—but readers also sought out the painful experiences of others as a form of readerly pleasure. Pain was no longer something to be avoided and repelled at all costs, but something deliberately to be sought out and enjoyed.

What becomes apparent from the decadent movement is its insistence on sensation as a primary good. Like Prescott's Sholto with his 'quivering nerves' and offended sensibility, Oscar Wilde offers the same ability to suffer but in a markedly different context. Dorian Gray is the archetypal decadent in 'his search for sensations',[123] his desire to make himself feel acutely. He has the sensitive body of the decadent that responds delicately to stimuli, as he finds himself 'vibrating and throbbing to curious pulses'[124] and finds, on contemplating old age, that 'a sharp pang of pain struck through him like a knife, and made each delicate fibre of his nature quiver'.[125] It is the conjunction of this sensitive body with the desire to follow sensation for its own sake that, at least in part, marks out the decadent experience. In keeping with Krafft-Ebing's judgement that 'pain is always a ready means for producing an intense bodily impression'[126] Rhoda Broughton's aesthete, Mr Chaloner, finds himself asserting that 'surely there is nothing so beautiful as the passionate

---

[122] *History*, 465–6.   [123] *The Picture of Dorian Gray*, 196.
[124] Ibid. 28.   [125] Ibid. 37.   [126] *Psychopathia Sexualis*, 140.

pulsations of pain!'[127] whilst it is Lord Henry, in Wilde's book, who claims that 'One could never pay too high a price for any sensation.'[128] It is clear that this leads easily to a linking of the decadent dandy and the experience of physical pain, though it is not clear that the suffering will be that of the one who feels it so exquisitely. Dorian Gray congratulates himself on having 'lived centuries of pain, æon upon æon of torture'[129] whilst recalling Sibyl Vane's last and shatteringly poor performance on the night she died, and in later years gloats over his collection of church vestments and the suffering associated with them:

In the long cedar chests that lined the west gallery of his house he had stored away many rare and beautiful specimens of what is really the raiment of the Bride of Christ, who must wear purple and jewels and fine linen that she may hide the pallid macerated body that is worn by the suffering that she seeks for, and wounded by self-inflicted pain.[130]

It is the pain of flagellation to which Wilde is referring here as Dorian Gray glamorizes this wounded, suffering body, gorgeously bedecked and exquisitely tortured, in the same way that Frederick Rolfe, 'Baron Corvo', dwelt on the painful martyrdoms of youthful saints in his poetic works.[131] Rolfe's poem 'Sestina yn honour of Lytel Seynt Hew', the saint who was flogged to death, in its treatment of the boy's Christlike flogging, follows closely in the footsteps of Swinburne in his poems from *The Whippingham Papers*. Whilst Swinburne's unfortunate Arthur finds his 'tender bottom[s] blushing like a rose'[132] the young St Hugh is treated in such a way that 'On hys whyte fleyshe theyr scourge made roses bloome'.[133] The difference between the two lies in the deliberate archaism of Rolfe's language rather than in any difference of sentiment. As Ellis Hanson suggests, the poet is 'aestheticizing a figure of horror into an icon of pleasure',[134] something to be looked at and

---

[127] *Second Thoughts*, 5. [128] *Dorian Gray*, 84. 65.
[129] Ibid. 135. [130] Ibid. 207.
[131] *Collected Poems*, ed. Cecil Woolf (Cecil and Amelia Woolf, 1974).
[132] *Whippingham Papers*, 13.
[133] Rolfe, *Collected Poems*, 38–9: 'Sestina yn honour of Lytel Seynt Hew Who was crucyfyed by ye Jewys atte Lincoln on ye Eve of Seynt Peter ad Vincula in ye yeare of oure Lord MCCLV', originally published in *Universal Review*, 15 Dec. 1888, 585–91.
[134] *Decadence and Catholicism* (Cambridge, Mass., and London: Harvard University Press, 1997), 338.

enjoyed; a process Brinsley-Richards clearly recognized in his own growing pleasure at watching an Etonian flogging.

John Davidson, in his novel *Earl Lavender* (1895), forcibly links flagellation and decadence, refusing to accept the God-based logic that pain is connected to punishment. It is no surprise that, at a time when the medical profession was refusing to accept that pain had a divine purpose, other groups, including the decadent frequenters of flagellatory brothels, should do the same. In the search for sensation Earl Lavender and his companion Lord Brumm visit a brothel where they 'were laved in warm water, then plunged into snow artificially prepared, and finally drenched in a shower bath of attar of roses[135] before taking their places in 'the Whipping Room'. Artificiality and unnaturalness, the qualities celebrated in the decadents' green carnation, are brought to the fore and celebrated in a novel that has little plot that does not deal with flagellation. It details the ceremonies of flogging that go on in the *demi-monde* at considerable length:

There were three couples present when Earl Lavender and Lord Brumm were led in; and two of the men and one of the women were being soundly flogged by the other three. The chastisers counted the lashes aloud, and in each case twelve were administered. As soon as the punishment had been inflicted, the seeming culprits gathered their robes about them, received the whips, which were of knotted cords, from the hands of those who had wielded them, and the punishers became the punished. Then the couples, having been thus reciprocally lashed, laid their whips on one of the couches, and tripped out of the room, dancing to a measure which was clearly heard, and evidently proceeded from a band of music in a neighbouring apartment.[136]

Again, there is the determination to refuse to allow pain to be read simply as punishment, for here 'the punishers became the punished', and, indeed the attribution of meaning to any of the events that take place in, what the book terms, the Underworld, is disallowed. In this elaborate ceremony and celebration of the whip the participants, as Davidson claims in the Note that

---

[135] *A Full and True Account of the Wonderful Mission of Earl Lavender, which lasted One Night and One Day: With a History of the Pursuit of Earl Lavender and Lord Brumm by Mrs Scamler and Maud Emblem* (Ward & Downey, 1895), 126–7.   [136] Ibid. 126.

precedes the novel, show their 'widespread contempt of the great commonplaces of life—love, marriage, and the rearing of children'[137] and attain—the reader presumes, though this is never made explicit—sexual pleasure through entirely non-procreative means. After a sound flogging—but one that stops at the drawing of blood[138] as a flogging in the navy would never had done—Earl Lavender finds that 'it was the whipping that roused all [his] senses'[139] until he 'never was so stimulated in all [his] life'.[140] Sensation is a goal in itself and valuable simply as such for those who are capable of experiencing it. Again, this vision is inflected by a sense of class, for the solid figure of Mrs Scamler who, against her will, is brought by Earl Lavender into the Whipping Room, represents a sturdy common sense that is played off against *fin de siècle* decadence. The 'incomprehensibility of the circumstances in which she found herself'[141] militate against her sense of what is right, and she cannot make sense of the flagellatory scenes in front of her eyes: 'It may be Hell, or it may be Heaven, or it may be Purgatory, but, thank God, we're not dead, Maud, and they can't do that to us!'[142] Hers is not the quivering, sensitive, and upper-class flesh of Dorian Gray, but the 'broad back'[143] and 'solid shoulders'[144] of the respectable middle classes. As such, for Davidson, she is incapable of escaping from the bounds of ill-thought through Christianity, and persists in reading the whippings administered in the Underworld as punishment: ' "Oh, my sins were very, very little ones; but ask me not to remember them all, for I can't and never could." '[145] For Earl Lavender the experience is different, and takes on a mystical and religious sense of its own, as the group floggings are described as an 'extraordinary ceremony'[146] and, waiting for a flogging, he 'clasped his hands on his breast'[147] in a pose that mimics religious veneration.

The persistent problem with flogging in any kind of penal or corrective setting becomes very apparent in the context of *Earl Lavender*, for it is the danger of the enjoyment of the one who does the flogging, or, indeed, of the one who is flogged. This is an issue that, whilst it clearly was on the agenda, was largely avoided, though hinted at by those who wrote about flogging.

[137] Ibid. p. ix.   [138] Ibid. 261.   [139] Ibid. 135.   [140] Ibid. 269.
[141] Ibid. 262.   [142] Ibid. 258.   [143] Ibid.   [144] Ibid. 262.
[145] Ibid. 259.   [146] Ibid. 127.   [147] Ibid. 128.

Mrs Walter enters the debate on the corporal punishment of children in her pamphlet *The Rod: Its Use and Abuse* (1889) in which she insists that 'The modern generation of children have in many cases got out of hand for want of proper punishment'[148] and adds, in a way that mimics G. W. Steevens's denunciation of the 'New Humanitarianism', that 'the nation has to thank the sentimentalists for much of the indiscipline and want of respect for authority'.[149] Hers is clearly a pro-whipping stance, with the usual justification: 'In using the rod we are acting kindly for the child and following out the teaching of the Bible.'[150] Yet at the end of her pamphlet a cautionary note is sounded, and she insists that 'where a pleasure is felt in administering punishment—be sure that the rod is not in good hands'.[151] She defends this by suggesting that the rod should only be used by 'those who possess the necessary control over themselves and their tempers'[152] and surely this is a hint (though a quiet one)—about the sexual pleasure potentially derived from the administering of a whipping—a pleasure which makes William Bennett, crusading against the retrograde and vicious infliction of penal whipping, ask why those in favour of flogging are 'so anxious to tear with the lash'[153] the backs of those found guilty of criminal misdemeanour.

And it is here that I want to turn finally, and briefly, to a persistent current in late Victorian writing—the desire to read about, and vicariously to enjoy, the infliction of pain—and to suggest by drawing this into alignment with Alexander Bain's squeamishness in the face of the sufferings of others that two completely different sets of expectations about physical pain could run alongside each other without either being negated. Bain, arguing the case for corporal punishment, but throwing a sop to the 'sentimentalists',[154] looks for ways of making physical punishment acceptable. Instead of flogging which is messy and bloody, Bain argues, electricity could be used 'to produce a painful condition of the nerves',[155] such that 'any amount of

---

[148] *The Rod: Its Use and Abuse* (Bristol: Henry Hill, 1889), 8–9.
[149] Ibid. 9.   [150] Ibid. 11.   [151] Ibid. 16.   [152] Ibid. 16.
[153] *The Lash! A Protest Against its Use in Punishment, as being Barbarous, Revengeful, and Unimproving* (Glasgow: T. Bennett, [1876]), 4.
[154] *Mind and Body. The Theories of their Relation* (2nd edn., Henry S. King, 1873), 75 n.
[155] Ibid.

torture might be inflicted'.[156] The electrified prisoner would not present a terrible figure as his pain would be invisible to the viewer: 'The punishment would be less revolting to the spectator and the general public than floggings, while it would not be less awful to the criminal himself.'[157] In ways that unintentionally parody the arguments of antivivisectionary writers, Bain advocates the invisibility of pain and extols its infliction without the necessity for drawing blood which would bring attention to the process. He mentions a plan for 'imprisonment with periodic floggings' suggested by Lord Romilly, but argues that 'The idea would be too painful to the community at large; while a more refined application of pain would pass unheeded, except by the sufferer.'[158]

For Arthur Machen, the author of the bloodthirsty Gothic novel *The Three Impostors*, acute pleasure is to be found in those very scenes at which Bain baulks: his enjoyment is evident. In the chapter 'The Decorative Imagination', Burton tells a story he calls the 'Novel of the Iron Maid', and in it Mr Mathias, with his collection of instruments of torture, provides a model for those Victorians who doted on the idea of torture:

It is my hobby, this sort of thing. Do you know, I often sit here, hour after hour, and meditate over the collection. I fancy I have seen the face of the men who have suffered, faces lean with agony, and wet with sweats of death growing distinct out of the gloom, and I hear the echoes of their cries for mercy. But I must show you my latest acquisition.[159]

This 'latest acquisition' is the agent of poetic justice, for Mathias gets caught in the arms of the relentless Iron Maid, 'a large statue of a naked woman, fashioned in green bronze',[160] and is strangled to death. However much moralizing goes on on the surface of the text—Burton claims to be 'sickened at the sight of the man and his loathsome treasure'[161]—Machen's book is a parallel collection of stories of pain and bodily mutilation to Mathias's collection of instruments of torture. With his continual references to unspeakable torment, Machen provides a series of tall stories which lead the reader away from the core story of the tortured young man with spectacles: in taking pleasure

---

[156] Ibid.   [157] Ibid.   [158] Ibid.
[159] *Three Impostors*, 193–4.   [160] Ibid. 194.   [161] Ibid. 195.

in the stories of inflicted pain, the listeners within the book, and by implication the book's readers, are implicated in sadism. The image of Lipsius, the torturer 'standing near and gloating over the refinements of [the man with spectacles'] suffering'[162] his undoubted pain, stands as a powerful image of the Victorian reader who took pleasure in the suffering of others.

What becomes apparent from the acute divergence in approaches taken by Machen and Bain is that this divergence is important precisely *not* because it invalidates the claims I have made about pain, but rather because it suggests the fluidity of pain, the way in which it is open to interpretation. Two contemporary discourses can use the same language for the same phenomenon, but in directly opposed ways: contrary readings do not disprove my argument, but rather validate it.

---

[162] *Three Impostors*, 280.

Bibliography

Note: The place of publication is London throughout the citation details in the Bibliography and footnotes, unless otherwise stated.

Adderley, Charles, *A Few Thoughts on National Education and Punishments* (Longmans, Green, 1874).

Alden, W. L., *Among the Freaks* (London, New York, Bombay: Longmans, Green, 1896).

Allbutt, H. Arthur, *The Wife's Handbook: How a Woman should Order Herself during Pregnancy, in the Lying-in Room, and after Delivery. With Hints on the Management of the Baby, and on other Matters of Importance, necessary to be known by Married Women* (R. Forder, 1887).

Allen, Grant, *Physiological Æsthetics* (Henry S. King, 1877).

Andrews, W., *Old Time Punishments* (Hull: Andrews, 1890).

'Another Murder and More to Follow', *Pall Mall Gazette*, 8 Sept. 1888, 1–2.

'A Possible Clue', *Pall Mall Gazette*, 10 Sept. 1888, 7.

Australie [Emilie Matilda Australie Heron], *The Balance of Pain: And Other Poems* (George Bell, 1877).

Autton, Norman, *Pain: An Exploration* (Darton, Longman and Todd, 1986).

Bailin, Miriam, *The Sickroom in Victorian Fiction: The Art of Being Ill* (Cambridge: Cambridge University Press, 1994).

Bain, Alexander, *The Senses and the Intellect* (John W. Parker, 1855).

—— *The Emotions and the Will* (John W. Parker, 1859).

—— *Mind and Body. The Theories of their Relation* (2nd edn., Henry S. King, 1873).

Barker-Benfield, G. J., *The Culture of Sensibility: Sex and Society in Eighteenth-Century Britain* (1992; Chicago and London: University of Chicago Press, 1996).

Baynes, Donald, *Auxiliary Methods of Cure. The Weir Mitchell System. Massage. Ling's Swedish Movements. The Hot Water Cure. Electricity* (Simpkin, Marshall, 1888).

Beer, Gillian, ' "The Death of the Sun": Victorian Solar Physics and Solar Myth', in Bullen (ed.), *Sun is God*, 159–80.

Bending, J. C., 'Pain Descriptions', MS notes in possession of author, 1993.

Bennett, Cyril, *The Massage Case*, 2 vols. (T. Fisher Unwin, 1887).

Bennett, William, *The Lash! A Protest Against its Use in Punishment, as being Barbarous, Revengeful, and Unimproving* (Glasgow: T. Bennett, [1876]).

Bentham, Jeremy, *An Introduction to the Principles of Morals and Legislation* (1780), ed. J. H. Burns and H. L. A. Hart (London and New York: Methuen, 1982).

[Berdoe, Edward], *St. Bernard's: The Romance of a Medical Student. By Æsculapius Scalpel* (Swan Sonnenschein, Lowrey, 1887).

[——] *Dying Scientifically: A Key to St. Bernard's. By Æsculapius Scalpel* (Swan Sonnenschein, Lowrey, 1888).

Bergonzi, Bernard, *The Early H. G. Wells: A Study of the Scientific Romances* (Manchester: Manchester University Press, 1961).

Bernard, Claude, *Introduction à l'étude de la médicine experimentale* (Paris: J. B. Baillière, 1865); trans. Henry Copley Greene as *An Introduction to the Study of Experimental Medicine* (New York: Macmillan, 1927).

—— *Physiologie Opératoire* (Paris: Bailliere et Cie, 1879).

Berridge, Virginia, and Edwards, Griffith, *Opium and the People: Opiate Use in Nineteenth-Century England* (London: Allen Lane; New York: St Martin's Press, 1981).

Besant, Annie, *On Eternal Torture* (Thomas Scott, [1874]).

—— *My Path to Atheism* (Freethought, 1877).

—— *The Meaning and the Use of Pain* (Adyar Pamphlets, 168; Adyar: Theosophical Publishing House, 1932).

[——] *Euthanasia* (Thomas Scott, [1875]).

[——] *On the Atonement* (Thomas Scott, [1874]).

Besant, Walter, *The Eulogy of Richard Jefferies* (Chatto and Windus, 1888).

Bevan, David (ed.), *Literature and Sickness* (Amsterdam and Atlanta, Ga.: Rodopi, 1993).

B. F., 'A Tale of a Hospital Ward. A True Story' (no publication details, [1898]).

Bigelow, H. J., *Surgical Anæsthesia: Addresses and Other Papers* (Boston: Little, Brown, 1900).

Bigland, Eileen, *Ouida: The Passionate Victorian* (Jarrolds, 1950).

Bolton, Gambier, 'Pictures on the Human Skin', *Strand Magazine: An Illustrated Monthly*, 13 (1897), 425–34.

Bonica, John J., *The Management of Pain* (Henry Kimpton, 1953).

—— 'History of Pain Concepts and Pain Therapy', *Seminars in Anesthesia*, 4 (1985), 189–208.

Braddon, Mary Elizabeth, *Lady Audley's Secret*, 3 vols. (Tinsley, 1862).

Brieger, Gert H., review of *The History of Pain* by Roselyne Rey, *Nature Medicine*, 1 (1995), 1207.

Brinsley-Richards, James, *Seven Years at Eton, 1857–1864* (Richard Bentley, 1883).

Brontë, Charlotte, *Villette* (1853), ed. Herbert Rosengarten and Margaret Smith (Oxford: Clarendon Press, 1984).

Brontë, Emily, *Wuthering Heights* (1847), ed. Hilda Marsden and Ian Jack (Oxford: Clarendon Press, 1976).

Brooks, Peter, *Body Work: Objects of Desire in Modern Narrative* (Cambridge, Mass. and London: Harvard University Press, 1993).

Broughton, Rhoda, *Belinda* (1883; Richard Bentley, 1887).

——*Second Thoughts* (1880; new edn., Richard Bentley, 1893).

Browne, Doreen R. G., 'Ritual and Pain', in Mann (ed.), *History of the Management of Pain*, 31–49.

Bruce, Charles, *The Book of Adventure and Peril: A Record of Heroism and Endurance on Sea and Land* (London and Edinburgh: William P. Nimmo, 1875).

Budd, Keith, *Pain* (Update, 1984).

Budd, Susan, *Varieties of Unbelief: Atheists and Agnostics in English Society, 1850–1960* (Heinemann, 1977).

Buettinger, Craig, 'Antivivisection and the Charge of Zoophil-Psychosis in the Early Twentieth Century', *Historian*, 55 (Winter 1992), 277–88.

Bullen, J. B. (ed.), *The Sun is God: Painting, Literature, and Mythology in the Nineteenth Century* (Oxford: Clarendon Press, 1989).

——'Figuring the Body in the Victorian Novel', in id. (ed.), *Writing and Victorianism*, 250–65.

——(ed.), *Writing and Victorianism* (London and New York: Longman, 1997).

Burdon-Sanderson, J. (ed.), *Handbook for the Physiological Laboratory*, 2 vols. (J. & A. Churchill, 1873).

Burgan, Mary, 'Heroines at the Piano: Women and Music in Nineteenth-Century Fiction', *Victorian Studies*, 30 (1986), 51–76.

Burke, Edmund, *Philosophical Enquiry into Our Ideas of the Sublime and the Beautiful* (1757), ed. Adam Phillips (Oxford: Oxford University Press, 1992).

Burney, Fanny, *Journals and Letters of Fanny Burney (Madame D'Arblay)*, ed. Joyce Hemlow with George G. Falle, Althea Douglas, and Jill A. Bourdais de Charbonnière, 12 vols. (Oxford: Clarendon Press, 1975), vi. 596–615: 30 Sept. 1811, 'To Esther (Burney) Burney'.

Burr, Anna Robeson, *Weir Mitchell: His Life and Letters* (New York: Duffield, 1929).

Burns, Robert, 'Address to the Tooth-Ache', in *Poems and Songs*, ed. James Kinsley (Oxford: Oxford University Press, 1969).

Butler, C. W., *The Light of Hope in the Mystery of Pain. A Sermon by the Rev. C. W. Butler. Preached in the Congregational Church, Eastwood, on Sunday Evening, June 23rd, 1878, on behalf of the London Missionary Society* (Langley Mill: Augustus Tucker, 1878).

Butler, Samuel, *The Notebooks of Samuel Butler* (1912), ed. Henry Festing Jones (Hogarth Press, 1985).

Bystrom, Valerie Ann, 'The Abyss of Sympathy: The Conventions of Pathos in Eighteenth and Nineteenth Century British Novels', *Criticism: A Quarterly for Literature and the Arts*, 23 (1981), 211–31.

Caesar, Adrian, *Taking it like a Man: Suffering, Sexuality and the War Poets. Brooke, Sassoon, Owen, Graves* (Manchester and New York: Manchester University Press, 1993).

Caine, Barbara, *Victorian Feminists* (Oxford: Oxford University Press, 1992).

Caird, Mona, *A Sentimental View of Vivisection* (Bijou Library, no. 3; William Reeves, [1893]).

—— 'The Evolution of Compassion', *Westminster Review*, 145 (1896), 635–43.

—— *Beyond the Pale. An Appeal on Behalf of the Victims of Vivisection* (Bijou Library, no. 8; William Reeves, [1897]).

Campbell, Harry, 'Pain and its Interpretation', *Lancet*, 10 Sept. 1887, 543.

—— *Headache and Other Morbid Cephalic Sensations* (H. K. Lewis, 1894).

Carey, John, *The Intellectuals and the Masses: Pride and Prejudice among the Literary Intelligentsia, 1880–1939* (Faber, 1992).

Carroll, Lewis, *Some Popular Fallacies About Vivisection* (Oxford: privately printed, 1875).

Cartwright, Lisa, *Screening the Body: Tracing Medicine's Visual Culture* (Minneapolis and London: University of Minnesota Press, 1995).

Cevasco, G. A. (ed.), *The 1890s: An Encyclopedia of British Literature, Art, and Culture* (New York and London: Garland, 1993).

Chadwick, Owen, *The Victorian Church*, 2 vols. (Adam and Charles Black, 1966).

Channing, Blanche, *The Madness of Michael Stark: A Story not drawn from Imagination* (James Clarke, 1900).

[Chatterton, Daniel], *Hell, Devils, and Damnation, or The Deeds of a Blood-Stained God and his Pioneer of Priggery, Jesus Christ, if True* (D. Chatterton, [1875]).

Christ, Carol T. and John O. Jordan (eds.), *Victorian Literature and the Victorian Visual Imagination* (Berkeley and Los Angeles: University of California Press, 1995).

Clarke, Edward H., *Sex in Education; or, A Fair Chance for Girls* (Boston: James R. Osgood, [1873]).

Cobbe, Frances Power, *Light in Dark Places* (Victoria Street Society for the Protection of Animals from Vivisection, [1883]).

—— *Life of Frances Power Cobbe, as Told by Herself. With Additions by the Author* (posthumous edn., Swan Sonnenschein, 1904).

[——] *Science in Excelsis* (Williams and Norgate, 1875).

Colenso, J. W., *Village Sermons* (Cambridge: Macmillan; Norwich: Thomas Priest, 1853).

Collins, Wilkie, *The Woman in White*, 3 vols. (new edn., Sampson Low, 1860).

—— *The Moonstone. A Romance*, 3 vols. (Tinsley, 1868).

—— *Man and Wife: A Novel*, 3 vols. (F. S. Ellis, 1870).

—— *Poor Miss Finch: A Novel*, 3 vols. (Richard Bentley, 1872).

—— *Heart and Science: A Story of the Present Time*, 3 vols. (Chatto & Windus, 1883).

—— *The Legacy of Cain*, 3 vols. (Chatto & Windus, 1889).

Collins, W. J., 'Pain and its Interpretation', *Lancet*, 20 Aug. 1887, 391.

—— 'Pain and its Interpretation', *Lancet*, 10 Sept. 1887, 543.

Connell, John, *W. E. Henley* (Constable, 1949).

Conquest, John, *Letters to a Mother, on the Management of Herself and Children in Health and Disease; embracing the Subjects of Pregnancy, Childbirth, Nursing, Food, Exercise, Bathing, Clothing, Etc., Etc. With Remarks on Chloroform* (1848; 5th edn. rev., Longman, 1858).

Conrad, Joseph, *The Secret Agent: A Simple Tale* (Methuen, 1907).

Cook, E. D. 'New Novels: *Heart and Science*', *Academy*, 28 Apr. 1883, 290.

Cooper, William M., *A History of the Rod in All Countries from the Earliest Period to the Present Time* (new edn., William Reeves, [1869]).

Corelli, Marie, *A Romance of Two Worlds: A Novel*, 2 vols. (Richard Bentley, 1886).

—— *A Romance of Two Worlds: A Novel* (Methuen popular edn., 1924).

Cosslett, Tess, *Women Writing Childbirth: Modern Discourses of Motherhood* (Manchester: Manchester University Press, 1994).

Cox, Edward W., *The Principles of Punishment, as applied in the Administration of the Criminal Law, by Judges and Magistrates* (Law Times Office, 1877).

Crowther, M. A., *Church Embattled: Religious Controversy in Mid-Victorian England* (Newton Abbot: David and Charles, 1970).

Crue, Benjamin L. (ed.), *Pain and Suffering: Selected Aspects* (Springfield, Ill.: Charles C. Thomas, 1970).

Dally, Ann, *Women under the Knife: A History of Surgery* (London, Sydney, Auckland, Johannesburg: Hutchinson Radius, 1991).

Darwin, Charles, *The Expression of the Emotions in Man and Animals. With Photographic and Other Illustrations* (John Murray, 1872).

——*The Formation of Vegetable Mould, through the Action of Worms, with Observations on their Habits* (John Murray, 1881).

Daston, Lorraine J., 'The Theory of Will versus the Science of Mind', in Woodward and Ash (eds.), *Problematic Science*, 88–115.

Davidson, John, *A Full and True Account of the Wonderful Mission of Earl Lavender, which lasted One Night and One Day: With a History of the Pursuit of Earl Lavender and Lord Brumm by Mrs Scamler and Maud Emblem* (Ward & Downey, 1895).

Davidson, J. Thain, 'Jesus Christ, the Healer of the Body. A Sermon', revised by the author in *Catholic Sermons No. V., June 1873. Preached in Islington Presbyterian Church, London, On Sunday Evening, April 20, 1873* (Edward Curtice and F. Pitman, 1873).

Dawson, R. B., *Livingstone: The Hero of Africa* (Seeley, Service, 1918).

Dean, Clarence L., *The Wonder Book of Freaks and Animals* (Barnum and Bailey, 1898).

——*The Official Guide. Book of Marvels in the Barnum & Bailey Greatest Show on Earth. With Full Descriptions of the Human Prodigies and Rare Animals* (Barnum and Bailey, 1899).

Descartes, René, *Discourse on Method* (1637), trans. John Veitch (La Salle, Ill.: Open Court, 1989).

Desmond, Adrian, and Moore, James, *Darwin* (Michael Joseph, 1991).

[Dicey, A. V.], Review of *Daniel Deronda* by George Eliot, *Nation*, 19 Oct. 1876, 245–6.

Dickens, Charles, *The Old Curiosity Shop* (1841), ed. Earl of Wicklow (London, New York, Toronto: Oxford University Press, 1951).

——*Bleak House* (1852–3), ed. Osbert Sitwell (London, New York, Toronto: Oxford University Press, 1948).

——*Little Dorrit* (1857), ed. Harvey Peter Sucksmith (Oxford: Clarendon Press, 1979).

——*A Tale of Two Cities* (1859), ed. John Shuckburgh (London, New York, Toronto: Oxford University Press, 1949).

Dixey, F. A., *The Necessity of Pain* (Oxford House Papers, no. 19; Rivingtons, 1888).

Dixon, Ella Hepworth, *The Story of a Modern Woman* (William Heinemann, 1894).

Dixon, James, *The Pain of the Present and the Happiness of the Future Life. A Sermon, Preached in Cheetham Hill Chapel, on Sunday Morning, April 10th, 1859* (Alexander Heylin, [1859]).

Douglas, M., *In Lionland: The Story of Livingstone and Stanley* (London, Edinburgh, New York: Thomas Nelson, 1900).

Dowie, Ménie Muriel, *Gallia* (Methuen, 1895).

Doyle, Arthur Conan, 'The Illustrious Client', in *The Case-book of Sherlock Holmes* (John Murray, 1927), 11–46.

Du Cane, Edmund F., *The Punishment and Prevention of Crime* (Macmillan, 1885).

du Maurier, George, *Peter Ibbetson, with an Introduction by His Cousin Lady ***** ('Madge Plunket'). Edited and Illustrated by George du Maurier*, 2 vols. (James R. Osgood, McIlvaine, 1892).

——*Trilby*, 3 vols. (Osgood, McIlvaine, 1894).

——*The Martian: A Novel* (1897; Harper, 1898).

Duff, Kat, *The Alchemy of Illness* (1993; Virago, 1994).

Earle, A. M., *Curious Punishment of Bygone Days* (Herbert S. Stone, 1896).

Ebbels, Arthur, 'On Vivisection', *Shafts*, 3 (1895), 10–11.

Ebensten, Hanns, *Pierced Hearts and True Love: An Illustrated History of the Origin and Development of European Tattooing and a Survey of its Present State* (Derek Verschoyle, 1953).

E. E. A. W.—One who attended the Church Congress Debate, 'A Sketch of the Church Congress Debate on Vivisection, October 6th, 1892', *Shafts*, 3 (1892), 12.

Eliade, Mircea (ed.), 'Suffering', in *The Encyclopedia of Religion*, 16 vols. (New York: Macmillan; London: Collier Macmillan, 1987).

Eliot, George, 'J. A. Froude's *The Nemesis of Faith*', *Coventry Herald and Observer*, 16 Mar. 1849, 2; rep. in George Eliot, *Selected Essays, Poems and Other Writings* (Penguin, 1990), 265–7.

——*Romola* (1863), ed. Andrew Brown (Oxford: Clarendon Press, 1993).

——*Daniel Deronda* (1876), ed. Graham Handley (Oxford: Clarendon Press, 1984).

——*The Mill on the Floss* (1860), ed. Gordon S. Haight (Oxford: Clarendon Press, 1989).

Elliott, Paul, 'Vivisection and the Emergence of Experimental Physiology in Nineteenth-Century France', in Rupke (ed.), *Vivisection in Historical Perspective*, 48–77.

Ellis, Havelock, *The Criminal* (1889; Walter Scott, 1890).

Ellmann, Maud, *The Hunger Artists: Starving, Writing and Imprisonment* (Virago, 1993).

Elston, Mary Ann, 'Women and Anti-vivisection in Victorian England, 1870–1900', in Rupke (ed.), *Vivisection in Historical Perspective*, 259–94.

Enright, D. J. (ed.), *The Faber Book of Fevers and Frets* (Faber, 1989).

Epstein, Julia L., 'Writing the Unspeakable: Fanny Burney's Mastectomy and the Fictive Body', *Representations*, 16 (1986), 131–66.

Essays and Reviews (John W. Parker, 1860).

Experiences of Flagellation. A Series of Remarkable Instances of Whipping Inflicted on Both Sexes, with Curious Anecdotes of Ladies Fond of Administering Birch Discipline. Compiled by an Amateur Flagellant (printed for private circulation, 1885).

Falkner, J. Meade, *The Lost Stradivarius* (Edinburgh and London: William Blackwood, 1895).

'Farini's Foreigners', *Punch*, 81 (3 Dec. 1881), 264.

Farrar, Frederick W., *Eric; or, Little by Little. A Tale of Roslyn School* (Edinburgh: Adam and Charles Black, 1858).

Flaybum, Lady Termagant, *Sublime of Flagellation: in Letters from Lady Termagant Flaybum, of Birch-Grove, to Lady Harriet Tickletail, of Bumfiddle-Hall. In which are Introduced the Beautiful Tale of La Coquette Chatie, in French and English; and the Boarding-School Bumbrusher; or, the Distresses of Laura* (George Peacock, n.d.).

Fletcher, Robert, *Tattooing Among Civilized People. Read Before the Anthropological Society of Washington, December 19, 1882* (Washington: Judd and Detweiler, 1883).

Forbes, Archibald, *Soldiering and Scribbling: A Series of Sketches* (Henry S. King, 1872).

Foster, J. Edgar, *Pain: Its Mystery and Meaning. And Other Sermons* (James Nisbet, [1891]).

Fremantle, Anne, *Three-Cornered Heart* (Collins, 1971).

French, Richard D., *Antivivisection and Medical Science in Victorian Society* (Princeton and London: Princeton University Press, 1975).

Froude, J. A., *The Nemesis of Faith* (2nd edn., John Chapman, 1849).

Gabriel, Messrs, *Painless System of Dentistry* (J. & A. Reeves, 1867).

Galton, Francis, *Inquiries into Human Faculty and its Development* (Macmillan, 1883).

Gant, Frederick James, *The Mystery of Suffering, Human and Theological* (Elliot Stock, 1900).

Garland, David, *Punishment and Welfare: A History of Penal Strategies* (Aldershot: Gower, 1985).

Gaskell, Elizabeth, *Mary Barton: A Tale of Manchester Life*, 2 vols. (Chapman and Hall, 1848).

—— *Ruth: A Novel* . . . (1853; Chapman and Hall, 1855).

—— *North and South* (1854–5), ed. Angus Easson (London, New York, Toronto: Oxford University Press, 1973).

Geison, Gerald L., 'Social and Institutional Factors in the Stagnancy of English Physiology, 1840–70', *Bulletin of the History of Medicine*, 46 (1972), 30–58.

Gibson, Ian, *The English Vice: Beating, Sex and Shame in Victorian England and After* (1978; Duckworth, 1992).

Gidley, Mick (ed.), *Representing Others: White Views of Indigenous Peoples* (Exeter: University of Exeter Press, 1992).

Gillies, H. Cameron, 'The Life-saving Value of Pain and Disease', *Lancet*, 13 Aug. 1887, 305–7.

Gilmour, Robin, *The Idea of the Gentleman in the Victorian Novel* (George Allen & Unwin, 1981).

—— *The Victorian Period: The Intellectual and Cultural Context of English Literature, 1830–1890* (London and New York: Longman, 1993).

Gissing, George, *The Unclassed* (1884; new edn., Lawrence and Bullen, 1895).

—— *The Nether World: A Novel*, 3 vols. (Smith, Elder, 1889).

—— *The Whirlpool* (Lawrence and Bullen, 1897).

Gordon, Jan B., ' "The Key to Dedlock's Gait:" Gout as Resistance', in Bevan (ed.), *Literature and Sickness*, 25–52.

Gore, Charles (ed.), Lux Mundi: *A Series of Studies in the Religion of the Incarnation* (John Murray, 1889).

Gore, George, *The Utility and Morality of Vivisection* (J. W. Kolckmann, 1884).

Gould, F. J., *The Agnostic Island* (Propagandist Press Committee, 1891).

Gould, Stephen Jay, *The Mismeasure of Man* (1981; Penguin, 1992).

Grand, Sarah, *The Heavenly Twins*, 3 vols. (William Heinemann, 1893).

—— *The Beth Book: Being a Study from the Life of Elizabeth Caldwell Maclure. A Woman of Genius* (Heinemann, 1897).

Greg, W. R., *Enigmas of Life* (Trübner, 1872).

Griffiths, Arthur, *The Brand of the Broad Arrow* (C. Arthur Pearson, 1900).

Grosskurth, Phyllis, *Havelock Ellis: A Biography* (New York: New York University Press, 1985).

Grossmith, George and Weedon, *The Diary of a Nobody* (Bristol: J. W. Arrowsmith; London: Simpkin, Marshall, Hamilton, Kent, 1892).

Gudgeon, Colonel, 'Te Umu-Ti, or Fire-Walking Ceremony', *Journal of the Polynesian Society*, 8 (1899), 58–60.

Haggard, H. Rider, *King Solomon's Mines* (London, Paris, New York, & Melbourne: Cassell, 1885).

——*She: A History of Adventure* (Longmans, Green, 1887).

——*Mr. Meeson's Will* (Spencer Blackett, 1888).

Hampson, Judith, 'Legislation: A Practical Solution to the Vivisection Dilemma?', in Rupke (ed.), *Vivisection in Historical Perspective*, 314–39.

Hanson, Ellis, *Decadence and Catholicism* (Cambridge, Mass., and London: Harvard University Press, 1997).

Hardy, Thomas, *The Trumpet-Major. A Tale*, 3 vols. (Smith, Elder, 1880).

——*A Laodicean; or, The Castle of the De Stancys. A Story of To-day*, 3 vols. (Sampson Low, Marston, Searle & Rivington, 1881).

——*Jude the Obscure* (Osgood, McIlvaine, 1896).

Harris, Ruth, *Murders and Madness: Medicine, Law and Society in the Fin de Siècle* (Oxford: Clarendon Press, 1989).

[Harrison, Frederic], 'Neo-Christianity', *Westminster and Foreign Quarterly Review*, NS 36 (1860), 293–332.

Hayman, Henry, 'Why We Suffer, An Attempt to Show the Economy of Pain', in *'Why We Suffer,' and Other Essays* (W. H. Allen, 1890), 1–109.

Hayter, Alethea, *Opium and the Romantic Imagination* (Faber, 1968).

Henley, William Ernest, 'In Hospital', in *Poems, 1898* (Oxford and New York: Woodstock, 1993).

Hennegan, Alison, 'Personalities and Principles: Aspects of Literature and Life in *Fin-de-Siècle* England', in Teich and Porter (eds.), Fin-de-Siècle *and its Legacy*, 170–215.

Henry, Teuira, 'Te Umu-Ti, A Raiatean Ceremony', *Journal of the Polynesian Society Containing the Transactions and Proceedings of the Society*, 2 (1893), 105–8.

[Hichens, Robert], *The Green Carnation* (William Heinemann, 1894).

Hilton, Boyd, *The Age of Atonement: The Influence of Evangelicalism on Social and Economic Thought, 1785–1865* (Oxford: Clarendon Press, 1988).

[Hinton, James], *The Mystery of Pain: A Book for the Sorrowful* (Smith, Elder, 1866).

Hithersay, Richard B. and Ernest, George, *Sketch of the Life of Saladin (W. Stewart Ross.) Freethinker and Journalist* (W. Stewart, [1887]).

Hodgen, Margaret T., *Early Anthropology in the Sixteenth and Seventeenth Centuries* (Philadelphia: University of Pennsylvania Press, 1964).

Hodgkiss, A. D., 'Chronic Pain in Nineteenth-Century British Medical Writings', *History of Psychiatry*, 2 (1991), 27–40.

Honeyman, W. C., 'Toothache: A Detective's Story', in *Toothache and Other Interesting and Amusing Stories. By Eminent Authors* (Edinburgh: William P. Nimmo, [1867]).

Hope, Anthony, *The Prisoner of Zenda: Being the History of Three Months in the Life of an English Gentleman* (Bristol: J. W. Arrowsmith; London: Simpkin, Marshall, Hamilton, Kent, [1894]).

Hopkins, Tighe, 'The Art and Mystery of Tattooing', *Leisure Hour*, 44 (1895), 694–8, 774–80.

'How the Poor Live', *Pall Mall Gazette*, 12 Sept. 1888, 7.

[Hughes, Thomas], *Tom Brown's School Days. By an Old Boy* (Cambridge: Macmillan, 1857).

Hugon, Anne, *The Exploration of Africa: From Cairo to the Cape*, trans. Alexandra Campbell (Thames and Hudson, 1993).

Hume, Fergus, *Tracked by a Tattoo. A Mystery* (London and New York: Frederick Warne, [1896]).

Hurley, Kelly, *The Gothic Body: Sexuality, Materialism, and Degeneration at the Fin de Siècle* (Cambridge: Cambridge University Press, 1996).

Hurter, H., *The Catholic Doctrine About Hell. From the Compendium of Dogmatic Theology*, trans. Kenelm Digby Best (London: Burns and Oates; New York: Catholic Publication Society, 1887).

[Hutton, R. H.], review of *The Island of Doctor Moreau* by H. G. Wells, *Spectator*, 11 Apr. 1896, 519–20.

Huxley, Thomas H., *Evolution & Ethics: The Romanes Lecture 1893* (London and New York: Macmillan, 1893).

Ignatieff, Michael, *A Just Measure of Pain: The Penitentiary in the Industrial Revolution 1750–1850* (Penguin, 1978).

Illich, Ivan, *Medical Nemesis: The Expropriation of Health* (Harmondsworth: Penguin, 1977).

Illingworth, J. R., 'The Problem of Pain: Its Bearing on Faith in God', in Gore (ed.), Lux Mundi, 113–26.

Indecent Whipping (no publisher, 1880?)

Ireland, William W., *On Idiocy and Imbecility* (J. & A. Churchill, 1877).

Jaguer, Jeff, *The Tattoo: A Pictorial History* (Horndean: Milestone, 1990).

James, Alice, *The Diary of Alice James* (1964), ed. Leon Edel (Harmondsworth: Penguin, 1982).

James, Henry, *The House of Fiction: Essays on the Novel by Henry James*, ed. Leon Edel (Rupert Hart-Davis, 1957).

James, William, *Psychology* (Macmillan, 1892).

James, William, 'Vivisection', *Nation*, 20 (1875), 128–9.

Jenkins, Roy, *Gladstone* (London and Basingstoke: Macmillan, 1995).

Kant, Immanuel, *Lectures on Ethics*, trans. Louis Infield (Methuen, 1930).

Kincaid, James R., 'Girl-Watching, Child-Beating, and Other Exercises for Readers of *Jude the Obscure*', in *Annoying the Victorians* (New York and London: Routledge, 1995) 233–47.

Kingston, William H. G., *Travels of Dr. Livingstone* (Routledge, [1886]).

Kinnear, Alfred, *Across Many Seas: A Story of Action from Crimea to Coronation* (Bristol and London: J. W. Arrowsmith, 1902).

Kipling, Rudyard, *Barrack-Room Ballads* (Methuen, 1892).

——*Kim* (Macmillan, 1901).

Krafft-Ebing, R. von, *Psychopathia Sexualis, with especial reference to Contrary Sexual Instinct: A Medico-Legal Study*, authorized trans. of the 7th enlarged and rev. German edn. by Charles Gilbert Chaddock (Philadelphia and London: F. A. Davis, 1892).

Lang, Andrew. *Rhymes à la Mode* (Kegan, Paul, French, 1885).

——*Modern Mythology* (Longmans, Green, 1897).

——'The Supernatural in Fiction', in *Adventures among Books* (Longmans, Green, 1905).

Lansbury, Coral, 'Gynaecology, Pornography, and the Antivivisection Movement', *Victorian Studies*, 28 (1985), 413–37.

——*The Old Brown Dog: Women, Workers, and Vivisection in Edwardian England* (Madison: University of Wisconsin Press, 1985).

[Lawrence, G. A.], *Guy Livingstone; or, 'Thorough'* (1857; Leipzig: Bernhard Tauchnitz, 1860).

Leffingwell, Albert, *The Vivisection Question* (New Haven: Tuttle, Morehouse & Taylor, 1901).

Lewes, George Henry, *Sea-side Studies at Ilfracombe, Tenby, the Scilly Isles, & Jersey* (Edinburgh and London: William Blackwood, 1858).

——'On the Dread and Dislike of Science', in *Versatile Victorian*, ed. Ashton, 317–26.

——*Versatile Victorian: Selected Writings of George Henry Lewes*, ed. Rosemary Ashton (Bristol: Bristol Classical Press, 1992).

[Linton, E. Lynn], *The True History of Joshua Davidson* (Strahan, 1872).

Lippington, G. C., 'Pain and its Interpretation', *Lancet*, 17 Sept. 1887, 594.

[Livingstone, David], *Livingstone's Travels and Researches in South Africa; including a Sketch of Sixteen Years' Residence in the Interior of Africa, and a Journey from the Cape of Good Hope to*

Loanda on the West Coast, thence across the Continent, down the River Zambesi, to the Eastern Coast. From the Personal Narrative of David Livingstone, LL.D., D.C.l. To which is added A Historical Sketch of Discoveries in Africa (Philadelphia: J. W. Bradley, 1859).

Loane, Marcus L., *John Charles Ryle, 1816–1900: A Short Biography* (James Clarke, 1953).

Logan, Peter Melville, *Nerves and Narratives: A Cultural History of Hysteria in Nineteenth-Century British Prose* (Berkeley and Los Angeles: University of California Press, 1997).

Lombroso, Cesare, 'Illustrative Studies in Criminal Anthropology', 3 pts. *Monist*, 1 (1891), 177–85, 186–96, 336–43.

——'The Savage Origin of Tattooing', *Popular Science Monthly* (Apr. 1896), 793–803.

Lombroso, Caesar, and Ferrero, William, *The Female Offender* (T. Fisher Unwin, 1895).

Lombroso Ferrero, Gina, *Criminal Man according to the Classification of Cesare Lombroso. Briefly Summarised by his Daughter* (Knickerbocker Press, 1911).

Looker, Samuel J., and Porteous, Crichton, *Richard Jefferies: Man of the Fields. A Biography and Letters* (John Baker, 1964).

Lyons, J. B., *The Citizen Surgeon: A Biography of Sir Victor Horsley. F.R.S., F.R.C.S., 1857–1916* (Peter Dawnay, 1966).

Macaulay, [J.], *Livingstone Anecdotes: A Sketch of the Career and Illustrations of the Character of David Livingstone, Missionary, Traveller, Philanthropist* (Religious Tract Society, [1886]).

MacCarthy, Mary, *Handicaps: Six Studies* (Longmans, Green, 1936).

McClintock, Anne, *Imperial Leather: Race, Gender and Sexuality in the Colonial Contest* (New York and London: Routledge, 1995).

Machen, Arthur, *The Three Impostors or, The Transmutations* (London: John Lane; Boston: Roberts, 1895): repr. as *The Three Impostors* (London: J. M. Dent; Vermont: Charles E. Tuttle, 1995).

——*Precious Balms* (Spurr and Swift, 1924).

MacKenzie, Jeanne, and Norman, *H. G. Wells: A Biography* (New York: Simon and Schuster, 1973).

M'Kinnel, Mary, 'Vivisection', *Shafts*, 2 (1894), 340–1.

[MacLagan, Douglas], *Nugæ Canoræ Medicæ: Lays by the Poet Laureate of the New Town Dispensary* (Edinburgh: Thomas Constable, 1850), 36.

Maehle, Andreas-Holger, and Tröhler, Ulrich, 'Animal Experimentation from Antiquity to the End of the Eighteenth Century: Attitudes and Arguments', in Rupke (ed.), *Vivisection in Historical Perspective*, 14–47.

Mann, Ronald D. (ed.), *The History of the Management of Pain: From Early Principles to Present Practice* (Carnforth, Lancs and Park Ridge, NJ: Parthenon, 1988), 31–49.

Mantell, Gideon, *The Journal of Gideon Mantell, Surgeon and Geologist. Covering the Years 1818–1852*, ed. E. Cecil Curwen (London, New York, Toronto: Oxford University Press, 1940).

Manton, Jo, *Mary Carpenter and the Children of the Streets* (Heinemann, 1976).

Manuel, Diana, 'Marshall Hall (1790–1857): Vivisection and the Development of Experimental Physiology', in Rupke (ed.), *Vivisection in Historical Perspective*, 78–104.

Marcus, Steven, *The Other Victorians: A Study of Sexuality and Pornography in Mid-Nineteenth-Century England* (1964; Corgi, 1969).

[Martineau, Harriet], *Life in the Sick-Room. Essays. By an Invalid* (Edward Moxon, 1844).

Martinet, Mrs, *The Quintessence of Birch Discipline. A Sequence to the Romance of Chastisement* (privately printed, 1870).

Maugham, William Somerset, *Liza of Lambeth* (T. Fisher Unwin, 1897).

Maurice, Frederick Denison, 'Concluding Essay: Eternal Life and Eternal Death', in *Theological Essays* (2nd edn., Cambridge: Macmillan, 1853).

Melville, Herman, *Typee; or, a Narrative of a Four Months' Residence among the Natives of a Valley of the Marquesas Islands; or, A Peep at Polynesian Life* (1846; John Murray, 1847).

Melzack, Ronald, and Wall, Patrick, *The Challenge of Pain* (1982; rev. edn., Penguin, 1988).

Meredith, George, *The Egoist: A Comedy in Narrative*, 3 vols. (C. Kegan Paul, 1879).

—— *One of Our Conquerors*, 3 vols. (Chapman and Hall, 1891).

Meredith, Owen (*pseud.*), *Lucile* (Chapman & Hall, 1860).

Milgate, Michael (ed.), *The Life and Works of Thomas Hardy* (Macmillan, 1984).

Miller, Jonathan, *The Body in Question* (London and Basingstoke: Papermac, 1978).

Mitchell, P. Chalmers, Review of *The Island of Doctor Moreau* by H. G. Wells, *Saturday Review*, 11 Apr. 1896, 368–9.

Mitchell, S. Weir, *Fat and Blood: and How to Make Them* (Philadelphia: J. B. Lippincott, 1877).

—— 'Civilization and Pain', *Annals of Hygiene*, 7 (1892), 26.

—— *Characteristics* (6th edn., Macmillan, 1899).

—— 'Heroism in Every-day Life', *Century Illustrated Monthly Magazine*, 43 (1902), 217–20.

——*Injuries of Nerves and their Consequences* (Philadelphia: J. B. Lippincott, 1872).

Moore, George, *Confessions of a Young Man* (Swan Sonnenschein, Lowrey, 1888).

——*Esther Waters* (1894); ed. David Skilton (Oxford: Oxford University Press 1991) (based on 1931 rev. text).

Morley, John, 'W. R. Greg: A Sketch', in *Critical Miscellanies*, 3 vols. (Macmillan, 1886) iii. 213–59.

Morris, David B., 'How to Read *The Body in Pain*', *Literature and Medicine*, 6 (1987), 139–55.

——*The Culture of Pain* (1991; Berkeley and Los Angeles: University of California Press, 1993).

Morris, William, *News from Nowhere or, An Epoch of Rest, Being Some Chapters from a Utopian Romance* (Reeves & Turner, 1891).

Morrison, Arthur, *Child of the Jago* (Methuen, 1896).

'Mosquito Phobia', *Punch*, 5 Sept. 1874, 104.

M.S.S., Review of *The New Priesthood* by Ouida, *Shafts*, 2 (1893), 173.

Munro, J., 'The Nerves of the World', *Leisure Hour* (1895), 18–22, 96–102, 183–7.

Murphy, Gardner, *An Historical Introduction to Modern Psychology* (London: Kegan Paul, Trench Trübner; New York: Harcourt, Brace, 1929).

Murphy, Howard R., 'The Ethical Revolt against Christian Orthodoxy in Early Victorian England', *American Historical Review*, 60 (1955), 800–17.

Nabokov, Vladimir, *Bend Sinister* (New York: Henry Holt, [1947]).

New Catholic Encyclopedia, 15 vols. (New York: McGraw-Hill, 1967).

Newman, F. W., *Life After Death? Palinōdia* (Trübner, 1886).

Newman, John Henry, *Discourses on the Scope and Nature of University Education. Addressed to the Catholics of Dublin* (Dublin: James Duffy, 1852).

Nietzsche, Friedrich, *The Gay Science, with a prelude in rhymes and an appendix of songs* (2nd edn., 1887), trans. Walter Kaufmann (New York: Vintage Books, 1974).

Noble, James Ashcroft, Review of *Heart and Science* by Wilkie Collins, *Academy*, 28 Apr. 1883, 290.

Nordau, Max, *Degeneration* (William Heinemann, 1895).

Notes and Queries, 18 Oct. 1862, 312.

Ogilvie, John. *The Imperial Dictionary of the English Language: A Complete Encyclopedic Lexicon, Literary, Scientific, and Technological*, new edn. rev. by Charles Annandale, 4 vols. (Blackie, 1882).

Oldfield, Josiah, *Myrhh and Amaranth. Two Lectures. I. Brother Pain and His Crown. II. Sister Drudgery and her Roses* (Sampson Low, Marston, 1905).

Ouida [Marie Louise de la Ramée], *The New Priesthood* (E. W. Allen, 1893).

——*Toxin and Other Papers* (copyright edn. [1894]; Leipzig: Bernhard Tauchnitz, 1896).

Owen, Richard, *Lectures on the Comparative Anatomy and Physiology of the Invertebrate Animals, Delivered at the Royal College of Surgeons, in 1843* (Longman, Brown, Green, and Longmans, 1843).

Paget, Stephen, *Sir Victor Horsley: A Study of his Life and Work* (Constable, 1919).

Patmore, Coventry, *Poems*, 2 vols. (2nd collective edn, George Bell, 1886).

Paul, Herbert, *The Life of Froude* (Sir Isaac Pitman, 1905).

Pearson, Karl, *The Grammar of Science* (Walter Scott, 1892).

Perkins, Judith, *The Suffering Self: Pain and Narrative Representation in the Early Christian Era* (Routledge, 1995).

Pernick, Martin S., *A Calculus of Suffering: Pain, Professionalism, and Anesthesia in Nineteenth-Century America* (New York: Columbia University Press, 1985).

Peters, Catherine, *The King of Inventors: A Life of Wilkie Collins* (Secker and Warburg, 1991).

Pick, Daniel, *Faces of Degeneration: A European Disorder, c. 1848–c. 1918* (1989; Cambridge: Cambridge University Press, 1993).

Porter, Roy, 'Pain and Suffering', in W. F. Bynum and Roy Porter, *Companion Encyclopedia of the History of Medicine* 2 vols. (London: Routledge, 1993), ii 1574–91.

Poovey, Mary, *Uneven Developments: The Ideological Work of Gender in Mid-Victorian England* (Virago, 1989).

——*Making a Social Body: British Cultural Formation, 1830–1864* (Chicago and London: Chicago University Press, 1995).

Power, A., 'The Nervous System', in *Sanitary Rhymes. The Present Series Consists of Personal Precautions against Cholera, and all kinds of Fever; and contains:- No. I.—The Skin. No. II.—The Blood. No. III.—The Nervous System* (T. Richards, 1871).

Prescott, E. Livingstone (*pseud.*) [Edith Spicer Jay], *Flogging NOT Abolished in the British Army. A Reasonable Inquiry Into the Present Abuse of the 'Cat' and Birch in Our Military Prisons. Based on Parliamentary and Prison Official Records, from 1887 to 1897, with an appendix of Statements of Prison Officials past and present, Correspondence in the 'Times,' 'Morning Post,' 'Daily Chronicle,'*

'Westminster Gazette,' 'Echo,' etc., full description by Eye-Witnesses of Punishments, and Illustrations, from photograph, of Government 'Cat' (Clapham: A Bachhoffner, 1897).

——Scarlet and Steel: Some Modern Military Episodes (Hutchinson, 1897).

Prestige, G. L., The Life of Charles Gore: A Great Englishman (London and Toronto: William Heinemann, 1935).

Purdy, D. W., Tattooing: How to Tattoo, What to Use & How to Use Them (D. W. Purdy, [1896]).

Quilp, Jocelyn, Baron Verdegris. A Romance of the Reversed Direction (Henry, 1894).

Reiser, Stanley Joel, Medicine and the Reign of Technology (Cambridge: Cambridge University Press, 1978).

Rey, Roselyne, The History of Pain (1993), trans. Louise Elliott Wallace and J. A. and S. W. Cadden (Cambridge, Mass. and London: Harvard University Press, 1995).

Richter, Stefan, Tattoo (London, Melbourne, New York: Quartet Books, 1985).

Ridge, W. Pett, Mord Em'ly (C. Arthur Pearson, 1898).

Ritvo, Harriet, The Animal Estate: The English and Other Creatures in the Victorian Age (1987; Penguin, 1990).

Robinson, Victor, Victory over Pain: A History of Anesthesia (Sigma Books, 1947).

Robley, [H. G.], Moko; or Maori Tattooing (Chapman and Hall, 1896).

Rolfe, F., Baron Corvo, Collected Poems, ed. Cecil Woolf (Cecil and Amelia Woolf, 1974).

Rollin, Bernard E., The Unheeded Cry: Animal Consciousness, Animal Pain and Science (1989; Oxford and New York: Oxford University Press, 1990).

Rorty, Richard, Contingency, Irony, and Solidarity (1989; Cambridge: Cambridge University Press, 1994).

Rosenfield, L. C., From Beast-Machine to Man-Machine (New York: Oxford University Press, 1940), 3–26.

[Ross, William Stewart], The Flagellants (new edn. by Saladin, W. Stewart, 1890).

——A Fearful Flogging, by One Who Endured It. Based upon a ms. in the Possession of Saladin (W. Stewart, 1894).

Rothfield, Lawrence, Vital Signs: Medical Realism in Nineteenth-Century Fiction (Princeton: Princeton University Press, 1992).

Rowell, G. A., An Essay on the Beneficent Distribution of the Sense of Pain (Oxford: G. A. Rowell, 1857).

Rowell, Geoffrey, Hell and the Victorians: A Study of the

Nineteenth-Century Theological Controversies concerning Eternal Punishment and the Future Life (Oxford: Clarendon Press, 1974).

Runciman, James, 'Discipline', in *The Ethics of Drink and Other Social Questions or, Joints in our Social Armour* (3rd edn. Hodder and Stoughton, 1893).

Rupke, Nicolaas A. (ed.), *Vivisection in Historical Perspective* (1987; London and New York: Routledge, 1990).

—— 'Pro-vivisection in England in the Early 1880s: Arguments and Motives' in id. (ed.), *Vivisection in Historical Perspective*, 188–208.

Ryder, Richard D., *Victims of Science: The Use of Animals in Research* (Davis-Poynter, 1975).

Ryle, J. C., *The Cross. A Tract for the Times* (5th edn., Ipswich: Hunt; London: Wertheim and Macintosh; Nisbet, 1852).

—— '*The Hand of the Lord!' Being Thoughts on Cholera. 2 Sam. xxiv. 14* (London and Ipswich: William Hunt, [1866]).

—— *Eternity! Being Thoughts on 2 Cor. iv. 18. Spoken in Peterborough Cathedral, on Dec. 23rd, 1877. With a Postscript containing some remarks on Canon Farrar's 'Eternal Hope.'* (William Hunt, 1877).

Salt, Henry S., *Consolations of a Faddist: Verses Reprinted from 'The Humanitarian'* (A. C. Firfield, 1906).

—— *Memories of Bygone Eton* (Hutchinson, [1928]).

Samuelson, James, assisted by J. Braxton Hicks, *Humble Creatures. The Earthworm and the Common Housefly. In Eight Letters* (John van Voorst, 1858).

Sandison, Alan, *Robert Louis Stevenson and the Appearance of Modernism* (Basingstoke and London: Macmillan, 1996).

Scarry, Elaine, *The Body in Pain: The Making and Unmaking of the World* (New York and Oxford: Oxford University Press, 1985).

Schupbach, William, 'A Select Iconography of Animal Experiment', in Rupke (ed.), *Vivisection in Historical Perspective*, 340–60.

Scutt, R. W. B., and Gotch, Christopher, *Art, Sex and Symbol: The Mystery of Tattooing* (1974; 2nd edn., rev., New York and London: Cornwall Books, 1986).

Sewell, Anna, *Black Beauty: His Grooms and Companions. The Autobiography of a Horse. Translated from the Original Equine by Anna Sewell* (Jarrold, [1877]).

Shattock, Joanne (ed.), *Dickens and other Victorians: Essays in Honour of Philip Collins* (Macmillan, 1988).

Shaw, George Bernard, *Cashel Byron's Profession. A Novel* (Modern Press, 1886).

—— Letter to *Saturday Review*, 28 Aug. 1897, 224.

—— *An Unsocial Socialist* (Swan Sonnenschein, Lowrey, 1887).

Shore, [Margaret] Emily, *Journal of Emily Shore* (new edn., Kegan Paul, Trench, Trübner, 1898).

[Shorthouse, J. H.], *John Inglesant; A Romance* (Birmingham: Cornish, 1880).

——Preface, *John Inglesant; A Romance*, new edn. (London and New York: Macmillan, 1883).

Showalter, Elaine, *Sexual Anarchy: Gender and Culture at the* Fin de Siècle (1990; Virago, 1992).

——*A Literature of their Own: From Charlotte Brontë to Doris Lessing* (1978; rev. edn., Virago, 1993).

Simpson, J. Y., *Answer to the Religious Objections advanced against the Employment of Anæsthetic Agents in Midwifery and Surgery* (Edinburgh: Sutherland and Knox; London: Samuel Highly, 1847).

——'Superinduction of Anæsthesia in Natural and Morbid Parturition: with cases illustrative of the Use and Effects of Chloroform in Obstetric Practice', in *Answer to the Religious Objections advanced against the Employment of Anæsthetic Agents in Midwifery and Surgery* (Edinburgh: Sutherland and Knox; London: Samuel Highly, 1847).

——*Anæsthesia, or the Employment of Chloroform and Ether in Surgery, Midwifery, etc.* (Philadelphia: Lindsay & Blakiston, 1849).

Smith, Protheroe, *Scriptural Authority for the Mitigation of the Pains of Labour, by Chloroform, and Other Anæsthetic Agents* (S. Highly, 1848).

Sollier, Paul, 'Idiocy', in Stedman (ed.), *Twentieth Century Practice*, xii. 257–368.

Spanker, Lady Gay, *Tales of Fun and Flagellation* (privately printed, 1896).

Spencer, Herbert, *Principles of Sociology*, 3 vols. (Williams and Norgate, 1876).

Spens, Walter Cook, *Jurisdiction and Punishments of Summary Criminal Courts (With Special Reference to the Lash); Being Answers to the Home Secretary's Queries to English and Scotch Magistrates* (Edinburgh: T. & T. Clark, 1875).

Stables, W., *Medical Life in the Navy* (Robert Hardwicke, 1868).

Stedman, Thomas L. (ed.), *Twentieth Century Practice: An International Encyclopedia of Modern Medical Science by Leading Authorities of Europe and America*, 20 vols. (Sampson Low, Marston, 1897).

Steevens, G. W., 'The New Humanitarianism', *Blackwood's Edinburgh Magazine*, 163 (1898), 98–106.

—— *With Kitchener to Khartum* (William Blackwood, 1898).

Steevens, G. W., *The Works of George Warrington Steevens*, ed. G. S. Street, 7 vols. (Edinburgh and London: William Blackwood, 1900–2).

—— 'Two Hospitals', in *Works*, Street, i. 300–3.

Sternbach, Richard A., 'Strategies and Tactics in the Treatment of Patients with Pain', in Crue (ed.), *Pain and Suffering: Selected Aspects*, 176–85.

Stevenson, Robert Louis, *Treasure Island* (London, Paris, and New York: Cassell, 1883).

—— *Strange Case of Dr. Jekyll and Mr. Hyde* (Longmans, Green, 1886).

—— *The Annotated Dr Jekyll and Mr Hyde*, ed. Richard Dury (Milan: Guerini, 1993) (an annotated edn. of the above).

—— *The Lantern-Bearers and Other Essays*, ed. Jeremy Treglown (Chatto and Windus, 1988).

—— and Osbourne, Lloyd. *The Ebb-Tide: A Trio and Quartette* (William Heinemann, 1894).

Stewart, Garrett, 'Reading Figures: The Legible Image of Victorian Textuality', in Christ and Jordan (eds.), *Victorian Literature and the Victorian Imagination*, 345–67.

Stoker, George, *Clergyman's Sore Throat and Post-nasal Catarrh. Causes, Symptoms, and Treatment for Speakers and Singers* (J. & A. Churchill, 1884).

Stubbs, Edgar, 'Elizabeth Brownrigg (?1720–1767)', in *Lives of Twelve Bad Women: Illustrations and Reviews of Feminine Turpitude set forth by Impartial Hands*, ed. Arthur Vincent (T. Fisher Unwin, 1897).

Stull, Bradford T., *Religious Dialectics of Pain and Imagination* (Albany, NY: State University of New York Press, 1994).

Sublime of Flagellation: in Letters from Lady Termagant Flaybum, of Birch-Grove, to Lady Harriet Tickletail, of Bumfiddle-Hall. In which are Introduced the Beautiful Tale of La Coquette Chatie, in French and English; and the Boarding-School Bumbrusher; or, the Distresses of Laura (George Peacock, n.d.).

Sutherland, John, *The Longman Companion to Victorian Fiction* (Harlow: Longman, 1988).

—— *Mrs Humphry Ward: Eminent Victorian, Pre-eminent Edwardian* (1990; Oxford and New York: Oxford University Press, 1991).

—— 'Is Heathcliff a Murderer?', in *Is Heathcliff a Murderer? Great Puzzles in Nineteenth-Century Literature* (Oxford and New York: Oxford University Press, 1996), 53–8.

[Swinburne, Algernon Charles], 'The Flogging Block. An Heroic Poem. By Rufus Rodworthy, Esq. With Annotations by Barebum Birch-ingham, Esq. . . .' British Library, Ashley MS 5256.

——*Lesbia Brandon: An historical and critical commentary being largely a study (and elevation) of Swinburne as a novelist*, ed. Randolph Hughes (Falcon Press, 1952).

——*The Swinburne Letters*, ed. Cecil Y. Lang, 6 vols. (New Haven, Yale University Press, 1959).

'Tattooing', *Boy's Own Paper*, 29 Mar. 1884, 412–14.

Teich, Mikuláš, and Porter, Roy, (eds.), *Fin de Siècle and its Legacy* (1990; Cambridge: Cambridge University Press, 1993).

Teleny or, The Reverse of the Medal. A Physiological Romance of To-day, 2 vols. (Cosmopoli, 1893).

Tennyson, Alfred, *Tennyson: A Selected Edition*, ed. Christopher Ricks (Harlow: Longman, 1989).

Thackeray, William Makepeace, *The Letters and Private Papers of William Makepeace Thackeray*, ed. Gordon N. Ray, 4 vols., (Oxford: Oxford University Press, 1945).

Thomas, Edward, *Richard Jefferies: His Life and Work* (1909; Port Washington, NY and London: Kennikat Press, 1972).

Thomson, Basil, 'The Fiery Furnace', in *South Sea Yarns* (Edinburgh: William Blackwood, 1894), 195–207.

Thornhill, Mark, *The Clergy and Vivisection* (Hatchards, [1883]).

——*The Morality of Vivisection* (Hatchards, 1885).

——*Experiments on Hospital Patients* (Hatchards, 1889).

Tibbits, Edward T., *Medical Fashions in the Nineteenth Century: Including a Sketch of Bacterio-Mania and the Battle of the Bacilli* (H. K. Lewis, 1884).

Toothache and Other Interesting and Amusing Stories. By Eminent Authors (Edinburgh: William P. Nimmo, [1867]).

'Touch and Taste in Animals', *Chamber's Journal of Popular Literature, Science, and Arts*, 5th ser. 9 (1892), 583–6.

T. R., *Hell and its Torments, as described by Eye-witnesses and Others. With remarks by T.R., Author of 'Substitution'* (London: Geo. John Stevenson; Manchester: John Heywood; Glasgow: W. Love; Edinburgh: H. Robinson, 1870).

Tregear, Edward, 'The Maoris of New Zealand', *Journal of the Anthropological Institute of Great Britain and Ireland*, 19 (1890), 97–123.

Treves, Frederick, *The Elephant Man and Other Reminiscences* (London, New York, Toronto, Melbourne: Cassell, 1923).

Trollope, Anthony, 'A Ride Across Palestine', in *Tales of All Countries*, 2nd ser. (Chapman and Hall, 1863), 228–86.

Tuke, Daniel Hack, *Illustrations of the Influence of the Mind Upon the Body in Health and Disease, Designed to Elucidate the Action of the Imagination*, 2 vols. (2nd edn., J. and A. Churchill, 1884).

Turner, James, *Reckoning with the Beast: Animals, Pain, and Humanity in the Victorian Mind* (Baltimore and London: Johns Hopkins University Press, 1980).

Unsigned review of *The Ebb-Tide* by Robert Louis Stevenson, *Speaker*, 29 Sept. 1894, 362.

Unsigned review of *The Island of Doctor Moreau* by H. G. Wells, *Manchester Guardian*, 14 Apr. 1896, 4.

Unsigned review of *The Island of Doctor Moreau* by H. G. Wells, *Speaker*, 18 Apr. 1896, 429–30.

Unsigned review of *The Island of Doctor Moreau* by H. G. Wells, *Guardian*, 3 Jun. 1896, 871.

Unsigned review, 'The Island of Doctor Moreau. By H. G. Wells. (Heinemann.)', *Athenaeum*, 9 May 1896, 615–16.

Venables, George, *A Stinging Rod for a Sinning Nation. A Sermon Preached in Burgh Castle Church, (Suffolk) after Reading the Queen's Letter for the Army in South Africa and Sufferers by the War, Sunday Morning, Jan 7th, 1900* (Norwich: Agas H. Goose, 1900).

Vidler, Alec R., *The Church in an Age of Revolution: 1789 to the Present Day* (Harmondsworth: Penguin, 1961).

Vincent, Arthur, *Lives of Twelve Bad Women: Illustrations and Reviews of Feminine Turpitude set forth by Impartial Hands* (T. Fisher Unwin, 1897).

'Vivisection and Cheek', *Punch*, 17 Jan. 1874, 28.

'Vivisection and Science', *Punch*, 19 Dec. 1874, 257.

[von Arnim, Elizabeth], *Elizabeth and her German Garden* (Macmillan 1898).

Voysey, Charles, *Dogma versus Morality. A Reply to Church Congress* (Trübner, 1866).

—— *The 'Sling and the Stone.' Aimed not against Men, but Opinions. Free Speaking in the Church of England*, 10 vols. (London: Trübner; Ramsgate: Thomas Scott, 1867): vol. I, pt. xi. 'Jehu and Hezekiah'; vol. II, pt. ii, 'Salvation'; vol. III, pt. iv, 'Bribes and Threats'; vol. III, pt. viii, 'God's Thoughts not Our Thoughts'.

—— 'Address to the Reader', in *'Sling and the Stone.'*, vol. ii, pp. 1–3.

—— *The Mystery of Pain, Death and Sin, and Discourses in Refutation of Atheism* (London and Edinburgh: Williams and Norgate, 1878).

Vrettos, Athena, *Somatic Fictions: Imagining Illness in Victorian Culture* (Stanford, Calif.: Stanford University Press, 1995).

Vynon, Frederic, *In a House of Pain* (London and Sydney: Remington, 1894).

Wainwright, Geoffrey, *Keeping the Faith: Essays to Mark the Centenary of* Lux Mundi (SPCK, 1989).

Walter, Mrs, *The Rod: Its Use and Abuse* (Bristol: Henry Hill, 1889).

Ward, Mrs Humphry, *Robert Elsmere*, 3 vols. (Smith, Elder, 1888).

——*Marcella*, 3 vols. (Smith, Elder, 1894).

——*Helbeck of Bannisdale* (Smith, Elder, 1898).

Waters, Amos, '"Ratto." A Photograph', *Shafts*, 2 (1894), 315–18, 331–4.

Webb, R. K., 'The Gaskells as Unitarians' in Shattock (ed.), *Dickens and other Victorians*, 144–71.

Wells, H. G., *The Time Machine: An Invention* (William Heinemann, 1895).

——*The Wonderful Visit* (London: J. M. Dent; New York: Macmillan, 1895).

——'Human Evolution, An Artificial Process', *Fortnightly Review*, NS 60 (1896), 590–5.

——'The Province of Pain', in *Early Writings*, 194–9.

——*The Island of Doctor Moreau* (William Heinemann, 1896).

——*The Invisible Man: A Grotesque Romance* (C. Arthur Pearson, 1897).

——*Experiment in Autobiography: Discoveries and Conclusions of a Very Ordinary Brain (Since 1866)*, 2 vols. (Victor Gollancz and Cresset Press, 1934).

——*Early Writings in Science and Science Fiction by H. G. Wells* ed. Robert Philmus and David Y. Hughes (Berkeley and Los Angeles: University of California Press, 1975).

Westacott, E., *A Century of Vivisection and Anti-vivisection: A Study of their Effect upon Science, Medicine and Human Life during the Past Hundred Years* (Ashingdon: C. W. Daniel, 1949).

[Whately, Richard], 'On the Origin of Civilisation. A Lecture by His Grace the Archbishop of Dublin. To the Young Men's Christian Association', in *Lectures Delivered before the Young Men's Christian Association, in Exeter Hall, From November 1854, to February 1855* (James Nisbet, 1855), 1–36.

'What is Pain?', *Lancet*, 13 Aug. 1887, 333.

'What is Wanted?', *Pall Mall Gazette*, 12 Sept. 1888, 7.

Wheeler, Michael, *English Fiction of the Victorian Period* (1985; 2nd edn., London and New York: Longman, 1994).

——*Death and the Future Life in Victorian Literature and Theology* (Cambridge: Cambridge University Press, 1990).

The Whippingham Papers: A Collection of Contributions in Prose and Verse, Chiefly by the Author of the 'Romance of Chastisement' (privately printed, 1888).

[White, William Hale], *The Autobiography of Mark Rutherford, Dissenting Minister. Edited by his Friend, Reuben Shapcott* (Trübner, 1881).

Wiener, Martin J., *Reconstructing the Criminal: Culture, Law, and Policy in England, 1830–1914* (1990; Cambridge: Cambridge University Press, 1994).

[Wilberforce, Samuel], 'Essays and Reviews', *Quarterly Review*, 109 (1861), 248–305.

Wilde, Oscar, *The Picture of Dorian Gray* (London, New York and Melbourne: Ward Lock, [1891]).

Wilkinson, C. Allix, *Reminiscences of Eton (Keate's Time)* (Hurst and Blackett, 1888).

Williams, E. R., 'Pain and its Interpretation', *Lancet*, 17 Sept. 1887, 593–4.

Williams, Rowland, 'Bunsen's Biblical Researches', in *Essays and Reviews* (John W. Parker, 1860).

Witmer, Lightner, 'Pain', in Stedman (ed.), *Twentieth Century Practice*, xi. 905–45.

Wohl, Anthony S., *Endangered Lives: Public Health in Victorian Britain* (London, Melbourne, Toronto: J. M. Dent, 1983).

Wood, A. Maitland, 'Are the Pain and Sorrow in the World Inconsistent with a Belief in God's Power and Goodness?', in Walsham How, Espin and A. Maitland Wood (eds.), *Hard Questions. A Course of Mid-day Addresses at St. Peter's, During the Mission at Chester, 1877* (Chester: Phillipson & Golder; London: Griffith & Farran, [1877]).

[Wood, Mrs Henry], *Trevlyn Hold; Or, Squire Trevlyn's Heir*, 3 vols. (Tinsley, 1864).

Woodham-Smith, Cecil, *Queen Victoria: Her Life and Times, 1819–1861* (Hamish Hamilton, 1972).

Woodward, William R., and Ash, Mitchell G. (eds.), *The Problematic Science: Psychology in Nineteenth-Century Thought* (New York: Praeger, 1982).

Woolf, Virginia, 'On Being Ill', in *The Essays of Virginia Woolf*, (ed. Andrew McNeillie), 4 vols. (Hogarth, 1994), iv. 317–29.

Index

Adderley, Charles:
  *A Few Thoughts on National
    Education and Punishments* 242
aestheticism 69, 92
Alden, W. L.:
  Among the Freaks 228-9
algometer, electrical 218-19
Allbutt, H. Arthur:
  The Wife's Handbook 57
Allen, Grant:
  Physiological Æsthetics 54, 192
anaesthesia 27, 55, 64, 68, 76, 241
  in childbirth 21, 57, 218
  dangers of 68
  enfeebling effects of 70
  in surgery 56, 63, 68, 130-1, 146
  and vivisection 120, 136
analgesia 76
analogy 88-9, 107, 109, 111
animal automatism 120
animals 207
  lack of pain in 183
  and language 101, 169, 186
anthropology 210
antivivisection:
  and documentation/quotation 136,
    137, 140, 144, 148
  and feminism 121
  and irrationality 137, 151
  and pictures 143-5
  and reading 136, 140, 142, 143,
    146-7, 150, 174
  and Robert Louis Stevenson 154
  and women 128, 137, 151-2, 161-
    2
antivivisectionary fiction 156-7, 158,
  159, 163, 167, 168, 175
aspirin 55, 72, 76
Association for the Advancement of
  Medicine by Research 119, 141
atavism 223, 231
Athanasian Creed 7, 23
atheism 32
atonement 7, 8, 10, 12, 16, 17, 21,
  24, 25
Australie:
  'The Balance of Pain' 42-4, 48

Autton, Norman:
  Pain: An Exploration 83

Bailin, Miriam:
  The Sickroom in Victorian Fiction
    91
Bain, Alexander 54, 146
  The Emotions and the Will 53
  Mind and Body 272-3, 274
  The Senses and the Intellect 53, 99,
    105, 149, 240
Barker-Benfield, G. J.:
  The Culture of Sensibility 180-1,
    192
Barnum and Bailey's Greatest Show on
  Earth 229
Bell, Charles 53
Bending, J. C. 110
Bennett, Cyril:
  The Massage Case 73
Bennett, William:
  The Lash! 272
Bentham, Jeremy 178
Berdoe, Edward:
  Dying Scientifically 80 n., 146
  St Bernard's 123, 127-8, 146-7,
    156-8, 166-7
Bergonzi, Bernard:
  The Early H. G. Wells 174
Bernard, Claude 165, 147 n.
  *Introduction to the Study of
    Experimental Medicine* 148
  Physiologie Opératoire 144
Berridge, Virginia and Griffith
    Edwards:
  Opium and the People 72 n.
Besant, Annie:
  Euthanasia 2, 27
  The Meaning and the Use of Pain
    110-11
  My Path to Atheism 26
  On Eternal Damnation 23 n.
Besant, Walter:
  The Eulogy of Richard Jefferies 73,
    105
B.F.:
  'A Tale of a Hospital Ward' 99

Bible 19
  authority of 6, 8, 10–11, 13, 16, 20, 21, 26, 28, 30
  historical criticism of 12, 29
  Old Testament cruelty 8, 15
Bigelow, Henry Jacob 146
  'Vivisection' 125
Bishop of Manchester 142
Blomfield, Bishop 12
Bolton, Gambier:
  'Pictures on the Human Skin' 230
Bonica, John:
  'Pain Concepts' 55
Book of Marvels, The 229
boxing 237
Boy's Own Paper 225
Braddon, Mary Elizabeth:
  Lady Audley's Secret 92
branding 221, 222
Brinsley-Richards, James:
  Seven Years at Eton 255, 270
Broad Church 7, 8 n., 12
Brontë, Charlotte:
  Villette 92, 94
Brontë, Emily:
  Wuthering Heights 128–9, 172, 197
Broughton, Rhoda:
  Belinda 63 n., 209
  Second Thoughts 92, 268–9
Browne, Doreen R. G.:
  'Ritual and Pain' 214 n.
brutalization 75, 120, 125, 132–4, 139, 146, 152, 154, 159, 162–3, 166, 255, 261, 265
Budd, Susan:
  Varieties of Unbelief 25, 26
Buettinger, Craig:
  'Anti-vivisection and the Charge of Zoophil-Psychosis' 137, 208
Burdon-Sanderson, John:
  Handbook for the Physiological Laboratory 118, 122, 148
Burgan, Mary:
  'Heroines at the Piano' 92
Burke, Edmund 97, 98, 99
Burne-Jones, Edward 230
Burney, Fanny 103
Butler, C. W.:
  The Light of Hope in the Mystery of Pain 35, 44–5, 46
Butler, Samuel 199 n.
Bystrom, Valerie Ann:
  'The Abyss of Sympathy' 94

Caird, Mona 123, 171
  Beyond the Pale 154, 157, 209
  'The Evolution of Compassion' 126, 129
  A Sentimental View of Vivisection 80, 142
Campbell, Harry:
  Headache and Other Morbid Cephalic Sensations 179–80
  'Pain and its Interpretation' 67
cancer 104
Carey, John:
  The Intellectuals and the Masses 202
Carlyle, Thomas 201–2
Carroll, Lewis 122
  Some Popular Fallacies About Vivisection 209
Cartwright, Lisa:
  Screening the Body 142
Chadwick, Owen 11
Channing, Blanche:
  The Madness of Michael Stark 80 n.
Chatterton, Daniel:
  Hell, Devils, and Damnation 32
Chelsea Hospital for Women 80–1, 218
Cheyne, George 180, 191, 194
childbirth:
  and anaesthetics 21, 57
  by Caesarean section 218
  and civilization 124
  as curse of Eve 21, 66
  in hippopotamus 186
  in novels 203–5
  pain of 66
  and savagery 125
  and working classes 124, 203
cholera 18–21, 60, 72 n.
chloroform 21, 27, 39, 56, 57, 68, 71, 76
Christ:
  physical suffering of 49
  and redemptive pain 48–9
Christianity:
  ethical revolt against 24, 28, 29, 64
  and silent suffering 99, 101
Church, Dean 16
civilization 126, 128, 130, 171–2, 173, 174, 197, 208, 213, 226, 236, 250
  enervating effects of 70, 75, 124, 205

and nervous development 194
and pity 129
and sensitivity 86, 123, 124, 125, 225
'civilized savage' 126, 130, 135, 138, 159
Clarke, Edward:
Sex in Education 194
class 92–3, 191, 196, 197, 199, 209, 232, 233–8, 243–4, 252–5, 258, 261–5, 271
clergyman's sore throat 71
Cobbe, Frances Power 122n., 123, 128, 134, 136, 143, 146, 153
and atonement 27
and eternal damnation 2, 27
Life of Frances Power Cobbe 27
Light in Dark Places 143–5, 148–9, 157
Colenso, John William 10, 12
Collins, Wilkie:
Heart and Science 80, 123, 126, 130–4, 135–6, 137–41, 150, 152, 156, 158
The Legacy of Cain 73n., 197
Man and Wife 135, 150, 204
The Moonstone 138, 238
Poor Miss Finch 94
The Woman in White 92, 138, 195, 221
Collins, W. J.:
'Pain and its Interpretation' 65–6
comparative anatomy 183, 184, 186
Conquest, John:
Letters to a Mother 124, 203, 205
Conrad, Joseph:
The Secret Agent 222n.
Cooper, William:
A History of the Rod 258, 266n., 267–8
Corelli, Marie:
A Romance of Two Worlds 191
corporal punishment 22, 46, 221
biblical justification 31
legislation 241
and social control 240
Cosslett, Tess:
Women Writing Childbirth 204
Coutts, Angela Burdett 162
criminality 126, 208–10, 216–23, 231–2, 237
criminology 53n., 210, 216–20, 227, 232, 260

crucifixion 49
Cruelty to Animals Act (1876) 118
curare 120

Dally, Ann:
Women under the Knife 71, 194n.
Darwin, Charles 47, 146, 185–8, 200, 207
The Expression of the Emotions 185–8
On the Formation of Vegetable Mould 188
Origin of Species 24
Daston, Lorraine 54
Davidson, John:
Earl Lavender 270
Davidson, J. Thain:
'Jesus Christ, the Healer of the Body' 48
death 38, 65, 95, 96, 100, 102
decadence 268, 270–1
decency 130, 175
decorum 84, 87, 140, 152
degeneration 125
delicacy 136, 180, 182, 191, 192, 224, 260
dentistry 68–9, 72
Descartes, René:
Discourse on Method 120
descriptions of pain 104–5
Desmond, Adrian and James Moore:
Darwin 185
deviancy 208
Dickens, Charles:
Bleak House 74, 115
Little Dorrit 71
The Old Curiosity Shop 90, 95
Oliver Twist 90
A Tale of Two Cities 90
Dixon, Ella Hepworth:
The Story of a Modern Woman 90
Dixon, James:
The Pain of the Present 33
Douglas, Lord Alfred 198
Dowie, Ménie Muriel:
Gallia 69, 73n.
Doyle, Arthur Conan:
'The Illustrious Client' 233n.
DuBois Reymond, Émile 218
Duchenne, Guillaume 185, 188
Duff, Kat:
The Alchemy of Illness 83n.

du Maurier, George:
  The Martian 106
  Peter Ibbetson 90
  Trilby 79–80, 192
Dury, Richard 154

Ebbels, Arthur:
  'On Vivisection' 151–2
electrical treatments 73
Eliot, George 24, 91
  Daniel Deronda 121, 177, 226–7
  The Mill on the Floss 184 n.
  Romola 93
Elliotson, John 150
Ellis, Havelock 126, 137, 208, 233
  The Criminal 216–20, 232, 263
Elston, Mary Ann:
  'Women and Anti-vivisection' 127,
  151, 166
Englishwoman's Domestic Magazine
  266
Epstein, Julia L.:
  'Writing the Unspeakable' 103
Essays and Reviews 10, 12, 16
esthesiometer 218–19
eternal damnation 5, 6, 7, 8, 10–13,
  21, 24, 25, 28, 106, 215
ether 55
eugenics 69
Evangelicalism 16, 30
evolution 67, 173
evolutionary scales 178, 184, 191,
  194, 196, 197–207, 237
evolutionary thinking 24, 47, 64, 65–
  6, 170
evolution of society 195
*Experiences of Flagellation . . . by an
  Amateur Flagellant* 258
experimental physiology 53, 117,
  150
experiments on hospital patients 80

fairground attractions 227–8
Family Herald 266
Farrar, Frederick:
  Eric; or, Little by Little 242–3
fire-walking 210–15
flagellant correspondence column
  266–8
flagellation:
  of Christ 49, 263, 269
  and decadence 270–1
  mortification of flesh 22, 269

and pornography 256–7, 258, 259,
  266
and sexual pleasure 257, 265, 271
see also flogging
flagellatory brothels 270
Flaybum, Lady Termagant:
  Sublime of Flagellation 267
Fletcher, Robert:
  Tattooing Among Civilized People
  222
flogging:
  in armed forces 259, 261–5, 271
  of criminals 240, 241
  and degradation 259–60, 262–5
  and formation of character 242
  pleasure in infliction of 255–6, 258,
    262, 265, 266, 271–2
  of school boys 74, 106, 240–1,
    242–56
  silent endurance of 242–3, 259,
    260, 263
  see also flagellation
flogging narratives 258–60
Forbes, Archibald:
  Soldiering and Scribbling 258, 259–
  60, 262, 263
'Foreign savage' 139
Foster, J. Edgar:
  Pain: Its Mystery and Meaning 32,
    35, 36, 40–1, 46, 47, 110
Foster, Michael 118
'freaks' 191, 208, 216, 226, 228–9,
  230
Freud, Sigmund 208
Froude, James Anthony 22, 24
  The Nemesis of Faith 25
Furniss, J.:
  The Sight of Hell 22–3, 106, 122–
  3

Gabriel, Messrs 68–9, 70
Gall, Franz 53 n.
Galton, Francis 62–3, 217, 232 n.
Gant, Frederick:
  The Mystery of Suffering 246–7
Garland, David:
  Punishment and Welfare 209, 241
Gaskell, Elizabeth:
  Mary Barton 11
  North and South 55–6, 100, 101
  Ruth 203
Geison, Gerald:
  'Social and Institutional Factors in

the Stagnancy of English
Physiology' 117–18
gentlemanliness 233, 235, 242, 261–5
Gibson, Ian:
The English Vice 240, 266 n.
Gillies, H. Cameron:
'The Life-saving Value of Pain and
Disease' 64–5, 95, 100
Gilmour, Robin 27
*The Idea of the Gentleman in the
Victorian Novel* 233
Gissing, George:
The Nether World 93, 106, 107,
164
The Unclassed 93, 100
The Whirlpool 74–5
Gladstone, William 22
Gore, Charles:
Lux Mundi 16
Gore, George:
*The Utility and Morality of
Vivisection* 141–2
gothic conventions 97–8, 99, 109, 134
Gould, Frederick:
The Agnostic Island 178
Gould, Stephen Jay:
The Mismeasure of Man 220 n., 231
gout 74, 93, 94, 130
Grand, Sarah 147
The Beth Book 134–5
The Heavenly Twins 195
Greg, W. R.:
Enigmas of Life 9–10, 22 n.
Griffiths, Arthur:
The Brand of the Broad Arrow 221
Gudgeon, Colonel 210, 212–14

Haggard, H. Rider 195
King Solomon's Mines 69, 93,
221 n.
Mr. Meeson's Will 228 n.
She 97, 98, 99, 135
Hall, Marshall 120 n.
Hampson, Judith:
'Legislation: A Practical Solution to
the Vivisection Dilemma?' 119
hangovers 93
Hanson, Ellis:
Decadence and Catholicism 269
Hardy, Thomas:
Jude the Obscure 197–202, 207
A Laodicean 221
The Trumpet-Major 72 n., 93

Harris, Ruth:
Murders and Madness 233–4
Harrison, Frederic 13
Hayman, Henry:
'Why We Suffer' 59 n.
Hayter, Alethea:
*Opium and the Romantic
Imagination* 72
headache 94, 106, 179–80
hell 7, 9, 17, 22–4, 25, 26, 28, 215,
241
Henley, W. E.:
In Hospital 103
Hennegan, Alison:
'Personalities and Principles' 208,
209–10
Henry, Teuira 210–11
heresy 10, 26
Hichens, Robert:
The Green Carnation 198
hierarchies of pain 34, 42, 85–6, 107,
180, 192, 196–207, 218
Hilton, Boyd:
The Age of Atonement 16
Hinton, James 30
The Mystery of Pain 30, 34–5, 40,
48, 49–50
Hoggan, George 147 n.
Holyoake, Austin 8
Holzapfl, Michael Joseph 144
Honeyman, W. C.:
'Toothache: A Detective's Story' 72
Hope, Anthony:
The Prisoner of Zenda 94
Hopkins, Tighe:
'The Art and Mystery of Tattooing'
224–5
Horsley, Victor 136, 155–6
Howard, Annie 229
Hughes, Thomas:
Tom Brown's School Days 106,
242
humanitarianism 69, 70, 140, 149
Hume, Fergus:
Tracked by a Tattoo 221
Hurley, Kelly:
The Gothic Body 47 n., 195
Hurter, H.:
Compendium of Dogmatic Theology
23
Hutton, R. H.:
review of *Island of Doctor Moreau*
169, 174, 175

Huxley, Thomas 173
  'Evolution & Ethics' 173
hysteria 61, 108, 189, 190, 208

idiocy 208, 217, 232
Illich, Ivan:
  Medical Nemesis 75–7, 189
Illingworth, J. R. 33
  'The Problem of Pain' 39, 44, 45,
  48
imperialism 74, 75
Indecent Whipping 266
insensitivity 37, 130, 132, 154, 158,
  159, 161, 190–1, 208–9, 210,
  216–20, 231, 232, 262
intensity theory 62
International Medical Conference
  (1881) 119, 121
Ireland, William W.:
  On Idiocy and Imbecility 232 n.

Jack the Ripper 159
James, Alice:
  The Diary of Alice James 82–3,
  103, 190
James, Henry:
  'Robert Louis Stevenson' 155, 163
James, William 1, 136
Jefferies, Richard 73, 102, 104, 105,
  107–9, 193
Jelf, R. W. 12

Kant, Immanuel 120
Kay, James Phillips 18 n.
Keate, Dr 245
Kincaid, James R.:
  Annoying the Victorians 197 n.
Kingsford, Anna 142
Kinnear, Alfred:
  Across Many Seas 261
Kipling, Rudyard:
  Barrack-Room Ballads 75
  Kim 211 n.
Klein, Emanuel 139 n., 171, 174
Koller, Karl 55
Krafft-Ebing, R. von. 208
  Psychopathia Sexualis 257, 268

Lancet 56, 64
Lang, Andrew:
  'Art's Martyr' 216
  Modern Mythology 210, 214–16
  'The Supernatural in Fiction' 98

Lansbury, Coral:
  'Gynacology, Pornography, and
  the Antivivisection Movement'
  117 n.
  The Old Brown Dog 121 n., 197 n.
laudanum 72
Lawrence, G. A.:
  Guy Livingstone 101
Leffingwell, Albert:
  The Vivisection Question 146
Lewes, G. H. 207
  'On the Dread and Dislike of
  Science' 20
  Sea-side Studies 37, 193–4
Linton, Eliza Lynn:
  Joshua Davidson 196, 202, 209
Lippincott, G. C. 67 n.
literary conventions 92–6, 177, 179
Livingstone, David 38
Lombroso, Cesare 53 n., 208, 216,
  218, 220 n., 222, 232, 237, 260
  'The Savage Origin of Tattooing'
  223, 224, 231
Lombroso, Cesare and William
  Ferrero:
  The Female Offender 234
Lombroso Ferrero, Gina:
  Criminal Man 218 n.
loss of faith 25
lunatics 138, 208
Lux Mundi 39

McClintock, Anne
  Imperial Leather 211
McGill pain questionnaire 104–5, 112
Machen, Arthur:
  Precious Balms 134 n.
  The Three Impostors 133, 273–4
M'Kinnell, Mary:
  'Vivisection' 148–9, 151
Maehle, Andreas-Holger and Ulrich
  Tröhler 117
Magendie, François 53, 150
manliness 42, 69, 70–1, 74, 75, 86,
  102, 113, 259–60
Mantell, Gideon 103
Manton, Jo:
  Mary Carpenter 140
Maoris 211, 213–14, 217, 224, 230
Marcus, Steven:
  The Other Victorians 256, 258
Martineau, Harriet 5–6
  Life in the Sick-Room 30, 102–3

Martinet, Mrs:
  *The Quintessence of Birch
    Discipline* 256–7, 258, 262
martyrdom 269
masochism 257
massage 73
mastectomy 103
Maudsley, Henry 54
Maugham, William Somerset:
  Liza of Lambeth 93
Maurice, F. D. 10–12
  Theological Essays 10, 11
Melville, Herman:
  Typee 224, 226
Melzack, Ronald and Patrick Wall:
  The Challenge of Pain 83, 104–5,
    108, 112
Meredith, George:
  The Egoist 74, 179
  One of Our Conquerors 94
Meredith, Owen:
  Lucile 41–2
metaphors of pain 74, 90, 91, 107–10,
    113, 235
  as lover 113
  as music 41–2, 256
  as Nietzsche's dog 74
  as sculptor 40, 42, 47, 110
military prisons 261–5
milk diet 73
Miller, Jonathan:
  The Body in Question 108
Mitchell, P. Chalmers:
  review of *Island of Doctor Moreau*
    168, 175
Mitchell, S. Weir 131, 146
  Characteristics 125
  'Civilization and Pain' 125
  Fat and Blood 73 n.
  Injuries of the Nerves 39 n.
  and Rest Cure 73 n.
moko 224
Monckton Milnes, Richard 252,
  254
Moore, George:
  Confessions of a Young Man 69
  Esther Waters 202–6
Morel, Benedictin Augustin:
  *Treatise on the Degeneration of the
    Human Species* 47 n.
morphine 55
Morris, David B.:
  The Culture of Pain 83 n.

Morris, William:
  News from Nowhere 66
Morrison, Arthur:
  Child of the Jago 93
Morton, William 55
M.S.S.:
  review of *New Priesthood* 149,
    161–2
Müller, Johannes 53
Munro, J.:
  'The Nerves of the World' 59
Murphy, Gardner:
  *An Historical Introduction to
    Modern Psychology* 53
Murphy, Howard 24, 25
music 41–2, 42 n., 80, 193, 256

Nabokov, Vladimir:
  Bend Sinister 115
nerves 59, 180, 195, 260, 265
  education of 181, 192, 196
  as electric wires 191
  excitation of 58
  refinement of 191–2, 195, 196
  and society 195
  as telegraph system 58–60
  and women 181, 192, 194, 262
  and worms 178, 179
nervous system 182, 183, 184, 194
neuralgia 79, 101, 106
neurological organization 180, 192,
    193–8, 202, 255, 259
neurology 53, 59, 180
Newman, Francis 24, 207
Newman, John Henry:
  The Idea of a University 233, 235
Newton, Isaac 180
'New Woman', the 69
Nietzsche, Friedrich 74, 111
Nightingale, Florence 91
Nordau, Max:
  Degeneration 127, 137, 209

Oldfield, Josiah:
  Myrrh and Amaranth 45
opium 55, 72 n.
Ouida 123
  The New Priesthood 131–2, 136,
    139, 147, 149, 153, 161, 164–5,
    171
  Toxin 153
ovariotomy 166
oversensitivity 124, 192

Paget, James 65
Pain:
  behaviour caused by 179, 235
  and bravado 220
  as character-building 37, 42, 82,
    242
  in children 46
  definition of 56–7, 79, 81
  as force for good 74
  and gender 70–1, 101, 113
  and imagination 61n.
  as index 77, 91, 95, 183, 196
  infliction of 92, 106, 126, 159, 193,
    217, 220, 232–9
  insularity of 82, 83, 105, 108–9
  invisibility of 79, 179
  medicalization of 75–7
  and memory 103–4
  as mystery 6, 18, 20, 29, 35, 46, 52
  as problem 6, 28, 29–31, 35–6, 42,
    52, 64
  protective function of 37, 38, 59, 65
  as punishment 44, 45
  and purification 112
  relativity of 35, 38, 44, 85, 86, 109,
    200, 250
  and sex 96, 113
  as sign of God's benevolence 37–8,
    39, 60, 64–5
  as spur to action 47, 49
  as symptom 189
  therapeutic advances 55
  universality of 67, 82–3, 89, 114
  use of 17, 22, 31n., 37, 60, 65, 113
  and violence 107
  and vitality 68
pain relief 55, 72, 76
pain tracts 190
painless man 190
parallelism, mental and neural 61, 189
Patmore, Coventry:
  'Pain' 111–14
patriotism 70
Pearson, Karl:
  The Grammar of Science 59n.
Pernick, Martin S.:
  A Calculus of Suffering 56n.
photography 185
phrenology 53n.
pianos 92
pleasure 42–3, 54, 62, 63, 112
Poovey, Mary:
  Making a Social Body 18

Uneven Developments 57
Power, Alfred:
  'The Nervous System' 59
Prescott, E. Livingstone:
  *Flogging NOT Abolished in the
    British Army* 263
  Scarlet and Steel 261–5, 268
Prince Constantine 227
prisons 217, 223, 231, 241
prostitutes 226, 228n., 230
'psychical analgesia' 137, 220, 232,
    233, 263
public schools 118, 240, 252, 253
Purdy, D. W. 227
Pusey, E. B. 13, 22n.

Quilp, Jocelyn:
  Baron Verdegris 95

'Ratto' 156
readerly enjoyment of pain 96, 268,
    272–4
Reiser, Stanley Joel:
  *Medicine and the Reign of
    Technology* 53n.
Research Defence Society 174
Rest Cure 73
Rey, Roselyne:
  The History of Pain 52, 68, 93n.
rheumatism 106
Rhodes, Frank 69–70
Richardson, Samuel 181
Richter, Stefan:
  Tattoo 232
Ridge, William Pett:
  Mord Em'ly 93, 95–6
Ritvo, Harriet:
  The Animal Estate 118n.
Robley, Major-General:
  Moko; or Maori Tattooing 224
Rolfe, Frederick:
  'Sestina yn honour of Lytel Seynt
    Hew' 269
Rorty, Richard:
  Contingency, Irony, and Solidarity
    114–15
Ross, William Stewart (Saladin):
  A Fearful Flogging 244, 245–52,
    257, 263
  The Flagellants 247–8
Rothfield, Lawrence:
  Vital Signs 92
Rowell, G. A.:

*An Essay on the Beneficent
Distribution of the Sense of Pain*
37–8, 39–40, 64–5
Rowell, Geoffrey:
Hell and the Victorians 6 n., 15
Royal Commission (1875) 119, 139,
171, 174
Royal Society for Prevention of
Cruelty to Animals 122
Runciman, James:
'Discipline' 195, 201
Rupke, Nicolaas:
'Pro-vivisection in England in the
early 1880s' 119
Ruskin, John 122
Ryle, J. C. 16–21, 27, 36
Cholera 19–20
The Cross 17
Eternity 17, 23

sadism 32, 256, 257, 262, 274
sailors 216, 220, 221 n., 229, 230
Salt, Henry:
'Hymn of the Flagellomaniacs'
265–6
Memories of Bygone Eton 245
Samuelson, James:
*Humble Creatures: The Earthworm
and the Common Housefly* 181–
2, 184, 185, 193, 199
Sandison, Alan:
*Robert Louis Stevenson and the
Appearance of Modernism* 158
savagery 75, 124, 125, 126, 128,
129–30, 164, 171–2, 195, 197,
205, 210–15, 217, 223–6, 231,
238, 250
savages 138, 192, 194, 230
Scarborough:
flagellation establishments of 256
Scarry, Elaine:
The Body in Pain 78–9, 82, 83,
86–9, 105, 109–11, 114, 249–50
Schiff, Moritz 165
'scientific savage', the 138
Scott, C. P. 107
secularism 8, 25, 28
self-mutilation 217, 225
sensation fiction 95–6
sensibility 42, 49, 98, 122, 123, 128,
130, 132–3, 134, 142, 147, 148,
150–1, 160, 167, 170, 180–1,
182, 195, 196, 255, 260

sensitivity 123, 124, 134, 181, 183,
185, 191–2, 193, 196, 200, 201,
205–6, 213, 224, 256, 264
sentimentality 118, 120, 127, 128,
166, 245, 272
servants 195, 205–6
Sewell, Anna:
Black Beauty 116
Shaftesbury, Lord 122, 140
Shafts 121, 127, 148, 152
Shaw, George Bernard:
Cashel Byron's Profession 162,
237 n.
and flogging 265–6
An Unsocial Socialist 105
Shore, Emily 103
Shorthouse, Joseph:
John Inglesant; A Romance 192–3
Showalter, Elaine:
A Literature of their Own 204
silent suffering 99–102, 106, 242
Simpson, James Young 21, 63, 66, 70
sin 44–5, 46, 47
slugs 198, 199
Smith, Protheroe:
*Scriptural Authority for the
Mitigation of the Pains of Labour*
131
societies for the protection of animals
118, 122
soldiers 70
Sollier, Paul:
'Idiocy' 232 n.
Spanker, Lady Gay:
Tales of Fun and Flagellation 106,
267
'spare the rod, spoil the child' 22,
252, 258
specificity theory 55, 62
Spencer, Herbert 54
Principles of Sociology 195
Spens, Walter:
*Jurisdiction and Punishments of
Summary Criminal Courts* 264
Stables, William:
Medical Life in the Navy 258, 260
Steevens, G. W.:
'The New Humanitarianism' 69, 74,
125, 272
Sternbach, Richard:
'Strategies and Tactics in the
Treatment of Patients with Pain'
77–8

Stevenson, Robert Louis:
　'The Character of Dogs' 154
　The Ebb-Tide 75, 233, 234–8
　Strange Case of Doctor Jekyll and
　　Mr Hyde 123, 130, 154–64, 165,
　　237–8
　Treasure Island 222
Stewart, Garrett:
　'Reading Figures: The Legible Image
　　of Victorian Textuality' 228 n.
stoicism 48, 69, 213, 225, 259, 260
Stoker, George:
　Clergyman's Sore Throat 71
Stull, Bradford, T.:
　Religious Dialectics of Pain and
　　Imagination 114
subconscious pain 61
Sutherland, John:
　'Is Heathcliff a Murderer?' 128 n.
　Mrs Humphry Ward 71–4
'Swedish rubbers' 72, 73
Swinburne, Algernon Charles 243,
　　252–6, 257, 265, 267
　Lesbia Brandon 243
　'Notre Dame des Sept Doulours'
　　113
　The Whippingham Papers 252–6,
　　269
sympathy 69, 98, 99, 105, 118, 122,
　　126, 130, 141, 150, 152, 163,
　　170, 171, 233, 260

tattooed lady 229
tattooing 210, 216–32
　and fortitude 220
　and Jewishness 226–7
　and money 227
　and sex 228 n.
tattooists 227, 230
Tawhiao, King 230
Teleny 62–3
Tennyson, Alfred 122
　The Princess 122 n.
'Te Umu-Ti' 210
Thackeray, William Makepeace 26–7
theosophy 110
Thomas, Edward:
　Richard Jefferies: His Life and Work
　　193
Thomson, Basil:
　South Sea Yarns 214–15
Thomson, Elihu 142
Thornhill, Mark 123, 176

The Clergy and Vivisection 142,
　　143
Experiments on Hospital Patients
　　80 n., 166
The Morality of Vivisection 140–3
Tibbits, Edward T.:
　Medical Fashions in the Nineteenth
　　Century 68
Tomasso, the Human Pincushion 190,
　　208, 229
toothache 68–9, 70, 72, 94, 104, 235
Topinard, Paul 231
torture 273
'Touch and Taste in Animals' 194
T.R.:
　Hell and its Torments 23, 24
Treves, Frederick:
　The Elephant Man and Other
　　Reminiscences 63
Trollope, Anthony:
　on eternal damnation 7
　'A Ride Across Palestine' 96
Trotter, Thomas 192 n.
Tuke, Daniel Hack 61 n.
Turner, James:
　Reckoning with the Beast 118, 134,
　　136, 143

ulcers 105
Unitarianism 6, 10

vaccination 21, 70
vegetarianism 127
Venables, George:
　A Stinging Rod for a Sinning Nation
　　241–2
vicarious pain 129, 130–2, 142, 151,
　　163, 263
Victoria, Queen 96, 98, 102, 121–2,
　　230
Vidler, Alec R. 13
visual signs of pain 105, 106, 179,
　　185–8, 191, 200, 251, 273
vitriol-throwing 107, 233–4
vivisection:
　and duty 141
　and fictional villains 153
　and foreignness 139
　of humans 80–1, 138, 165–7, 168
　and legislation 119
　and G. H. Lewes 193
　limitations of animal model 166
　as metaphor 121

and professionalization of medicine
118, 120–1
and scientific knowledge 54, 141
versus surgery 149–50
von Arnim, Elizabeth
Elizabeth and her German Garden
124 n.
Voysey, Charles 10, 14, 23, 26, 29,
30–2, 33, 36
and the Bible 14–15
and corporal punishment 46, 241
on eternal damnation 15
and morality of Old Testament 15
The Mystery of Pain 6–7, 32, 33–4,
183, 184, 201
The 'Sling and the Stone' 14, 29, 69
Vrettos, Athena:
Somatic Fictions 70 n.
Vynon, Frederic:
In a House of Pain 90

Walter, Mrs:
The Rod: Its Use and Abuse 272
Ward, Mrs Humphry 71–4, 89
Helbeck of Bannisdale 106
Marcella 92, 105–6
Robert Elsmere 204
Waters, Amos 157
Wells, H. G.:
Experiment in Autobiography 173 n.
'Human Evolution, An Artificial
Process' 171–2
The Invisible Man 160 n.
The Island of Doctor Moreau 75,
123, 133, 167–76
'The Province of Pain' 170 n.
The Time Machine 173 n.
The Wonderful Visit 172
Whately, Richard 225–6, 232
'What is Pain?' 56
Whipping Act (1861) 241
Whippingham Papers, The 252–6

White, William Hale:
*The Autobiography of Mark
Rutherford* 100–1
Wiener, Martin:
Reconstructing the Criminal 241
wife-beating 93
Wilberforce, Samuel 13
Wilde, Oscar:
The Picture of Dorian Gray 69,
121, 268–9, 271
Teleny 62–3
Wilkinson, C. Allix:
Reminiscences of Eton 244–5, 252,
253
Williams, Rowland 10, 12–13, 29
'Bunsen's Biblical Researches' 8 n.
Willis, Thomas 180
Wilson, Andrew 183–4, 185, 194, 195
Wilson, George 63–4, 70–1
Wilson, H. B. 10, 12, 14,15, 16, 28–9
Witmer, Lightner:
'Pain' 61, 77, 188–91, 200
Wohl, Anthony S.:
*Endangered Lives: Public Health in
Victorian Britain* 18
women 194, 204, 218, 224, 226, 228,
234, 260, 262
Wonder Book of Freaks and Animals
229
Wood, A. Maitland:
'Pain and Sorrow' 49
Wood, Mrs Henry:
Trevlyn Hold 100, 101
Woolf, Virginia 82
'On Being Ill' 83–6
working classes 93, 124 n., 184, 203–
7, 262
worms 178, 181–5, 188, 191, 193,
197–9
writers' cramp 72

Zoophil-Psychosis 137, 208